AF668356

John Lang

John Lang

Wanderer of Hindoostan
Slanderer in Hindoostanee
Lawyer for the Ranee

Amit Ranjan

NIYOGI
BOOKS

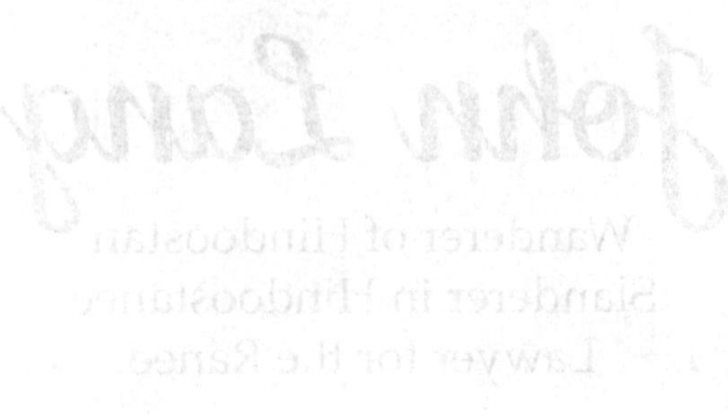

Published by
NIYOGI BOOKS
Block D, Building No. 77,
Okhla Industrial Area, Phase-I,
New Delhi-110 020, INDIA
Tel: 91-11-26816301, 26818960
Email: niyogibooks@gmail.com
Website: www.niyogibooksindia.com

Editor: Vibha Chakravarty Kumar
Design: Shashi Bhushan Prasad
Cover design: Sadhvi Jawa

ISBN: 978-93-91125-05-9
Publication: 2021

Printed at: Niyogi Offset Pvt. Ltd., New Delhi, India

To Mom…

And to Alice, whose name rhymes with 'gallus'.

Praise for the Book:

Amit Ranjan's page-turning chronicle of the life and times of John Lang—an obscure Australian lawyer and writer who made his career in India, representing the Rani of Jhansi—presents readers with a diversion that is, in equal parts, history and literary delight.

Prof. Kama Maclean
History Chair, South Asia Institute, University of Heidelberg, Germany

Amit Ranjan has written a remarkable book. At once a history of literature and an expedition into the culture and politics of a forgotten 19th century India, it is also, in a way, a song to the process of literary criticism and the potential it holds for self-discovery, threaded through by Dr Ranjan's eye for coincidence and rhyme in history and language. The fascinating John Lang took his own fiction's inspiration from Boccaccio's meta-stories; here Amit Ranjan turns Lang's life into another intertextual metanarrative, a journey across novels and plays, newspapers and court depositions, that traces a winding trail from Lang's world into ours. It deserves the attention of any reader interested in the connected histories of world literature.

Dr Carlos Grenier,
Florida International University, Miami, USA

Amit Ranjan's relentless pursuit of the intriguing John Lang has culminated in a most valuable book for those seeking to better understand the *longue duree* of Australia's Asian context. Further, the work highlights the powerful witness of an Australian who, through his own colonial background, was uniquely positioned to cast a critical gaze upon British colonialism and its legacies during a momentous period in Indian history.

Prof. Sean Brawley
Professor of History, Macquarie University, Sydney, Australia

Ranjan writes with a quirky intelligence playfully moving between archival documentation, oral tradition, anecdote and his own storytelling skills. He places the personage of Lang center stage in the world in which he moved—India, Australia, Britain—and assesses his legacy. He speaks with an affectionately critical eye and articulates fresh and nuanced perspectives on the collusion and collision of race and gender, colonial politics, the legal system, and the literary world. Ultimately, the joy of reading comes from the spirited narration that tests shifting boundaries of visions of truth and ethics, history and fiction.

Prof. Stephanos Stephanides,
Founding faculty of University of Cyprus

Epigraph

Pablo Picasso could draw Realistic portraits very well. But then, he chose a form of his own.

—Dr Saugata Bhaduri, who apart from being an astute academic, is also the famous actor who essayed the role of Fooko in the famous play *The True Story of Fooko, Shoe Kriya and Fooko in Just Three Acts, Mind the Commas, Please.* In a private conversation, over something from Malibu.

New Delhi, April 2011

I have fallen in love with India. I have even worked on the sets of a Bollywood film. The best thing is that Indians speak English so well. I have had some amazing conversations, but I miss out on something. The punch line in an Indian-English conversation is always in Hindi.

—Ida Hattemer-Higgins, famous German-American writer, at a conversation at the Haseraghatta Bar, under the evening star.

Bengaluru, December 2010

O Jhansi-ki-rani-ka-lawyer-ka-scholar! What if someone steals your mad ideas? That person will be called Jhansi-ki-rani-ka-lawyer-ka-scholar-ka-chor.

—Anahita Mukherjee, super reporter, at the Pyrmont Bridge.

Sydney, May 2010

Catherine Tekakwitha, who are you? Are you (1656–1680)? Is that enough? Are you Iroquois Virgin? Are you the Lily of the Shores of the Mohawk River? Can I love you in my own way? I am an old scholar, better-looking now than when I was young. That's what sitting on your ass does to your face.

—Mr Leonard Cohen, in *Beautiful Losers.* Almost two score years ago.

Time present and time past. Are both perhaps present in time future. And time future contained in time past.

—T.S. Eliot, in 'Burnt Norton', *Four Quartets* (1941).

CONTENTS

FOREWORD

One would think this is a book only about John Lang, the 19th century Australian-turned-Indian, barrister-cum-author-cum-maverick. The John Lang who was born in Sydney in 1816, studied in England from 1837 to 1841 to become a barrister, and sailed off to Calcutta in 1842 to practise law there till 1845. The John Lang who also started the remarkable journal *The Mofussilite*; who relocated—along with his journal—to Ambala in 1846; to Meerut thereafter; then to Agra in 1857 and back to Meerut in 1859, and died in Mussoorie in 1864. The John Lang who is buried in a rather difficult-to-find grave in Camel's Back Road cemetery in Landour, Mussoorie.

The John Lang who, in his short life of 48 years, produced no less than 23 novels or serialised volumes of fiction, one travelogue, some plays, and five volumes of poetry—apart from numerous other pieces in journals and periodicals, making him practically the first substantial author in Australian literature. The John Lang who routinely published anti-East India Company tracts in his journal, fought as a lawyer against the Company on several occasions—including, most famously, for Laxmi Bai, the Rani of Jhansi, thus making him a notable player in India's own (post) colonial history.

The John Lang who, thus, ought to be a major figure in the chequered histories of British imperialism and a pioneer in Indo-Australian political and cultural relations, and yet languishes in obscurity—generally overlooked by official historiography. A Lang in need of a language of re-inscription in public memory.

Well, that this book, for sure, minimally is.

It is indeed a meticulously researched work on John Lang—his life, his exploits, and his literary output. Amit Ranjan spent nearly a decade chasing this elusive and yet so important figure down musty archives and dusty by-lanes, through ghostly cemeteries and ghastly bureaucratic tangles, across India and Australia. In that chase, Ranjan has collected an incredible corpus of material and anecdotes, which is presented here to piece together the complex jigsaw puzzle that John Lang seemingly is. All this has been buttressed with several fellowships to visit Australia and the US for conducting this research—a full-fledged doctoral dissertation emerging out of the process, and numerous publications and media appearances on the subject.

While Ruskin Bond was indeed the first to have attempted to bring John Lang out of the bushes in 1964—by discovering his shrubbery-ridden grave in Mussoorie a century after his death, and writing about him and his stories—Lang was still to remain in utter obscurity for four more decades. It was only in late 2002, when Rory Medcalf, the then spokesperson of the Australian High Commission in India, started researching on Lang in collaboration with Australian scholar Victor Crittenden—resulting in a book by Crittenden on John Lang in 2005. There was also the unveiling of a plaque at Christ Church, Mussoorie, on 15 August 2005 by the Australian High Commission in memory of the 'barrister, writer, journalist, wanderer, and editor of *The Mofussilite*, the first Australian-born novelist...a brilliant and restless soul'.

Amit Ranjan began his research on John Lang around this time. It will not be an exaggeration to say that, while the couple of efforts mentioned above may have sown early seeds of Lang revival, it is Amit's sustained enterprise over the years that has brought Lang to greater public attention. There is a plethora of academic events and publications blossoming on Lang now.

This book does indeed bear out the toils and the fruits of such singular pathbreaking research: the almost mystical pursuit by a young Indian scholar, for nearly a decade, of the elusive and yet most brilliantly colourful and historically significant persona of John Lang.

And yet, this book is much more than just that. Amit's search for Alice Richman—beyond the local Pune lore about a suicidal white woman in love with a local lad, and whose ghost still haunts the campus—led him on a track that would eventually take him to John Lang, veritably though mostly unknown, the most prominent of the Australians living in 19th century India.

This book could thus be more properly described as fundamentally stemming from a quest for Alice, and incidentally leading on to John Lang. He does not come alone in this book, but is accompanied by a most curious cast of characters. More interestingly, this book also leads us to encounter some major figures of India's first war of independence in 1857—the Rani of Jhansi who, as mentioned earlier, employed Lang as her lawyer against the Company; and the noted rebel Nana Sahib, whose image was curiously replaced by that of Lala Jotee Persaud—a contractor and supplier of provisions to the East India Company—in the official records of the Company. These, and numerous such trivia involving the motley of Lang's lived universe—brigands, forgers, charlatans, detectives, phrenologists, occultists and the like—paint a most vibrant picture of the complex networks of mid-19th century colonial India. Something no traditional historiography can provide.

Far from being just another piece of sound academic literary-historical work and a well-researched biography of a lesser-known author who needs to be repatriated to the canon, this book is an exuberant exercise in passion—a passion that could set one off on a late night foray into the unknown just to look up some obscure tomb, or to pick up some obscure discursive thread. Amit's is an exercise that demonstrates how variegated, yet connected, our little histories are.

In fact, this book is not on a John Lang, but on a lone *jang* (a lonely battle) fought by Amit Ranjan as he struggled not just through the accumulated debris of the past to ferret out little known but interesting facts about the world as we know it, but also against presumptions as to what style and what form the output of such an exercise should be laid out in. Poetic, anecdotal, dealing with the ephemera and yet delivering layers of tangled truths, this book is research at its colourful best—a Lang portrayed not in languid noontide when the blazing monochromatic sun burns out all shades from the palette, but one conceived of and executed at dusk...when the owl of Minerva spreads its wings, welcoming, in the multi-hued twilight, the speckled stardust to follow.

Professor Saugata Bhaduri
Centre for English Studies
Jawaharlal Nehru Uuniversity
New Delhi
14 July 2019

PREFACE

Stories forgotten, or lying in the cold, find their own time to be told.

And so be it. This manuscript has taken eight years, since the time of its writing, to take the form of a book; and so, perhaps, it needs a new preface. The original preface was the chapter that is my letter to Mr Lang. The letter will give a fair overview of Lang—his times and age, and his language—so I will keep this short.

Lang, after his death in 1864, remained a fairly well-known writer for another 50 years or so. After roughly 1915, he was cast into the annals of obscurity, for he was not supported by British critics; they called him a 'hospital bed writer'—someone who could only criticize the British administration in India, and someone who could only show the dark side of the moon.

In the 1960s, John Earnshaw, a Lang enthusiast, took it upon himself to piece together Lang's life. However, his focus was largely on Lang's Australian period, which only extended to his early youth. Thereafter, Victor Crittenden, a librarian by profession, took the baton from Mr Earnshaw and republished some of Lang's works. When I met Mr Crittenden in 2010, he was an 86-year-young man who was hopeful of republishing all of Lang's works by 2016—which would be Lang's 100th birth anniversary. However, destiny did not will so: Mr Crittenden passed on before Lang's birth centenary. There was some interest amongst a handful of Australian scholars and diplomats, notable of which are Rick Hosking and Rory Medcalf. However, apart from Mr Crittenden, there was no one obsessing over this matter.

Long before Lang, I was haunted by—and hunting for—someone else in 2007: Alice Richman, a South Australian woman who had died in Pune in 1882. Hers is a lone grave at Pune university, shrouded in myth and mystique, with an epitaph that read: 'Died at this very spot, and is buried at this spot'. She was no military general or a civil servant, so the clues were scant. A year later, while randomly flipping through an old poetry book, I chanced upon a poem titled 'On the Death of Alice Richman' written by Margaret Thomas. Alice, from here on, decided the course of events. Through Alice, I learnt about the South Australian Baptist Mission, which helped tame 'wild' Australian women and induct them into their fold; about camels that were exported to Australia; about Melbourne girls who married Indian princes, and so on.

And I found John Lang—his wit, grit, and invectives were incentives enough to pursue him. He became my research subject; I went to Australia, and that's where I met Victor and Rick. The latter indulgently took me to Alice's village in Melrose, where there was a letter waiting for me from a man I had never met.

When I came back to India, someone stole my backpack, which also contained a pen drive on which I had assiduously taken pictures of Lang's newspaper issues. It was 8 GB of data lost, and had me wandering on the streets of Delhi looking for a University of New South Wales backpack. A month wasted in that pursuit, but I realised I still had enough material to write a fat thesis for my PhD.

An interesting set of events took place in 2014. I was looking forward to publishing my doctoral thesis as a book and had been writing in newspapers, and about Lang. Suddenly, there was an interesting piece of news doing rounds: that the Indian PM gifted his Australian counterpart with John Lang documents to demonstrate how far back the relations between the two countries went. I was not acknowledged. However, it was also a backhanded compliment. Lang had finally found an afterlife. I was invited to write articles in various newspapers but I remained anxious, for my manuscript was still a manuscript. A couple of big publishers promised to publish it but they took forever, and the matter lost its 'newsworthiness'.

Somewhere, Alice decided this would be the year that her story should be told at her grave; the event got covered on the front page of a leading newspaper. She also decided that this is the year Lang should be booked in a book.

Stories forgotten, or lying in the cold, find their own time to be told. And so, here it is.

—Amit Ranjan
Paris, September 2019

A LETTER FOR MR LANG

To,

John Lang Esq

Camel's Back Cemetery

Mussoorie, India

John Lang, who are you? Are you (1816–1864)? Is that enough? Are you, or were you? A writer? A translator? A journalist? A traveller? A wanderer? An Emancipist? A gentleman? An Australian? An Indian? A Brit(ish)? A polyglot? An illegitimate son? An illegitimate father? A legitimate lawyer? A Jew? Or a Christian? An alcoholic? A phrenologiphiliac? The best friend of Lala Jotee Persaud?

(Interceptor of this letter, please do not think that I am just playing around with words—he will answer all questions with a 'yes', except maybe the one about an illegitimate son.)

John Lang, let us play the game of 'Can You Answer in Questions?' You can see that I am good at it. I will ask a question, and you will answer in question, and I will answer in question, and so on. Whoever answers in an answer, loses a point.

But what's the point? You will answer in silence, and it is difficult to understand if silence is a question or an answer.

They keep stressing in the classroom these days, 'question the question'—which seems like an answer to me; and 'read the silences'. The first task is accomplished with this game, but the second—to read the silences—I tell you, is a difficult one.

Last year, just when the very hot summer was setting in in my country, I ran away to the winter of your country of birth. Before going, I met a buffalo and asked her this question: 'Are you proud that you are black, for if you were white, you would be holy buff like holy cow?' The buffalo did not answer, she merely chewed her cud, and slid into a nearby pond; and I exclaimed to myself '*Gayi bhains paani mein*'.

I told this story, just as I have told you, to a writer friend from America. She said that she loves India, and that it is very convenient for her here because everyone talks in English, but that she feels incapacitated at the end of an interesting story because the punchline is always in Hindi. I translated 'Gayi bhains paani mein' as 'the buffalo has gone into the water' but it was clear to both of us that she was right.

You learnt this fact as soon as you arrived in India in 1842, from Australia. You grew up in Sydney, studied law in England, went back to Sydney, where your belligerence was no good for your career—and so you set sail for where the fortune was—India! You also learnt Hindustani and Persian within six months, argued your cases in the courts in these languages and beat the John Company at its own game (that's what the East India Company was called informally, wasn't it?). You knew how to deliver the punchline in Hindustani. The black boy with blue eyes in one of your stories delivers the perfect Hindustani punchline to the British officers, 'Khuda Lord Karein', which idiomatically translated would be 'May God make you an English Lord', but legitimately translated, it would be 'May God do God'.

A famous writer—so famous that even you would know her, and of course much more famous than you—asked a question: 'Can the subaltern speak?'

She answered the question herself, but the answer was so long that it has taken scholars three decades to figure it out.

It would be best to play the game of 'can you answer in questions?' with her and perhaps question her question with, 'Can the subaltern not speak?'

Her question then would be, 'Do you think the answer is "yes"?' My retort would be, 'Do you think the answer is "no"?'

This would exhaust all questions, and exasperated, she would answer in 'yes' or 'no'.

You see, this is how you score points in this game. And given that her initial question is the basic question, and her final answer is the basic and the only answer, she would have answered her question with one word, and that would save us a lot of work.

By the way, your subaltern hero, the black boy with blue eyes, could absolutely speak. He was a 'box-waller' who peddled sundry goods in his box—knives, combs, perfumes—to the British army officers. They kicked him and made fun of him, and he replied with good humour that in heaven there will be no black and white, and that there, therefore, they would not kick him.

But you, the narrator, while narrating all this, say that all native Hindustani box-wallers are scoundrels. At the same time, you are vocal about the atrocities meted out to the poor boy. A scholar told me that the 'I' in the story is not you, but 'I, the narrator'. But if you are the narrator, and apparently chronicling Indian life, the 'narrator' will have some of your eye in it.

Perhaps you were writing in English, and so you had to please your English audience a little bit while drawing home the real point—that's smart, I must say. Or perhaps you had both the ruler and the ruled in you. So, let me ask you this: Are you a racist?

I see that you have, yet again, answered with silence, and I do not know if your answer is a question or an answer.

And so, I will not play the game of 'Can You Answer in Question?' with you. I'd rather play the game with the famous writer; after all, she asks a question right at the beginning. Besides, she is much more famous than you, and it is practical to play with more famous gamesters—one also stands the chance of getting famous. This could be fallacious, though; your close friendship with Charles Dickens didn't result in any fame for you.

Remember the party at Henry Vizetelly's house where you got drunk and told stories after stories from India? And Dickens matched you story for story, joke for joke, also from India?

Then you learnt Dickens had never been to India.

Dickens was an imaginative man, you see. All that you wrote in his *Household Words* went under the great man's name. But then you must remember that he was a man of *Household Words*, while you were a wanderer.

A wanderer must tell his tale and wander off again in search of another tale. Then there was another gatherer, Tom Taylor, who gathered stories from everywhere and tailor-made them to produce intriguing plays. Your play became his play. But, let's be fair…you can't call this plagiarism. Mr Taylor defined originality in an original way and said that an adapted play is 'new' and a considerably adapted play is 'new and original'.

Oh, by the way, did you know your ghost saved a man? In 1918, in the First World War, a guy called Maurice Hamonneau got shot in his heart. But, not quite. He was carrying a book in his left breast pocket, which is what the bullet pierced, except the last 20 pages.

The novel was Rudyard Kipling's *Kim*. You'll ask what your ghost has to do with this. Well, your formula of marrying a British soldier with an Indian woman of 'low birth', and of an orphan British child brought up by an Afghan dealer—that was used by Kipling. And that was only 20 pages, the rest were his own. You would say, 'Oh well, such standard Bollywood formulas are used by everyone.' But then, Kipling acted in your play. He knew your books very well and learnt the formulas from there.

Do you feel hurt hearing all this? There's no need—a retired veteran librarian in Australia, Mr Victor Crittenden, has republished some of your works.

Also, Mr Crittenden has claimed for you, what I think is not yours. Remember the novel *Violet, the Danseuse?* It was a rage across Europe, but it was way before your time; it was published when you were 19. If you wrote that, you were a teenage prodigy who did not have such a prodigious adulthood, for nothing ever matched *Violet*'s success.

Mr Crittenden also claims for you the poems by a poet called 'Epsilon' who wrote poems about the sea, and other things. That's poetic justice—at least we can claim for you anonymous and pseudonymous works, if in your time, your works were claimed by others as theirs.

Henry Vizetelly tells me—in a letter he left for me six score years ago—that at the party at his house you drank like a fish. He tells you loved good Scotch, but that the good Scotch loved you more—it reduced you to a wiry frame.

He's not the only one who tells about your intoxicated-ness. Remember William-Forbes Mitchell, that soldier who fought in the battle of 1857? You won't believe, he turned a writer 35 years later, and wrote a book about his reminiscences of 'The Mutiny'. He tells about the party a day before the judgement on the Jotee Persaud case was pronounced. He tells that John Exshaw was the ruling 'spirit' of the day, and spirited by that spirit, you declared that the jury members were a bunch of 'damned soors'.[I]

That's another example of Hindi punchline. You came from England in 1851 to fight the case of Lala Jotee Persaud, who had provided provisions for the John Company in the Anglo-Sikh wars, and instead of being paid up Rs 37 lakh, he landed in the court facing charges of fraud. You cooled your heels listening to the prosecution for a week, and then you made all the witnesses contradict each other. And so, drunk with the success that was going to come next morning with the judgement, you uttered profanities at the party. You were challenged by your friends if you could say the same things in the courtroom, and you accepted the challenge. You told the jury that the case stank like the pork that you had on the ship on your way to India from England; that this aspect stank like the head—pointing to the head of the jury; that that aspect stank like the legs—looking at another member, and so on.

I 'Soors' is the Hindustani word for pigs.

You won the case, and the bet. You would say being drunk is good because you win every time, but well, that's also what landed you in jail.

You thought you had acted smart by selling your newspaper *The Mofussilite* before the commencement of this case—so that whatever you wrote would not go under your name. While arguing the case, you were sober and did not accuse any jury member of anything. But obviously you had had some John Exshaw at night and had ghost-written in supposedly-not-your newspaper that a jury member—Colonel Mactier—had acted cowardly in the Kotah campaign of 1824. And there you were, proud and drunk at your sleuthing capabilities, showing off how well you knew things that had happened much before you came to India. 'Vanity of vanities, all is vanity'—never read that? You were too busy practising your Latin and quoting Byron to be bothered by Dr Johnson. If you had to write all this about Colonel Mactier, you could have written it under 'Letters to the editor' rather than under court proceedings, that Mr Lang accused such and such of cowardice.

So, despite all your arguments, the Johnnies of the John Company tightened the noose on you, and you landed in the Calcutta jail. There, instead of writing a prison diary, you started running a newspaper from the prison. Are you a 20th century don to be running business from a jail? That's why you could not write a history book like Nehru, or a historical book like Gandhi. Jail is a place for meditation and writing history and historical stuff.

There are at least two instances where you should have been confined to the environs of the jail. Just because Lord Ellenborough, then Governor-General had a fascination for elephants, and kept using elephant metaphors to describe political situations, and just because he organised an exhibition of paintings of elephants, you christened him Lord Elephantborough. He was a smart, lean man, and your christening him so would lead to the posterity thinking he was fat. This is an unpardonable offence, Mr Lang.

On another occasion, you lampooned Governor-General Hardinge so much that he got exasperated and walked into your office in Meerut and asked you why you write against his policies so much. Drunk on John Exshaw early in the morning, you had the audacity to ask his lordship if he had come to India to earn money. The Lord replied that he was a poor man in need of money, and so, indeed, that was one of the reasons. You said that you had come for the same pecuniary reason, and that writing against him helped your newspaper sell better than writing for him would do. The Lord was pleased with your candidness; but let me tell you, that's no way to behave with a Governor-General. You should definitely have been sent to the jail for this rudeness.

Never mind the two trips to jail—for after Calcutta you landed yourself in a Vienna jail as well. After all you won the case of your best friend, Lala Jotee Persaud. And he gave you three lakh rupees for winning that case in 1851! And that too after having called the jury a bunch of 'damned soors'! And the Lala presented you with a life-size portrait of his, gold brocaded and all, and you carried it about on your person always.

What mischief you played with the portrait!

You thought no one remembered; but William Forbes Mitchell did. In 1857, they were hunting for a portrait of Nana Sahib, the scourge of the British at Cawnpore.[II] And the illustrator of *Illustrated London News* walks in to your house in England and he sees the portrait of the Lala, thinks it must be Nana, has it copied and published. You did resist—I am sure it was a token resistance—but you did have fun at the cost of both the gentlemen.

Nana's henchmen thought the engraver was silly to have sketched him like a Marwari banker; and Lala's supporters were happy that he looked so much like Nana; and the poor Lala contemplated a plastic surgery lest he be confused for Nana and sent to the gallows!

II Present-day Kanpur

Do you know that your mischief created history? Till date, Lala's picture is printed as Nana's in history books. And till date I am hunting for Lala Jotee Persaud's descendants to show them the picture of their great ancestor.

I soon understood that reading books and rummaging through archives is not enough to hunt down descendants. I revised my methodology from reading historical times to reading revealing rhymes: I found one academic called Motee Persaud, in the USA. Motee rhymes with Jotee, and Persaud is Persaud. Thus, I concluded that Motee Persaud must have something to do with Jotee Persaud.

I sent an email, but it didn't work because his services had been terminated, for there was a case sub-judice against him. With much difficulty, I found a friend of his who forwarded to Motee Persaud my email that spoke about his great-grandfather and your best friend.

Motee Persaud, I do not know why, through his friend refused an interview. I just wanted to tell him that he should hire a lawyer with the surname Lang, and then he would surely win the case.

There's something else that you did that has gone down history's pages, without anyone knowing you were responsible for it.

Ever heard of Fisher's Ghost Festival in Sydney? But how would you have heard? The festival started some 90 years after you made Camel's Back your permanent address. [What a place for permanent residence—your fluid fetish didn't leave you even at the end—you thought there must be a lot of intoxicating fluid stored in Camel's Back, didn't you?] Remember the story of Fisher's Ghost that you wrote in *Tegg's Magazine*, and thereafter in various places? Well, it was a court case you had heard of as a child. Fisher—though his name differs in writings of other writers—was a convict in New South Wales, who had earned his freedom and acquired a lot of property. (see plate 4) He wanted to go back to England; so, he gave his neighbour the right to sell his property and thence send the money to him. Fisher was assumed to have gone to England; his property was sold off by the neighbour—but then his body was discovered in a pond. It was found out that the neighbour had murdered him and grabbed all his wealth. The neighbour was tried and hanged in public; his body was used for medical study, and phrenologists studied his brain.

One of the things in your will, Mr Lang, is that you wanted your brain to be examined by a phrenologist. I am sure, the fascination comes from the Fisher case.

Anyway, the Fisher case became a rage, and some writers wrote stories about it. But there, you came up with your mischief once again. You inserted a ghost into the story—that an old man saw a ghost every day upon Fisher's property, and that the ghost pointed towards a pond. The old man, also a drunkard (you think only drunk men are capable, don't you?) went to the pond, had it thoroughly searched, and fished out Fisher's body.

The story was forgotten, and then suddenly resurrected in the 1950s with a Fisher's Ghost Festival in Campbelltown, in Sydney. They, of course, don't know that they owe their celebrations to your mischief. I was at the festival last year, and it was a grand! It looks like my country's Republic Day parade, with ghosts showing off everything in the community—cars, latest fashion, old tanks, latest dance moves that kids have learnt, yoga teachers and astrologers and what not. You must make your ghost go there this year; it'll be fun.

And that would be homecoming for you, too. You never went back to Sydney after having left in 1842. You went to study at Cambridge at the age of 19, in 1835, and got thrown out for your drunken tricks.

Mr Crittenden calls them 'Botany Bay tricks' after the stories of clever convicts you wrote under the title *Tales from Botany Bay*. However, unfazed, you entered the Middle Temple, and came out a barrister. The issue of your 'convict origins' always bothered you, and you married a pretty lady from a distinguished family before you returned to Sydney in 1840. You joined the Emancipist group back home, to champion the issues of currency lads. A lawyer without a brief, you overshot yourself and spoke things on the behalf of a judge. He, instead of patting you on the back for your wit, reprimanded you. You fought with your mother and had no clue what to do in life. You took the cue from your brother-in-law and decided that India it shall be—the jewel in the crown of the British Empire.

Here, you became a successful lawyer, journalist, and writer. You also went to England a few times with your ambition to become another Charles Dickens. You would drink with the famous writer and write stories for his journals, but never become as famous as him in England.

In India, your name would always be in circulation. Rolf Bolderwood—you wouldn't know him; he was a famous Australian writer just after your time—tells in early 1900s that your novels sold like hot cakes at the railway stations in Madras Presidency.

However, your father's homeland, England, would elude you. And you would never go back to your mother in Sydney; even at her death in 1858. Was the fight so irredeemable? Your father Walter Lang died nine months before you were born, and your mother Elizabeth got married again—to Joseph Underwood, the famous businessman and whaler who already had four kids. She had four more children with him. The 10 children, including your elder brother Walter, grew up in the huge estate called Ashfield Park, in Sydney. Walter died young, and you were the only child left from your mother's first marriage.

I went to Ashfield Park last year. The estate has been brought down; the huge land was auctioned a hundred years back and subdivided to form a suburb called Ashfield. It has a huge immigrant population now; you can find a lot of Chinese stores there. There's a curious tower, built by an eccentric genius who used the tower as an observatory to study stars. This is now the office of Brahmakumaris, one of the many spiritual cults of India.

Yes, the West still believes it is material and India is spiritual, and therefore the need for heavy imports. There's a church in Ashfield that your mother got built, and that's where her grave lies. I laid a wreath upon her grave while a wild rabbit played about. There, the forever-jolly Dr David Reeve clicked my pictures, to be printed in an Indian newspaper.

But do you know what they did to the picture? They made a cutout of my frame, holding your portrait, and they cut out your mother's grave. It seems they took your fight with your mother, without knowing, a little too seriously. And what did they print in the background? Some sketch of the Rani of Jhansi—not even a good sketch at that. That's your brand value today—*Jhansi-ki-rani-ka-lawyer* (Lawyer of the Rani of Jhansi). That's what you are known for, throughout the books on the rebel queen of 1857: the English lawyer who the Rani had summoned to try and save her kingdom.

Once this article appeared, about me wasting time on you and your ancestors, several other stories spawned in Indian newspapers about a rare portrait of the Rani. There are no likenesses of the queen, and the only account about what she looked like is in your description, which has been used several times. There was this guy who copied a claim about a rare portrait of the Rani on his blog, and this was picked up by the papers. Such sensational stories crop up like identical mushrooms in our media, and die out equally soon, too.

So, your account of the Rani was in circulation quite a bit last year, without anyone mentioning your Australian origins. But that's your doing—you posed as an Englishman all through. You were gifted a portrait by the Rani, apart from camels and slaves. What happened to that portrait? Must have been with your son, who was born to Margaret Wetter and you. Wetter was barely out of her teens, and you were pushing 40—married, with three kids, and separated from your wife. Quite a ladies' man you were, Mr Lang! The child was illegitimate, for getting a divorce was nearly impossible, but you did get it eventually.

John Livingston Lang was the name of the boy; do you know he went to become an officer in the Indian Civil Service? Not quite your type, but I am sure he did well for himself. He got posted in Burma. During the Second World War, when the Japanese were invading, Livingston Lang's family fled from Burma to India, and then to England. And so, all your letters, chatters, scandals, chandeliers and Rani of Jhansi's portrait must have been left behind in Burma.

I must find them some day. That may be a little unsettling for you, for right now your personal life is shrouded in mystery. One has to glean from your chronicles, as well as your fictional work. When you make an Englishman fall in love with an Indian woman in many of your stories, I see your shadow in the man; and when you, the narrator, tell about some English hero of 'India he loved, England he despised', I almost get the feeling he is your mouthpiece.

But what India was it that you loved? You hobnobbed with the masses and the classes of India as well as the British authorities. You were mesmerised by the common workers and the faqirs of India, and snakes who listened to human beings; you got 'shampooed' by Nana Sahib's henchmen; you fought cases only for Indians; you played billiards with their arch rivals, the British army officers, as well. Somewhere, it's also the luxury of colonial India, isn't it? Your hero of *The Wetherbys* is distraught on returning to London—there are no mansions, no servants at his beck and call, no one to bear his palanquin.

I think, above all, you are a storyteller, and that that's your consuming passion. Life is a stage, and you want to record it and write about it feverishly. But it works the other way around as well—you want to live it because you want to write about it. Your wife and kids leave you, you get drunk, and are forever drunk it seems, and it is a story for you. That's the predicament of a writer—to write what you live or to live what you write.

You make stories out of all the people you meet. You meet the Rani of Jhansi and describe her waning beauty. The queen in purdah gives you a glimpse, so you think, because women want their beauty to be noticed. You write about her features—well-shaped nose, stout but pretty, and with great charms. And then that image haunts you and it becomes a white heroine, Jenny Dale, with the same description in the novel *Three Calendars*.

By the way, our television channels are much more imaginative than you. In a serial about the Rani of Jhansi produced by Zee TV, they have converted one meeting of yours with the Rani into a love affair. She even plays cricket with you. (Since I haven't yet posted this letter in nine years, I must tell you more—no such luck of even featuring as the Rani's lawyer in the 2019 film—*Manikarnika*. Kangana doesn't like to share the stage, you see. But you wouldn't have minded, would you? You are so used to falling in love with the women you meet and describing them like a true ethnographer. You praise someone's feet, someone's fingers and someone's features with whatever half stolen glances you manage.)

Empiricism of the Victorian age gives you an excuse to indulge lavishly in this exercise. However, otherwise you seem to be of a different time. You spoof the Victorian novel—you make three men fall in love with the same woman, and she falls back in love with all the three because they all look alike in the 'Calendar dress' (*Three Calendars*).

One of your white heroes marries a low caste Indian woman, earns a lot of money and is hacked to death by thugs; the wife doesn't report the matter because the man wanted to live under a pseudo-Indian identity; the son has black skin and blue eyes; he is to become 'the first black earl' but gets lost in Europe ('Black and Blue').

After reading stories of this kind, who would say magic realism is a genre of late 20th century? There is a writer of magic realism by the name of Gabriel Garcia Marquez. He got the Nobel Prize, and when he was asked how he wrote the real as if it were magical, or vice versa, he said it is the reality of his land—there is nothing magical about it. Half your novels revolve around female protagonists, in an age when women wrote under male pseudonyms. One of your widowed heroines has a bachelor tenant and doesn't care about gossip. No wonder you were considered a writer of trifles. You took realism a little too seriously.

Did you know that both your daughters from your first marriage married into Italian nobility? And did you know, unlike your stupid second son who wrote nothing but file notings of the government, your younger daughter Lucilia became a writer? Her work about Luca Della Robbia, the Italian Renaissance artist, is one of its kind. I have read letters between her and an American scholar, Allan Marquand, and I must tell you she is a fine scholar.

But none of your progeny turned out as adventurous as you (after all, only intoxicated people are able). I have read a story in a 19th century Sydney newspaper, of how you intervened at the court of an Indian king—where a man was pleading his case to the king. You thought you could help the pleader frame his argument properly. He, instead of thanking you, got furious; and lifted you, and threw you into the crowd. You once jumped off a ship into the ocean waters to save a child. I think it could have been any child, and it was a wonderfully wild thing to do; but Mr Crittenden feels that it was your son—Livingston Lang, for no one jumps into the ocean to save other people's children.

There was one man in your family who was equally adventurous—your maternal grandfather, John Harris. He was convicted for stealing eight silver spoons and sentenced to death by hanging. (I have also stolen a spoon on a Turkish Airlines flight, by the way; but that was in air, so the offence doesn't fall under any country's law). Harris's sentence was commuted to transportation to America. He escaped, and was convicted for trying to escape, and again sentenced to a hanging. The judge again changed the sentence to transportation (they needed labourers in colonies after all) to New South Wales. He arrived with the First Fleet at Sydney in 1788 and found a way out of the mess. He proposed a night watch because convicts would steal from convicts, and he became one of the first policemen of Sydney. He married a convict woman, who would bear him a son, and two daughters. He set up a rum trade which was destroyed by the governor. He sailed to England with the son, never to return, leaving the two daughters in the custody of a man named James Larra. The elder daughter would be your mother, and the younger one would create a huge scandal by running away with a penniless captain, very much like Wickham in Jane Austen's *Pride and Prejudice*.

All this about your grandfather I read in an unpublished book written by one of your Australian descendants—Laurence Halloran. Not a direct descendant, of course, but from your mother's huge second family. The book was given to me by Liz Parkinson who lives at the Entrance in Sydney, and who feeds a hundred beautiful birds in her backyard every evening. She has also written a book about your second family, the Underwoods. Anyways, Halloran wrote this unpublished book to contest the fact that you were Jewish. Mr Crittenden thinks that you denied your convict origins by posing as a British gentleman, and your Jewishness by getting buried with a New Testament. John Harris, the spoon-stealing policeman turned rum-trader, once swore under the Old Testament at a court, and that is taken as evidence of his Jewishness by Jewish historians, especially Rabbi John Levi. Halloran is distraught that his ancestor could be Jewish. And so, there are a series of letters in the 1970s between the Rabbi and Halloran, on the subject whether John Harris was too Jew or not too Jew. I pinched the letters from the Jewish Historical Society in Sydney. The last letters are catfights between the two, each swearing that he will not speak to the other ever again! I went to Melbourne to tease the Rabbi about the catfights, but he was quite pleased that someone is writing about one of the first illustrious Jews of Australia.

Christian or Jew, I think your religion was to wander and write. Perhaps you got buried with the New Testament because you wanted to read the stories you had never bothered to read before, or because you liked the narrative strategies in it. From what I know of you, you may as well have said, 'Atheism is a non-prophet organisation.'

I went to Camel's Back in Mussoorie with a bunch of friends two years ago to ask you this question, but couldn't find you among so many slumbering men, women, and children. Young men—they died of cholera mostly, I think, or 'spirits'. You yourself write in your novel *The Wetherbys* about how men in the British Indian Army got promoted not by their virtue, but because their seniors died—either of cholera or some other tropical disease, or of alcoholism. You also write that the widows quickly remarried within the regiment because widows couldn't stay in the army barracks. Thus, there are battles where men are lost—supposed dead, their widows remarry, and these 'lost' husbands come back to claim their wives, and there are duels between the dead and the living husbands!

You love pulling the leg of the Empire, don't you? Anyway, when we went to Camel's Back, it was raining heavily—everything was covered with moss, and it was impossible to find you even though the beds are arranged pretty much chronologically. I had thought (1816–1864) would help, but it didn't. So, we played hide-and-seek, splashed in mud puddles, clicked pictures with crosses and told each other ghost stories. We met Ruskin Bond, too, to ask where you're slumbering, for it was he who had discovered your final abode 40 years ago. That, too, didn't help.

But tell me Mr Lang, do you think I went to Melbourne last year just to tease the Rabbi about his catfights? Come on, you're a writer—you are supposed to understand narratives. No guesses? Well, I went to meet Susan and Scott, and to fly in a helicopter over the Seven Sisters, and to take photographs of kangaroos in the wild at Kyneton. But above all, I went to meet Dr John McArthur.

Don't ask me if he is an academic doctor or a medical one, because I don't know. I also don't know whether he is dead or alive. I don't even know what he looks like. He had left a letter for me at the Melrose Historical Society (MHS). He had sent a letter to MHS asking if they knew anything about Alice Richman. He was interested in Alice Richman because he is a descendant of Charles Summers, the tutor of the famous 19th century artist Margaret Thomas; and Thomas was a close friend of Alice—so close that she wrote a very moving poem about her death. Dr McArthur also attached a print-out of a blog, which was mine, saying that there's an Indian guy interested in Alice, too.

You would ask, 'Who the muck is Alice?' Well, Alice Richman is (1856–1882) and someone I am mesmerised by. She is slumbering in the eponymous Alice Garden in Pune University, and I met her four and-a-half years back. She was born at Melrose, South Australia, and had gone to Bombay to visit her illustrious uncle, Governor Sir James Fergusson in 1882, when she and her aunt fell to cholera. Don't ask me why I am mesmerised like a firefly—for that, you'll have to read the story I have written about her. The person who wrote Alice's epitaph is boring and doesn't describe people like you do. He doesn't say whether she had beautiful eyes, or whether her cheeks were like rose; merely that, 'She was born at Melrose'. I have been hunting for her ever since. I got interested in Maragaret Thomas because she was a friend of Alice, and Dr John McArthur got interested in Alice because she was a friend of Margaret. Now do you see the connection?

But Dr McArthur and I could not connect. Using the data gleaned from the letter he left for me, I emailed him, but it bounced back. I phoned him from Sydney, and he did not answer. I went to Melbourne to meet him in person, but he did not answer the door. I went to the death registry office, but they would not divulge 'personal information.' I have no proof for any of this, Mr Lang, because my camera got stolen at the Sydney airport on my way back to India, but you have to take my word for it. My hunt for Alice shall continue.

Mr Lang, let us clear the air, let us get even. Do you think it matters to me whether you wrote 20 odd novels, 50 odd short stories and 100 odd poems? Or that you ran a newspaper for 20 years, that you fought the cases of Rani of Jhansi and Lala Jotee Persaud? That you knew seven languages, that you could sketch very well, that you drank John Exshaw, that you knew a lot of Latin phrases, and that you sued and were sued?

Do you think I care for auditing your oddities? The question is rhetorical…and so, the answer should be 'no'. But maybe the answer is 'yes'.

Sometimes, when an exasperated friend asks me what my problem is—which is also a rhetorical question—I tell her/him a whole list of my problems. Anyway, what and who matters is Alice. You were incidental. I was just looking for Australians who lived in India in the 19th century to know more about her, when you popped from nowhere. So, I have indulged you a bit, but don't be under any illusion that you are more important than Alice.

I have been to your birthplace, but Sydney is a major city today—one does end up there. But I have also been to Alice's birthplace, which is Melrose—300 km north of Adelaide—and no one ventures there. There, I even went to the abandoned estate of the Richmans (or should it be Richmen?) in the Richman Valley with Professor Rick Hosking. We saw a water tank in the ground in the sprawling, lush field, and the professor told me that 'tank' is a Sanskrit word. Isn't it incredible? I always thought that the Hindi word *tanki* had appropriated the word from the English 'tank'. He told me that the Sanskrit 'tanka' had a variant 'tankha' in Marathi, which the colonisers of Goa, the Portuguese, took back to Europe. There, it was borrowed by English; with the British, the word came back to India, and was taken by Hindi. You can verify it from any etymological dictionary, Mr Lang. However, the point is that the word's origin is forgotten in its own land.

And well, this is what happened to you. An Australian (of course, it was New South Wales then) underdog travels to England, creates ruckus on travelling back to Sydney; sails to Calcutta, and later gets jailed in Calcutta; is left by a wife, gets a new wife; fights cases, drinks John Exshaw; travels to England to rub shoulders with Dickens and gets a shoulder-ache instead, and returns to India—for 'India he loved, and England he despised'. Laut ke buddhu ghar ko aaye (The fool returns home). Another punchline in Hindi. Australia, your place of birth, forgets you as you just did not write enough about them. You wrote a few stories with convicts as protagonists which they consider good, but that's not good enough. James Paull, one of the librarians at the University of New South Wales, asked me, 'You are researching about John George Lang! But why!?'

India forgets you, despite so many novels set in India, despite the famous cases fought by you, despite Rudyard Kipling, who took inspiration from you. You were too wild with your drinking, praising beauty, and fathering an illegitimate child to be remembered by history. You exist on a page of a history book about Rani of Jhansi as the British lawyer who was summoned by her, and who described her physical features.

England—would they want to remember you at all with all your scandalous novels? For example, the one about a widow living under the same roof as a bachelor, or would they want to remember you after the humiliating defeat of the John Company at your hands in the Jotee Persaud case? The case even rocked the House of Lords, did you know that? Would the critics give a chance to an upstart from the colonies in front of Dickens and Thackeray? No wonder, 'India he loved, England he despised'.

So here you are, like the 'tank', lost to your places of origin. All of them are your places of origin—Australia for your birth, and your larrikin childhood; England for your study of law and your literary ambitions; India for all that you did—courtrooms, editorial office, midnight oil burnt to write those books, and the languages you learnt and translated from. And like the word 'tank' informed about your origin by a stray scholar to a stray scholar.

That is why, Mr Lang, it is important to have a passport. What passport do you have? John Lang, are you (1816–1864)? Is that enough?

Do you know Henry David Thoreau, the great experimenter with solipsism who wrote Walden is (1817–1862)? Your (birth year–death year) circumscribes his (birth year-death year) and he is more famous than you. Do you see my point? To be a famous writer, your (birth year–death year) should be circumscribed by the that of a less famous writer. You can't do much about it, can you? But there is another writer who is (1816–1864): Fidelia Fiske. Do you know of her? She was the first graduate from Mary Lyon's Mount Holyoke Female Seminary in South Hadley to go on a foreign mission. She landed in Persia, after a book and a dream, to serve Christ's children the same year as you came to India.

In literary history books, they begin writing about any writer with a (birth year–death year) type bracket. It is depressing, since there is a begin date and an end date. Like medicines. Even for the writers that are alive, they write it as (1930–). The authors of such books never write such a bracket under their own name when they begin a book. So, Mr Lang, if your genre of writing does not fit under the general trend of your bracket, you are an outcast.

I am a part of a marathon relay. Rolf Bolderwood noticed your novels still selling 40 years after your passing. John Earnshaw wrote letters to the Tilak Memorial Library in Mussoorie in the 1960s, and to several libraries in Australia and England enquiring about you. He has scribbled on a copious amount of paper about you. However, in the end, all that he wrote was 35 pages—and you are not even a writer of great importance for him but just the first Australian-born novelist—Ruskin Bond discovered your grave four decades ago and wrote a couple of pieces. Mr Crittenden decided to make your biography his passion in his sixties, in the 1980s. He is still going strong and intends to celebrate your 200th birthday in 2016. Rory Medcalf, a former

Australian diplomat, had a plaque installed for you in the church in Mussoorie where you got married the second time. And I… I met you exactly a dozen dozen—or should we say gross[III]—years after you took to (after) living in Camel's Back. But do not think that I am a part of this relay marathon. Everyone else discovered you through your writings. I chanced upon you because of Alice.

I am supposed to write a book about you, Mr Lang. Should I use footnotes or endnotes? Your feet could never be tied by notes—the bank ones, or the literary ones. So, let us use endnotes. Notes are best counted at the end. And I promise you, I shall not discipline and punish, just because you went to jail twice. In deference to your wanderings, I shall not let the matters be deferred or differed. I shall follow the Orwellian formula. There, you would say Orwellian means '1984'—that it means dystopian. That's how proper nouns become abstract nouns. Orwellian is what Orwell says in his essay 'Politics and English Language—that certain kinds of writing are used to dress up a simple statement and give an air of scientific impartiality to biased judgements. I shall make my biases clear, Mr Lang.

I shall keep writing about you till Alice tells me her story. I shall Lang-u-ish with your Lang-u-age. And there's an incentive for that if I keep sitting and writing. Mr Leonard Cohen says in his novel *Beautiful Losers*: 'I am an old scholar, better-looking now than when I was young. That's what sitting on your ass does to your face.'

Here's a limerick for you Mr Lang:

> There was a wayward wanderer
> O! That incorrigible squanderer
> Spirits he would drink
> Spirited, he would think
> That lonesome philanderer!

III Gross (Noun) is an amount equal to 12 dozen; hence a dozen.

To end, I really respect your last wish on your gravestone, 'Bar at Law.' But they don't—there's no Indian court with a bar yet. Of course, lawyers who are also writers cannot quite get into the spirit without some spirit. Hope this letter will make them respect your last wish better.

By the way, Mr Lang, do you know why 'gallus' rhymes with Alice?

Waiting for a larrikin reply,
Anagrammatologically yours,

A.R. 'Risque'
333, Sutlej, JNU.
10 April 2011

Stories Forgotten, or Lying in the Cold

I had come off edge,
I was in college.

So I read many romances,
Also attended a few seances.

So we raised toasts,
And summoned ghosts.

But for every vice,
There is a versa.

So ghosts can also beckon,
And have their share of fun.

They carelessly drop a tale,
Some curious cat follows the trail—

And marvels through their pages,
Travels through their ages.

Stories forgotten,
Or lying in the cold,
Find their own time,
To be told.

The title of the above poem, *Stories Forgotten, Or Lying in the Cold*—and also the title of this chapter—is inspired by John Lang's novel titles that have the 'either/or' structure. For example, *Too Clever By Half, Or the Harroways* (1848)[1]; *The Wetherbys, Or Chapters of Indian Experience* (1853)[2]; *The Secret Police, Or Plot and Passion* (1859)[3]; *My Friend's Wife, Or York You're Wanted* (1858)[4]; *Botany Bay, Or True Tales of the Early Days of Australia* (1859)[5]; and *Captain Macdonald, Or, Haps and Mishaps at Capias Castle* (1858)[6]. A quick glance at these titles suggests that the 'or' has the functionality of 'colon (:)', where the second half is the description of the first half.

However, this assumption became suspect when I found a rare version of the novel mentioned last, at the Mitchell Library in Sydney, which bore the title *Captain Macdonald, Or The Bailiffs Outwitted* (1860)[7].

The author of these works, then, can be assumed to be fond of 'aliases'. A quick glance at the title of the novels also shows three different locales where the novels are set: Australia (*Botany Bay*), India (*The Wetherbys*), and England (*Haps and Mishaps at Capias Castle*). There is also a fourth locale which is hidden in the title *The Secret Police*, and this locale is continental Europe. 'Secret Police' here refers to the secret police of Joseph Fouché that helped him find adversaries to the rule of Napoleon in France.

These four settings point at the different 'aliases' that the author lived under: an Australian-born Emancipist (of convict origins, born: 1816); a 'gentleman' lawyer—as opposed to currency lad[I]—settled in colonial India; a British student, writer and journalist—he ran a newspaper *The Mofussilite* from Umballa,[II] Agra and Meerut at different points of time (1845–1864); and the fourth, which is embedded in the previous two 'aliases'—a scholar who knew his Latin and continental history as well as anyone else.

I A term used to denote convict origins

II Present-day Ambala

Lang uses Latin phrases in many of his works; furiously so in *Mr Flax* (1863), but also cleverly, so that the plot is not lost to the lay reader, who would have considered him 'showing off' even in his times. European history and literature also find a prominent place in his smaller works like the short story 'Dresden China', 'The Secret Police' (1859) and 'Love's Last Sacrifice' (1863).

One paradoxical alias in Lang's life is that he was a lawyer, a 'legal' man, who fathered an 'illegal' child in India with Margaret Wetter.

It is, however, a joke more at our legal system than at the poor 'rich man' (Lang used to charge hefty fees for his cases). The term 'rich man' has been cleverly inserted. It is also a joke because Lang had, for long, been separated from his first wife who was living in England in the 1850s but could not get a divorce because of the rigid divorce laws. One of Lang's preoccupations in his writings is to lampoon the legal system that was arduous, slow and farcical.

I call it '*our* legal system' because Lang's writings on it can be passed off as 21st-century Indian English writing about jurisprudence in India. In the chapter 'Military Matters' in *Wanderings in India (1859)*[8], Lang narrates the story of a court-martial case involving 'two boys'. The Major who is also the narrator of the incident says, 'Who thought (it) proper to quarrel at the mess-table, and to make use of a certain little word, not altogether becoming (of) gentlemen, if applied to one another'. The major tells the narrator that 'this is the seventh court-martial held in this station within the past two months, and with the exception of one case, the whole of them were unnecessary'. At the commencement of the trial, both boys 'wished to' plead guilty but are told by the Deputy-Judge-Advocate-General in a 'low tone of voice': 'No don't do that; say Not Guilty'.

What ensues is a story that spans 30 pages and 30 days, which involves betting amongst army personnel as to what would happen, and ends with the Commander-in-Chief himself swearing at the jury and saying the court was derelict in its duties and that the severe reprimand which the Court awarded was a mockery which 'stunk in the nostrils' and that 'prisoners were to be released from arrest and return to their duty without receiving it'.

Lang ends the chapter with: 'If it be inquired by the reader whether the above description of a Court-Martial in India is a fair specimen of what usually transpires at these tribunals, I reply, emphatically, "Yes", and I make the assertion after having watched the proceedings of no fewer than eighteen Courts' Martial during my sojourn in the East Indies.'

The professional aliases of Lang are fairly evident by now—lawyer, journalist, writer. Under these heads, too, there are aliases. So, the lawyer also becomes a convict and goes to 'gaol' twice—once in Calcutta, and the second time in Vienna. The competitive journalist himself supplies news surreptitiously to vernacular newspapers. The writer dabbles between novel, poetry and drama, with a facility for various languages.

I have a theory about this liaison with aliases, which has something to do with the title that had a hidden alias of Lang vis-à-vis the settings of his novels—*The Secret Police, Or Plot and Passion*. The theory is that the liaison with aliases, at least (and at most) in titles of novels, is a subconscious effect of the looming presence of Tom Taylor.

Tom Taylor, or Sartor Resartus,

or Tailor-Re-Tailored

In the Mulini Press edition (2008) of John Lang's *The Secret Police, Or Plot and Passion*, the editor Victor Crittenden, in his introduction, draws the timeline of the publication of this novella:

> **1856:** First published as a serial in Lang's journal *The Mofussilite* in January as *Plot and Passion, Or The Cytherean Cohort. A Dramatic Story.*
> **1859:** The magazine *The Welcome Guest* published it as just *Plot and Passion*. This magazine was edited by Henry Vizetelly.
> **1859** (later in the year): Ward & Lock, London, published it as *The Secret Police, Or Plot and Passion.*

The Tom Taylor play, simply titled *Plot and Passion*, was performed first in 1853. The play was a huge success and ran for many years not just in England, but Europe, America and India as well. The roots of the '*liaising-with-alias* syndrome' lie somewhere here.

In various 19th century sources, the play is documented as having been co-authored by Taylor and Lang. However, Mr Taylor opined that he had been magnanimous to grant co-authorship to Lang, since Lang had given Taylor an idea, and that had been Lang's only contribution. Lang, on the other hand, maintained that the novel was not taken from the story of the play, but that the play was dramatised from his story.

Lang claims in his newspaper *The Mofussilite* of 4 January 1856 that he had started to write the novel sometime in 1847, and that he had put it aside unfinished, thinking it would make a better play. Between Lang's beginnings of the novel in 1847 and the production of the play in 1853, there are six years, and that would have been enough for him to do a little research about Tom Taylor.

Tom Taylor (1817–1880) started his career as a journalist and was associated with *The Punch* magazine. He was a professor of English at University College, London, for a couple of years; he was also a lawyer and, later, a public servant at the Board of Health. Being a playwright was his part-time activity, but he is credited with 100-odd plays.

The above account would make for a short obituary, but an obituarist called G.E.M., in *The New York Times* (18 July 1880) ignored all these details and harped only on his plays. He mentions 53 of them and points out that there is little originality in Taylor, that some plays were co-authored, some were adaptations and so on. The obituary reads like the famous Mark Antony 'Brutus is an honourable man...' speech for the most part. Here is a sample:

> Among the many able and popular playwrights of the century, Tom Taylor has long held a foremost place; and when we compare him with some of his associates—especially with Brougham and Boucicault, whose names are naturally suggested by his own—I think it will be found that his work ranks higher than theirs. I will make an attempt...to gauge the value of his labour...and this will lead me to consider his claim as an 'original' dramatist, and the much mooted charge that he was, in fact, nothing more than a clever adapter—a brain worker in other men's brains... it must be admitted that Taylor's popularity has been during the last 15 years genuine and widespread. He began what may justly be termed his vocation—for he had several avocations—at a late date of life, though it is not true that his taste for the stage and the drama was a growth of after-time.

That Taylor had to make the claim of 'originality' is itself quite telling. One can go on about the documents pertaining to Tom Taylor and 'originality', but after perusal of several documents, one finds Thomas Purnell's *Dramatists of the Present Day* (1871)[1] particularly outstanding. Going by this book, the most original aspect of Tom Taylor seems to have been his definition of originality. Purnell begins his chapter on Tom Taylor as follows:

> Just as Napoleon maintained there is no such word as 'impossible,' Mr. Tom Taylor holds there is no such word as 'original.' He does not know what it means, or he attaches to the term a meaning different from what it usually receives.

The bone of contention here is Taylor's play *The Fool's Revenge* (1869) which the critics said was just a translation of Victor Hugo's *Le roi s'amuse!* (1833) while others described it, more contemptuously, 'as a mere rifacimento of the libretto of Verdi's *Rigoletto* (1851)'.

Purnell says that the truth of these statements is denied by Taylor in the preface to the play. Taylor admits that the play originated on the suggestion of an actor to adapt *Rigoletto*, and that he perused Hugo's above-mentioned play to get inspiration. Within the play, the motives of the Jester, the machinery by which his revenge is diverted from its intended channel, and the action in the court subsequent to the abduction of the daughter—are according to Taylor, his own; and 'these features, I conceive, give me the fullest right to call *The Fool's Revenge* a new play, even if it is disentitled to the epithet "original" which is matter of opinion'.

Purnell goes on to say that a close examination of most of Taylor's plays shows that 'the originality of almost everything Mr. Tom Taylor has done is, to use his own words, matter of opinion'.

Purnell's jibe continues, and he congratulates Taylor on having invented new ideas of originality, for they are not identical with those of other men, but unfortunately 'it has not yet found general acceptance'. Purnell proceeds to recount how he had been at one of

Tom Taylor's 'new' plays, and started chatting with a drama critic sitting next to him. Purnell praised Taylor; the critic nodded in the affirmative but said that most of the ideas were, unfortunately, not of the 'reputed playwright'.

One is tempted to quote the entire conversation as recounted by Purnell, and one shall give in to it partly, for apart from the wonderful dialogue, the conversation also provides a lot of context to the mid-19th century drama. Here is what goes on between Purnell and his friend:

> Upon my observing that there were good points in some of Mr. Taylor's plays, my neighbour admitted the fact; but he supplemented his admission with the remark that what I had admired belonged to other men than the reputed author. "Surely,' said I, '*A Sheep in Wolf's Clothing* was written by Mr. Taylor?'
>
> 'Ah,' said my new friend, evidently commiserating my ignorance, 'I perceive you have not read *Une Femme qui d'teste son Mari*, by Madame de Girardin.'
>
> 'Well,' said I, 'what of *Still Waters Run Deep*?'
>
> 'There is a sort of thing called *Le Gendre*, by Ch. de Bernard,' was the reply.
>
> 'I suppose you will admit that the drama *To Oblige Benson* is the creation of the gentleman whose name appears on the title-page?' I remarked.
>
> 'You have never read *Un Service le Blanchard*,' was the rejoinder.
>
> 'Well, what of *The Hidden Hand*?' was my next question; 'the scene is in Wales, and the persons of the drama are Welsh.'
>
> 'I refer you to *L'Ai'eule*, by A. Dennery,' was the answer.
>
> 'Surely you will admit that *Payable on Demand* is the invention of Mr. Tom Taylor?' I asked.
>
> 'I take the liberty of referring you to *Feurige Kohlen*,' was the curt reply.

> I then instanced *Babes in the Wood, An Unequal Match*, and *Victims*.
>
> 'It is clear to me,' said my interlocutor, 'that M. Cormon was before your time.'
>
> I began to be confounded. 'May I ask you,' said I, turning to my informant, and looking him steadily in the face, 'if you have seen the play entitled *Nine Points of the Law*?'
>
> 'I have,' was the reply of my imperturbable informant, 'and I have also read *Clover Cottage*, by Savage. I suppose I need not inform you,' continued my communicative friend, 'that Madame Pfeiffer had something to do with *'Twixt Axe and Crown*; that Mr. Gilbert is not altogether unacquainted with *Mary Warner*; that *Plot and Passion* was claimed by John Lang; and that Mr. Taylor's most popular drama, *The Ticket-of-Leave Man* is a version of MM. Brisebarre and Nuz's *Leonard*.'
>
> All this information was not altogether new to me: still, I desired to encourage the conversation. 'May I venture to ask,' said I, 'if you have reason to suppose the drama we are now witnessing is derived from any foreign original?'
>
> My friend was expanding his crush hat. 'Certainly not,' he replied with emphasis, pointing to the stage, whereon they were roasting Mrs. Rousby; 'I know no other dramatic author who, left to himself, would conceive the notion of presenting before an audience such brutal realism as that.'
>
> And my friend left.[2]

I shall concentrate on two aspects: Taylor's idea of 'originality' and Taylor's vacillation about Lang as a co-author of the play, *Plot and Passion*. We shall stay with Purnell on this. Purnell tells that this 'notice' was published in the journal *The Athenaeum* (for which he worked as the drama critic) under the pseudonym 'Q' and that Taylor entered a lengthy correspondence with the said journal to defend his position. The correspondence in its entirety has been published in Purnell's book.

Taylor, in his reply to Q's notice in *The Athenaeum*, says that every dramatist owes something to someone while writing his play; that Shakespeare was the greatest borrower of all. Taylor, however, adds that due credit must be given to collaborators, and that he has always done that when such has been the case. He claims several plays as his original, but 'pieces, like *Plot and Passion*, *Masks and Faces*, *The King's Rival*, *The Loves of a Life*, I have worked in partnership, but may claim, at least, half the honours of invention, as well as dramatic treatment'.

Taylor, here, is clearly acknowledging Lang as the co-author of *Plot and Passion*. This play is not just important because of John Lang connection, but because this is one of the few plays that sustained Taylor's reputation.

Q, in reply to Taylor's defence, tells the case of Mr Davies, who had complained to *The Athenaeum* in July 1859 that Taylor's play *The Contested Election* bore strong resemblance to his own play *Our Town*—which was written before Taylor's work. Taylor had replied saying that he had come to know about Davies' play only after the gentleman had sent him a letter about it, and that he was 'wholly at a loss to account for the resemblances he appeals to in proof of his inference'. He also says that Davies' play was similar to his because they both were talking about corruption in public affairs. Purnell infers that 'this therefore is not the only instance in which something occurs to Mr. Taylor which has already occurred to another distinct mind'. Purnell comes to the subject of *Plot and Passion* and asks why the name of John Lang had not appeared on the title page of the printed play bills.

Taylor, in reply, says that Q does not know theatrical practices very well, that the author seldom sees the play bills when they are printed (insinuating that Lang's name, and other names having been left out are not his fault).

Taylor, in this reply, theorises originality in a rather original way:

> But I have no doubt that, in the play-bills announcing my pieces, the usual practice has been followed, viz., of describing adapted plays as 'new,' unadapted as 'new and original.'

This seems to be a curious Taylorian theory; it goes on to show how old words acquire new meanings—even the word 'new'.

Peter France talks about James Robinson Planche's defence of Taylor[3], and says that his defence of a practice, which by present-day standards would be termed plagiarism, is a curious one. This is Planche's (1795–1880) defence:

> The crime [reliance on French sources], if it be one, carries its own punishment along with it — a poor, bald, literal translation fails, and a clever spirited one succeeds...The mere literal translator, whatever be the merit of his work, cannot lay claim to its *invention*... There is much more art required to make a play actable than a book readable, and in cases of adaptation and reconstruction, where only the plot or a portion of it has been taken, and the dialogue wholly or the greater part of it rewritten—why is the dramatist, however humble, to be denied the privilege so kindly accorded by Q to Shakespeare, Moliere and Boucicault?[4]

Planche, here, is obviously talking of French plays that Taylor had adapted, and not the ones where he did not credit his collaborators. The number of French plays adapted for the English audience at this time was mind-boggling, and France says that both Taylor and Planche took great pains to suitably alter the originals to suit the English taste.

The reasons for popularity of French plays can be gauged from this article in *The Musical World* (1853):

> ... every character is made subservient to one grand end, namely, the gradual and artistic evolution of the plot, and the success

> achieved affords convincing proof that action should ever be the first object in a dramatist's eye. Character and dialogue are, of course, indispensable aids, but they are subservient to action. The French dramatists are well acquainted with this fact, and hence the great care, attended with such gratifying results, which they always pay to construction. English authors are beginning to see the matter in the same light.[5]

Curiously enough, the above statements are from a review of *Plot and Passion,* where Mr Taylor is thus lauded for being an English author who is beginning to 'see matters in the same light' that everything else is 'subservient to action'. What the author of this piece, J. Alfredo Novello, does not know is that Lang probably had a hand in the play, and that one characteristic feature of his writings is that actions take primacy over settings. This is because Taylor was an established playwright—however suspect his originality be—while Lang had just arrived in England from India to further his literary career. Most of Lang's works are immediate, rushing from dialogue to dialogue, constructing fast-paced action. For example, in *Wanderings in India*, there is barely any flora and fauna; he gets straight into his Indian characters, and the action they're involved in. In 'My Experience in Austria', there is barely any description of Vienna; Lang instead gets straight into the circumstances of his being jailed and the events thereof.

Even *The Athenaeum* (in the 18 March 1854 edition), while talking about the best plays of 1853, says this of *Plot and Passion*: '... as a specimen of the prose-play of the highest class, it will maintain a permanent reputation'. It, however, adds that the play—originally ascribed to Tom Taylor alone—was 'written in conjunction with Mr. John Lang'—to whom it does much credit.

So here is *Plot and Passion*, which would not 'cease to run till a majority of the two million and odd inhabitants have seen it', and which is a 'prose-play of the highest class', and about which Tom Taylor admits initially to Q that half the credit should go to John Lang, after which he does a volte face. Lang says in the preface to the 1859 Ward and Lock edition of *The Secret Police, Or Plot and Passion*:

> The reader is requested to observe that the story of the 'Secret Police; or, Plot and Passion' is not taken from the play of 'Plot and Passion' (of which the author of these pages is the joint author with Mr. Tom Taylor), but that the play 'Plot and Passion' was dramatized from the story.

This, thus, is Taylor's about-turn in *The Athenaeum* in reply to Q's allegations (this is, of course, many years after Lang's stated preface, and seven years after Lang had died in 1864, and thus in no position to defend his earlier claim):

> 'Q' asks why the name of John Lang has never appeared on the title-page of 'Plot and Passion,' as having a right to 'half the honours of invention'. Simply because John Lang never wrote a line, suggested a character, or invented an incident of the play. Mr. John Lang, it is true, called my attention to the story on which the play is founded, that Fouche employed a body of abandoned women, whom he called his Cohorte Cytherienne, to lure his enemies within his reach. Mr. Lang suggested this as a good subject for collaboration of Mr. C. Reade and myself, who were then working together. Mr. Lang himself afterwards wrote a play and a story on the subject…My play was written without consultation, collaboration, or communication with Mr. Lang, and during his absence from London. Mr. A. Wigan knows the circumstances of the case, but as they affect private character, though not mine, I am unwilling to introduce them into a public correspondence…

Taylor says something very interesting: Lang wrote a play parallelly, and that it was never performed. As a 19th-century critic would have said, the novaturient wishes of Lang were rejected. Lang never said he wrote a play; he said, he had begun writing a novel on the subject in 1847, but thought it would make a better play; and that the (Tom Taylor) play was dramatised from his novel. Had Lang written a parallel play, he would probably have published it in his newspaper. Also, Taylor talks about personal circumstances which Mr A. Wigan, one of his lead actors, knew. One wonders what such a private circumstance could have been.

However, it clearly shows that Lang was exploited in the case, being a newcomer to the London scene. Therefore, this is the 'liaising with alias' theory: Lang knew of Taylor's reputation as an inventor of new definitions of originality, and therefore, he had to keep several 'alias' titles in mind, just in case Mr Taylor kept one for himself. This is evident in the three different titles that Lang had to play with while publishing his novel. Lang also probably cracked an in-joke in the title, *Plot and Passion*. The plot was his, so was the passion; but the credit would go to Mr Taylor. Perhaps, after whatever private circumstances that Taylor mentions, Lang suggested this title, and the joke was lost on Taylor.

The theory, of course, is half in jest, and it is commonly known that several 19th century writers kept such titles which had 'This, Or That' structure. However, 'half-in-jest' theories, when ingested, lead to serious matters, for jokes always come at a cost. This time the joke is not just on Mr Taylor, who's probably just a symptom, but at Victorian drama as well as at canon formation. Victorian drama was prolific in quantity. *The Athenaeum* of 18 March 1854 says that there were around 180 new plays in 1853, besides about 50 foreign pieces. Out of these 200 odd plays, the journal says that the expert critics do not hold more than five in positive light.

Borrowings from the French by the English was so rampant in mid-19th century that it included works of all kind, ranging from scientific to literary. Purnell has this to say about this trend:

> The practice of appropriating foreign skill appears to me to be on the increase, and Englishmen are not ashamed to call themselves authors of what has been conceived and executed by others. Within the last year or two there have appeared several French works…These have been issued in this country, not with the names of the respective authors, but with those of the persons employed to translate the books, who announce in a preface that they are under deep obligations to the original writers. When one of the works goes into a second edition, the preface is omitted…Dramatic authors are more liable to this treatment than men of science, and dramatic authors obtain even less credit than their scientific brethren. English writers take French plays, 'adapt' them, and then exhibit their imagination, not in their work, but in the belief that they themselves are the authors of the pieces produced. Of these, Mr. Tom Taylor appears to be a prominent and popular representative…Most of his plays owe something to somebody other than himself. With his views of originality, Mr. Taylor could supply every stage in London. The area of his resources is almost unlimited…

The case of *Plot and Passion,* vis-à-vis Taylor and Lang, also somehow vindicates Planche's claim that making a play riveting is much tougher than making a book readable, for the play of Tom Taylor was much more well-known than Lang's novel. Winton Tolles, a mid-20th century critic, also points to this well-known facet of Taylor: '...the British playwright Tom Taylor considered it quite legitimate for a play to be described as a "new" one if it considerably altered its source.'[6]

Mr Taylor, in short, re-tailored various fashions and retailed them in the Victorian market.

It seems that despite what happened in this case, Lang continued his collaborations with Taylor, and co-authored another play titled *Dawk Bungalow* with him, which was published in Lang's newspaper.

The Death of Abe Lincoln,

or The Birth of Tom Taylor

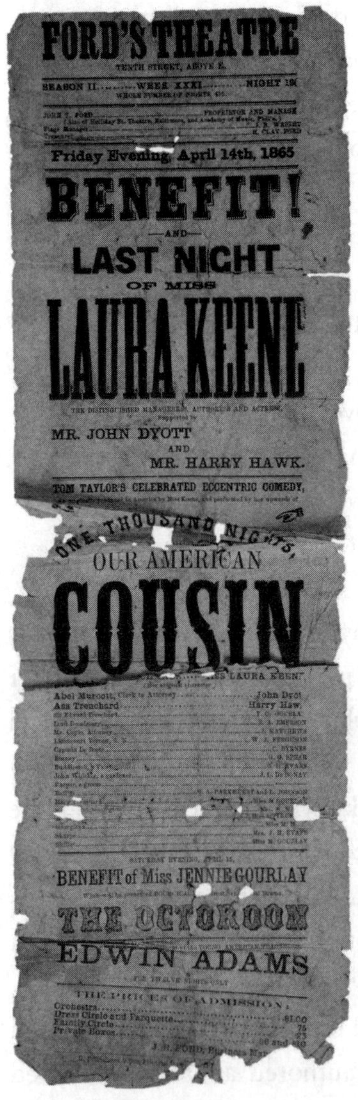

Our American Cousin play bill

Tom Taylor has not been included along with Dickens, Thackeray, Rossetti & Co. in the canon despite his hundred odd plays. For all their jibes, even Purnell and others acknowledge his widespread fame. Even though this work, too, derides Taylor, it also gives him ample space—despite and because of John Lang. However, there's one incident which etched the name of Taylor forever in history.

This is the fateful evening on which Abraham Lincoln was shot dead by actor John Wilkes Booth, who was supposed to be acting in the Tom Taylor play, but was not, that evening. One is almost tempted to say that this play was also jointly written by John Lang, but *The New York Times* obituarist G.E.M (mentioned earlier) has someone else as the nominee for 'the inspirer of yet another Taylor original.' G.E.M tells that *Our American Cousin* 'in its early shape was suggested by the story of a young American backwoodsman whom Sir

Edward Poore, one of Taylor's friends, came across during the hunting expedition in the West.'[1]

This play would make Taylor's name survive, for the assassination of Lincoln is never mentioned without the name of Taylor. It is noteworthy that Taylor was the editor of *The Punch* journal,[2] and certain anti-Lincoln articles are conjectured to have been written by him. After the assassination of Lincoln, Taylor wrote a tribute poem for the former.[3]

John Wilkes Booth, the assassin, was a part of the play troupe and knew the play very well. He would wait for the moment that was the funniest in the play, so that the audience would be writhing with laughter, and distracted, so he could shoot. Therefore, he chose Act III, Sc II, which had the following 'funniest' line: 'Well, I guess I know enough to turn you inside out, old gal—you sockdologizing old man-trap.'[4]

The context in the play is that an American comical 'rube', Lord Dundreary, is visiting his snooty British cousins, where he is accused by Mrs Mountchessington of not being used to good manners of the society. Dundreary, who became a prototype for several such characters—and that indeed shows Taylor's prowess—hollers back to the lady with the 'sockdologizing' line.

One would not be able to find 'sockdologize' in the dictionary, but Sarah Vowell, in her 2005 book *Assassination Vacation* (which is a book about three famous American assassinations), is determined to find out the meaning, and she asks the two tourist guides at Ford's theatre to tell her. The guides look up several old dictionaries and tell her it means 'manipulative'[5]. Neither Vowell nor the guides think that the line is funny enough, but that the last words heard by Abe Lincoln were 'you sockdologizing old man-trap'.

Ken Ashford tells that 'sockdologizing' was a popular slang in mid-19th century America. It means a forceful or decisive blow, something that settles a matter and leaves nothing else to follow, a knockdown blow, a 'conclusive remark, or blow, which leaves no possible response'. He conjectures that though the word is dead, its variants live on in phrases like 'he gave me a sock in the jaw' or 'sock-it-to-me'[6].

Tom Taylor, of course, sockdologised his critics with this play that ran for a thousand nights, and with the 'sockdologizing line' that had the audience in splits in every single show, so much so that it was particularly chosen as the time for assassination.

On the matter of *Our American Cousin*, I could have well argued that the irreverent style of writing in the play is quite Lang-ish, so this could well be a John Lang 'co-authored' play. But poor Edward Poore would, again, have been excluded. Also that Taylor, for all his 'originality', is not remembered for his 100-odd plays but for writing this play, during the performance of which Lincoln was shot.

> *History is fickle,*
> *in what it decides to pickle*
> *to serve the posterity, and*
> *what it lets trickle through its moment.*

Taylor, of course, owes a lot to Lang but there's another writer who, off the course, owes something to him.

What Shaw Saw, or The Seed Planted

The writer who, of course, owes something to Lang is Bernard Shaw. The first play that Shaw saw at the age of seven-and-a-half was *Plot and Passion.*

Dan H. Laurence, in the introduction to his book, *Bernard Shaw Theatrics* (2005)[1], tells that there was never a time—as Shaw reminisced about himself—that he could not read. Shaw remembered having read news reports of American Civil War at the age of five. 'He was equally precocious in regard to his theatre going experience. His first play, at seven and a half, he reminisced, was Tom Taylor's crime drama *Plot and Passion.* As with his reading, Shaw's theatre indoctrination came so early that it seemed thereafter a natural part of his life.'

Shaw wrote about his boyhood experiences in his criticism, as well as his prefaces and lectures. Laurence says that it is from these that we learn that '*Plot and Passion,* a three-act play, starring Frank Huntley and Sidney Bancroft, was performed in a single bill at Dublin's venerable Theatre Royal following a full-length pantomime *Harlequin Puss in the Boots, Or, The Fairies of the Gossamer Grove.* The latter, a hodgepodge of vaudeville, mime, ballet and farce, starred the popular Mrs Burkinshaw as Puss, and the versatile clown Hildyar, who Shaw recollected, shot a policeman into multiple segments, and that the play featured "roller skaters who crashed together in the middle of the stage and disappeared shrieking down the grave trap". The child's escort on this January evening in 1864 presumably was his mentor George John Lee, his mother's singing teacher...'

The part about *Puss in the Boots* has been included here to glimpse at mid-19th century English theatre—quite in the vein of Mrs Rousby being roasted on stage in a Tom Taylor play. This is in great contrast to *Plot and Passion,* which was praised for its rounded characters and meaningful action.

Shaw, despite boasting about his political news-readings, does not remember the controversy surrounding Taylor, or that Lang was featured as a co-author initially. However, given that Shaw watched *Plot and Passion* in 1864—a good 11 years after the first production—the fact of Lang's association with the play would have died out, as Lang, too, had died the same year. However, when Purnell's book *Dramatists of the Present Day* came out in 1871, Shaw was 14—equally into reading and theatre—and he did miss out on an important and sensational book of his time, which would quite surely have excited a teenaged Shaw.

In retrospect, why would Shaw never go back to the first play he watched? Why would the name of Tom Taylor (who died when Shaw was 23) not excite him to find out more about him? Why would his childhood memory not trigger questions about where it all started?

Childhood memory is curious and romantic; perhaps a frozen moment that one doesn't want to tamper with. This 'idea' of memory is problematised by Laurence arguing that Shaw does not remember who he saw performing that evening. The names of the actors, then, are insertions by Laurence and other critics/historians through archival study; or by Shaw himself through archival study out of curiosity.

If the latter is the case, Lang proves to be unlucky again. Shaw also did not seem to have an interest in the Raj narratives that were being published by Dickens and others in their journals, for he does not mention Lang anywhere in his very vividly recorded life. Another reason could be that most of these journals had anonymous writers, with only the name of the editor known to public.

For example, *Household Words* is a journal known only by the name of Dickens, though many writers contributed to it, including

Lang, who published as many as 22 pieces in the journal. This, of course, was revealed through researches much later.

Laurence tells that Shaw could not recall whom he had seen perform that evening because at that time, in Shaw's words, it 'seemed all real to me'.

Laurence goes on to say, 'Moreover he had to be forcibly removed from the theatre at the end because "after the falls of the curtain three times in *Plot and Passion* I could not be persuaded that it would not presently go up again"'.[2]

The date of performance of this play was 20 January 1864, one learns from A.M. Gibbs' *A Bernard Shaw Chronology*[3].

Since Shaw was fond of recalling his boyhood events, and of weaving them into his literary pursuits, I shall take the liberty to recount an incident where I owe something to Shaw. It was the interview for admission to my erstwhile undergraduate college. I was sitting outside the interview room, where I started chatting with a pretty girl dressed in shorts (one mentions this because the violation of the dress code would be her undoing, or so she would recount), and she told me about the million books she had read, which was mostly Dickens.

My turn came after hers, and since I was cautious, my answer to their question 'what do you read?' was 'newspapers'.

In school we had to study Shakespeare, Shaw, John Steinbeck, Oscar Wilde, among the literary big names, but I felt 'newspapers' would be the safest start. I was, after a while, asked what literary works I had read, and I mentioned several works, and finally, very hesitantly, *Saint Joan* by Bernard Shaw, which I had devoured several times. They noticed the hesitation, and pounced on me, and the little trick worked. I was pelted with questions about Shaw and *Saint Joan*, and I was able to answer them with comfort.

With Shaw's *Saint Joan* began my formal academic career in literature; and such a twist of curious coincidence that Shaw's theatrics began with John Lang's *Plot and Passion*.

Plot and Passion continued to be a favourite and a much-performed play for a long time after its first production in 1853. Yet another account of its performance is in 1883, and the mention of this performance would also lead to yet another unacknowledged debt to John Lang, not just in terms of authorship of *Plot and Passion*, but in terms of another very important book that saved a man's life.

The Book That Saved a Life,

or Kim, or What

The first part of the above title is fairly easy: 'The book that saved a life, or Kim', implying that a book called *Kim* saved a life. The second part, 'Kim, or What', involves a trans-lingual pun or an explanation, which is that *Kim* in Sanskrit means 'what'; this shall problematise the easiness of *Kim,* with the question, 'What or who is Kim?'

However, let's first get into the tale of the book that saved a life. It was published in the 1952 *Kipling Journal*, and has been recounted variously. In 1918, during the First World War, a French soldier was caught in the middle of an intense gunfire. The soldier, Maurice Hamonneau, got a bullet aimed straight at his heart; it was on the right path, but was stopped by a book that the soldier was carrying in his left breast-pocket. A release from the Library of Congress (USA) where the book is now kept, says, '...the French legionnaire and the last survivor of the artillery attack near Verdun in the First World War, lay wounded and unconscious for hours after the battle. When he regained his senses, he found that a copy of the 1913 French pocket edition of *Kim* by Rudyard Kipling had deflected a bullet and saved his life by a mere twenty pages.'[1]

In 2007, Debra Wynn, of the Library of Congress, presented a paper at The Kent Conference,[I] where she spoke about the rare Kipling material housed in the library.[2] She told of the grateful Hamonneau who sent his battle-scarred copy of *Kim*, along with his Croix de Guerre

---

I The Kent Conference was held in September 2007 at the University of Kent in Canterbury. It was sponsored by the Kipling Society to mark the centenary of Rudyard Kipling's Nobel Prize for Literature.

military medal he subsequently received, to Rudyard Kipling. 'Kipling, of course, is flabbergasted and deeply moved,' told Wynn. 'He accepts these valuable tokens on the condition that they would be returned once Hamonneau has a son. The collection of fourteen letters documents the budding friendship from the initial contact in 1918 until 1932 when at Hamonneau's request, Kipling returns the medal and the copy of *Kim* back to Maurice Hamonneau for Hamonneau's son, Jean.'

In a short video that History Channel made on the subject in collaboration with the Library of Congress,[3] the Chief of Rare Books and Special Collections, Mark G. Dimunation, shows the 'injured' book. It is a French edition of *Kim;* the bullet hit half-an-inch from the top of the book, and pierced through all but the last few pages. If the book had been twenty pages lesser, that would have been the end of Hamonneau.

When Kipling returned the book and the medal for Hamonneau's son Jean, he wrote a letter to the little boy: 'My dear little Jean, when you are old enough to listen, and not just be listened to, your papa will tell you the story of an ancient war and how he was saved from being killed by a bullet which was turned away from his heart by a book of mine...' Dimunation reads out a funny moment where Kipling gives the young boy some advice, 'You should always go to the battle with a book in your left pocket. Such books should never be less than three hundred and fifty pages. And it is of the first importance that book should always be in the pocket: the left breast pocket...'[4]

Kim (1901)[5] is, of course, one of the most celebrated works of Rudyard Kipling. The book was made into a film in 1950.[6] According to the official trailer of the film, its highlights are events 'conjured by witchcraft, palaces that gleam like sapphires in sun, strange bazaars filled with forbidding men of a 100 races…threat of wild bandits who roam the Khyber pass...strange land of princes and beggars… and perfumed harem girls.' It claims to be 'a monumental motion picture (that) brings you the magical fascination of the bizarre East.'[7]

One feels the need to mention the official trailer of the film because it spells out the politics of the post-Raj British psyche, as well as that of the acclaimed author, Mr Kipling. The construction of the Orient with its harem girls and witchcraft is quite in-your-face here, and almost obviates the necessity to talk about the Occidental fetishisation of the Orient that various works about postcolonialism engage with. In a story in Lang's *Wanderings in India*, an army officer tells the narrator that Lord William Bentick had planned to raze down the Taj Mahal because under its magnificence, the Victorian buildings paled to insignificance, and because the natives would think that the British had no confidence in their hold over India.

Lang, in that sense, is quite different from the Anglo-Indian writers—in always depicting the mirror image, with Indians thinking of the British as barbarians who dance with women other than their wives, for example. Lang's position is also not that of a radical rebel, for he carries with him the vantage position of 'a gentleman' and conforms to social mores of the day. His position is much more complicated than that of the India-born Rudyard Kipling, whose construction of India is generally exotic.

To put matters in context, and to get an insinuation into Kipling's worldview, let's summarise Kipling's celebrated work. Kim, or Kimball O'Hara, is an orphan who works for an Afghan horse trader in Lahore. Kim's 'white' parents died, leaving their son to fend for himself in the teeming bazaars of Lahore. Since he is well versed with the customs and Hindustani language, Kim, who also has a set of documents from his deceased father, is able to camouflage himself as a native. Street smart that he is, he changes into his English clothes whenever he anticipates being caught by the police for running errands for his mentor, Mehbub Ali.

Kim meets an old Tibetan Lama who is wandering in search of the 'River of the Arrow' to attain Moksha.[II] Legend has it that Lord

II Freedom from the "cycle of death and birth." Also known as Samsaara, the Wheel of Things, in Buddhism.

Buddha shot an arrow into the air, this river sprang from where the arrow struck. Kim decides to become the Lama's *chela*[III] and starts journeying with him on the Grand Trunk Road. This is one adventure. The other begins after Kim learns about the Great Game—a secret service run by the British government to catch native anti-social elements who might be conniving with Russians. Kim is recruited by a British officer to carry a message to an officer in Umballa[IV] as a part of this mission.

The twist in the tale comes when Kim is forcibly separated from the Lama, once identified through his father's Masonic certificate. The Lama, thinking it would be in the best interest of the child, also wants Kim to go away. The boy goes to Lucknow, where he gets good education. Kim keeps in touch with the Lama through letters, and thus continues to be a part of the espionage mission at Simla during his vacations.

After three years, when he completes his schooling, Kim is commissioned to be a part of the Great Game. He also gets a break during which he rejoins the Lama; they travel to the Himalayas at the behest of Kim's senior and colleague, Hurree Chunder Mookherjee. Here, Kim manages to get some confidential documents from Russians who have a plan to undermine the British authority in the region. When the Russian agents start looking for their documents' thief, Mookherjee befriends them to lead them astray. Meanwhile, the Lama, unwittingly, gets into trouble with the Russians. Kim shows great espionage acumen in rescuing the holy man.

The guru and *chela* travel to the plains—after the Lama realises that the river he has been looking for is in the plains, and not the hills—and the Russian documents are delivered to the government. Mehbub Ali, the Afghan mentor of Kim, comes to meet him. The Lama finds the river and attains Enlightenment.

III disciple (chela is used throughout the novel *Kim*).

IV Present-day Ambala.

Kim's future path is left to the reader's imagination—whether he would take the spiritual path of Tibetan Buddhism, or government espionage that would win him medals and accolades. Kim, however, says to the Lama, 'I am not a Sahib. I am thy *chela*.'

Kipling creates an easy dichotomy between the material and the spiritual in a classical way. The West is in its material pursuit, and the East in its spiritual one; and the boy—a crossover between the two—is at the confluence, an embodiment of both. The spiritual quest is in trouble, and it is the bravery of the Western man that can salvage the situation. During his childhood, too, whenever the 'native Kim' is in trouble, he changes into 'Western Kim' to save himself.

A performance of the play *Plot and Passion* took place in Lahore in December 1883. This performance is important because Rudyard Kipling played the role of Desmarets, the villain in the play. (see plate 2) According to Sandra Kemp and Lisa Lewis, editors of *Writings on Writing by Rudyard Kipling*: 'The large railway complex at Lahore (with junction and repair yards) had its own staff theatre. Here on 20 and 22 December 1883 *(sic)* the Lahore Amateurs performed a play *Plot and Passion* by Tom Taylor and John Lang (1853), in which Rudyard Kipling plays Desmarets, a principal part.'[8]

The Library of Congress also possesses an invitation card for the above-mentioned play. This invitation, with hand-written notes by Kipling, was for one of his lady friends.

Debra Wynn, in her conference paper,[9] presented the postcard as 'a hand-lettered and illustrated theatre program…drawn by Rudyard Kipling for a performance of the 1853 Tom Taylor play *Plot and Passion*'. (*She, of course, misses John Lang…like everyone*).[10] William M. Carpenter[V] indicates that this program card was given to Miss Plowden, a close friend of the Kipling family.

V The Library of Congress has the postcard with Rudyard Kipling's handwriting in the William Carpenter collection. William M. Carpenter, of Evanston Illinois, was said to have in his possession several Kipling related memorabilia which is now part of the Library of Congress Kipling catalogue.

On the back of the card is a poem with 12 lines of a verse from 1883. The text of this poem is included as the final two stanzas in 'Preadmonisheth ye ghoste of Desmarets', a six-stanza verse cited in Andrew Rutherford's *Early Verse by Rudyard Kipling, 1879–1889.*

Kipling got rave reviews for his performance. The writers who have written about Kipling have always attributed the play to John Lang, as well as to Tom Taylor. One does not know about Kipling himself though. Having the first part of the chapter's title 'The Book that Saved a Life, or Kim'—the novel *Kim* saving a life— sorted, let us come to the second part of 'or What'.

Kipling (1865–1936) obviously knew of John Lang (1816–1864). Lang was a famous public figure in India; both as a writer and a lawyer, and reviews of Lang's novels were carried out by almost every reputed journal of the time. Most of Lang's novels were set in India, and he was a principal Anglo-Indian writer writing novels set in India. It seems that the character of Kim is, in part, inspired by the writings of John Lang.

There are three stories in Lang's *Wanderings in India* that explore the issue of Anglo-Indian children. These were published variously in Dickens's journal *Household Words* (1856) and the American journal *The Living Age* (1856).[11] The three stories are 'The Mahommedan Mother', 'Black and Blue' and 'Marching'. The three stories explore the fate of Anglo-Indian children born out of different kinds of wedlock. The father, of course, remains a white, army man. Even the radical Lang could not explore the possibility of a native man with a white woman. It's only much later (in 1924), in E.M. Forster's *A Passage to India*, that a native man's platonic liking for a white woman results in some reciprocation, but it also results in massive trouble for the man.

Coming back to the Lang stories, the first story obviously has a Muslim mother, the second one has a native woman of not just very low caste, but also of 'black complexion'; the third story has an orphaned child of white parents, being brought up by an Afghan merchant.

It is from the third story that *Kim* draws its inspiration particularly. Lang, in 'Marching', recounts a journey to Agra he undertook with a lieutenant. Of the several stories 'connected with the war in Affghanistan' that the officer tells him, one interests Lang in particular.

The lieutenant had stayed at a friend's place in Meerut sometime in the early 1850s, when an 'Affghan dealer came to the house with several commodities from Caubul'[VI] to sell. [It is interesting to note that Lang does not use the term 'Caubuli-wallah' though the term 'Kabuli-wala' is very much ingrained in the 20th century Indian psyche through popular depictions in films and stories, as well as visits by real Kabuli-walas. Rabindranath Tagore also wrote a story titled 'Kabuliwala']. The lieutenant tells Lang that, 'to talk to these dealers is rather amusing at times, especially when you know their habits…and peculiarities…it is like meeting with an old friend, and one lingers as long as possible over the business of the bargain and sale… We had him for at least an hour in the verandah before my friend's wife would decide upon what she would take. This matter concluded, the Affghan inquired if the lady would buy a kitten—a Persian kitten…'.

The picture that Tagore paints of the Kabuliwala is very similar—that of meeting an old friend, of lingering over business, for the lingering is more important than the business itself. Lang further recounts in 'Marching' that upon the buyers not being able to see any kittens with the Caubuli-wallah, the merchant takes out the kittens from his *chogah*:[VII]

> 'Here,' said the merchant, putting his hand into a huge pocket at the back of his chogah (a sort of gaberdine), and withdrawing, one by one, no less than sixteen of these little animals (all males). For more than the hour…this living

VI Present-day Kabul.

VII (also choga) A loosely-worn long-sleeved robe.

> bustle had remained perfectly motionless, and had not uttered a single sound; but now, when they saw the light, and were placed upon all-fours, they ran about and mewed—bushy tails on end—after the most vigorous fashion imaginable. There they were! Kittens as black as the blackest ink, kittens white as the whitest snow, kittens as yellow as the yellowest gold, and kittens piebald, brindled, and grey.

The above paragraph shows the playful, evocative manner of Lang's writing. It is also a creation of the Exotic East in a certain way, but one gets the flavour of a 'lived' experience.

In the story, after two cats have been bought, the lady of the house is interested in fruits. The dealer, who does not have them on his person, promises to send them with a boy the following day. The next day, a boy comes with the fruits; and though he talks in Hindustani, his skin colour is pale, and eyes are blue. The lady of the house notices something about the boy and asks everyone present to observe all facial features of the boy, 'especially his smile', and 'even the shape of his fingers' and guess who the boy looks like. The lady, her husband and the lieutenant then write down the name of the person whom they thought 'the boy looked like'. All of them had named a dead soldier named Percy. When an army major and his wife come to the house and see the boy, the couple, too, immediately recognise him as Percy's. The boy, when asked about his origins, says he is a 'Mahommedan, and an orphan'.

The party then summons the dealer and asks him how he came to possess the child. It is revealed that the he bought the boy as a slave from a trader, who had got him from 'a native woman in Caubul'. The dealer, in turn, questions them if they thought the boy was of English parentage, and asks them the amount they are willing to pay for him. When the dealer would not part with the boy for 'even half a lac rupees', the English party point out to him that slavery was not permitted in the British dominions.

At that point the dealer says the boy is free, and can choose where he wants to stay. In reality, the dealer has been trying to verify if the white people were earnest about adopting the child. He even asks for the *nishan* (insignia) of the deceased boy's father. Once the Afghan is satisfied that his boy is in good hands, he decides to let go of the boy for no money, promising to return whatever the child's father left for him. The boy, who has been listening to all this drama unfold, raises a furore that he will not go to the 'home of infidels'.

There are various similarities between the boy of this story and Kipling's Kim. Kim is an orphan, born of white parents; he is brought up by an Afghan trader, and is perfectly at ease with all the hustle and bustle of 'Hindoostan'. He is recognised by an Englishman who knew his father, and it is with great difficulty that he can be made to adopt a new identity. All the elements present in the story by Lang as well. The rest of *Kim*'s narrative is Kipling's, where Kim delves into the seeking of the holy river, and being a part of the Great Game.

A copy of *Kim* saves Hamonneau's life by deflecting a bullet aimed at his heart. All but 20 pages of the book were pierced. The first 20 pages is all that Kipling draws from Lang, which got pierced. The last 20 save the man's life. Yet again, Lang is out of luck—to be shot through, and unknown.

It is not that I am trying to contrive a case for Mr Lang. There are others who concur with this idea, albeit less vociferously. B.J. Moore-Gilbert notes that the narrative of *Kim* follows in a tradition of Anglo-Indian fiction featuring abandoned British orphans, particularly John Lang's '*Who Was the Child*?' (1859) and F.M. Crawford's *Mr. Isaacs.*[12] Joseph Bristow also makes the same case via Moore-Gilbert in his book *Empire Boys: Adventures in A Man's World.*[13]

Moore-Gilbert, however, has the name of the story wrong; a lot of 19th century books had, on the left pages, the name of the book, and on the right pages, the event that would be happening in the narrative in those two pages. So, the chronicle/chapter called 'Marching' in

Wanderings in India has right page headers that read 'An Affghan Dealer', 'A Lost Child', 'Questions and Answers' 'Who Was the Child?' etc. Of these, 'Who Was the Child?' would have seemed the natural title of the piece to Moore-Gilbert.

Fact is stranger than fiction—the adage is ably proved by the case of Maurice Hamonneau being saved by a book. However, a more intriguing thought would be that fiction and fact belong to some common realm, or that fiction informs fact.

In his novel *Will He Marry Her?*[14], Lang describes the situation where the hero of the story is wounded in action:

> [Augustus] Reckless, who, as the hero of this story, claims our greatest attention, received two wounds—one in the breast (which would have killed him had not the point of the instrument pierced, in the first instance the little book which was in the pocket of his undress jacket); and the other in his leg, a very bad wound, which was dangerous and painful for some time.

The saviour book in question was gifted to Augustus by his cleric brother, Robert. It was a book of Burial Service, which Augustus could have a need for on the battle field, for though 'you cannot give yourself a Christian burial; but there may be times when you would desire to give it to others'. His two other elder brothers—Charles, the lawyer, and John, the doctor, gave him a bottle of brandy to be used only in dire need, and a case of surgical instruments, respectively. Augustus promised that he would always carry all these 'invaluable presents' with him on the battle field, in 'the breast-pocket of my undress jacket'.

(While reading the novel *Will He Marry Her*, the moment Augustus promises to carry it in his 'breast-pocket', I knew what was coming, for I had read the case of Maurice Hamonneau before reading this novel. And that is what exactly happens 112 pages later in the novel—Augustus gets shot at, and is protected by the book.)

Will He Marry Her? was written in 1858. In a real-life script played out exactly 60 years later, Hamonneau would be saved from a bullet by the book *Kim* in his breast-pocket—a book inspired by a story from John Lang.

Lang writing fiction in which a book becomes an armour against a bullet for a fictional character; Kipling getting inspired by another tale by Lang, and writing his own book; this book acting as an armour against a bullet for a real man in a real war—is prime material for great ponderings-over for those who seek connections and patterns in this mysterious world.

The Story of Isaacs,

or The Other Half of Kim

At this point, it would be a good idea to discuss Francis Marion Crawford and his novel *Mr Isaacs*, for this book is also said to have inspired the genesis of *Kim*. Crawford is remembered in America, but does not figure anywhere in the British literary canon, despite the fact that he had taken the pains to travel to England from America at the publication of his first book *Mr Isaacs*, for he ought to have been present in Britain on the day of the publication to secure copyright. This was recounted by Crawford himself[I] to Major Pond[1]. Crawford (1854–1909) was the son of an American sculptor, and brother of Mary Crawford Fraser[II]. Major Pond tells, 'At the age of twenty-two he returned to Rome to study at the University of Rome. There one of the professors interested him in Buddhism and the other Oriental mysteries. This professor, who recognised the young pupil's aptitude in languages, advised him to go to India and study Sanscrit, and then returning, he could readily obtain a professorship.'[2]

Crawford sailed to Bombay with a hundred pounds but soon turned a pauper. He met the editor of the *Bombay Gazette*, who informed him that the editor of the Allahabad *Indian Herald* was in need of a good man. Major Pond says:

> Would he take the position? 'Would a duck swim?' said Mr. Crawford and off he went to Allahabad, a thousand miles away. There he learned that the 'good man' was supposed to fill the

I The account is of Major Pond's interview with FM Crawford in 1900. Major Pond, a prolific public speaker and writer, died in 1904.

II Mary Crawford Fraser, better known as the American writer Mrs Hugh Fraser, known for her various memoirs and historical novels.

> posts of reporter, managing editor and editorial writer, with now and then a turn at type-setting. Thus none of the sixteen hours of the working day would be wasted. But Mr. Crawford couldn't afford to grumble.[3]

Crawford's Indian stint would be the hardest 18 months of his life. He would go back to Italy, and then to America in 1880. On the way to America, the ship would break down and Crawford's physical toughness would be great help in maintenance of the ship. Crawford would go on to study 'Sanscrit' under Professor Charles Lanman. He stayed sometimes with, interestingly, Uncle Sam Edward Harkins, and quotes Crawford, 'As was perfectly natural, we began to exchange stories while smoking, and…with a great deal of detail, my recollections of an interesting man whom I met in Simla.'

This man's story would become the novel called *Mr Isaacs*. The original man was a diamond dealer called Mr Jacobs. By and by, Crawford would remember a chance meeting with an intriguing Buddhist monk, and he would introduce him to the plot. Macmillan and Co. agreed to publish the novel, and Crawford travelled to the English soil to secure copyright. It seems that in an age of fluid definitions of originality espoused by the likes of Mr Taylor, an author had to be physically present to insist his authority.

When Crawford returned to America, he found that his work had become a roaring success. The novel would run into 12,500 copies, which is a bestseller even by today's standards. The first two novels of Crawford were the only ones to have crossed the 10,000-print mark.

Let us have a look at the plot of *Mr Isaacs*. The novel opens with an American-brought-up-in-Italy journalist, Mr Griggs, landing in Simla to gather news that would sell, for Simla was the hub of British political and social affairs. There he meets a rich merchant, Mr Isaacs, by whom he is mesmerised. At first, Mr Griggs thinks Mr Isaacs is an Italian because of his finesse and skin tone. Mr Isaacs, in a conversation then, alludes to a German proverb about angels passing by a house. Isaacs can also speak English very fluently, and with a British accent, which makes Griggs think the merchant must have gone to an elite institution like Oxford or Cambridge. Isaacs finally ends Griggs' curiosity by telling him that he is a 'Zoroaster by birth but Mussalman by faith, sold as a slave in the Turkish market'. Isaacs explains that his master was kind to him due to his fair skin and great mental and physical abilities. Isaacs points to the South star, Sirius, and tells Griggs that whatever word Griggs might use for 'kismet', it 'allotted me a somewhat happier existence than generally falls to the share of young slaves in Roum'[4].

Isaacs got a chance to go for the Haj pilgrimage to Mecca, where after he got on a ship that was sailing to Bombay. In Bombay, however, he got arrested because he touched some sweets on a Hindu's plate. The British upheld the decadent caste laws of Hindus, by which if a Muslim man touched the food of even a low-caste Hindu man, it would become impure. The judge of the case, understanding that the man is poor and new to the country, acquits him and gives him a rupee to fend for himself. Isaacs would never forget this gesture of John Westonhaugh; when time comes, he would reciprocate.

The rest, as they say, is history (for the novel). Abdul Hafiz-ben Isak changes his name to Mr Isaacs for the convenience of the British tongue and becomes a renowned diamond merchant. In the story that ensues, he falls in love with an English lady called Katherine Westonhaugh, who would turn out to be the sister of the judge who had given Isaacs the rupee of *kismet*. The backdrop is of the Second Afghan War (1878–80), and Isaacs saves an Afghan revolutionary called Shere Ali from the British hands, assisted by Griggs and Ram Lall, a Buddhist mystic. In the end, Isaacs disappears after leaving all his wealth for the judge.

The novel hovers around the principal characters, their psyches, worldviews and energies. The saving of the Afghan from the British police is just one of the events. The historical setting is not important to the novel. Priya Joshi rightly points out that the figures in this novel 'are not to be understood in relation to the historical moment… Crawford draws his reader's attention to the biographical and psychic details that create and motivate his protagonists, as this, he insists, is the central point of *Mr Isaacs*'[5].

Coming back to Kipling and *Kim*, while the first part of Kim's genesis—his background—is inspired by Lang's account of the orphan child in *Wanderings in India,* the second part draws heavily from *Mr Isaacs.* B.J. Moore-Gilbert's suspicion is not unfounded. *Kim* is also set during the Second Afghan War, and has the rescuing of the Buddhist monk as one of the important events. In *Mr Isaacs,* the Buddhist monk aids in rescuing Shere Ali. While *Mr Isaacs* has a Zoroastrian protagonist who can pass off as an Italian, an Anglo-Indian, or anyone; that ambivalence is done away with in *Kim*—that character is taken from Lang's story. Lang never delves into the matter of adult Anglo-Indians; he always looks at the fate of such children. Kipling, with the aid of Crawford's work, develops it. The spiritualist is a part of the espionage mission in Crawford's novel, whereas he would need to be saved by the Anglo-Indian in *Kim.* Kipling uses his characters as voices for different kinds of worldviews and ways to live. Crawford, on the other hand, dislocates his characters from the historical moment—only apparently, for his characters are very much of their own times—to engage with basic human emotions.

Lang leaves his story at the child howling and saying that he does not want to stay with infidels; Crawford creates a fluid identity for his protagonist, and in the only intrigue of the novel, a Persian, a white man, and a Buddhist monk collaborate to take on the might of the British empire. Kipling's Kim, however, does well to be taken away from his vagrant ways, is educated and employed in a great espionage mission, with the help of which he is able to save his spiritual master.

Kipling places his protagonist very much in a historical time, and perpetuates the stereotypes of the 'civilising white man' and 'mystic Orient'[III]. One would think that it is outsiders to the system—Lang who had come from a convict-origin-Australian past; and Crawford, who had come from Italy—who are able to challenge the (Edward) Said-ian notions of Orientalism.

Maurice Hamonneau also owed his life to two other people apart from Kipling. Perhaps it would interest his grandchildren to know that.

There are two other reasons why we are discussing Crawford: one, he bears striking resemblance to Lang—almost his alias in afterlife—and two, Crawford is part of an important debate over Realism in the 19th century. Lang's narratives also challenge this trope of the 19th century. The difference is that Crawford theorised, Lang didn't. The similarities between the two men of letters is striking. Major Pond tells us (in 1900) that almost all portraits of Crawford show him smoking. Contemporary accounts about Lang—and there are not many—talk about his drinking and smoking habits too. William Forbes-Mitchell, in his book *Remiscences of the Mutiny* (1893), writes about a party on the eve of the pronouncement of the judgement of a case that Lang has been a lawyer in, where Lang is drunk enough (in 1851) to call the jury a 'parcel of damned *soors*'.[6] Henry Vizetelly recounts a party in 1857, where Charles Dickens was also present, and tells about Lang's love for smoke and alcohol, and how the latter habit had 'unstrung every nerve in his wiry frame'[7]. Lang, himself, incessantly keeps smoking in *Wanderings in India* (in the chapters 'Himalayan Club', 'Marching' etc.) That is, of course, no great point of comparison between two men of letters, and Crawford was not an alcoholic. But nonetheless, the above points give an insight into Lang's boisterous personality, and also his alcoholism—which would be his nemesis.

III Joseph Bristow in his book *Empire Boys: Adventures In A Man's World* argues that B.J. Moore-Gilbert writes in *Kipling and 'Orientalism'* that Edward Said's idea of the Occident creating a monolithic, mystical Orient is challenged in works like *Kim*.

Coming to the more serious similarities, Crawford had an interest in languages, and a tremendous facility for learning them—by the time he was 15, he knew English, French, Italian, Swiss and German; later, he added Sanskrit, Hindustani, Russian and Turkish to his list. Lang knew English, French, Italian, Hindustani and Persian very well. He was a voracious reader, and his novels would be peppered with Latin and French quotations, as well as quotes from writers like Byron, Molière etc.

Lang and Crawford, both, were editors of radical newspapers of their time. While Lang was the owner and editor of *The Mofussilite* for around 20 years (1845–1864), Crawford was the editor of the *Indian Herald* in Allahabad for 18 months (1878–1880). We have already seen how Crawford spent the most overworked 18 months of his life serving this newspaper. Lang also almost single-handedly wrote his entire newspaper; he would also write serials of his novels in the paper. *The Mofussilite* almost always troubled the government. Crawford, in his brief stint in Indian journalism, wrote about self-rule almost five years before the Indian National Congress was founded.

Another instance of Lang's larrikin, boisterous, and witty attitude is recounted by Lieutenant Colonel Balcarres D. Wardlaw Ramsay,[8] where he tells about Sir Henry Hardinge (later Lord Hardinge), the governor-general at the time of the Second Anglo-Sikh War, being very irritated by the articles against him written in *The Mofussilite.* The governor-general was so irked, that when he was in Meerut, he summoned John Lang to explain his position. This is what ensued:

> When Lord Hardinge was on his way home, he passed through Meerut and sent for Mr Lang, addressing him as follows:
>
> 'Now Mr Lang, I am going home and I should like to know why you have so persistently abused me. Speak without reserve, I shall not be annoyed.'

> 'Well,' replied Mr Lang, 'will your lordship answer a question first?'
>
> 'Certainly.'
>
> 'Why did your lordship come out to India?'
>
> 'For several reasons.'
>
> 'Did not the wish to make money somewhat influence you?'
>
> 'Certainly,' said Lord Hardinge, 'for I am a poor man.'
>
> 'Well, then,' said Mr Lang, 'I came to India for the same reason; and I found I could not make money faster than abusing your lordship's policy. If I could have made as much by praising it, it would have given me greater pleasure. It is a simple question, not of principle, but of "L.s.d".'[IV] Lord Hardinge was delighted with this frank avowal.

Both Crawford and Lang tasted success in countries not of their birth—Crawford in America, and Lang in India—with both being popular in British literary circles as well. They were both outsiders to their systems, which is probably the core of their appeal—they could write with a certain detachment and a certain freedom from biases that other Englishmen held in the colonies. Both writers also wrote with a deep interest in the psychology of their characters, and used lots of dialogues to bring out their worldviews. The settings of their novels spanned a huge geographical range—India (*Mr Isaacs* as also later works), America (*Dr Claudius*), Russia, Turkey, Europe for Crawford; Lang's settings were in India (most of his novels begin in England, and a character is sent off to India), Australia (two books of short stories about convicts), and Europe (*Dresden China, An Experience in Vienna*). These two people are not unique in the 19th century context—the bustling trade and other connexions between various colonies of the Empire as well as other places—prompted

IV L.s.d stands for £, shillings, pence (drachmas), and is an idiom popular in the 19th century.

the rise of many such wanderers and dissenters. Both these writers were also very successful in their time—Crawford's sales figures say it all; and Lang was known to almost every important man of the Empire and reviewed in important journals of the time. Both were later forgotten by history, despite having written prolific amounts in their short lives; Lang lived till 48, Crawford till 55—and Lang wrote over 20 novels, and Crawford, 36. Crawford is still relatively known when compared to Lang, who is quite lost. Another very important point of commonality—which is one of the reasons why literary history has treated them with ignominy—is that both wrote against the conventions of writting of the time.

Lang had his novels strewn with female protagonists, and that, with tremendous agency; for example, in *Three Calendars*, Jenny Dale has her affections for not one but three men because they all look alike when in the 'Calendar Dress' and not alike when they are not in the said dress. The 'Calendar Dress' is not described, and becomes an ambiguous reason for such behaviour. The magical dress critiques the standard mode of writing of the day—namely Realism—while Lang maintains the stylistics of the time.

Crawford, in *Mr Isaacs*, does not make his characters adhere to the stereotypes attached with their affiliations or political standing but explores possibilities for them, besides making the protagonist a self-made man who has risen from being a slave to someone who can pass off as an Italian, a British or an Indian. Crawford also theorised about the novel form and wrote a book about it.

Of course, there are problems in the novels of both Crawford and Lang, but they are not, in Crawford's words, 'what they call realism'. He speculates about this singularly unique man who he had met in Simla through this novel. Crawford is interested in telling a story based on a character he has met. Lang, to take the example of *Three Calendars* again, is almost spoofing the Austenian romantic realism, for the novel has three girls and three men. The other two girls simulate the idea of a usual romantic novel, for the reader to soon discover that it actually turns out to be an understated spoof. Both the writers draw from experience of meeting unique characters, and their own experiences—not that they are singularly unique in this. While Lang's early novels—*Raymond, Mazarine, Will He Marry Her?*—are replete with seemingly autobiographical references about university life, Crawford's character Mr Griggs in *Mr Isaacs* is an American-Italian journalist very much like him. Both the writers play with, challenge, and critique the Empire, but are not able to cross over when it comes to the taboo—of a white woman marrying a native colonial man. *Mr Isaacs*, for all his wealth and charming personality, is unable to marry Katherine. In Lang's stories Anglo-Indian children are all born of wedlock between a white man and Indian woman, but not the other way around.

So here are these two very successful novelists of the 19th century, from both of whom Kipling borrowed for his novel *Kim*, and ended up being far more famous than either of them. Both were polyglots, writers, dissenters, newspaper men who made the British government squirm, novelists with an urge to usurp realism that seemed unreal to them, and both were forgotten by the canon, especially Lang, as a writer of trifles. Even John Earnshaw, who spent almost two decades (1950s and 1960s) researching on the life of John Lang, makes light of Lang's literary work with his own Victorian sensibility, and steers clear of it mostly. His research, in the end, seems to be because Lang was the first Australian-born novelist, and not because he was a fine novelist. The Indian memory is because Lang represented the Rani of Jhansi in the Doctrine of Lapse case—which he lost by the way, within a week—and not because he wrote 15 novels set in India, or because he gave new dimensions to journalism of dissent.

What's interesting here is that all the various things said about both Lang and Crawford have been gleaned from 'reminiscences'. Lord Hardinge summoning Lang is from Ramsay's reminiscences, Lang getting drunk and calling the jury a bunch of pigs is from William

Forbes-Mitchell's reminiscences, Lang's problem of alcoholism is from Henry Vizetelly's reminiscences; various aspects of Crawford's personality are from Major's Ponds reminiscences. Interestingly, all these writers are military men except for Vizetelly, and this insinuates the inclination that army men of the 19th century had for writing about their exciting historical times. History, apparently, does not treat reminiscences as verifiable sources, for they may carry the biases of their writers. However, in this very context, has history not shown its own biases in forgetting two men who were prolific in their time?

One wonders if Francis Marion Crawford, who came to India in 1878, had heard of John George Lang, who had died in Mussoorie in 1864.

The Italian Connexion[I]

or The Legal Man Who was an Illegal Father

I wonder if F.M. Crawford had heard about John Lang. I need not wonder if Lang had heard of Crawford; the latter was 10, still four years away from smoking, when the former died of his drinking habits. However, my desire that the two men of letters should be connected somehow is fulfilled through a daughter of Lang. Lucilia Lang, who later became Lucilia Marchesa Burlamacchi, wrote in 1900 *Luca Della Robbia*,[1] a book about the famous Renaissance artist by the same name. She begins her book with the following:

> 'Genius,' as Marion Crawford justly says, 'means, before all things, great and constant creative power; it means wealth of resource and invention; it means quantity as well as quality.'

Burlamacchi's definition is probably apt for both Lang and Crawford—both had great and constant creative power, and could draw resources from their many travels, experiences and imaginations; the quantities produced by both are immense; the quality was suspect for the Victorian critics. It is interesting that till Burlamacchi's work came, Luca Della Robbia was considered a minor artist, but not after that. One hopes the same for Lang.

Lucilia married and settled down as L. Marchesa Burlamacchi at Lucca. Marion Crawford was also born at Lucca. Not much is known about Lucilia's life—the one book that she wrote resurrecting Della Robbia is what she is known by. *Luca Della Robbia* was a part of the

I. Chiefly it's an old-fashioned spelling of 'connection' in British English. It also means 'link,' something that connects two ideas.

series 'The Great Masters In Painting and Sculpture' commissioned by George Bell and Sons, which included works on Velasquez, Raphael, Andrea Del Sarto and other artists.

Lucilia's work received rave reviews and became a classic for any further work on Robbia. *The Athenaeum* conjectures (rightly so) that she is an Englishwoman, though without knowing it:

> Despite her Italian title and name, the author, if such we may call her, writes like an Englishwoman, and treats her unusually fresh subject in a manner and mood which are by any standards very scholarly.[2]

When it comes to 'gut feelings', this journal gets the facts about the father and the daughter correct, without quite knowing it for fact.

The exhaustive nature of the work is pointed out by Francis A. Hyett: 'A catalogue of all the known works in (Andrea Della) Robbia ware, that are in churches or public galleries in Europe, is given by the Marchesa Burlamacchi her Luca Della Robbia.'[3]

That the 'Marchesa Burlamacchi' was a daughter of John Lang is attested to in a few places. Colin Roderick and John Earnshaw in their 1963 article on John Lang[4] tell that Lucy's two daughters, Aimee and Lucy, married into Italian families. When applying for probate on her mother's death on 17 August 1874, Aimee, then Countess Riccardi, described her mother as 'the widow and relict of John Lang, late of Calcutta in the East Indies, Barrister at Law', and gave her successive address as '37 York Street Portman Square in the County of Middlesex, afterwards of 16 Pizza dello Statuto Turin in the Kingdom of Italy but late of Casa Manzi Viareggio Tuscany'. It thus appears that the widow died at the home of her younger daughter Lucy, at this time 'Lucy Manzi, formerly Lucy Burlamacchi'.

Lang's first wife Lucy died 10 years after him—he died on 20 August 1864, and she on 17 August 1874. It is also interesting to see the use of the word 'relict' by Aimee. Relict means widow, and to use the same term twice would be tautology. 'Relict' in its original Latin sense also connoted 'relinquished'. Things between the former husband and wife had turned very sour just before his death.

In 1863, Lucy Lang filed a suit in the High Court of Calcutta to settle the issue of alimony with her former husband. *Allen's Indian Mail* published the summary of the trial:

> HIGH COURT of CALCUTTA.—Lucy Lang v. W.C. Hurry and others…This was a suit to recover the sum of a lakh and fifty thousand rupees from Lalla Joteepersaud and William Cobb Hurry. It appeared that Mr. John Lang, the husband of the plaintiff…was the legal adviser of Lalla Joteepersaud, who had made a settlement…upon Mrs. Lang…The Advocate-General said…that Mrs. Lang should accept Rs. 90,000 in lieu of all claims, that the money should remain in the hands of Mr. Hogg, the Administrator-General, and a release be obtained from the children as they came of age…Mr. Peterson was present… His examination was conducted as follows…I am brother of Mrs. Lang. She has three daughters and one son. The eldest daughter is married to Count Adolphe Ricardi, a major in the Italian army. She was of age before she married...The second of the children is William Bland Lang, who was of age last year…The third child is Lucy; she was twenty years of age last April. She is living at Pisa. The name of the fourth is Margaret; she was born in the latter end of 1844. I saw the whole family eleven months ago…Mr. and Mrs. Lang have not lived together for many years. She obtained a divorce, a mensa et thoro from him…The father has abandoned his family and has provided nothing for them… Joteepersaud told me that he was paying the money for the benefit of Mrs. Lang, because he could not trust her husband.[5]

There are many interesting things to note in this lawsuit. First, let us have a look at the issue of divorce. 'A mensa et thoro' is a Latin phrase which means 'from bed and board'. Lectric Law Library's Lexicon explains, 'a divorce a mensa et thoro', as 'a separation of the parties by act of law, than a dissolution of the marriage. It may be granted for the causes of extreme cruelty or desertion of the wife by the husband. This kind of divorce does not affect the legitimacy of children, nor authorise a second marriage'[6].

One does not know under what circumstances Lang and his wife Lucy were separated, but that the two had been separated for a considerable time is insinuated in the above account. As stated, this kind of divorce does not authorise a second marriage, but Lang did go ahead and marry a second time in 1861.

Colin Roderick and John Earnshaw, in their 1963 article on John Lang write of Lang's second marriage:

> At Mussoorie, on the 11th May 1861, Lang married a second time. The name of the bride was Margaret Wetter. Both parties were living at Landour at that time, but whence Margaret Wetter came, what age she was, and what happened to her after Lang's death are not yet known…No record of this divorce (Lang's divorce from Lucy) appears to exist in England or in the records of the Commonwealth Relations Office, which succeeded the India Office in 1947.[7]

Lang's obituary notice published in his own newspaper *The Mofussilite* on 26 August 1864 mentions that once, a child had fallen off a ship, and Lang had jumped into the sea to save the child. Mr Crittenden, however, in an interview with me in May 2010, conjectured that the child was Lang's own, for no one would jump into the sea so spontaneously to save anyone else's child.

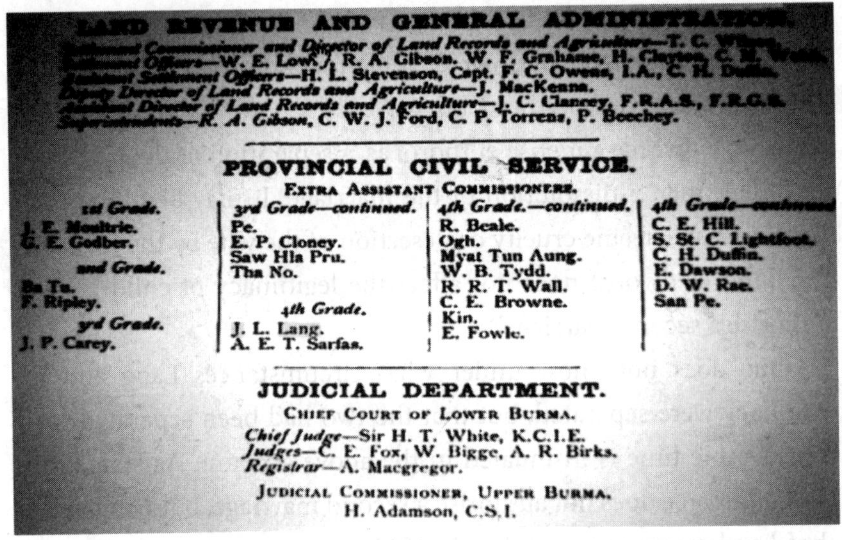

LAND REVENUE AND GENERAL ADMINISTRATION.

Settlement Commissioner and Director of Land Records and Agriculture—T. C. Wilson.
Settlement Officers—W. E. Lowry, R. A. Gibson, W. F. Grahame, H. Clayton, C. M. Webb.
Assistant Settlement Officers—H. L. Stevenson, Capt. F. C. Owens, I.A., C. H. Duffin.
Deputy Director of Land Records and Agriculture—J. MacKenna.
Assistant Director of Land Records and Agriculture—J. C. Clancey, F.R.A.S., F.R.G.S.
Superintendents—R. A. Gibson, C. W. J. Ford, C. P. Torrens, P. Beechey.

PROVINCIAL CIVIL SERVICE.

EXTRA ASSISTANT COMMISSIONERS.

1st Grade.	*3rd Grade—continued.*	*4th Grade.—continued.*	*4th Grade—continued.*
J. E. Moultrie.	Pe.	R. Beale.	C. E. Hill.
G. E. Godber.	E. P. Cloney.	Ogh.	S. St. C. Lightfoot.
2nd Grade.	Saw Hla Pru.	Myat Tun Aung.	C. H. Duffin.
Ba Tu.	Tha No.	W. B. Tydd.	E. Dawson.
F. Ripley.	*4th Grade.*	R. R. T. Wall.	D. W. Rae.
3rd Grade.	J. L. Lang.	C. E. Browne.	San Pe.
J. P. Carey.	A. E. T. Sarfas.	Kin.	
		E. Fowle.	

JUDICIAL DEPARTMENT.

CHIEF COURT OF LOWER BURMA.

Chief Judge—Sir H. T. White, K.C.I.E.
Judges—C. E. Fox, W. Bigge, A. R. Birks.
Registrar—A. Macgregor.

JUDICIAL COMMISSIONER, UPPER BURMA.

H. Adamson, C.S.I.

Mr Crittenden is of the view that the family of the son born of Lang's alliance with Wetter settled in Burma and fled to India during the Second World War when the Japanese were attacking. Thereafter, Lang's son, John Livingston Lang, fled to England with his family. All of Lang's papers and property, therefore, may well be buried somewhere in Burma.

After thorough inquiries in official gazettes, I managed to find John Livingston Lang. The India List and The India Office List for 1905, published by Harrison and Sons—who claim to be 'booksellers to His Majesty and H.R.H. Prince of Wales'—cites the presence of 'John Lang' as well as 'J.L. Lang'. There is John Lang, magistrate and collector in Bengal Service; there is J. Lang, magistrate and collector, 3rd grade, in Bengal Land Revenue; and there is J.L. Lang, extra assistant commissioner, 4th Grade, in Burma Provincial Civil Service (1903) (above). It is the last one which, most probably, is John Livingston Lang, the son of John Lang and Margaret Wetter.

The High Court proceedings summarised by *Allen's Indian Mail* mention four children from the John Lang-Lucy Peterson marriage.

This is the first time that a research work mentions a fourth child. Crittenden as well as Roderick & Earnshaw mention only three children. The fourth child, Margaret, born 'in the latter half of 1844', has not been talked of by anyone—probably because she did not marry into a prominent family like her two elder sisters. The birth of Margaret is recorded in *The Indian Mail* in the list of births—she was born on 4 October 1844 in Calcutta.[8]

This High Court case is the only document that talks about Lucilia Lang's pre-marital life. It says that she turned 20 in April 1862, which means she was born in April 1842.

There seems to be a little discrepancy here, for the second child William Bland Lang, Roderick and Earnshaw say, was born on 6 November 1841:

> They (John and Lucy) appear to have taken up residence with Lang's mother at Ashfield Park and to have entered the emancipist social circle, since Lucy's next child, born on 6 November (1841), was on the 28th baptised William Bland Lang by Rev. J.K. Walpole of the parish of Ashfield. Bland was one of Underwood's friends, and as one of the leading medical men he very likely attended Lucy Lang (in her pregnancy).[9]

After the death of John Lang's father, his mother, Elizabeth, remarried. Her second husband was Joseph Underwood, a trader and a sea-man—mentioned above.

If William was born in November 1841, then Lucy, the third child of the couple, could not have been born in April 1842—as suggested in the testimony of Andrew Peterson in the 1863 High Court case. That there is a year gap between the two children, and that they were born in 1841 and 1842 is also clear from the 1863 court proceedings: 'William Bland Lang was of age last year', and 'Lucy, the third child was of twenty years last April'.

One of the two dates is wrong. Given that the court testimony is by the children's uncle, one is inclined to believe that Roderick and Earnshaw have got William's birth date a little later than it should be.

About Margaret, the fourth child, then, the only things known are that she was born in 1844, and that she was unmarried in 1863. An obituary of John Lang published in *Allen's Indian Mail* wrote, 'His eldest son is a lieutenant in the Royal Artillery'[10]. William Bland Lang, at this time, was 23 years old. This obituary also states, 'Lang has three grown up children'. It misses Margaret. This shows that Lang's personal life was not well known to people.

I have, however, been able to find more About William Bland Lang. There is an article that appeared in *Illustrated London News* on 12 April 1856, which is titled 'Crimean Heroes and Trophies at Woolwich'. The front page shows Sergeant Christy and Sergeant Samuel McGifford of 4th Battalion and 'Trumpeters Gritten and William Lang—with banners taken from churches of Sebastopol and what looks like a captured Eagle'.[11]

The picture (plate 3) shows a young boy, and is attested to as a 'lad' in the book Realism and Politics in Victorian Art of the Crimean War (1984).[12]

The Journal of the Society for Army Historical Research (1933) describes the 'lad' William Lang as:

> …barely thirteen years old when he first heard the whistling of cannon-balls on the banks of the Alma…The night after the battle he was found by an officer lying under the bush, nearly dead from exhaustion. He was wrapped in a horse-rug, and carried to one of the camp fires, where he speedily recovered. He sounded his trumpet at Balaclava, at Inkerma, and during the whole siege...

The battle of Alma commenced on 20 September 1854 and is considered the first battle of the Crimean War (1853–1856). In 1854,

William Bland Lang was 13 years old and living in England with his mother. The Royal Artillery which he became a lieutenant in, as attested in *Allen's Indian Mail* of October 1864, was also involved in this battle and the subsequent war. In the 19th century, young children took up vocations, even if they were from a well-off family. John Lang himself had served in the navy, possibly on a warship (*Warspite*) in his teenage, as is told in his obituary in *The Mofussilite*.[13] In *Household Words* in 1857, Lang in 'Himalayan Club', writes, 'Jack Apsley and I were midshipmen together, some years ago, in a line-of-battle ship that went by the name of the House of Correction'[14]. Lang's connection with *Warspite* is suspect,[15] but he did have something to do with ships and expeditions in his teenage. Lang's father and step father Joseph Underwood were both seafaring merchants.

The idea of young lads taking up vocations despite their family connections comes across in Lang's novel *Ex-Wife* as well, in which Eva Merrydale's son proposes that he would take up the trade of a carpenter. Lady Merrydale is reduced to penury and the circumstances of the narrative make the young boy Merry express his wish:

> Here am I nearly eight years of age, and strong enough to pull a boat, or carry a heavy weight, or dig in a garden. For my part, I should like to be a carpenter…[16]

The lady's pride is hurt on hearing this from her young son, but she remembers how her husband, Sir George Merrydale, had in his teenage, taken a fancy to becoming an ironsmith, and how his parents had built a workshop for him.[17] Lady Merrydale thus would give in to her own son's wish, and 'allow him to make himself acquainted with the art upon which his mind was set'.

Ex-Wife is a novel in which Lang imbues Eva Merrydale with his own personality, but his wife Lucy's circumstances—thus, the ex-wife has to go through travails and take up various vocations to support herself and her child; some of the vocations she chooses are what Lang was dabbling in when he was in Europe during 1854–59—translating from German and French, and writing stories for magazines.

In fact, one of the stories titled *Love's Last Sacrifice* mentioned by Eva was actually published by Lang in *The Mofussilite* in 1863. The novel has several autobiographical elements, and father and son taking up vocations in their boyhood could allude to Lang and his own son. Also, Lang was very fond of music; in an account titled *Keranees*, Lang tells that he had employed a Keranee—a term for the mixed race of Indo-Portuguese people—to act as his messenger and sing his epistles to the recipients. He had also employed Keranees to entertain him with their music and verses.[18] The young William could have imbibed this taste from his father, and insisted that he wanted to be a trumpeter. However, all this is conjectural and the 'lad' William Lang, the trumpeter of the Crimean War, may or may not be William Bland Lang.

A rough timeline of Lang's progeny is this:

1839 — John Lang marries Lucy Peterson. (2nd February)[19]

1840 — Aimee Lang born. She would become Amie Riccardi after marriage.

1841 — William Bland Lang born, named after Emancipist and surgeon, William Bland. (November 6, date suspect)

1842 — Lucilia Lang born (April). She would go on to become Lucilia Burlamacchi and Lucilia Manzi post-marriage(s).

1844 — Margaret Lang, youngest of Lang-Lucy wedlock, born on October 4.

1861 — John Lang remarries in May. The name of the bride is Margaret Wetter.

Unknown date (between 1855 and 1864)—John Livingston Lang born.

Despite knowing about his offspring, it has been difficult to trace any of Lang's direct descendants. One, however, finds descendants from Elizabeth's (John Lang's mother) other family through marriage—the Underwoods. One of these descendants, Liz Parkinson, has written a detailed book about the family, *The Underwoods: Lock, Stock and Barrel* (1989).[20] The author's introduction in the book says that this is her 'first book' which 'sprang from a desire to locate the missing Underwood money'. Interestingly, she didn't find any!

However, she 'found a good story in the process of researching all the genealogy, and dealings and court cases relating to the Underwood family'. The other noted descendant is Laurence Halloran who contestes the idea that John Harris—the maternal grandfather of John Lang—was Jewish. He produced a monograph on the subject.

I, on the other hand, have been able to trace the line of Lang's eldest daughter, Aimee. We already know that she married an Italian count, Conte[II] Adolphe Riccardi. Adolphe/Adolfo, who was the Aide-De-Camp (ADC) to the king of Italy, and Amie had just one child, a daughter named Fede Maria Riccardi, who married Thomas Cubitt of England. This is recorded in Melville H. Ruvigny's book *The Nobilities of Europe*. Following is the information given in this book:

> 27 May 1904 [R.L. 16 Dec 1905]
>
> Thomas (Cubitt, now [R.L. 10 Dec 1904] Riccardi-Cubitt), 1st Count Riccardi-Cubitt (Conte Riccardi-Cubitt) [Italy]; b 8 May 1870; cr. As above by King Victor Emannuel III; m 23 May 1893 Fede Maria *suo jure* 1st Countess (Contessa) Riccardi [Italy 3 May 1903] da. And h. Of Adolfo (Riccardi), 3rd Count Riccardi [Sardinia], Col. And ADC to the king of Italy and has issue.
>
> Heir (to the mother's title): Charles Cyril, Contino Riccardi (son), b 28 Jan 1896.[21]

II (Count is known as Conte in Italy)

Suo jure means 'in her (or his) own right'.[22] It is used for the nobility in the sense that the person in question is entitled to a title in her own right, rather than one acquired through marriage. Fede Maria was the last of the line of the Riccardis since there was no son, and therefore, her husband would have to become the first Count Riccardi-Cubitt to preserve the line. King Emmanuel III crowned her husband Thomas Cubitt as Thomas Riccardi-Cubitt in 1904.

The *Genealogical and Heraldic History of the Landed Gentry*, founded by Burke, has more information to offer about Aimee and Adolfo. Under the entry of Thomas Riccardi-Cubitt, this is what is written:

> Italian title in this country by Royal Warrant 16 Dec 1905. B 8 May 1870; educ. Eton and Merton Coll. Oxford, BA; m 23 Nov 1893 the Countess Fede Maria Riccardi (RRC medal and medal of queen Elizabeth of Belgium) only surviving child of Adolfo, Count Riccardi of Vercelli, Piedmont. Col Italian army and ADC to the King of Italy, and Aimee, his wife, dau. Of John Lang, barrister-at-law.[23]

The above account from Burke's peerage cross-checks the fact that Aimee was John Lang's daughter, and that Fede Maria was the only surviving child of Aimee. We also get more information about Thomas Cubitt and Fede Maria. We also get to know from 'Royal Styles and Titles' in UK National Archives that the title to Cubitt[24] was specially granted by the King of Italy to preserve the royal line.[25]

We know from the first of these three accounts that Contin Charles Cyril Riccardi-Cubitt was the heir to the title of his mother in 1905, and that he was born in 1896. After this, I lost the lineage plot till I encountered the name of Monique Riccardi-Cubitt, an art historian, journalist, and writer. I have been able to reconstruct the rest of the story of Aimee Riccardi's descendants, through Monique's biography.

Monique married Michael Riccardi-Cubitt. Her biographer says this about her husband's family:

> Her husband, Count (Michael) Riccardi-Cubitt, was her father's age. Issued from an ancient Italian aristocratic family, he became for her a father and a mentor. His great grandfather (Adolfo) had served as an aide de camp to three kings of Italy at the court of the House of Savoy in Turin. Thomas Cubitt, his English ancestor, a carpenter by trade, became an architect and a property developer, a close friend of Queen Victoria and Prince Albert. He transformed the London urban landscape, developing new districts, such as Pimlico and Belgravia, proud to the end to be known as a master builder. Their house in Pimlico had been built by the family firm in 1840.[26]

The great grandfather (on the maternal side) mentioned here is obviously Adolphe Riccardi. That Thomas Cubitt was an accomplished architect and property developer is interesting, because elsewhere, he is talked of as a carpenter. Given his proximity to nobility, it is not surprising that he married into nobility. One was almost hoping that it would be a story of a fairytale romance between a noble and a subaltern. The short biography has more details about Thomas Cubitt, most of which we already know:

> Michael Riccardi-Cubitt's grandfather converted to Catholicism at Oxford under the influence of Cardinal Newman. He married an Italian Contessa, Contessa Fede Riccardi, the last of a long and prestigious line, and in order to assure its survival, he took on her name and title in 1904 by Royal Warrant of King Victor-Emanuel III of Italy, endorsed by Edward VII of England in 1907.[27]

We get to know more objective details about the Riccardi-Cubitt family from the Doddington family history website. Thomas Cubitt's father had married into this family. Thomas Cubitt died at the age of 80, in 1950. According to the website, he and Fede Maria had four children—Charles Cyril Cubitt (1896–), the one mentioned as the heir and three daughters: Vera Alicia Maria Cubitt, Theodora Fede Maria Cubitt Sister of Charity and Monica Yolanda Cubitt.[28]

These details are also attested in Marquis of Ruvigny's *The Plantagenet Roll of the Blood Royal: The Mortimer-Percy Volume* (1911).[29] It is interesting to note that Vera Cubitt also wrote a book on Catholic faith in 1913, titled *The Pearl of Great Price.*[30] Given that Vera's grand-aunt Lucy Burlamacchi had written the book about Lucca Della Robbia in 1900, the two ladies probably would have known each other. Vera married Flight Lieutenant W.A. Meade in 1917.[31]

Another Interesting family history here is that the first Count Riccardi-Cubitt, Thomas, gave up the title of Count in 1944, six years before his death. However, his grandson Michael used the title. A notice was published in the London Gazette on 2 June 1944, where Thomas Cubitt said in a notice dated May 25 that after 21 days of the publication of the notice, he would drop his title and be called just Thomas Cubitt.[32]

Following are the details given in the Doddington history for Conte Charles Cyril Riccardi-Cubitt:

> Charles Cyril Cubitt
> Charles married Gladys Louisa Violet Crake on 10 November 1919.
> Children from this marriage were:
> 72 M i. Michael Francis Vandeleur Cubitt was born on 18 Sep 1920.
> 73 M ii. Lt Victor Barrington Cubitt was born on 28 Apr 1922 and died on 27 Jun 1944 at age 22.

> 74 M iii. Capt Charles Desmond Cubitt was born on 24 Jun 1924 and died on 22 Oct 1958 at age 34.
>
> Charles married Diana Muckerman on 21 Oct 1958. Diana died on 22 Oct 1958. death: both he and wife killed in plane crash, 22 Oct 1958.

There seems to have been streak of tragedy in this this family: Lt. Victor Cubitt died the age of 22, it seems, in Second World War. Captain Charles Cubitt died at the age of 34—both he and his wife died in a plane crash—just a day after their wedding. This would have an effect on Michael Francis Vandeleur Riccardi-Cubitt, the first born, and the husband of Monique, for the latter's biographical note says that Michael had gone into depression and ultimately committed suicide.

Michael's marriage to Monique was not his first marriage. His first marriage was with Lavinia French. A peerage website that borrows its information from Burke's Peerage (107th edition) has the following information:

> Lavinia Marie French was born on 28 October 1928.[i] She is the daughter of Hon. Bertram Leo French and Maud Mary Dease. [ii] She married, firstly, Michael Francis Vandeleur Cubitt, son of Major Charles Cyril Cubitt, on 8 October 1968. She married, secondly, Major John Norman Pembroke Watson in 1971.
>
> From 8 October 1968, her married name became Cubitt. Her marriage to Michael Francis Vandeleur Cubitt was annulled in 1970.[33]

There are more details about the life of Count Michael Riccardi-Cubitt in Monique's biography:

> Count Riccardi-Cubitt was educated at the Benedictine college of Ampleforth, and in time became a Knight of Honour and

> Devotion of the Sovereign Military Hospitaller Order of St. John of Jerusalem, of Rhodes and of Malta. At the beginning of the war he was the youngest officer in the British army... Carrying on his action in Military Intelligence during the war, he studied the Arab culture and language at the Middle East Centre of Arabic Studies, MICAS, in Jerusalem, entering the British Intelligence agency, MI6...When they met (Michael and Monique),[34] he was living in London where he had opened his own consulting company for public relations between London and the Middle East...She visited Lebanon and Saudi Arabia after his death, giving lectures at the American University in Beirut and The National Museum of Riyadh.'[35]

Monique's bio-note says that Michael's 'prisoner of war experiences deeply affected her and... Her husband's suicide at the end of a long-standing depressive illness marked a decisive turn in her life. She took on his spiritual heritage, remaining loyal to his ideals in death as in life... She sought to realise the dream he had given up when he had left Lebanon, *to be a bridge between the East and the West*, in order to reconcile in her own life the Atlantic and the Mediterranean, as much as the Orient and the Occident...Her love for her husband, a mystic, poet, nature lover and accomplished sportsman, found its source in this common passion. In this union of similar souls, Monique Riccardi-Cubitt sought to reconcile Eros, the youthful earthly love, with Anteros, his twin brother, the divine sublimated love of maturity, father and protector of all the arts'[36].

I established an e-mail correspondence with Countess Monique Riccardi-Cubitt in hope that there may be letters between Aimee and her mother Lucy Lang still preserved. The hope was soon shattered. Initially, Monique did not believe that Lang could have been a great grandfather of her husband Michael Vandaleur Cubitt through a mixed paternal-maternal line. Here is a part of that correspondence:

> It somehow feels SO unlikely somehow, and I do wonder if there could be ANOTHER John Lang, it is quite a common name. Do you have FOR SURE the decadence *(descent)* of Lang with AMY as a daughter? For my part I have to disappoint you in saying that ALL the family archives have been lost in the sale after the war of the family estate Eden Hall in Kent by my father-in-law (Charles Cyril Cubitt), whom I never knew since he had died before my marriage. The family villa at Bordighera in Italy had been looted by the Germans during the war, and was sold too at the same time. Count and Countess Riccardi-Cubitt died of grief in a convent few years later.[37]

Hence, one more source of the possibility of perusing any John Lang papers that might exist is exhausted. The Count and Countess mentioned towards the end of the e-mail are Thomas Cubitt and Fede Maria, the grand-daughter of John and Lucy Lang. After I convinced Monique that it is the same John Lang, Monique wonders why Michael Cubitt never told her about John Lang:

> I am really perplexed as to WHY my husband NEVER mentioned this Australian ancestor novelist and orientalist! Also WHERE did his daughter Amy or Aimée meet Count Adolfo Riccardi, who was a general, hence a soldier and courtier at the Court of Savoy in Torino. I did find out the entry of his wedding to AMY DI JOHN LANG in 1862 in the *LIBRO DELLA NOBILITÀ ITALIANA,* two years before her father's death in India, but not WHERE.[38]

Andrew Peterson answered that question in the 1863 court case—the marriage took place at Leghorn. The answer to Monique's question as to why her husband never told her about Lang is probably simple—

that Michael Cubitt had not heard of John Lang. Michael would have known his paternal ancestors, that is Charles Cubitt, Thomas Cubitt and upwards; and on the maternal side of his grandmother Fede Maria—the royal Riccardi family. Also, Aimee Riccardi (née Lang) would barely have liked to talk much about her father John Lang, who had got married to Margaret Wetter just a year before her own marriage. The court case of 1863 clearly tells—also with the absence of Lang in the court—that the relationship between the father and the children was strained. Monique tells in another e-mail that the Riccardi-Cubitt family was mired in stories of intrigue:

> It is NOT a pretty story but a story of power and greed on the part of the son Cyril [son of Thomas Cubitt and Fede Maria Riccardi] and his wife Gladys Cubitt, born CRAKE, my mother-in-law. As well as for Monica, last daughter of Thomas and Fede Riccardi-Cubitt, who was determined to become more British than the British, and despised her parents, their values and their inheritance. She also hated my husband for being the physical and moral heir to the Italian title. He was the only one to speak and feel Italian, in fact he spoke five languages…
>
> What you do not seem to realize is that my husband's family were ashamed of their Italian connections and that my husband's father renounced the name RICCARDI-CUBITT and title during the war; my husband, heir to the name, title and estate, was deprived by his own father of his legitimate inheritance, both morally and materially, and never recovered from the loss. It was at the root of his mental illness and hence cause of his suicide. He took on the name and title again, against his own family's wishes after the death of his father. But all this has little to do with John Lang's story I dare say.
>
> Everything to do with this family has been greed, betrayal, snobbism, manipulation, to the point that the Cubitt aunt,

> Monica, refused to let my husband be buried in the family grave with his parents, which was his right and possession as the heir. She had him cremated and his ashes scattered against his wishes and mine. So, as you can see it does bring back a lot of unhappiness and suffering for me.[39]

Count Thomas Riccardi-Cubitt had denounced his title in 1944. To my query as to how the title still remains in the family, the countess told me that the title was given by a royal warrant and cannot be annulled. She added that Thomas Cubitt gave up the title because he was under the pressure of his son Charles Cyril and daughter-in-law Monica to do so. She further adds:

> As for my husband he reassumed what was his rightful inheritance which had erroneously been given up publicly for political reasons, since as I mentioned earlier a Royal Warrant cannot be broken ... It just shows the family's hysterical and neurotic behaviour which denied and destroyed their own inheritance needlessly, humiliating their parents in the process and making them homeless in forcing them to sell their estates in 1945 ...[40]

It is interesting to see that Charles Cubitt had an inferiority complex about his Italian heritage, and that he forced his father to give up his royal title because it essentially emanated from Italy. It is almost reminiscent of Lang's constant denial of his convict heritage and fabrication of an identity of a gentleman—the difference is that Lang was denying a convict past, and Charles was denying a royal past. If Charles did know about Lang, and if he was so parochial, he would barely have liked to mention Lang, who was of convict origin and not on good terms with Charles' grandmother.

Monique is right in pointing out that 'all this has little to do with John Lang's story'. However, I thought it important to integrate the story of Lang's descendants—for as Monique wrote, 'It is an extraordinary story—that of this John Lang, unknown to his own descendants'.

In terms of genealogical research, this is, to my belief, an important step. By the way, Lang also believed in endlessly connected meta-stories, for he was immensely inspired by immensely intertextual and hyperlinked texts like the *Arabian Nights* and *The Decameron* by Giovanni Boccaccio, both of which find constant mention in his work.

More importantly, it is remarkable that there are several points of similarity between Lang and his descendant Michael Cubitt, four generations down the line (John Lang—Aimee Riccardi née Lang—Fede Maria Riccardi-Cubitt née Riccardi—Charles Cyril Cubitt—Michael Riccardi Cubitt). We have seen that Michael was very interested in Arab culture, studied about and strived for confluence of the East and the West—which also was a prime interest of Lang (his interest in India, and scholarship of Persian and Arabian literature). In Monique's biographical note, Michael is told to be 'a mystic, poet, nature lover and accomplished sportsman', all of which Lang also was.

Lang, in fact, got married through a sport—that of hunting. He had gone hunting with friends, broken a leg, and ended at Lucy's house, whom he impressed and married.[41]

Lang was decidedly a poet, and an accomplished one in his own right—his poetry appeared in his newspaper through 1845 to 1864, and his novels were strewn with verses written by him. Lang had great interest in mysticism and occult—there are several articles about mesmerism in *The Mofussilite* in 1845; in *Wanderings in India,* Lang recounts having been healed by a faqir who simply stared at him and cured him. Lang is known to have loved nature, children, animals, and birds.[42]

If we so contrive it, there is trivia that matches, too. Michael Cubitt went to jail as prisoner of war; Lang went to prison in Calcutta, albeit on a charge of libel against a colonel who he had called a coward.[43]

Michael Cubitt was employed by MI6, the British intelligence agency, while Lang was charged with spying and jailed for three days on suspicion in Vienna in 1854.[44]

Michael knew five languages; Lang perhaps knew more—he decidedly knew English, Hindustani, Persian, French, German,[45] and Latin (perhaps Greek[46] too)—there are Hindustani phrases strewn through his works, and he says in *Wanderings in India* that he spent a long time in Oude (a princely state in the Awadh region of North India until 1858) learning the language[47]; his translations of Persian poetry of Sadi of Shiraz, and the prose tale *Goolistan* appeared in *The Mofussilite* (the former in 1863, the latter in 1845); every single novel of his has several Latin phrases; and he had won the gold medal in Sydney College for study of Classics,[48] and his first work was a translation of Horace's first satire.[49]

Lang married Margaret Wetter in 1861, and perhaps had a child with her, who entered the Bengal Civil Service. Except for the children from Aimee, Lang's descendants through his five children are unknown. For the ease of the reader, I have prepared a family tree depicting various threads of this chapter, which appears on the next page.

Based on all the data I collected, this is John Lang's family tree that I have prepared. This depicts the convoluted chain of relations that connects Lang to our contemporary times.

Family Tree leading fro

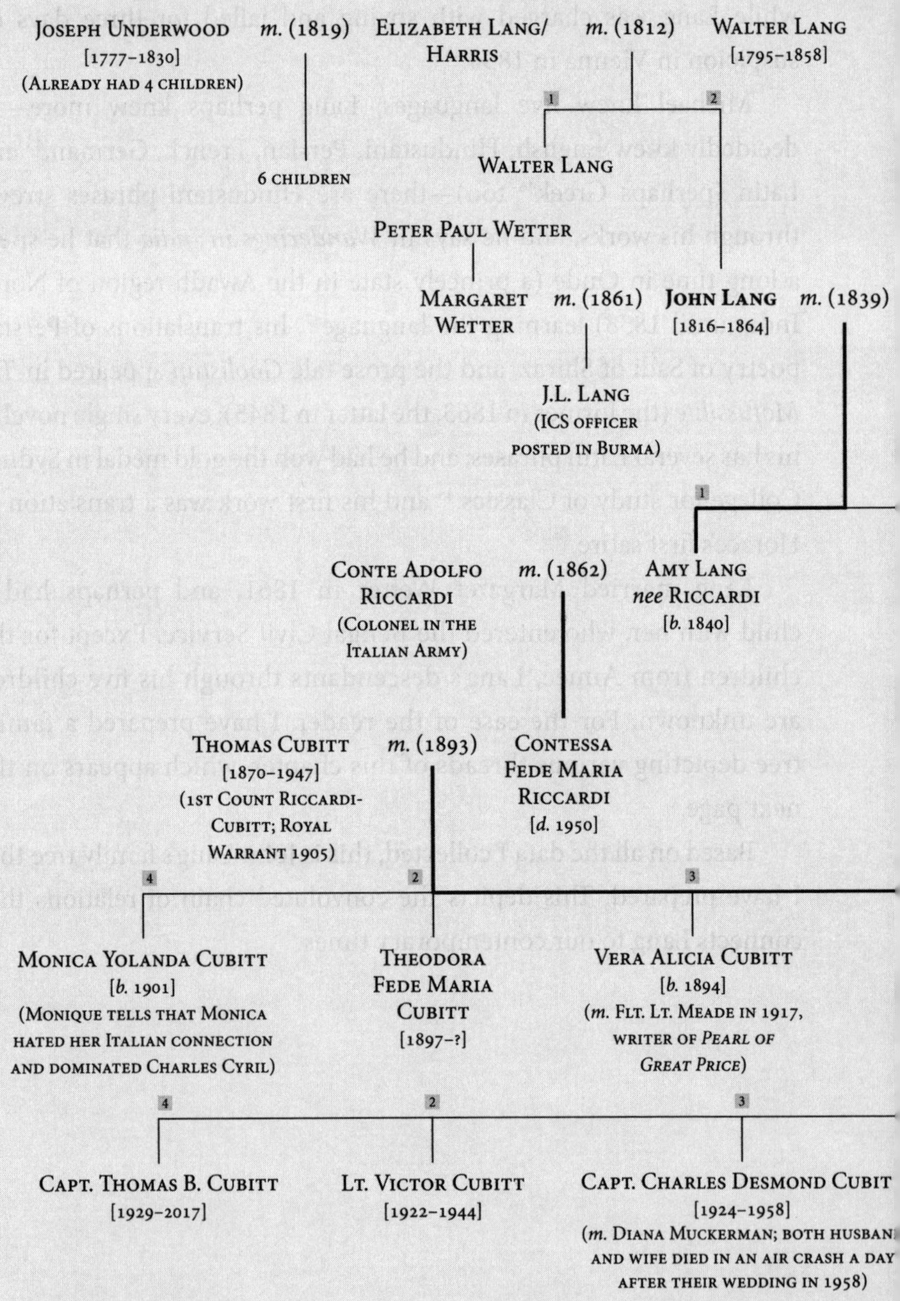

ohn Lang to Michael Cubitt

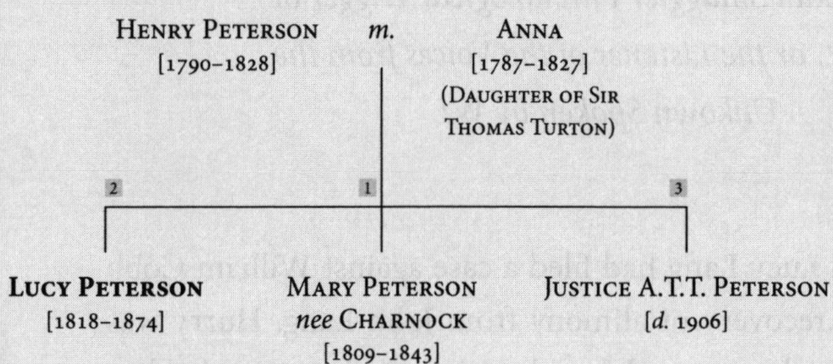

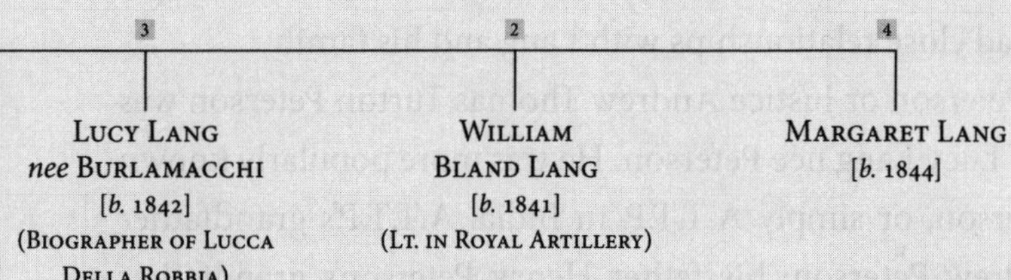

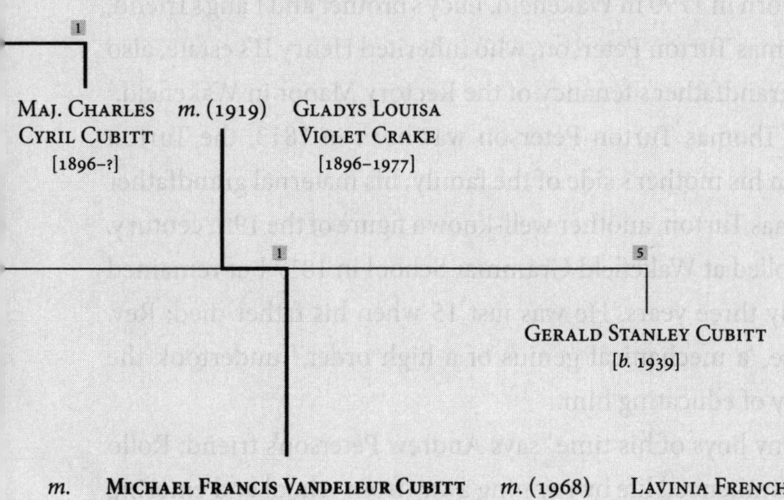

William Cobb Hurry,

or the Skull Smuggler Phrenological Trigger or A.T.T.P., or the Listener of the Voices from the Unkown Spoken by WL

We now know that Lucy Lang had filed a case against William Cobb Hurry in 1863 for recovery of alimony from John Lang. Hurry was representing Lang in the case and must have been a close friend of his. On behalf of Lucy, Andrew Peterson spoke and told the court how the settlement was to be carried out. Both Hurry and Peterson are unique figures, and had close relationships with Lang and his family.

Andrew Peterson or Justice Andrew Thomas Turton Peterson was the brother of Lucy Lang née Peterson. He was more popularly known as A.T.T. Peterson, or simply A.T.T.P. in India. A.T.T.P.'s grandfather was also Andrew Peterson; his father Henry Peterson's grandfather was also Henry (see plate 7). That makes it Henry Peterson s/o Andrew Peterson s/o Henry Peterson s/o Andrew Peterson. Andrew I's son Henry II—who also happened to be a friend of Lang's father, Walter Lang—was born in 1790 in Wakefield. Lucy's brother and Lang's friend, Andrew Thomas Turton Peterson, who inherited Henry II's estate, also secured his grandfather's tenancy of the Rectory Manor in Wakefield.[1]

Andrew Thomas Turton Peterson was born in 1813; the Turton part was from his mother's side of the family; his maternal grandfather was Sir Thomas Turton, another well-known figure of the 19th century. Andrew enrolled at Wakefield Grammar School in 1817 but remained there for only three years. He was just 15 when his father died; Rev. John Michele, 'a mechanical genius of a high order,'[2] undertook the responsibility of educating him.

'Like many boys of his time,' says Andrew Peterson's friend, Rollo Massy, 'he commenced life by running away from school and entering the career of a sailor; he rose rapidly in his calling, but a serious illness in India, together with the advice of the doctor who attended him, caused him to return to England and study for the Bar. As a Barrister he was successful from the first; returning to India, he rose to be the leader of the Calcutta Bar, and was for a time a judge of the High Court of Calcutta.'[3]

Earnshaw and Roderick contend that Andrew Peterson's influence on Lang would have been a lot. When Lang had to face hostility in Sydney from 'exclusives'[I] in 1841, his wife would have advised him to follow her brother's example. Andrew Peterson's presence in India might have been a reason for Lang to go to India. After that, however, it does not appear that Peterson had much influence over Lang's legal career. Lang was in the legal profession in India 1845 onwards, but apart from the case he fought for Jotee Persaud in 1851 and the case of Rani of Jhansi in 1853 Lang doesn't seem to have fought cases for such celebrities—at least it appears so from the copious court documents of the 19th century. On the other hand, A.T.T. Peterson's name appears throughout mid-19th century as a lawyer, and later, as a judge.

Lang and Peterson were friends—their fathers Walter Lang and Henry Peterson had also been friends—and had various common interests, but in my opinion vis-à-vis the legal profession, Lang did not have much to do with Peterson.

A.T.T. Peterson was a very well-known man in India. His fame can be gauged from the fact that in 1863, a book was published bearing the title *Public Dinner at Calcutta to Mr. A.T.T. Peterson.*[4] Peterson may have been in Calcutta at this time to be a witness in the 1863 Lucy Lang case.

Peterson had a house at Tetaglun, 14 miles from Calcutta, close to the military cantonment of Barrackpore.[5] He had varied interests and used to keep newspaper cuttings on various subjects—medicine being one of them. Cholera was a ravaging disease in those times, with most medical men busy trying to find a cure for the dreaded

I Descendants of free people, as opposed to the descendants of convicts.

ailment. Peterson used to collect cuttings about cholera. In a letter to Dr John Chapman dated 4 March 1866, Peterson tells that he kept a newspaper cutting from *The Times* of 11 October 1865 about curing cholera with the help of ice. He tells that one day a native was brought to his house in a very bad state of cholera. According to Peterson, he referred to Chapman's article and then describes, in great detail, how he administered to the ill man, and says that after the application of ice, the patient did not vomit even once.[6] This is what he describes of the following morning:

> ...To my surprise, I found him sitting up and smoking the everlasting hookah, which, rightly or wrongly, I took away from him, and made my servants make him a good mess of chicken broth, which he speedily demolished.[7]

Peterson ends the letter saying the natives believed that he had performed some 'Jadoo,' and that he let them retain that belief.[8]

Along with the hunt for the cure for cholera, there was another pseudo-science that was in vogue in the 19th century—mesmerism. Considered path-breaking in mid-19th century, it was hoped that mesmerism would herald a new era in medicine and surgery. In 1846, James Esdaile published his observations in a book entitled *Mesmerism in India, and its Practical Application in Surgery and Medicine.*[9] Lang's newspaper *The Mofussilite* constantly carried out articles about mesmerism. In 1845, a year before Esdaile's book was published, there were a series of articles in *The Mofussilite* about mesmerism. Some of these articles of 1845 are: 'Mesmeric facts'[10]; 'Weekly summary of the news: Mesmerism'[11], 'The man must be good actor indeed who can play a serene, and composed part, while a doctor is taking off his leg, or arm.'

In the first issue of Lang's newspaper *The Mofussilite,* of 2 August 1845, there appears a short article with reference to mesmerism:

> ...when men shall be woke after the separation of a limb, or women after the extraction of a cancer, with less consciousness of what has passed than if a fit of indigestion had troubled them with a nightmare, how many valuable lives will be saved, now sacrificed to the fear of pain, and how much agonizing sympathy will be spared to the relatives and friends of the afflicted.

The same issue quotes from *The Hurkaru* newspaper of Calcutta about mesmeric feats of Esdaile.[12] The colonies were an experimental ground for the scientists of 19th century. Various branches of science were also used to define the Orient, circumscribe it. It was hoped that these branches of science would help the enterprise of colonisation better. The article quoted above also says that mesmerism did not have an effect on a European subject. This also, in a way, insinuates that the European mind was stronger and less amenable to external influences. The article goes on to say:

> Some water was mesmerised. Certain natives who drank it were thrown into a mesmeric state, but it had no effect on a European officer, who ventured to take a large draught of it. In one case, a patient was struck with the mysterious influence just as he was in the middle his potation. It was like magic—as if he had been touched with the wand of an enchanter. The lips closed on the rim of the tumbler—where the stiffened hand still held it. These are strange facts and show that there is something more in nature than is dreamt of in the philosophy of men in general.

Nineteenth century is indeed full of such exotic tales. The 'natives' were affected, but they may have been paid off to put up a performance. Poverty was great and it was not difficult to 'buy' natives in experiments like these, or in the courts. In the famous case that Lang won for Jotee

Persaud, he won it partly because most of the witnesses perjured themselves and changed their statements.[13]

Interestingly enough, on the same page of the newspaper as the 'mesmerism' article, is a sarcastic piece written by Lang about 'forms of law' which tells that 'there is a story about an indictment showing that forty Napoleon Bonapartes were in existence at one and the same time'.

That titbit aside, Lang, in his travelogue-autobiography *Wanderings in India*,[14] provides a counter-point to the subtle insinuation that the European mind was less amenable to external influence. This is when Lang gets treated of a headache by a native mesmerist, who obviously was not a mesmerist, since mesmerism was a new science having taken its name from Dr Mesmer of Vienna, while the native doctor had learnt his art from his forbears, Lang describes the 'native' doctor thus:

> The native doctor was a tall, thin Mussulman, with a lofty forehead, small black eyes, long aquiline nose, and finely chiselled mouth and chin. His hair, eyebrows, and long beard were of a yellowish white, or cream colour. Standing before me in his skull-cap, he was about the most singular looking person I ever beheld. His age did not exceed forty-four or forty five years.[15]

This is the way Lang describes most of the people he writes about. This exactitude is very characteristic of 19th century writing. Lang recounts a tale of meeting a doctor in Bijnor where he was seized with an attack of tic-douloureux, and had been persuaded by one of his host's servants to summon this native doctor. The native doctor 'mesmerises' Lang:

> Seating himself in a chair immediately opposite to me, he looked very intently into my eyes. After a little while, his gaze

> became disagreeable, and I endeavoured to turn my head aside, but I was unable to do so. I now felt that I was being mesmerized. Observing, I suppose, an expression of anxiety, if not of fear, on my features, he bade me not to be alarmed. I longed to order him to cease; but, as the pain was becoming less and less acute, and as I retained my consciousness intact, I suffered him to proceed. To tell the truth, I doubt whether I could have uttered a sound. At all events, I did not make the attempt. Presently, that is to say, after two or three minutes, the pain had entirely left me, and I felt what is commonly called, all in a glow. The native doctor now removed his eyes from off mine, and inquired if I were better. My reply, which I had no difficulty in giving at once, was in the affirmative; in short, that I was completely cured.[16]

Lang asks the doctor if he had heard of Dr Esdaile and mesmerism, to which the doctor replies that he has heard of mesmerism, but that his talent he had discovered on his own, and that there are several such healers like him across India. The doctor also informs Lang he is not the first European who the former has cured. He tells that there was a cattle sergeant who he had cured of drinking madness by 'locking up his eyes' as he had done in the case of Lang. He tells of another similar success that he had with an alcoholic:

> 'But,' he exclaimed, energetically, 'the most extraordinary case I ever had, was that of a Sahib who had gone mad—'drink delirious.' His wife would not suffer him to be strapped down, and he was so violent that it took four or five other Sahibs to hold him. I was sent for, and, at first, had great difficulty with him and much trembling. At last, however, I locked his eyes up, as soon as I got him to look at me, and kept him for several hours as quiet as a mouse, during which time he had no brandy,

> no wine, no beer; and, though he did not sleep, he had a good long rest. I stayed with him for two days, and whatever I told him to do he did immediately.'[17]

The 'native doctor' goes on to show the various certificates he had got from his various clients. Lang returns to the subject of certificates on another occasion in *Wanderings in India* while describing his stay with Nana Sahib, where all of Nana's servants get character certificates written by him, to preserve, to impress their kin, and to seek future employment. It is interesting that this legacy of 'character certificates' still lives on in India. Lang tells about the certificates of his healer, Mustapha Khan:

> I proceeded to examine very carefully every one of his many certificates; not that I was in any way interested in them, but because I knew it would afford him great pleasure. In all, they were quite as numerous as those which English charlatans publish in testimony of their skill in extracting corns. They were more elaborate however; for it is by the length of a certificate that a native judges of its value—just in the same way that Partridge, when Tom Jones took him to see *Hamlet,* admired the character of the King, because he spoke louder than any of the company, 'anybody could see that he was a king.' As for myself, I sat down and covered a whole sheet of foolscap in acknowledgment of my gratitude to Mustapha Khan Bahadoor, for having delivered me from unendurable torments.

The above statement shows Lang's propensity to allude to literary references in any kind of situation. He does it in all his works, and he did in the court case of Lala Jotee Persaud in 1851—he quoted from Shakespeare's *Twelfth Night* at length in the court to prove a point.[18] Such statements as above—the literary allusion excepted—may be considered Orientalist and disparaging of the Indian people, but the fact that Lang has included this story, and mentioned Esdaile in it, and said that what Mesmer was then doing was a common practice amongst Indians, goes on to show that his ideology is quite different from what can be interpolated by quoting him out of context.

Lang also tells in this story that he gave the doctor a cheque for 100 rupees, which he did not use for a long time. The doctor, upon being asked later, said he intended to keep it as an 'imperishable memorial from a European gentleman, and that he would not part with it for ten times the amount in gold and silver'[19].

There are more such instances in *Wanderings in India* where natives attach a lot of value to something given to them by a European. This legacy, again, continues in some way or the other not just in India, but in most former colonies. It goes on to show how, through the enterprise of colonialism and its various vehicles, the native populations were made to feel inferior about themselves. It reminds one of Franz Fanon's idea that the colonised seek liberation within the limits set by the coloniser.[20] Even though the native doctor is confident of his capabilities and has many certificates, he needs to keep the cheque from Lang who is surprised because he thinks he is 'insignificant'.

Lang mentions mesmerism in his novels as well. In *Ex-Wife*,[21] Mathilde tells Eva that Colonel Stair 'nearly died of laughter yesterday when I told him of Sydney Smith replying to the mesmerist, "*Do you feel anything now?*"—"Yes, a most profound contempt for your ridiculous pretensions."'

Lang had ambivalent views on these issues of pseudo-science. In his newspaper issues of 1845, he seems to be taken in by the new wave. However, by 1859, he seems to have rethought these issues and offers his counter-points and 'laughs' through the examples of the native doctor and Sydney Smith.

In the 6 September 1845 issue of *The Mofussilite*, there appeared a long poem about mesmerism. Instead of typing out the poem, I have used snippets from the newspaper.

Original Poetry.

HOOGHLEY MESMERIZERS AND DITCH SCEPTICS.

Still must I listen to the harshest note
That e'er escaped a feathered songsters throat?
Still must I listen to the constant cry
That all my mesmerism's all my eye?
Coma the vision of a dreaming ass,
And catalepsy nothing but a farce?—
Not mention patients whom to sleep I lull,
Lest by Ditch Doctors I be dubbed "a gull"?
Prepare! As counselled by the *Englishman*,
I'll search, and write,—and publish all I can.—
Mesmeric art! my glory and my pride!
Beloved as fondly as by Bridegroom bride,
I'll fight thy battles, be it inch by inch,
And from the contest will I never—flinch.
No more will I, than would an Alexander,
Be frighten'd by a goose, or even gander.
Nor while my fortunes will afford a bed,
Whereon to lie my mesmerizing head,
Will I give in to them a single point!
Forsooth the times* *are* sadly out of joint!
Can I not charm a Hogman by a squint?
Then who'll deny that there is *something* in't?
Can't I with nothing than pure water stronger,
Send fast asleep the beautiful Alonga?
Or pass to slumber, in an instant, Nobee,
The wife of Pittumber, the Judge's *Dhobie*?
Or cut a wen from off the neck of Genda
And she unconscious, if to sleep I send her?
Or can't I so entrance a simple lout,
That sticking pins in him wont make him shout?
Or cant I serve, without a wince, or cry,
A Patient, as a child would serve a fly,—
Pull off his legs, without the slightest pain,
Then blow, and bring him to himself again?
What signifies the thickness of a wall?
Save me from thickheads, and you grant me all!

* * * * * * *

When Galileo said the earth went round,
To listen to his doctrines who was found?
Did not they tell him that his brain was turned,
And if he said such things, he should be burned?
(Conscious that burning was beyond a joke,
His words he swallowed, and his *doorbeen* broke.)

* * * * * *

When Watt, they tell us, first got up his steam,
And made head way against the wind and stream,
Did not the multitude their garments rend,
And swear the world was coming to an end?
When Koster first, on wooden types did strike,
Off fifty copies, which were all alike,
Did not the art upon the mind *impress*
Ideas of Witchcraft,—neither more nor less?

(*To be continued.*)

* Query rhymes?—Ed.

☞ We have published the above fifty lines, but unless the author takes one side or the other,—and comes to the point, we shall not give insertion to any more of the Poem.—Ed.

In my opinion, the poem is written by Lang. It has the irreverent and careless attitude of Lang with rhymes like ass/farce. At the end of the poem, the 'Ed' says that the poet is not decided about his position vis-à-vis mesmerism, and no more of this poem will be published till the author states his position.

This is Lang filling in the side column of the page and being done with it, at least I would think so. He left many of his serials unfinished after he got bored of them. In 1861, he left a novel *The Detective* unfinished, saying he had lost the manuscript.

Coming back to issue of science, quirks and Peterson— after retiring from the Calcutta High Court, Peterson became a Spiritualist; that is to say, he started believing that the spirits of the dead could be contacted through séances. Andrew Peterson was interested in both ideas—spiritualism and socialism. He came in touch with an uneducated and 'sensitive' William Lawrence, whom he used as a medium to contact spirits. Lawrence was charged with fraud and imprisoned for a few months, after which he entered the services of Peterson.[22] With the help of his 'medium' William Lawrence, Peterson contacted the 'controls' or the spirits, and wrote a book in 1885, called *Essays from the Unseen, Delivered through the Mouth of W.L., a Sensitive, and Recorded by A.T.T.P.*[23] The 'controls' range from Aristotle, Pythagoras, and Julius Caesar to various of A.T.T.P.'s 19th century contemporaries—including Henry Lawrence, and even Jotee Persaud. The spirit of Henry Lawrence talks about John Lang and *The Mofussilite*; and Jotee Persaud remembers Lang and his family very fondly.

A.T.T.P. was told by a 'control', Sir Christopher Wren, that he should build a tower at Sway, in England.[24] The tower built in the 1880s reached a height of 218 feet, and is the tallest tower built only of concrete without any reinforcements. (see plate 3)

Benedict Le Vay says that Sway Tower is aptly named, 'for it was built to prove it wouldn't, but nearly did'. Vay says that Peterson wanted to prove the efficacy of the Portland cement concrete blocks without reinforcement. He persuaded local workmen to assemble the blocks like a giant Lego kit into the slim 218-ft-high tower entirely without scaffolding. Built in the Indian Gothic style between 1876 and 1879, the main tower is a hexagonal turret taking a spiral staircase up 330 steps and has 11 rooms. On top is the Mughal-style lantern for the view but the judge was refused permission for the light, since it would send wrong signals to seamen. Peterson had, among his various curiosities, also researched about the efficacy of cement and he, in the time to come, was proved right, in times to came, indeed.[25]

Let us now turn towards the other man mentioned in the 1863 case, W.C. Hurry. He was a friend of Lang, but died a year before the case filed by Lucy Lang began. Hurry was a man of varied interests and perhaps therefore, he never married.[26] Hurry was a botanist who had great interest in propagation of Guinea grass in India as fodder for the cattle. In a series of correspondences in 1836 with John Bell, the secretary of Agricultural Society in India, Hurry discussed propagating this grass by seed so that it can be sent by *daak*[II] all over India; he discusses the fact that coolies cannot distinguish between weed and Guinea during wedding.

Hurry thought that this grass was of great importance because 'In my own family want of Guinea Grass is always discovered by the inferiority of the butter'[27]. Hurry was also an 'energetic and able secretary of landholder's society'[28]. Hurry was also the editor of the *Englishman* for some time.[29] This could well be the reason for beginning of a long friendship between Hurry and Lang. The main vocation of Hurry was a business, and he was an assignee of Alexander and Co. He had interests in indigo factories.[30] He is known to have been involved in several court cases involving indigo plantations. Lang mentions his travels to Tirhoot indigo factories—perhaps on an invitation from Hurry—and in an article titled 'Inundation In Bengal' in the *Household Words* in 1853 describes the flood that destroyed all the crops. This is a piece of adventure writing where Lang tells how he proceeded into the inundated landscape despite warnings of all and sundry. He, however, juxtaposes his privileged position—of having 'palkee-bearers' who waded in the waters carrying him, and of the luxury to indulge in such adventure—with that of the common Indian farmers who had lost everything in this flood:

> A famine in India is an awful spectacle; but, while it lasts, an inundation is even more horrible. The wretched people do not

II daak – The Hindi word for post

> beg, while they weep. Money can procure nothing when there is no single article to be sold. It is not until the dangers are over that they ask for assistance…Even from the south of Bengal thousands upon thousands crowded to Calcutta, for a pittance whereon to subsist. So rapid was the rise of the water in many places that before the indigo planters could bring their boats to remove the plant which had been cut, it was carried away and lost…In obedience to Lord Hardinge's orders, boats laden with rice were despatched to several districts…It is one thing for a mass of rich people to afford charity to a destitute few; it is another thing for a few, who have to work for their own living, to feed millions of despairing mendicants thrown suddenly on the world. The scene, when the waters rapidly surround a village, is heart-rending in the extreme.[31]

Lang mentions Hurry with relation to court cases in India on another occasion. Lang was a bitter critic of the legal system in India, both of the East India Company and of the legacy left by the Mughals, by which most cases up till Lang's time were argued in a jargon that was a mixture of Arabic, Persian, and Hindustani:

> There was at Bijnor a native munshi who was a very good scholar; and, as I was anxious to read Hindoostanee and Persian with him (the more especially as I much enjoyed the society of mine host and his assistant)…I studied for several hours a-day, besides attending the Court House regularly, to listen to the proceedings, and acquire some knowledge of a most extraordinary jargon, composed of a little Hindoostanee, a little Persian, and a good deal of Arabic. This jargon is known in India as the language of the courts. A good Persian and Hindoostanee scholar cannot understand it, unless he is accustomed to it. Many magistrates and judges have insisted

> upon having pure Hindoostanee spoken; but to no purpose. Up to a recent period, Persian mixed with Arabic was the language in which legal proceedings were conducted—Persian and Arabic being as foreign languages to the people of India as English, German, or French. And, when the order went forth that Hindoostanee was to be used, the native officers of the courts, and the native lawyers who practised therein, complied with it by putting a Hindoostanee verb at the end of each sentence, and using the Hindoostanee pronouns, retaining in all their integrity (or rascality) the Persian and Arabic adverbs, prepositions, nouns, adjectives, and conjunctions.[32]

Hurry was involved in a court case regarding a land dispute between two Indian 'zemindars', Wyoodyechund Dutt and Isserchund Dutt.[33] Lang grounds his criticism with the case of Hurry, who had been in India several years, knew Hindustani well and yet could not follow the court proceedings:

> An indigo planter in Tahoot, who spoke Hindoostanee perfectly, having lived amongst the natives for upwards of twenty years, assured me that he did not comprehend a single sentence of a decree in court Hindoostanee, that he heard read out to him—a decree in a case to which he was a party. What is even more absurd, each court has its own peculiar jargon, so that the magistrate or judge, who from long experience has acquired a thorough knowledge of the jargon of his own court, has very great difficulty in comprehending the jargon of another court. This might be altered by fining any officer of court, or native lawyer, who, in matters connected with a suit, used words and phrases unintelligible to the mass of the people; but the order would have to emanate from Government. No magistrate or judge would venture on even an attempt to bring about so desirable a reform.[34]

There, then were various common interests between Lang and Hurry—English journalism in India, plight of indigo farmers, Hindoostanee language and critique of the legal system in India. There was one more thread, which is in my opinion, the most important one, that made the two friends come together—their shared interest in phrenology.

William Cobb Hurry's interest in phrenology led him to procure skulls of deceased men from his sources abroad. In Tasmania, there was a cannibal by the name of Pearce who had been hanged. To study it, Hurry procured his skull from the surgeon who had conducted the post-mortem of the body. Hurry, despite not being a medical man, was a member of the Phrenological Society. This, once again, like the case of A.T.T.P., shows the excitement amongst wealthy Englishmen in the 19th century to be a part of all that seemed to be historical. There are several such characters who were interested in various knowledge systems and pursued it with zeal in the 19th century, including Lang.

Pearce, an Irishman originally, was convicted in County Monaghan for stealing several pairs of shoes. At Tasmania's west coast, he earned a secondary punishment at the infamous Macquarie Harbour for being rebellious.[35]

The export of skulls from Australia to various parts of the Empire was not an uncommon practice during that time. *The Australian* newspaper reported in 1827[36] that 15 months after the establishment of Sydney Phrenological Society, there was a new trend of a curious export from the colony—that of skulls. It said that a great phrenologist had sent as many as 20 heads of aboriginals who had fallen in skirmish with settlers.

In his book about popular sciences in the 19th century, Roger Cooter argues that phrenology—like other sciences and pseudo-sciences of the 19th century—resulted in intellectual ferment, and that it was not merely a curiosity, that it had subtle ideological implications.[37] Phrenology was a system of studying human psychology through shapes of skulls; and this could easily become a vehicle of racial discrimination, as Charles Darwin's theories would also become around the same time.

In Australia, phrenology led to the belief that aboriginals could not be civilised because the shape of their heads did not resemble those of 'civilised' people. This was proved systematically by attributing qualities to various parts of the skull, which were missing in these aboriginal people—who had carried out a civilisation quietly for thirty thousand years or so.

An Act of the Parliament in 1772 made it mandatory that the bodies of criminals hanged by capital punishment for murder be dissected for medical study. Despite this Act, the number of bodies that could be legitimately secured by medical teachers met only a fraction of the demand. Thus, secretive trade in corpses illegally exhumed from graveyards or stolen from workhouse infirmaries characterised the British medical economy.[38]

John Lang would have known about these smugglings of skulls from Australia to various parts of the British Empire, for he regularly corresponded with his family and friends in Australia, and he knew a smuggler himself—William Cobb Hurry. Descriptions of foreheads form a constant part of Lang's depiction of characters, though not necessarily in conjunction with the word 'phrenology'. In some places, the preoccupation with the emerging science is visible. In *Wanderings in India,* Lang tells that he had been witness to an execution. When the man is hanged and pronounced dead, and the body is brought down, Lang examines the deceased and says,

> A finer head, in a phrenological point of view, I had never seen, and across the naked chest was suspended the sacred thread, indicating that the culprit was a Brahmin.[39]

At this point, Lang asks his host who had taken him to witness the scene whether it wasn't true that the most diabolical crimes in

India were committed by Brahmins—the hanged man's crime was the murder of a seven-year-old girl for taking a bangle from him. Lang is trying to connect phrenology with criminality here—an enterprise that we have seen was the preoccupation of the Australian phrenologists of the time—but his juxtaposition of 'fine forehead', 'thread across the chest' and the murder of a little girl make him perplexed. Lang offers a scathing critic of caste through his host's reply who says that it was not at all odd that the men of highest caste committed the most heinous crimes:

> Do you not know that they (Brahmins) believe nothing can hurt their pure souls after death; and hence their comparative recklessness in this world? There was a Brahmin hanged here, about a year ago, who, just before he was turned off, made a speech such as that made by Napoleon on paper to Sir Hudson Lowe—'You may convict me of what you please; you may make me a prisoner; you may, if you like, shackle these limbs, and consign me to a dungeon; but you will find that my soul will be just as free, just as proud, as when it awed all Europe!'[40]

The reader may assume that this could be an Orientalist attitude. It is misleading, as has been pointed earlier, to quote Lang sans the complete context of his narratives. He is equally sarcastic of the barbarous way in which the executions took place:

> They are not adepts in the art of hanging in India; it took the culprit at least ten minutes to die. At times I feared, so desperate were his struggles, that he would break the beam, snap the rope, or bring down the whole apparatus. In the days of Henry Fielding, the vulgar used to speak of hanging as 'dancing on nothing,' and this horrible idea the Indian culprit on that morning amply realised.[41]

After the man is 'cut down', Lang tells:

> The cutting down of the culprit, as soon as it was discovered that life was extinct (for as there was no crowd of pickpockets and vendors of cakes and ginger-beer to take a moral lesson, the prescribed hour was unnecessary) was quite as primitive as the foregoing part of the operation.[42]

Lang, it seems from this narrative, knew the principles of phrenology as told to him by medical men of the time, but finds his learning at odds with his findings. He returns to phrenology with a long, elaborate chapter about a professor of phrenology in his novel *Will He Marry Her?*. The account is a spoof of the phrenological enterprise, for Augustus Reckless takes a misshapen cast of his own head from a sculptor named Massaroni and passes it off as a criminal's to professor Linney, who shows great interest in it and indulges Reckless, detailing what was wrong with the man whose skull's cast had been brought in. Lang, in his usual sarcastic manner, cuts out a tailor-like picture for Professor Linney:

> Mr. Linney, the Professor of Phrenology, prided himself on going 'twice as far as even Deville.' He divided the head into something like sixty or seventy parts; and after manipulating the cranium for some fifteen minutes—looking immensely serious all the while—he would run on thus, his assistant taking down his words as they were from time to time uttered in a loud, grave voice:—'Keep down 29, 37; raise up 16, 22… keep down 4, 11, 13; raise up 18, 19, 20; expand 2, 5; contract 1, 12, 39; and the result will be, that, in the course of a year, your head will be considerably altered in shape, and your abilities proportionately increased.' Linney, in fact, measured a head for a complete suite of character and talents, just in the

same way that a tailor measures a body for a complete suite of clothing.[43]

Augustus gives the cast to the professor and tells him that it is a cast of the head of a criminal who was convicted for his parents' murder. What ensues between Linney and Augustus should be quoted verbatim, to show Lang's wit as well as sound knowledge of the subject:

> 'I am greatly obliged to you, Mr. Reckless,' Linney began, 'for bringing me the cast of this head. It is, indeed, a splendid specimen, and completely proves the soundness of my theory. This man, sir, was not deficient in ability—in intellect; but just put your finger upon his 'Firmness.' In *his* case it amounted to obstinacy. And then observe this frightful development of 'Combativeness,' and then his enormous 'Acquisitiveness.' Those three organs…had a complete ascendancy over Benevolence, Conscientiousness, and Veneration. What was the result? The gallows! Had he, as he might have done, raised up his 6, 24, 32, and depressed his 21, 16, 11, this man would have been, perhaps, an ornament to society.'
>
> 'Poor wretch!' sighed Reckless. 'But if you look at the back of the head, it is comparatively small; and according to first principles, his intellectual predominated considerably over his animal or vicious propensities.'
>
> 'We must not be guided by first principles, Mr. Reckless. That is the great mistake. Besides, this man was evidently of a very sanguine temperament.'
>
> 'Sanguinary, you mean?'
>
> 'It amounts to the same thing, sir. Had he been of a bilious or lymphatic temperament, his brain would probably have been less active.'
>
> 'What about his ideality?'

> 'Well-developed. But then look at his 67—his Caution. His 67 acted as a check on his 39. Caution is to Ideality what a log and chain is to the human leg.'
>
> 'Then why did not Caution step in when he entertained the idea of killing his parents?'
>
> Here Mr. Linney pursed his lips, looked mysteriously into Reckless's eyes, tapped with his huge forefinger the apex of the cast, and said, with an air of confidence, and in an extremely grave voice, 'Here, sir here! His 21—his leading organ—his Obstinacy—this was the rock on which this man split.'
>
> 'No; it was upon himself that he split,' said Reckless, playing on the word, and inwardly smiling, rather contemptuously. 'He confessed. It was thus that the murder was discovered. What organ induced him to confess?'
>
> 'Here it is! His 80—his Hope!' Linney scratched the organ with his thumb-nail.
>
> 'Hope of what, Mr. Linney?'
>
> 'Pardon in this world, and of forgiveness in the next. There must have been a terrible struggle going on for some time...' Here Linney leant over the plaster of Paris cast, and gazed at it very intently for at least two minutes.[44]

The comic and sarcastic tone of the conversation and the use of two puns—sanguine (cheerful)/ sanguinary (bloodthirsty); and split (Lenny comparing the man's obstinacy with rock)/ split (Augustus insinuating split personality)—suggest that the narrative is dismissive of Linney's enterprise. However, Reckless's dismissal is not so emphatic:

> Meanwhile Reckless put to himself these questions, and made inwardly the following remarks: 'Is this man an impostor? That is to say, does he know that he is talking nonsense? Does he really believe in the science to the extent that he professes? I

> will give him the benefit of the doubt, and ask him to sup with me; and he shall manipulate every head in the company if he likes—Parry's included.'[45]

Lang affects a mocking tone in this episode: this very tone was the reason of his journalistic success. In his journalism, too, Lang used the same technique of combining sensationalism with acute knowledge of the subject, which lent credence to sweeping statements.

In this account, Lang, cleverly, is alluding to himself through the first qualities of the cast declared by Linney—'the man was not deficient of ability—in intellect,' he had 'firmness' amounting to obstinacy, 'combativeness' and enormous 'acquisitiveness'. Lang was intelligent and considered himself so; he was obstinate; he was combative and took on the East India Company through the gall of his pen and oration throughout his career, and he is known to have had a facility for very fast learning without the need for re-referring sources once he had had a look at them.[46]

Curiously, the obituary of Lang in *The Mofussilite* tells that Lang had always wished for a post-mortem after his death and the finding was that 'his brain weighed eight ounces less than the average, in the human adult'. The obituarist adds that 'however, that it was peculiarly notable on account of the excess of "grey or cortical substance" so called, to which the physiologist has traced the seat of thought and intelligence.'[47] (see plate 2)

This lesser weight is in consonance with head being small, and 'intellectual predominated' resonates with 'excess of grey or cortical substance'. Fiction manifested into fact once more in the after-life of Lang.

Out of the several cases of anatomization, dissection, and phrenologification that happened in 19th century Australia, Lang knew one case very well. This was the hanging of George Worrall in Sydney in February 1827. Frederick Fisher, who was a convict transported from England to New South Wales for forgery of banknotes, earned a ticket-of-leave (which entailed that he could be a free man, but not absolutely pardoned) and amassed a fortune. He went back to England after many years, handing over the rights to his neighbour Worrall to sell his property. At this moment, there were suspicions among some people that Fisher had been murdered, and his body was found by an aboriginal tracker in a pond near his house in Campbelltown, Sydney. A case commenced against Worrall, the neighbour, and he was pronounced guilty. Worrall maintained throughout the trial that he was not guilty, and the public sympathies were with him on the day of the hanging. It was declared that Worrall had confessed his crime just before the hanging. This declaration may just have been to placate the public—one does not know if Worrall actually confessed. As we have already seen, it was mandatory at that time to dissect the body of a person convicted for murder.

The *Monitor* said that Worrall did not die instantly, but that he showed symptoms of life five minutes after he was hanged. It went on to say that his 'body, we understand, was given to one of our Sydney practitioners, as a subject for anatomical and phrenological experiment; the sentence of law having awarded dissection'.

By the Act of 1752, titled An Act for Better Preventing the Horrid Crime of Murder, the judge was empowered to order that the body of the murderer was to be hanged in chains. If he did not order that, then the Act required that the body was to be anatomised, that is, dissected by surgeons, before burial.

Peter Linebaugh in the preface of his book *The London Hanged* says that the Tyburn riots[48] were an 'earnest battle of loved ones against the surgeons for possession of the condemned corpse, and it showed the scorn evinced in word and deed by Tyburn crowd against law and authority'[49].

I have chosen to print snippets of the Worrall trial news for three primary reasons. First, we find no mention of any ghost, not just in himself in this second confession, alleging the commission of the murder to have originated in accident—a blow, he said, aimed at a horse, killed Fisher; but the train of succeeding circumstances controvert such a story. At half-past nine, every preparation being completed, the drop fell; the rope by which he was suspended was of unusual shortness, he appeared to be instantaneously released from pain, but the mortal struggle was not, in reality, over; for after a lapse of near five minutes he shewed symptoms of returning animation, to the great pain of the witnessing crowd. Worrall was a tall, muscular man, apparently about 36 years of age. His body, we understand, was given to one of our Sydney practitioners, as a subject for anatomical and phrenological experiment; the sentence of the law having awarded dissection.

A copy cutting from The Monitor 10 Feb 1827

Execution.

George Worrall, who was convicted on Friday last of the murder of Frederick Fisher, yesterday suffered the dreadful sentence of the law. Till about 5 o'clock on the morning of his execution, he persisted in asserting his innocence, when he was at length induced to acknowledge to a gentleman, who had sat up with him during the night, that he, alone had perpetrated the murder, but positively affirmed that it was not his intention at the time to do so. He stated, that on the unhappy day when Fisher met his fate, they were going together with a bottle to get some rum, and in passing the paddock, discovered there was a horse there. Worrall said he jumped over the fence on one side, and Fisher on the other, leaving the bottle outside; that then he seized part of the paling, and made a blow which he intended for the horse, and that he did not know of the deed he had committed till his return from the pursuit, when he saw Fisher lying weltering in his blood; he added, that on seeing this dreadful spectacle he became confused, and was afraid if he made any disclosure he should be accused of the murder. This induced him to hide the body among some reeds, but his anxiety increased till he had deposited the body where it was eventually found. He also acknowledged that it was his full intention to hang the two men who were apprehended, in order to save himself, but now he acquitted them, or any other, of having any participation in the crime, and, we believe, he acknowledged the justice of his sentence to the Reverend Gentleman who assisted him in his devotions. His behaviour on the scaffold was manly and becoming, and he seemed absorbed in the contemplation of an awful eternity. The Rev. Gentleman at length took his leave —the executioner adjusted the cap—and

A report detailing the supposed confession made by Worrall. The victim, Fisher, went on to become the subject of Fisher's Ghost tales. Sydney Gazette, 6 Feb, 1827 (p 124)

Execution announcement 6 Feb 1827 Sydney Gazette

Sydney Gazette but also the other newspapers that covered the trial and the execution in 1827. Later, however, this story gets connected with a ghost—the ghost of the slain man, Frederick Fisher.

Secondly, this trial, perhaps, became famous because Worrall was considered innocent by the public and the statement of confession was added as an afterthought. Also, as a corollary, there was the issue of dissection of the body of an innocent man for phrenological experiments. Thirdly and most importantly, it is an issue of a huge unacknowledged debt to John Lang by the people of Campbelltown in Sydney.

Fisher Dead is More Powerful Than Fisher Alive

or The Festival's Celebrations Its Author Deprive

The trial of Worrall and his subsequent hanging became legendary. The legend would have faded out, but for the intervention of a ghost. Various versions of this story came into circulation that added a ghost to the story. These stories said that Fisher's ghost sat upon the rail in front of his house, and this was noticed by a man, who became suspicious. He reported the matter and subsequently an aboriginal tracker found Fisher's body, whereupon the case against Worrall—the names differ in different stories—commenced.

One of the first such stories to appear was 'Fisher's Ghost: A Legend of Campbelltown'. It appeared in the first issue of *Tegg's Magazine*, published from Sydney in March 1836, and printed by H. Bull. The story was reprinted in the same year in *The Sydney Gazette* and *New South Wales Advertiser* in the same month, with a leader advertising *Tegg's Magazine.*[1]

The story of Fisher's ghost appeared in one of the first issues of *The Mofussilite* in 1845. This was clearly written by Lang. It appeared in the *Household Words* in the 5 March 1853 issue again. At that time, this was not attributed to Lang but we know from Anne Lohrli's book entitled—*Household Words: A Weekly Journal, 1850–1859, Conducted by Charles Dickens: Table of Contents, List of Contributors and Their Contributions, Based on the Household Words Office Book in the Morris L. Parrish Collection of Victorian Novelists, Princeton*[21]—that the work is Lang's for sure. The long title of the book is self-explanatory to show that.

I The title of the book is so long because Lohrli consulted office book of *Household Words* and used the information about who was paid what sum for what article. This was done to definitively point out what was written by who in the journal famous only by Dickens's name.

Thereafter, the story appeared many times, and several under Lang's name. Lang expanded the story to about 20 pages when he published his collection of Australian stories called *Botany Bay, Or True Tales of the Early Days of Australia* (1859)[3]. This book, towards the end of Lang's life, was reclamation of his Australian identity. Lang, in the preface, talks about his indiscretion in 1842 when he ran into a conflict with the Exclusivists, and when he spoke against the Emancipist proposal of autonomy for New South Wales. This book ran into several editions, and is the book by which Lang is known in Australia. The story also appeared under other names like *Fisher's Ghost And Other Stories of the Early Days of Australia* (1920).[4]

The legend of Fisher's ghost grew and various literary works—stories, poems and plays—were written about it subsequently. In 1956, the legend resurrected when an annual festival, by the name of 'Fisher's Ghost Festival' was started in Campbelltown. The festival, is held in early November every year, spans 10 days and I had this opportunity to attend in 2010. The festival is a thrilling and inclusive community festival of Campbelltown in south-west Sydney—which resembles India's Republic Day parade—with various organisations of the locality marching through the main street along with dancers, army tanks, school children et al. It is a spectacular carnival in which most of those parading down the road wear ghost costumes. It is primarily a children's festival. One wonders about the connection between children and ghost stories—they seem to always be interconnected.

The Fisher's Ghost Festival maintains a website[5] which talks about the Fisher and Worrall case in brief, and has a poem about the incident, which is as follows:

Frederick George James Fisher
A convict he had been
Arrived on the Atlas transport

In the year 1816
Freedom soon was his
And Campbelltown showed much charm
That this was where he settled
On his thirty acre farm
Disaster struck June 17
The year 1826
Fred Fisher had disappeared
So a twenty pound reward was fixed
Then a ghost was seen pointing
To the banks along the creek
Blood was found on the bridge
From where the ghost did speak
On the last day of October
Fred's body had been found
Black natives solved the mystery
Buried three feet underground
George Worrall was arrested
Convicted by the Supreme Court
His life on earth was terminated
Justice had been bought

According to the website, the author is 'unknown' and it does not have any reference to any prose works. Upon enquiries made in Campbelltown, no one knew that John Lang had written a story called 'Fisher's Ghost'. Even to English literature students, this story is known through Lang's more known text in Australia, *Botany Bay* or True Tales of Early Australia.

Whether Lang is the originator of the ghost legend is a matter worth inspecting, but there is no doubts that Lang made the legend survive a century with his various versions of the tale in *Tegg's Magazine, The Mofussilite, Household Words* and *Botany Bay*. Lang's contribution has been such that the legend became a household matter, for numerous versions of the story came into currency in late 19th and early 20th century—and they all had their root source in Lang's story. It is to John Lang, then, that Campbelltown owes its legacy, and yet does not know about it.

In my interview with him in May 2010 at Canberra, Victor Crittenden contends that Lang conjured the ghost. He argues that Lang was fascinated by works of Shakespeare and that he probably had *Hamlet* in his mind when he wrote the story. There is no doubt that Lang was an avid reader of Shakespeare—he quotes from the bard quite often in his works—but this is not proof enough that the ghost tale was not already in currency when Lang wrote the story. Crittenden's idea of 'conjuring' probably emanates from the narrator's voice in Lang's story which says:

> As for the story about the ghost, very, very few put any trust in it. Bulwer was then a very young gentleman, and had never dreamt of writing about Eugene Aram; nor had Thomas Hood contemplated his exquisite little poem on the same subject. Nor had the murder of the Red Barn been brought to light through the agency of a dream. The only instances of ghosts coming to give evidence of murder were those of Banquo and Hamlet's father—and Shakespeare was not considered an authority to be relied upon in such a case as that of Fisher.[6]

John Lang clearly knew the related cases and texts. He, here, is making two points—one that the story of the ghost was generally not believed, and hence hinting that the ghost-sighter David Weir (Farley) stood suspect himself; and two, in stating that Shakespeare cannot be relied upon as an authority in Fisher's case; Lang is hinting that his inspiration for the story is not Shakespeare but that the story was in currency in Sydney.

It is characteristic of Lang to weave his various sources into his narrative. In most of his texts, he refers to his sources and similar literary references through the narratorial voice. For example, In *My Friend's Wife, Or York You're Wanted*, the narrator York refers to Maryatt, thus acknowledging Maryatt for having used the phrase 'York, you're wanted' in one of his novels. Eugene Aram was an English philologist who had murdered his friend Dan Clark, but no evidence had been found even though Aram was suspected. The skeleton of Clark turned up one day—like Fisher's ghost—to give testimony against Aram. After the discovery of the skeleton, Aram confessed to the crime, and tried committing suicide a day before he was to be hanged. Aram committed the murder because he had found out that Clark was having an affair with his wife. Aram's vicissitudes are detailed in Bulwer Lytton's novel *Eugene Aram*[7] and in Thomas Hood's poem *The Dream of Eugene Aram, the Murderer*.[8]

Andrew Lang, in his 1903 book *The Valet's Tragedy and Other Stories*[9] has a chapter about the 'yarn' of Fisher's ghost entitled 'The Truth About Fisher's Ghost' (the article first appeared in *Blackwood's Magazine*, 1897). He says that the 'yarn is much dressed up' in Lang's *Botany Bay* version.[10]

Andrew Lang has a point, for the *Botany Bay* story is a much longer version than John Lang's earlier stories. In *Botany Bay*, John Lang has dramatised the plot much more, though he keeps very close to the actual events as he would have read in the newspapers. The time gap between the murder and the discovery of the body is originally four months, which Lang increases to 15, to introduce pathetic fallacy—that the murder was so foul that it would not rain till it was discovered. The heavens preserved the blood stains, the evidence of the murder. Also, in Lang's *Botany Bay*, after the discovery of the body, there is a torrential downpour like never before, as if the heavens were weeping.

John Lang, however, retains the fact that the public sympathies were with the supposed murderer till the morning of hanging, and that it was a last moment confession by the convict that vindicated the jury.

Andrew Lang, the writer of this critique of Fisher's ghost 'yarn', by the way, is not connected to our subject John Lang. Andrew Lang also had a brother called John Lang, and the two Lang brothers were prominent writers of early 20th century. Andrew's brother, John Lang, was a writer of children's tales, who had me quite confused in the initial phase of my research.

Andrew Lang tells that the ghost appeared before the *Tegg's Magazine* story of 1836, which could be attributed to our John Lang, but Andrew doesn't attribute the *Household Words* version of the story to John Lang. It is only in late 20th century that the authorship of articles of *Household Words* could be definitely attributed.

Andrew Lang tells that the ghost story had appeared in Robert Montgomery Martin's *History of British Colonies Vol IV*, in 1835.[11]

Earnshaw says that Martin had spent time in New South Wales and knew the story first hand.[12] Lang would have read this story and built upon it. According to Andrew Lang, as told to him by Martin's friend, Martin was present at the trial, and had often told the friend the tale and discussed it with legal officials.[13] The ghost story, that means, was already in currency just after the trial even though no newspapers mention any such thing. After the trial, this 'yarn' would have been told by someone amongst the local population—Martin reported it in his book—from where John Lang took fancy to it. Lang was the populariser of this story for sure, and in fact, the parent of many further legends.

Andrew Lang conjectures about the origin of the story. He says that there were lacunae in the trial: the murder took place in June 1826; the hanging of George Worrall in February 1827. During the trial, a witness revealed that he had observed blood stains on the fence of Fisher's house; this is where the search for the body had commenced. The witness did not tell by whom the blood stains were seen. This is the gap that was filled by the ghost story.

John Lang has retained most of the witnesses in his story—albeit under changed names—and has used them to, vibrantly and vividly recreate life as it was in early Sydney. Andrew Lang, on the other hand, conjectures that the jury were told the ghost story, who did not make it public, for it would further weaken the case, that was already weak and based on circumstantial evidence:

> Worrall's condemnation is said to have excited popular discontent, as condemnations on purely circumstantial evidence usually do. That dissatisfaction would be increased if a ghost were publicly implicated in the matter.[14]

Andrew Lang compares this case with the case of the murder of a market-gardener William Edden in England in 1828. Edden went missing and his wife reported that she had seen her husband's ghost with a hammer in his hand. The wife deposed before the authorities maintaining her story of the ghost, but in the report of the trial, it was not mentioned. Andrew Lang says that in the Worrall case, the same strategy was used by the authorities—to keep the ghost out. Andrew Lang further states that in another 18th century trial, Jacobites had laughed at a ghost story, and this had resulted in acquittal of the accused.

Andrew Lang tells that he had been given a copy of Rusden's *History of Australia* (1883) by the author himself, who had given a summary of the Fisher's ghost story in his book.[15] Rusden had been told the story by the doctor of James Farley, who is supposed to have seen the ghost. Rusden told Andrew that Farley often used to have nightmares about the ghost. (In John Lang's story the name is changed to David Weir.)

In *Australian Stories Retold* (1887), W.H. Suttor writes: 'It has been suggested that the ghost having been seen at all was a mythical growth of a later day...I have the authority of a correspondent who was intimately connected with the gentleman who had the charge of the police when the murder was done, that Farley's story did suggest the search for the body in the creek.'[16]

Andrew Lang further write:

> But, Mr. Suttar thinks that Farley invented the tale as an excuse for laying information...if Farley knew the facts, and had the ghost to cover the guilt of peaching, WHY DID HE NOT PEACH? He only pointed to a fence...[17]

He, however, contends that there was no need for Farley to be an undercover informer. In this matter, if Andrew Lang is right, then perhaps a needle of suspicion points towards Farley, for he may have conjured the ghost story to draw the suspicion away from him. In John Lang's story, David Weir's (Farley) wife tells him that he must keep quiet about sighting a ghost lest people think he himself was the murderer and was using a decoy to indict Smith (Worrall of Lang's story).

Lang clearly knew that this idea was also in currency that Farley could have been the murderer and made up the story to have Worrall incriminated. Andrew Lang, after these particulars of his research, concludes that in his opinion the case for the ghost stands.

From these accounts, it is clear that the ghost story did exist before the trial. However, whether the ghost was actually sighted or was made up by Farley is difficult to tell. What Andrew Lang is using as a proof—the hallucinations of Farley as told by Farley's doctor later on—can go against Farley. He probably was the murderer and perhaps never reconciled with the idea of having sent an innocent man to the gallows.

Andrew Lang's book is from 1903; the John Lang cycle of Fisher's ghost stories starts in 1840s. Interestingly, all the arguments given by Andrew Lang are present there in John Lang's narration. This shows the lawyer's mind at work. Unless one reads Andrew Lang's much later and very astutely researched work, one won't be able to realise the amount of thought Lang had put into this story without having at hand all the books that Andrew Lang perused.

As already mentioned, Lang never failed to write a caustic remark or two against the legal system of any place. In most of his works, the judiciary of British India and England are subject of his gall, and in 'Fisher's Ghost', Lang takes the opportunity to extend his bilious words towards the Australian judiciary.[18]

That is the story of Fisher's ghost, and how it was not conjured by John Lang, but made a part of the folklore by him.

That adds into the list of unacknowledged debts to Lang, which started with Tom Taylor and *Plot and Passion.* Lang's association with Tom Taylor or vice versa didn't really create any ripples. What did create a stir—rather whole lot of turbulence—in the literary world was one of Lang's stray comments on an Edgar Allen Poe poem.

Poe's Woes,

or Ravens, Roosters and Pigs

Edgar Allan Poe, the celebrated American writer, in 1846 wrote a poem called 'The Raven'[1]. An 1856 edition of Poe's collection of poems says 'no single poem ever had greater success in America'[2]. Known for its internal rhyme and alliteration besides the esoteric, dark, brooding theme of exploring the subterranean terrifying truths of human psyche, the poem is a classic today. It is a narrative poem in which a talking raven visits a distraught lover and adds to his distress by saying 'Nevermore' repeatedly. The lover slowly descends into insanity.

The poem was followed by an essay called 'The Philosophy of Composition' in the *Graham's Magazine* in April 1846.[3] In this essay, Poe uses his own poem 'The Raven' to show the process of creation of a piece of literature, and to make his theory stand out against contemporary theories of spontaneity as essential in creation of poetry as espoused by Coleridge and Wordsworth. He makes three basic points—one, that literary works should be short; two, that writing is very methodical and that the writers who do not admit to this would 'positively shudder at letting the public take a peep behind the scenes'; and three, that there should be a unity of effect—that the writer should know what the end of a work is and only then decide the matter of form, rhyme, plot etc.

Analysing his poem 'The Raven', he says that 'the death...of a beautiful woman' was the subject he chose as it 'is unquestionably the most poetical topic in the world, and equally is it beyond doubt that the lips best suited for such topic are those of a bereaved lover'. The dead beloved is named Lenore in the poem.

This would be a good point of entry for Mr Lang. In 1858, he wrote a novel *Will He Marry Her?* The novel's heroine's name is Leonora, coincidentally, quite similar to Poe's Lenore. Lang's novel ends in 'the death...of a beautiful woman' Leonora. This makes Lang's novel stand testimony to Poe's philosophy of composition: the novel is long, which is an aberration for Lang's works which are mostly short; the writing is indeed methodical with a decided agenda of subverting the hero's classist and racist ideologies; there is a unity of effect—despite the stated subversion, the half-caste heroine—born out of the wedlock of a white father and 'sable' mother—is killed just after her marriage to the white hero. Such unity of effect is contrived cleverly to subvert Victorian norms and morality, and, in the end, affect a moral lesson that such marriages are ordained to end in death and despair.

At this point, the reader would think that Lang perhaps took inspiration from Poe's poem and essay while writing his novel. However, in writing this novel, Lang, who was boisterous in his exterior and subtle when writing, was subtly writing back to Poe while contriving several other things through his writing. Lang, earlier, had created a little stir in the literary world by his off-hand comment about 'The Raven.'

The story is that a friend of Lang's read out Poe's poem to him—when Lang looked up from his book and said that it was very good Persian, and quoted the original Persian poem. This was published in *Tait's Edinburgh Magazine* of 1855 in which the writer of the article 'Reading Raids' says that:

> When we ask for the *most* original writer yet produced by America, we are at once directed to Edgar Allan Poe and reminded of 'The Raven: a Poem.'* We, personally, have nothing to object against the statement that Poe is the most original of American authors, so long as in admitting the 'originality' we are not supposed to yield him the *very highest* rank in the literature of the New World. We give Poe the foremost place in his class, but that class is not the highest...only let the 'glory' be

> that of a wonderful combination of qualities, and not that of a real individuality of genius.[4]

The writer, who began mildly, goes on to jibe at Poe and his 'philosophy of composition' and gets provocative:

> A work of genius is the result of the spontaneous and harmonious exercise (or outflow) of any number of faculties, excited to such a degree of activity that the product shall be homogeneous (we mean no pun), and exclude the idea of *process*. With all that Poe has written (as far as we know) *fully* present to our minds, we are prepared to deny that he has left behind him any such work. We concede to him—
>
> 1. Extraordinary, perhaps unparalleled, powers of analysis, and of retention;
> 2. Great command of language;
> 3. Very great imitative and constructive tact;
> 4. An ideality sufficiently intense to tinge, (but not to saturate and deeply colour), all his conceptions:
> 5. All these receiving a special direction from a love of the wonderful and mysterious, and a gloomy *morale,* in which a sense of the terrible was an over present influence.
>
> This combination of powerful elements does not, however, make the thing called *genius.* The mere fact that we *can* dissect Poe's work, draw woof from warp, pass the light through the prism, resolve the product into its constituents; that we find what we are admiring is, chemically speaking, a mixture and not a solution.

The article is so caustic that it almost seems ghost written by Lang. The writer is insinuating at retention, imitation, colouring but not sufficient colouring—in short, hinting at plagiarism. If the reader would have noticed, there is an asterisk (*) in the first quote, which has a footnote that reads:

> It is current talk in literary circles, that this production (which has provoked as many parodies as anything ever written, with the exception of Wolfe's 'Burial of Sir John Moore at Corunna') is a paraphrase from the Persian. It was Mr. 'Mofussilite Lang, who hearing it repeated by a literary friend, is said to have looked up from his book with 'Hallo! That's very good Persian!' instantly quoting the original. Poe was a good Persian scholar.

Lang perhaps did not know that he would be quoted in the *Tait's Magazine*, or perhaps being the irreverent character that he was, he caused himself to be quoted. However, this seemingly casual comment from Lang, and it finding its way into this magazine, spawned various literary debates about Poe and originality.

Theodore Watts-Dunton, English critic and poet, wrote in a letter:

> ...I wish someone could say whence arose the extraordinary talk that was current in London some years ago, and which often got into print, about 'The Raven' being an adaptation from Persian! The most definite form the story took was this: Mr Lang—Mr 'Mofussilite' Lang according to a paragraph in Tait's Magazine...[5]

As is evident from Watts-Dunton's letter, this was a literary scandal and talk of the town—yet another Botany Bay[I] trick pulled off by Lang.[6] Botany Bay is where Captain Cook had landed in Australia,

---

I Botany Bay is the place where Lieutenant ajor (later Captain) James Cook, along with botanist Joseph Banks and the crew of HMS Endeavour first stepped on the land mass that is now called Australia, in April 1770. In the following two decades, the British Empire established a penal colony at Sydney Cove, somewhat north of Botany Bay. The people of England, however, misidentified that area, too, as Botany Bay.

and the term became a metaphor for convicted people. *The Morning Star* newspaper also took up the matter and said that Poe had merely translated the poem from a Persian original.[7]

I have not found any article written by Lang that definitively revealed which poem Poe had translated; and, interestingly enough none of the newspapers and journals that made this allegation cited the name of the poem either. 'Mofussilite' Lang's name was cited, and Edgar Allan Poe would have come to know of the man was had cast a blemish on his reputation. To date, this issue remains unresolved, and I have not chanced upon any 20th century work that takes up this matter and delves into it.

Poe was a good Persian scholar—as attested by *Tait's Magazine* and *The Morning Star.* Lang, also, was decidedly a good Persian scholar. He had learnt Persian to understand the court proceedings in India which were, till mid-19th century, held in a mixture of Persian, Arabic and Hindustani. Three years into his stay in India, he knew Persian very well, for, August 1845 onwards, Lang published his translations of Persian tales with the title *Goolistan* in *The Mofussilite*. He learnt some Persian at Bijnore as well. He tells in *Wanderings in India* that when he was in 'Oude for six months', he spoke nothing 'but Hindoostanee and Persian'[8]. In 'Mahomeddan Mother' from the same book, Lang tells that he spoke with Doonea, the distraught mother, in Persian. In 1863, he published the translation of poetry of Sadi of Shiraz in his newspaper. Lang's obituary in *The Mofussilite*[9] called him 'one of the best Persian scholars, which ever came to India'.

Lang also boasts about his facility for learning languages—Persian being one of them—in *Wanderings in India*:

> It was not long before I made up my mind to become a wanderer in the East. I had no occupation, was my own master, and had

> a large tract of country to roam about in. My first step was to acquire a knowledge of Hindoostanee and of Persian. By dint of hard study, at the end of six months I found myself capable, not only of holding a conversation, but of arguing a point in either of these languages...[10]

Lang having an intelligent mind and a retentive memory is also mentioned in Lang's obituary in *The Mofussilite*: 'his memory perfectly wonderful; it's natural power enabling him to dispense with the usual drudgery of study and reference'. The obituary also called Lang's wit 'ever ready', and 'his marvellous memory continually flashed forth appropriate illustrations from the ancient classics'. *Tait's Magazine*, then, may not be exaggerating when it says that Lang looked up from a book and said, 'Hallo! That's very good Persian' upon listening to Poe's poem.

Lang's scholarship of Persian and Arabic was well-known long after his death. *The Saturday Review*, while reviewing Palmer's translations of Egyptian poet *Beha-Ed-Din Zoheir's* poetry,[11] compared Palmer's translations with those of Lang:

> The song of Hafiz, well-known to Anglo-Indians, is popularly called *Taza-ba-taza,* because these words, 'freshly fresh' recur regularly at intervals. Mr Palmer begins:
>
> *O! minstrel sing the lay divine,*
> *Freshly fresh and newly new,*
> *Bring in the heart-expanding wine,*
> *Freshly fresh and newly new—*
>
> and so on for four more verses. We recollect a version of the same song by the late John Lang, author of *The Wetherbys* and other novels, in which this *refrain* was not always translated, and the effect was rather happy:

> *O! minstrel sing a song to me*
> *As fresh and new as it can be;*
> *And let the liquid verses flow,*
> *Taza-ba-taza, nau-ba-nau.'*[12]

Interestingly, Persian survived in India, despite the Mughal Empire in ruins; both Anglo-Indians[II] and Hindu chieftains knew and used Persian. Given that Lang's newspaper was decidedly for the Anglo-Indians, it is evident that Englishmen, too, knew a lot of Persian and Arabic phrases.

Lang, in his novels, always showed off his scholarship of languages. Even where a certain character is not supposed to know a language, he somehow contrives them to know the phrase he wants to quote. For example, in the novel *Ex-Wife*, Lady Eva Merrydale has never been to the East but knows a phrase which Lang wants to quote, courtesy her tenant (Mr Penderfield):

> To mingle with them in their social conversation was like (I know the simile is a very trite one) 'stumbling on an oasis in the desert. The Persians have a proverb—
>
> 'Humjins ba humjins kunad parwaz,
> Kabooter ba kabooter, baz ba baz'
> Which means (so poor Mr Penderfield told me)—
> 'Class with class should wing its flight—
> Dove with dove, kite with kite.'[13]

I was struck when I read this phrase in Lang's novel, for my memory of this phrase is from a rather risqué Bollywood song of the 1980s, 'Ek Do Teen Char' from a film called *Waqt Ki Awaz* (1988).

At one level, Lang's interest in Indian and Oriental languages could—in 20th century parlance—be called 'Orientalist' but the

II In this context, Anglo Indians means English people who lived in India during those times.

endeavour wasn't just of an Oriental scholar who wanted to study his subjects. His learning was out of a desire to mingle with Indian people, as well as a need; many of the 'Mofussil' court proceedings were in these languages. To run his newspaper, too, Lang needed news from vernacular newspapers and his learning would have proven handy. *The Mofussilite*'s intelligence on affairs of Punjab before the Anglo-Sikh wars (1845–50) was considered authoritative even by the army, and this must have been owing to Lang's companionship with locals and knowledge of Hindustani and Persian.

Besides, Lang visited several royals of India—Raja of Darbhanga, Nana Sahib, Tatya Tope, Rani of Jhansi, etc. His knowledge of Indian languages would have impressed them quite a lot. Besides these matters of business, Lang also had a keen interest in avenues of confluence of East and West. In an account in *Wanderings in India,* an Indian boy Shumsheer[III] who is Lang's 'khidmutgar', speaks English well, having had been in the service of assistant magistrate of Bijnore. He juxtaposes the image of his 'page' with himself reading many pages from a Persian book.[14]

Lang first realised his facility for learning languages when he was learning Latin at Sydney College. James Sheen Dowling wrote that Lang 'was a clever, bright fellow, a good scholar, who had a remarkable faculty for writing Latin verses; he wrote them with the greatest of ease, to the envy of fellow pupils.'[15]

According to Earnshaw, Lang's first piece of writing—the translation of First Satire of Horace—was the first translation of classics by a 'native Australian'; it was published in Sydney, printed by lithography on 1 December 1835.[16]

There are no recorded instances of Lang's tempestuous and fun-loving personality before his college days, where he got suspended for writing some verses that irked the authorities. James Dowling wrote:

III Lang explains that it is a Persian name meaning 'sword'

> He wrote English verses as well, and it is said that through exercising, not wisely, this gift at Cambridge, he brought himself into trouble with the heads of the college.[17]

Lang's prose is strewn with Latin phrases. In the story 'Mr Flax' published in *The Mofussilite* in 1863, there is an excess of Latin phrases—mostly untranslated. This, however, is an embellishment, for the story flows easily despite characters quoting Latin authors to each other incessantly.

Besides an interest in Persian and Latin, Lang also had an avid fascination for *The Arabian Nights*. He alludes to the tales from the legendary book in several places in *The Three Calendars* and *Ex-Wife*. Together, with Boccaccio's *Decameron*, the tales from *The Arabian Nights* form an important influence on Lang's writings. Lang's writing is a curious mix of bildungsroman and the frame narrative, where one story circumscribes the other, and the spiral thus formed is endlessly regressing.

This, then, was the story of Lang and his scholarship of languages and his fascination for the literature from the East. Unless Lang is playing a 'Botany Bay trick', he could very well be right about Poe passing off a Persian poem as 'The Raven.'

Lang had a fascination for birds and animals, and perhaps this had led him to read and remember a poem about a talking raven in Persian. Lang was always in for such curiosities. *The Mofussilite* often reported curious news about birds and animals. One such news article, published in 1845 is about a court case involving raven's brother crow, titled 'The Value of a Crow' where a Scottish agriculturist has to prove in court why crows are more valuable to farmers.[18]

Lang's newspaper was a mix of such curious stories from across the world, along with political and legal affairs of India and the British Empire, literary pages in which Lang wrote along with several contributors. One regular feature was Lang's spat with the editor of *Delhi Gazette* who was pro-government over some issue or the other.

The same page that carries this great revelation about the value of crows also carries a news item about 'An Astounding Scientific Discovery'. It said that according to a Professor Bronson, if human blood be seen under an oxyhydrogen microscope and magnified 20 million times, 'all the species of animals now existing on earth, or that have existed during the past' would be found. When a person is healthy, they would be living under harmony, but when a person is diseased, they would be at war with each other. He also stated that if a dead cat were to be thrown into the water, and the water then examined under microscope, there would be found every species of the cat family. Thus, the blood of lower animals is composed of its own kind, while the human blood is all inclusive.[19]

There is another story in *The Mofussilite* in August 1858 about a court case where an Indian man who had invited guests for lunch felt that the rice had been defiled by the looks of a cock brought in by a guest. Perhaps, this man, in a Jungian fashion, knew the word 'cockatrice'. This mythical based, with a cock's head and a serpent's tail, could kill merely with its glance.

> It appears that a bearer had invited several of his confreres to partake of a magnificent 'dejeuner sans fourchette,'[IV] consisting of boiled rice and some 'methais,' but that whilst the former was being cooked, a cock belonging to a European Gentleman had the presumption to look at the rice, probably arguing to himself that as a cat may look at a king there could be no harm in his looking at the rice. The bearer, however, thought differently, summoned the owner of the cock before the judge of the Small Cause Court and claimed damages, on the ground that he and his friends could not partake of the rice, which had become defiled by the cock

IV Lunch without fork

> looking at it. Now whether the eyes of the cock could produce such awful contamination, was the contending point…and from the arguments adduced on both sides, the cock was rapidly rising into celebrity and notoriety, and I don't know where the matter would have ended, had not the judge put a stop to it by decreeing, that as God had created the bearer, and the European gentleman, as well as the cock, each had a right to look at the other; that the suit was a vexatious one, and that the bearer should pay Rs. 16 to the defendant as compensation for having caused him so much annoyance and trouble. Had the matter come before the senior magistrates, the decision would in all probability have been, that the bearer should receive damages for not having 'puck-rowed' the cock; that the European gentleman would eat the rice defiled by the looks of the cock, and that the cock itself be roasted for the benefit of all parties concerned. I do not know whether the cock engaged counsel for the occasion, but anyhow he appears to have had the best of the argument, as the dispirited bearer threw away in disgust the rice, which the cock is said to have enjoyed uncommonly.[20]

Even though Lang was not in India in 1858, this article appears to have been written by him—it is laced with his gall and sense of humour. Lang was a bitter critic of the caste-system in India, and has a hearty laugh at the various prejudices in the Indian society. In the novel *Will He Marry Her?*, Baboo Zemindar goes to meet Leonora in England, and there he heartily partakes of alcohol and beef because there is no Indian around to see him.

There is a pig story in the very first issue of *The Mofussilite,* of 2 August 1845, where the Corn Laws are criticised:

> A thousand years hence antiquarians will derive the vulgar saying, 'Please the pigs,' from the Corn Laws. In Australia and

> the United States pigs are fattened on corn, because men are not allowed to eat it in England…If the Corn Laws, then, are preserved for no other end, it cannot be denied that they serve to please the pigs of Australia and America.
>
> In the Free Trade Bazaar an Australian pig, well fattened on wheat, should be exhibited in juxtaposition with a Dorsetshire labourer, in exemplification of the blessed working of the protective system, which gives the beast what it refuses the man. Certainly our law-makers have a secret sympathy with the pigs.[21]

Given all the different ways animals were used metaphorically to mock the authorities in his newspaper, Lang could very well have written his own *Animal Farm*. In fact, these articles are milder compared to some written by Lang's bilious ink.

That, then concludes the story of pigs, cocks, ravens and the ravenous shadow cast on Poe's reputation by Lang's language. There are many literary debts to Lang, and he tried to clear the debt of some Iranian compatriot by talking about the Persian original of 'The Raven'. There are still more unacknowledged debts to Lang. There is one that a famous writer of a detective classic owes him.

Undeclared Cards on Dickens's Table

or The Lord Who Was Sable, or Flights of Fancies of The Flying Fish Frustrated

In her introduction to *Unequal Partners: Charles Dickens, Wilkie Collins, and Victorian Authorship*, Lillian Nayder tells that Wilkie Collins attended on 14 June 1870 the funeral of Charles Dickens, Collins' friend and publisher for 27 years.

In a letter to Catherine Beard, Collins wrote that he was shocked and grieved; but, in another letter to his agent William Tindell, he wrote that Dickens's funeral put him behind with the proofs of his book.

Nayder points out that Collins mourned his lost day rather than his lost friend—and this was a value Collins learnt from Dickens himself. Dickens taught Collins that writing novels could be a lucrative profession if they were mass produced and serialised in an era of rapid industrialisation. The journal *Household Words* appeared only with the words 'Conducted by Charles Dickens'—not attributing any article to anyone. In 'factory like conditions' Dickens paid Collins by the column and, at one point, also employed him as a staff writer at five guineas a week, while Dickens himself made over a thousand pounds a year.[1]

At the end of *Unequal Partners...*, Nayder writes Dickens was much influenced by Wilkie Collins, and this was reflected in his books such as *Edwin Drood* (1870),[2] and even *The Tale of Two Cities* (1859).[3] In the preface to *The Tale of Two Cities* Dickens acknowledged that he was influenced by Collins's drama of *Frozen Deep*. However, this was not a matter of elevating Collins's position, it was rather a lament that Dickens lost his masterly touch under the influence of the 'inferior' Collins. For half a century, this remained the mainstay of Dickens criticism—that in imitating Collins's intricate plots, Dickens lost the 'magic' of literary genius.[4]

Another name in this conglomerate of 'unequal partners' is our currency boy gentleman. John George Lang, in 1853, went to England from India, despite having an established newspaper business and a flourishing legal career in India. Lang returned to India the same year and became the counsel for Rani of Jhansi, but went back to England again in 1854. A Tasmanian newspaper *The Courier* reported in 1853 about Lang's prosperity in India, and his journey to England:

> The friends in the colony of Mr J. Lang, the barrister, son of Mrs Underwood, of Ashfield park, and who proceeded to India in 1842, will be glad to hear that he is now residing in great comfort in London, having made a handsome fortune from £40,000 to £50,000 in the east by his profession and the conduct of his newspaper, the Mofussilite. Mr Lang is now writing a novel, 'Ellen Orford' which is publishing in Frazer's Magazine, and he is also a contributor to Household Words, Punch and other like periodicals of the day.[5]

As is visible, with two established vocations in India, Lang was, in pecuniary terms, probably better off than Dickens. Lang had also been publishing his literary works in *The Mofussilite*. Then what made Lang go to England and stay there for a long stretch of five years?

One reason could have been his family—his wife Lucy and their four children were in England, and he may have been reconciled with his family for a brief period. The only other reason that could take—or indeed had taken—Lang across the seas would be his literary ambition. He had already published a few novels as serials in his newspaper, and brought out book editions from The Mofussilite Press, but publishing from India and publishing from England were two very different matters.

His earlier work was inspired by Dickens's *Pickwick Papers*, and as Sir Philip Sidney would have said, Lang had the 'huge desyre' to become bigger than his idol. Lang went to England, made many literary friends—including Charles Dickens, and wrote several articles in the latter's journal *Household Words*. Dickens wanted articles from India in his journal, and John Lang was his special man. A century and a half later, Dickens is a household name, whereas the name of Lang's household, or even Lang's name, is barely known. Lang realised that the journal that bore the title 'Conducted by Charles Dickens' would not do him much good. Some of the articles published in the journal, he republished in books *Wanderings in India* and *Botany Bay*.

Lang published quite a few novels when in England—*The Wetherbys* (1853), *The Forger's Wife*, *Three Calendars* (1854), *Captain Macdonald* (1857), *Will He Marry Her?* (1858), *My Friend's Wife* (1859), *Ex-Wife* (1859), *Botany Bay* (1859), *Wanderings in India* (1859), and *The Secret Police* (1859)—and met with considerable success. However, Lang's works were generally much shorter while the demand in the market was for voluminous novels. He could barely bring himself up to it, since he loathed long descriptions of nature or characters of people. His stories were fast-paced, laced with action and dialogues, and usually finished around hundred pages. He did attempt two long novels—*Ex-Wife*, and *Will He Marry Her?*—both over 300 pages. These two novels sold, but got bad reviews because the former made a strong statement against class, while the latter took a strong position against racism. This was the fate of most of his novels—as Lang invariably provided a scathing critique of colonialism in India or made his heroines stronger than his heroes. The critics generally said that he was a writer of wit and capability, but could not put it to use.

Clever though he was, Lang did not realise that making, and keeping, the critics unhappy would lose him to posterity. So, Lang was a successful 'railway novelist' and his books were advertised as 1s and 2s[I] railway novels, but not a favourite of the critics.

After five years in England, Lang was in a hurry to return to India, and produced a flurry of books—five in 1859 before leaving for India.

I 's' here stands for shillings. Lang's novels sold at railway stations for a shilling or two.

Minus his wit, his eye for scandal and his provocative writing, his newspaper was floundering; and he was probably missing India—his narrator in 'Black and Blue' in *Wanderings in India* says about one of his protagonists, 'India he loved, England he despised'.

John Earnshaw of Australia was the first researcher to unearth fundamental facts about John Lang, 90 years after his death. I went through several of Earnshaw's epistles in the Mitchell Library in Sydney. Earnshaw wrote to the library of Victoria and Albert Museum in London, asking for information on Lang articles had been published in *Household Words* (HW). The letter was redirected to Leslie C. Staples, who conducted the journal *The Dickensian* (founded in 1905).

Staples replied, in a letter dated 25 March 1954, saying that the museum which had passed her the letter was not in possession of the HW Contributor's Book. She wrote that the original Contributors' Book was inherited by R.C. Lehmann from W.H. Wills who was a correspondent of HW. According to Staples, the book was in possession of Mrs Lehmann, 'whom you may be interested to know is the mother of Rosamund Lehmann the novelist, Beatrix Lehmann the actress, and John Lehmann the author'. Mrs Lehmann allowed Staples to make a copy, from which she prepared an index which she forwarded to Earnshaw. She told Earnshaw that the index did not include the prices paid.

In all, the number of John Lang articles in *Household Words* can be counted to be 33.

Anne Lohrli got hold of an HW account book in Princeton and published *Household Words: A Weekly Journal, 1850–1859*[II] in 1973. In her summary of John Lang, Lohrli touches upon Lang's alcoholism. She writes that *Too Clever by Half* went through 12 editions, and *Botany Bay*, too, had several editions. Lohrli says that Dickens wrote to his correspondent, Wills, saying that Lang's article 'was very droll'

II The complete name of the book is *Household Words: A Weekly Journal, 1850-1859, Conducted by Charles Dickens: Table of Contents, List of Contributors and Their Contributions, Based on the Household Words Office Book* and housed in the Morris L. Parrish Collection of Victorian Novelists, Princeton but he objected to the various technical terms that Lang had used, and asked Wills to remove them or paraphrase to make the terms clear.[6] Lohrli came up with the following list which is an improvement upon Staples' work:

Fisher's Ghost vii, 6–9. March 5, 1853
Tracks in the Bush xvi, 93–96. July 25, 1857
An Illustrious British Exile xix, 454–56. April 9, 1859
A Special Convict xix, 489–91. April 23, 1859
Baron Wald xix, 537–41. May 7, 1859
Three Celebrities [lead] xix, 553–57. May 14, 1859
Kate Crawford xix, 596–600. May 21, 1859
Miss Saint Felix xix, 613–17. May 28, 1859

The 8 items repr., with 5 additional stories, as *Botany Bay. By John Lang, Esq., Barrister-at-Law.* London: William Tegg, 1859. Pub. in *H.W.* acknowledged.

The Mahommedan Mother vii, 339–46. June 11, 1853
Black and Blue xiv, 276–82. Oct. 4, 1856
The Himalaya Club [lead] xv, 265–72. March 21, 1857
Wanderings in India [1st 2 instalments = lead] xvi, 457–63. Nov. 14, 1857, and 11 following nos. (not consecutive), ending xvii, 254–60. Feb. 27, 1858

The 4 items repr., with 2 chaps. of additional material, as *Wanderings in India: and Other Sketches of Life in Hindostan. By John Lang.* London: Routledge, Warne, and Routledge, 1859. Pub. in *H.W.* acknowledged.

Wedding Bells vi, 551–52. Feb. 19, 1853
Wolf Nurses vi, 562–63. Feb. 26, 1853
An Inundation in Bengal vii, 53–54. March 19, 1853
Starting a Paper in India vii, 94–96. March 26, 1853
Hovelling xv, 139–42. Feb. 7, 1857
An Experience of Austria xv, 381–84. April 18, 1857
Invisible Ghosts xvi, 109–111. Aug. 1, 1857
A Human Waif [chip] xvii, 595–97. June 5, 1858
The Abors [chip] xviii, 204–205. Aug. 14, 1858
A Bad Name xix, 477–80. April 16, 1859
Bad Bargains xix, 610–13. May 28, 1859

List of titles written by JL for Household Words in Anne Lohrli's work

Lohrli, thus, puts the number at 34. That is quite a lot of hard work to have gone unacknowledged.

In the summary about Lang in her book, Lohrli provides another snippet of interesting information; that *Forger's Wife* (1853) 'is dated from Vienna'.

We know that the autobiographical tale 'An Experience in Austria' is about incidents of 1854.[9] Lang's wife Lucy lived in Italy for some time…and two of his daughters married into Italian nobility. Perhaps, there was some family connection in Austria, as well.

Now, a question emerges due to the 34 pieces of John Lang in *Household Words* 'conducted by Charles Dickens'—what could have been the reasons for Lang's anonymity in the British journals?

In the 19th century, there were several dictionaries for

pseudonymous literature. The most renowned one, coincidentally, is by a man called J. Laing—*Dictionary of Anonymous and Pseudonymous Literature of Great Britain.*[8] The situation was not different from what it is today, the literary giants did not want to let the new talent come up, as we have seen in the case of Tom Taylor and Charles Dickens.

In Lang's novel *Secret Police*, or *Plot and Passion*, the characters of Fouche and Jerome are mouthpieces of Lang's own opinions about various matters—from politics to love to literature. In a letter to his sister, Jerome, who has escaped to England, and is trying to make a living there as a writer, writes:

> To take a leading place in literature is indeed no easy task. The young author, if he be successful, becomes an object of jealousy with those who are older and above him in the same pursuit; he also becomes the victim of cabals engendered by his compeers. Moreover, he has too frequently the misfortune to have his works judged by fools before they are permitted to reach the public eye. And, unlike other citizens, the man of letters generally holds to nothing, and is without aid. In short, he resembles the flying fish. If he rises a little the birds devour him. If he dives the fishes eat him up![9]

The 'flying fish' metaphor is apt for Lang—with Taylor on one side, and Dickens on the other; with Lang's own radical ideology on one side, and a clique of Victorian critics on the other. Lang is taking a direct dig at the critics with 'fools who judge the books before they reach the public eye.'

This is also an ironic premonition as to how Lang's work will be received. In a review of *My Friend's Wife* and *Plot and Passion, The Calcutta Review* began with saying that the latter was a higher effort (primarily perhaps, because Tom Taylor had borrowed from it), and moves to deride Lang in no uncertain terms:

> '*The Secret Police* is decidedly a higher effort. It is an attempt at the melodramatic as the former *(My Friend's Wife)* is at the comic. The story is well known from the play *Plot and Passion*. Fouche and his 'Cytherean Court' are introduced to us, and the main interest centres in an effort made to discover the author of certain Junius-like letters written against Fouche and Napoleon. Marie St. Cyr, a lady of exquisite beauty, is engaged to procure clear proofs of the authorship, by winning the love of the writer…she finds out the author, Jerome Lagrange, and induces him and his sister to accompany her to Paris where they are given over to Fouche. But as the Minister is about to send his prey to prison, Marie avows her love for him…they are married; they take up their abode at Dresden and there give shelter to Fouche when, as a fallen Minister, he is forced to flee from France.
>
> We fear Mr. Lang is incorrigible. There is hardly one of his works from the perusal of which we do not rise with the regret that he has so abused his wonderful powers.'

Lang also had a fixation, a complex, of posing as a gentleman and of denying his convict and Emancipist origins. It was considered below a gentleman's dignity to work or write for money. This complex led Lang to concoct a fictional identity for his deceased father Walter Lang, who had been a seafaring merchant. Lang's marriage certificate says his father was a Captain in the Army;[10] his obituary says the same: 'He was the posthumous child of Captain Lang, Military Secretary to General Lachlan Macquarie, Governor of New South Wales.'

Lang's father and foster father Joseph Underwood, both were very wealthy merchants; but, traders were not gentlemen.

Gentlemen were landed gentry with exquisite tastes. Lang was acutely aware of this, and even though he posed as a gentleman, his novels would show the gentry as decadent, and the commonfolk as industrious. In the novel *Ex-Wife,* Sir George Merrydale speaks for Lang and tells his erstwhile maid, Mathilde, that men of gentry make bad armymen but their presence is required for the commonfolk in the military to be led by example, to see that their lords sacrifice a life of luxury to serve the nation.

Lang, it is known, was friends with several army officers in India. The bulk of subscribers of *The Mofussilite* were, in fact, army men. Yet, criticising the British Army was one of Lang's main preoccupations, a subject to which he returns repeatedly in *The Wetherbys*, which is primarily a military novel, *Three Calendars*, *Too Clever By Half*, *Wanderings in India*, and *Will He Marry Her?*

Lang often chided 'gentlemen' in his works. In *Plot and Passion*, Jerome Legrange, too, expresses the idea of a gentleman not working for money. He says that a writer, considered above want, is respected, and adds that 'an author's poverty is too often a black mark against merit'.

> When they know how hardly we are pushed for the wherewithal to keep body and soul together, they exhibit towards us rudeness, impertinence, and frequently, contempt. Only those who depend on literature for a livelihood know the struggles, the disappointments, the delays, the heart burnings, that men of letters experience.[11]

We now know how Collins worked for Dickens at five guineas a week, even though Dickens took several ideas from him. Lang, here, is also alluding to the double jeopardy—the flying-fish situation a writer is faced with: if he poses as a gentleman, he would not want his name with his work for that would mean that he writes for money. On the other hand, if he declares that he works for money, no one would want him in the first place.

Frederic Perkins, in his book *Charles Dickens: A Sketch Of His Life and Works* (1870), recounts the tremendous physical energy of

Dickens by the dint of which even after a late-night party, he could play "leap-frog' at seven next morning.[12] Perkins quotes a friend who was at a party where both Lang and Dickens were present:

> But, good as he (Dickens) was, the genial side of his nature shone out with pre-eminent brilliancy. He was…ever ready to enter the whim which for the moment pleased the company best, and to add his ever flowing humour to the common amusement. We must not forget the laughable incident at Garrick's Head, a rather noted tavern of the older type, in Bow-Street, London. It was late in the evening. Father Prout, the inimitable wit, was at hour, as usual smoking a long 'Churchwarden', and late John Lang, editor of *The Mofussilite* (Of Upper India), author of 'Ex-Wife', and many other excellent novels; Mr WBB Stevens, solicitor to the late Sir Robert Peel; George Grant, ex-judge of the Sudder Adawlut (Bombay); Mr LH Stocqueler, and Mr Thornton Hunt, the editor of London Telegraph, were all, if truth must be told, slightly under the influence of the different liquids they had imbibed during the evening.

After this, the friend describes a little battle of tales between Lang and Dickens:

> At this little supper, Father Prout, by a series of manoeuvres, elicited story after story of real facts and scenes experienced by the Indian barrister and journalist, treasured in his extraordinary memory…Dickens capped story after story with his own. When Lang was mournful, Dickens was pathetic; when Lang was in the earnest, Dickens was solemn; when Lang was merry, Dickens literally boiled over with fun, and the most singular thing was that Dickens's stories were laid in Bengal, and the northwest provinces of India, with which Lang was

> thoroughly familiar. Every minute detail was told with such vivid accuracy that the whole party were astonished, and Mr Lang refused to believe that Dickens had never been to India, for while his own stories were founded on fact, Dickens's were the fruit of imagination of the moment. This, perhaps, showed his versatility more than anything he published.[13]

Here again, Lang's extraordinary memory is mentioned. This 'storytelling' contest is very important metaphorically—Lang could not defeat his idol and rival in the literary field; the narrator also says that 'this perhaps showed his versatility more than anything else'.

Dickens had not been to India, yet he was able to match tale with tale—better imagined ones than Lang's experienced ones. After all, *Household Words* was 'conducted by' Dickens and he knew all the stories from his writers.

That is the story of just one of Dickens' 'unequal partners'. We have seen that Dickens took inspiration from Collins and he received flak for 'lowering his standards' by doing so. What is interesting is that Collins, in a couple of his works, took inspiration from Lang. This has almost gone unnoticed by critics who focus their attention on the Dickens-Collins equation.

One work where Collins seems to have taken inspiration from Lang is *The Moonstone* (1968). In Lang's 1858 novel *Will He Marry Her?*, 'Shaitan Ka Heera' or Devil's Diamond forms an important sub-plot. It is not overtly stated, but it is clear in the narrative that all who possess the diamond have had ill luck. This is also the main idea of Collins's detective novel that went on to become a prototype.

The other place where Collins borrows from Lang is in his 1872 novel *Poor Miss Finch*.[14] In this novel, the white hero Oscar Dubourg turns dark blue as a result of the treatment of epilepsy. Oscar's race gets changed overnight and Collins constructs his plots around the vicissitudes of Oscar to examine the ways in which racial identities were constructed and construed in Victorian England. Oscar's blind beloved Lucilla must overcome her racial prejudice to marry him. Her blindness becomes a metaphor for the blindness of English society at large—Lucilla cannot see, but she can hear and believe. Collins is clearly making the point that seeing is not believing, but that believing is seeing.

One is delighted to find in Wilkie Collins a thinker and a storyteller ahead of his time. However, Lang may have influenced him into that thinking through *Will He Marry Her?*—a novel that revolves around the marriage of the half-caste daughter of a British army office and a black Indian woman, to a pure caste British man. Lang's heroine Leonora dies immediately after she marries the 'hero' Augustus and she turns black in death, and the hero's mother gives him a moral lesson that such marriages are not ordained by heaven. This, however, is Lang's ploy to mock his British reading public—he reaffirms the readers' faith in racism after having taken them through a 400-page journey of questioning their beliefs and making a fool of the racist hero, and a true heroine out of Leonora.

Collins was the sub-editor of *Household Words* and he had obviously not just read but also edited Lang's works. Another idea that Collins takes from Lang is sending one of his characters to India for an Indian sub-plot, which is characteristic of almost all of Lang novels written between 1853 and 1858.

Another influence on *Poor Miss Finch* is, again, Lang. The story 'Black and Blue' by Lang first appeared in *Household Words* in 1856.[15] Lang also included it in his *Wanderings in India.*[16] In this story, a white man marries an Indian woman who is black and has a son with her who is black, but has blue eyes. He is called 'black and blue' by people and he goes on to inherit a huge fortune left by his forefathers. In my opinion, this story, together with *Will He Marry Her?* form the core inspirations of Wilkie Collins's lesser known *Poor Miss Finch.*

Lillian Nayder in her essay 'Blue Like Me' tells that Collins, in making Oscar turn blue, may have been inspired by Thomas Watson's

Lectures on the Principles and Practice of Psychic,[17] a medical text that talks about the disfiguring effects of curing epilepsy with silver nitrate. Nayder then says that there was another source for the conception of such a character and it was John Lang:

> ...a journal article identifying those who are 'blackish blue' as the children of interracial articles—the so called 'half-castes' of British India. Written by John Lang and published in *Household Words* in 1856, shortly after Collins became one of Dickens's staff members, 'Black and Blue' describes the marriage of a renegade English aristocrat Francis Gay, and 'a young Mahommedan girl,' converted to Christianity before their wedding.[18]

'Black and Blue' is easily one of Lang's best stories in which Lang's wit, sarcasm, anti-colonial ideas, anti-racist stance, anti-class opinions, his love for India and his knack for telling uncannily dark stories with almost magical plots come into play. The 'Black and Blue' story—which is temporally set in 1816—begins with:

> Forty years ago there went out to India, in the good ship Globe, Ensign the Honourable Francis Gay, a younger son of the Right Honourable the Earl of Millflower. The ensign was in his nineteenth year, and was proceeding to join his regiment, which was stationed at Chinsura.[19]

Gay's father hoped he would never return, for he had been 'expelled from no fewer than seven schools', he had forged his brother Lord Larkspeare's signature, he was also 'guilty of a deed of violence', and his parents feared that he would be hanged, for 'in those days such a deed of violence was capital offence'. The narrator tells that Lord Millflower's four other sons were all 'steady' but rather 'dull beings'. Francis was gifted, witty, and 'the reprobate'. What Francis was in want of was 'feeling', for 'of feeling, he was in his youth, wholly destitute'[20].

In framing Francis' persona, Lang heavily borrows from his own life. Lang's mother married Joseph Underwood in 1819 after her first husband, the father of Lang, died in 1816. Underwood already had four children, and these are, probably, the 'dull beings' referred to. We also know that Lang was expelled from Trinity College for his 'Botany Bay tricks'. Lang was known to be witty and bright, but troublesome. This image remained with him all his life.

After Francis arrived in Calcutta, for several months he 'conducted himself with wonderful propriety', but by degrees 'the Honourable Francis fell off' and within a few days, there was no one who wanted to talk to him. It was decided that he would be court-martialled and dismissed on his next offence:

> '…The next time you are intoxicated on the parade ground, or the next time you use bad language in the mess-room…you will forfeit your commission.' Being the son of an earl, he was entitled—many colonels think—to every possible chance of redemption. Had he been the son of a commoner, he would, most probably, have been court-martialled and cashiered for the very first offence.[21]

This decadent image of a young ensign is a constant in Lang's works. In *The Wetherbys, Father and Son* (1853), Robert Wetherby is a similarly decadent person who rises in ranks by his connections, as also by the death of his seniors. This was one of Lang's standing jokes that in India, officers gained promotions due to the death of their seniors at the hands of cholera or malaria, rather than by their talent.

After the chastisement, Francis mends his ways for a while, and the officers, too, extend their hands to their former friend. Francis, however, is not interested: 'The whole regiment thought proper to cut him; and now he thought proper to cut the whole regiment.'[22]

Francis then starts learning Hindustani and Persian—Lang, like himself, made his heroes Indian and learn these languages. Francis mixes with only the 'natives' by the day, and by the night, he continues his studies. He begins living and dressing like natives, and abstains from drinking. He becomes vegetarian, and auctions off all his furniture. The narrator says that Francis could have said—

> The grape's juice my bosom never cheers;
> I am more than Moslem when the cup appears.[23]

This is the usual Lang, quoting from Byron. This is from Byron's *Corsair*.[24] The next thing Francis does is to attempt to convert a young Muslim girl, the daughter of a 'Bheestie' (water-carrier):

> She was not like the natives of India, but more like those of Africa. She was coal black, and had thick lips and wavy hair. She was short for her age—fourteen years—but thickset, with powerful limbs.

This is another Lang curiosity—turning his Indian heroines 'coal black'. In *Will He Marry Her?* Leonora's mother is also very black, and so is the artist Rooder who has made the likeness of Leonora. At the same time, Lang makes it very clear that Indians in general are not black, and that the standard ideas of racism do not apply in India. He says in 'Black and Blue':

> Colour is no criterion of high caste or rank in India. The late Maharajah Rooder Singh, of Darbungah, whose family—to borrow a phrase from 'Burke's Peerage'—is one of stupendous antiquity, had the complexion of an African; while his younger brother, Basdeo, who now sits on the throne, is far fairer than his Highness the Maharajah Duleep Singh.

Francis Gay later in the story becomes tanned enough to pass off for an Indian:

> Constantly moving about in the sun had tanned his once fair face; and neither from his appearance—for he was dressed as a native—nor from his speech, could the natives themselves detect that he was a European. He gave out that his birthplace was Nepaul, where the natives are sometimes born with blue eyes.

In my opinion, by turning Francis Gay tanned brown, he is making identities fluid: that Europeans can assimilate into India as Indians. On the other hand, he makes his strongest characters in these stories decidedly black to wage a war against racial stereotypes, to leave no ambiguity that his characters are lovable despite being 'coal black'.

Lang also takes on the caste prejudices in India. Despite being born low, Francis' beloved changes his fortunes through her talent for keeping accounts.

Francis wants to, and gets to, convert his beloved, Jehan, to Christianity. For converting this low caste Muslim black girl, Francis is considered a lunatic within his regiment. It is not just the army men who hold this view, but the chaplain himself—who is supposed to have Francis married—who says, 'I am sorry, Mr Gay, that I cannot with sincerity offer you my congratulations'. To which, Francis replies, 'My good sir, I did not ask them'.

The chaplain is perplexed and reports the matter to Colonel Role, who reasons with Francis to no avail, whereupon the Colonel speaks about the matter to the General who delivers a 'long and violent speech'. Mr Gay, with the most courteous tone, replies that the General had the authority to reprimand him on official matters but that in personal matters, he had no business to speak. Gay then threatens to report the presence of dubious characters in the General's House:

> 'Now tell me, general, which of us, think you, sins the most, and sets the worst example to the men, European and native, in this station?—I, who wish to marry this good Christian girl; or you, who have in your house—.'
>
> Mr. Gay then made mention of two very discreditable members of the general's establishment.[25]

Lang writing in mid-19th century is not exaggerating. Long after the British rule in India was established, and almost heading towards its last lap, long after the Doctrine of Lapse had ceased to exist, a white woman's marriage to a 'native' prince was still scandalous. In 1915, Molly Fink of Melbourne married Marthanda Bhairava Tondiman, the king of the princely state of Padukottai, and 19 years elder to her. The king, who was also a cricketer, had gone to Australia on a cricketing tour and received very bad press for wearing clothes like an Englishman. When the couple went to India, the British Government of India refused to recognise the marriage, and the king was forbidden from buying any property in any part of the Empire. An attempt to poison Molly was made when she was pregnant with his child, who would be curiously named Marthand Sydney, after the name of the city he was born in.[26]

Coming back to 'Black and Blue', the General and Colonel discuss such behaviour of Francis, and agree that the man is insane. A committee of doctors is appointed to examine the young man who has converted a black low caste Indian woman who he intends to marry.

> They (the doctors) reported that Ensign the Honourable Francis Gay was not only of sound mind, but one of the most intellectual young men in the station; and that he had explained to their entire satisfaction certain conversations which he had frequently held with himself in Chinsura, at the mess table.[27]

Here is the opportunity for me to quote the oft-quoted Michel Foucault, and I shall not let go of it. 'People know what they do; frequently they know why they do what they do; but what they don't know is what they do does'[28].

Francis Gay knew what he was doing and why, he did not know what the consequences of his doings would be. He did not know that he would shake up a belief system involving a whole regiment from General to the common soldier. Another quote from *Madness and Civilisation* would sum up the Honourable Francis Gay's situation:

> ...if you are not like everybody else, then you are abnormal, if you are abnormal, then you are sick. These three categories, not being like everybody else, not being normal and being sick are in fact very different but have been reduced to the same thing.[29]

The Francis-Jehan marriage takes place, and is witnessed by the whole station out of curiosity to see 'the tall and handsome English aristocrat, and beside him his coal-black bride, dressed in garments of red silk, trimmed with yellow and gold tinsel'.

Jehan, who is now Ellen after her christening, and Mrs Ellen Gay after the marriage, had a great eye for accounts, and she invested her husband's savings into money-lending business. The couple have a son who 'had light blue eyes, exactly like those of his father; but his complexion was quite as black as his mother's'. The child is christened Ernest Augustus George Francis Frederick after the names of Gay's brothers, including himself.

Francis gets promoted in the army as his seniors die of cholera. He leaves the army for he is worth one lac rupees, courtesy his wife's money lending business. In the story, Francis Gay becomes a dealer of precious stones, and trades under the name of Mustapha Khan. He gives his birthplace as Nepaul[III] where there are people who have

III Present day Nepal.

blue eyes. His wanderings take him a long time; three years per wandering, the narrator says. He wanders off and no one knows his whereabouts.

The scene returns to Europe where all of Sir Millflower's sons die, except the youngest, Frederick. Earnest dies during grouse-shooting, Augustus is lost in a vessel, George dies of small-pox. Sir Millflower makes enquiries about Francis, to no avail.

From here, Lang turns from wit to death in the story. Lang has combined all his faculties together to write, what I think is, his best story. This story almost foresees the coming of magic-realism.

Deaths by cholera, small pox, ships lost in the sea, deaths during game hunts were all too common in the 19th century. In my visits to 19th century graveyards of Delhi, Calcutta, Mussoorie, and McLeodgunj, I noticed that many of the epitaphs spoke of the eternal sleepers as people in their prime—all dead of cholera, plague, malaria, or small-pox.

Lang is at his best in this story because he is talking about a wanderer. Even in his novel *Ex-Wife*, Sir George Merrydale wanders for 12 years on a ship called *Wanderer*.

Wanderer was what Lang too, was—between Australia (1816–1838), England (1838–1841), Australia (1841–1842), India (1842–1853), England (1853), India (1853–54), England and Continental Europe (1854–1859), India (1859–1864), South America (sometime in his teenage), and Camel's Back Cemetery (1864–). Lang gives his verdict in 'Black and Blue':

> He (Francis) had never written to his family since his arrival in India, and had not received letters from any member thereof. India he loved, England he detested, and would not have taken up his father's title (even) if it had been a dukedom.[30]

Once, Francis alias Mustapha Khan goes to the Raja of Pulbecala to sell jewels. The Raja buys only a cat's eye-ring.

The cat's eye-ring, or 'Lehsunia' as it is known in Hindi, is a good luck charm. Lang is insinuating that all the jewels remain with Francis, but his good luck charm is gone. This also adds one more element to Lang's curiosities—gemstones. In *Will He Marry Her?*, as already insinuated, a gemstone plays a major role in the plot and several things are told about stones in that novel. The good luck having gone out of Francis's hands:

> On his way back to Delhi, at a place called Kunda ka Serai, a band of robbers attacked the jewel-merchant. They hacked him to pieces with their swords, but they spared his wife and the boy. The whole of their treasures was stolen; even the rings from Ellen's ears and fingers, and the gold bangles which Chandee (the son Ernest Gay) wore upon his arms.

The reader does not even realise that Francis has been killed. After building up a plot, Lang suddenly collapses it by hacking Francis to pieces at the hands of random thugs. But that is how life was. Traders carried all their worldly possessions on their person, and they were attacked by thugs in forests, and their stories came to a full stop before the bildungsroman of their narratives could reach their conventional denouement.

Another account in *Wanderings in India* has Lang sitting in a village sketching an old man and two little children. In some time, a hailstorm arrives; one so furious which Lang says he hadn't seen anything like in India ever before. Lightning strikes and burns a hut. Inside the hut are the two children lying dead. Lang is struck by the fact that there is no grieving.

To Lang, fatalism seems to be the creed of the people in India. This, a postcolonial may argue, is Orientalist. However, it must be pointed out that in this same book Lang also talks about the materialistic lives of kings and queens in India. It is, however, just an observation of a philosophy, and Lang describes it very poetically:

> 'The matter-of-fact way in which the natives of India regard the death of their relations or friends is something wonderful to behold. It is not that their affections are less strong than ours, or their feelings less acute. It is that fatality is the beginning and end of their creed. They are taught from their childhood to regard visitations of this character as direct and special acts of God—as matters which it is not only futile, but improper to bewail.'[31]

Another interesting 'fact-let' is that Lang talks about 'sketching' the two children. Lang was a good artist. Illustrations in *Too Clever By Half* (1853) I think have been done by Lang because some of them are signed 'M', which stands for 'Mofussilite'.

In *Ex-Wife,* the divorced wife Eva Merrydale takes up various vocations to support herself and her child. One of them is sketching. She also starts learning mechanical likeness—taking lessons from a 'Dagurrean artist' which insinuates at the excitement about photography in its initial days, and Lang's interest in it. Unfortunately, however, there are no known photographs or even likenesses of Lang.

This brings us back to the sketch of the two children—Lang draws the two children playing happily moments before they die, making the sketch to be the last thing between life and death.

Lang may have been a railway novelist of his time, but the workings of the writer were very intricate, carrying the legacy of all the numerous books he had read. Lang, it seems, here had Keats's *Ode On a Grecian Urn* (1820) in his mind.

In 1863, Lang wrote a story in *The Mofussilite,* called 'Dresden China'.[32] In this story, a professor named Boettger fails to make gold for the Elector of Saxony, and is, in turn, jailed. But, when a precious china vase in the Elector's household is broken, Boettger makes an exact replica. This is story of the birth of 'Dresden China' in Europe. The stupefied Elector orders Boettger's release. But when the guards to give the old professor the happy news, he is found dead.

This is the same theme as in the dead children and the sketch, and as in Keats's famous poem—that of art transcending mortal human beings, of works of art becoming an after life, of works of art becoming repositories of histories and souls.

Lang wrote something interesting in *Wanderings in India* about Kanpur—he tells that all the leather trade for which the city was famous for, and indeed is still famous for, was started by the Chinese:

> Cawnpore, until recently, was chiefly famous for its harness, boots and shoes, bottlecovers, cheroot-cases, helmets, and other articles made of leather. A nest of Chinese settled in the bazaar many years ago and introduced the manufacture of such matters.[33]

We have seen two examples of curious foretelling by Lang earlier—one, that a man would get shot in the heart and be saved by a book, and two, that Lang's brain would be small when examined by a phrenologist. In 'Dresden China', Lang concludes the story with:

> Even after Dresden shall have crumbled into ruins, will this great discovery preserve her name in the annals of the world.[34]

The last lines are obviously in keeping with the idea of further augmenting the theme of the story about art and mortality, by including the idea of ideas. Art would outlive the man, and man's idea would outlive art, too.

Curiously, Lang is proven right by history. Dresden did crumble to ruins: it was bombed and destroyed in the Second World War.

If the reader thought that the story of 'Black and Blue' was over with the sudden death of Honourable Francis Gay, such is not the case. I am paying a tribute to Lang's love for *Arabian Nights* and Boccaccio's *Decameron* in using the frame narrative and telling stories within stories.

While reading the story, I was so taken aback by the sudden twist in the narrative—when Francis is killed by the thugs at 'Kunda ka Serai'—and the verisimilitude of an actual incident is so well constructed by Lang that I immediately went searching whether a man called Francis Gay ever lived. Given that Lang often changed names in his narratives, it was a futile exercise. I then started looking for places, thinking I could get leads from there. 'Pulbecala' does not exist, neither does a similar sounding name. Since Francis was travelling from Pulbecala to Delhi, I started looking for road routes from what is now Pakistan to Delhi—because the story mentions something about north-west.

Finally, I found it in a geography book called *Historical Routes of North West Indian Subcontinent, Lahore to Delhi,*[35]: mentioned as 'Kund Ki Surye'. The British geographers would not have been able to pronounce 'Sarai', thus, made the spelling 'Surye', Lang knew Persian very well and, therefore, does not make the mistake. The place does not exist anymore.

Back in 'Black and Blue,' Ellen, the widow of Francis, does not report the matter to the police, for investigations would reveal that her husband was a white man, which he wanted to be concealed after having donned the identity of Mustapha Khan. This is the most poignant moment in the story and the most irrational one as well—the choice between respecting a deceased husband's wishes or bringing his murderers to the scaffold—an unimaginably difficult choice indeed.

The mother and son start afresh in Delhi, and set up a jewellery business. Chandee or Ernest Grey, having inherited the wandering genes of his father, takes up the profession of a 'box-waller' or peddler. A box-wallah is someone who has a box full of articles. The boy sells his articles to army men. Lang somehow brings army into the picture to pour his gall in all his stories. The army men call the boy 'black and blue' because he has blue eyes and black skin. They buy things from him, and often kick him and have a good laugh at his cost. Black and Blue takes it all in his stride:

> 'Ah, well! I know! You rich white gentlemans—I poor black devil. I pray all day all night that ensign be made leeft'nunt; leeft'nunt, capitaine; capitaine, capitain-meejor; meejor, kunnull; kunnull, meejor-jinneral…I get so much kick and so many bad words. God make us all—black and white; all equal right up above. You want blacking? Here you are. Very good blacking—quite genuine; only one rupee a bottle. I suppose you not got ready money! Very well, I wait till pay-day come. I very poor man. You my master. Khuda Lord Kuren.' The meaning of this expression, with which most natives wind up a speech to an European, signifies, May God make you a lord![36] (WI: 72)

Lang, here, paints the picture of the arrogance and racism of army men in very evocative and repulsive terms:

> There were several young officers in the bungalow, chums of the lieutenant; and, while the bargaining was going on, they began to tease Black and Blue. One removed his turban with the point of a stick; another sprinkled him with his eau de Cologne; a third touched the tip of his great toe (he had left his shoes, out of respect, in the verandah with the lighted end of a cheroot). Black and Blue howled with pain, whereupon the two roared with laughter.[37]

Black and Blue, in agony, says to the young officers:

> God make us all. When fire burns black man, black man feels as much pain as white man. In hell, you rich gentlemans sing out just as much as poor box-waller.[38]

At this point, a doctor comes into the story, who is struck by the 'black and blue' appearance of the boy and reminded of something. It is brought to the readers' notice that the doctor had cured a little boy years ago for dog bites, and that he suspects it was this very boy. The doctor meets the mother, and even though she is reluctant to reveal her history, she cannot feign to not know the doctor to whom she owed her son's life.

The doctor makes enquiries and confirms that Black and Blue alias Chandee alias Ernest Gay would inherit Sir Millflower's property. This discovery does not change the attitude of the army men, who still bully him and mockingly calling him 'my lordship'.

While the army men make fun of Black and Blue, the narrative mocks at class system and earldoms through Chandee's naivete:

> 'Look here, Lord Black and Blue. Why don't you go home and upset your uncle? Turn him out of his title and estates—eh? You would be sure to marry some beautiful girl.'
>
> To this Black and Blue would respond:
>
> 'What do I want with title and beautiful gal! This is my home, and I got good business, good many friends, and two or three very beautiful gal.'
>
> 'Where, Black and Blue?'
>
> 'Ah! that is my business.'
>
> 'Well, what will you sell your title for?'
>
> 'Well, what you offer?'
>
> 'One hundred rupees'
>
> 'Say one hundred and twenty-five.'
>
> 'No.'
>
> 'Well, take it—there. Give money, and I give receipt. You write it out; I sign it. Sold one title to Ensign Matheson for a hundred rupees.'
>
> 'But there are two titles, you ass; one an earldom, and the other, a viscounty.'
>
> 'Well, you take the two; give two hundred rupees for both.'

> 'No. The one I have already bought is the biggest and of the best quality; the other is the small one, and of inferior quality.'
>
> 'Well, I make reduction in price; take one with the other, and give me one hundred and seventy-five rupees. That can't hurt anybody that wants a title.'[39]

The narrator says that for all the earldom and viscounty that was going to herald upon Black and Blue, there were no takers for this Othello; nobody would give their white sister to this Black prince.

The matter of Black and Blue's curious story enters the newspapers, and it becomes talk of the town. An attorney tries to convince the boy and his mother that he should journey to England to claim the title. The attorney would take a small percentage to accompany the lad. There is divided opinion about whether the boy should make the journey, but finally he gives in to the attorney's wishes.

The two leave, and nothing is heard ever after of either the boy or the attorney. That is the end of the story of Black and Blue, as abrupt as his father's death.

We have seen earlier that Dickens was criticised for following the example of Collins and attempting intricate plots. My opinion is that Dickens's inspiration comes from Lang, even if it is twice removed. Wilkie Collins, who borrowed the idea of the 'cursed stone' from Lang, also learnt the art of intricate plots from him.

Lillian Nayder contends that Chandee/Ernest Gay is defined as the Other by his skin colour, whatever his class be.[40] This is the problem with most of the postcolonial scholarship—easy conclusions from sections of a text that ignore the context. Lang is not defining Chandee but questioning such definitions. Our discussion on 'Black and Blue' shows that Lang subverts all authority in this story.

In *Will He Marry Her?* too, Lang kills his half-caste heroine suddenly. There are two strategies at work here: either it is placating a British readership with such conclusion, or lamenting that all such beautiful people reach such an end because of deep social prejudices.

Nayder emphatically observes: 'In spite of the equality of races in the eyes of God, however, Lang clearly intends this article as a warning against interracial unions, which deprive the sons of Englishmen of their place in the "civilized" world.'[41]

Nayder, again, has fallen into the same trap by taking some words as Lang's and others as the narrator's. In trying to theorise about the 'Other' and the Occidental assumption of 'civilisation', she has missed the context.

Lang puts the words into the boy's mouth that everyone burns equally well in hell precisely to satirise Victorian ideas about racial identity. If Lang wanted to warn Englishmen about interracial marriages, he would not have made Francis Gay delete his European identity. He would not have made the Honourable Francis Gay say, 'India he loved, England he despised'.

'Black and Blue' is closely tied with the novel *Will He Marry Her?*—Lang takes his criticism of Victorian social identities further through a white woman, like the white man Francis.

Will He Marry Her? or Will She Marry Him?

Will He Marry Her? (1858)[1] should have been named *Will She Marry Him?*—for Augustus Reckless, the protagonist of the novel—an impetuous character with several prejudices and wavers—from the moment he sets his eyes on Leonora Ornsbie, is sure of his affection. The uncertainty is only on the part of the dark-eyed, dark-haired heroine who asks him to come to the East if he wants to marry her, and when he is in the East, tells him that they can be married only in the West.

Let us begin with the plaudits. *Will He Marry Her?* is credited with starting a new minor literary trend—that of an interrogatory title for a novel. The new style of title to works of fiction—first started by Edward Lytton in *What Will He Do With It?*[2] then adopted by Mr. John Lang, in *Will He Marry Her?* and followed by a host of minor scribes since—as said in the journal *Town Talk*, in 1859, is, 'we understand, to be the fashion of the coming publishing season'[3]. (see plate 5)

At the age of 42, 16 years after he first set foot in India, John Lang wrote his most voluminous (452 pages) and ambitious novel in *Will He Marry Her?* There is a hurriedness and impetuosity in Lang's personality, which is reflected in most of his writings as well, including this one. He builds great plots, gets weary of them, and collapses them to denouement quickly, like in *The Three Calendars*, and *Haps and Mishaps at the Capias Castle.* The same happens in *Will He Marry Her?* too—the writer unspools a number of threads, and in the end, is just too keen to wrap them up quickly. He was considerate of the reader, and this is said in the earnest—for Lang's descriptions are always short and pithy; his concern is pacing the plot and the psychologies of his characters.

To write this novel, Lang draws from the entire corpus of his resources. His most abiding interest was relationships between lovers, and strong portrayals of women—and he explores both these themes with élan in *Will He Marry Her?*. Augustus Reckless is reckless to the point of being flippant, while Leonora is sound, grounded, mysterious, and determined.

Lang draws tremendously from his own life, and distributes personal incidents among his several characters; he makes his characters talk about—college life at Cambridge, military matters in India, legal matters in the British Empire, mysterious gems, horses, phrenology, etymology—practically everything he had an interest in. He makes almost all his characters well-versed with European literature to be able to quote something on matters of importance. Even the native Rani who speaks broken English is able to comment on love and valour by giving the example of Dryden's translation of *The Iliad*:

> 'She talked of Helen and of Paris…and was very angry with Helen for not killing Paris when he came to her, after having run away from Menelaus.'
>
> "Jo Deryden Sahib bola—such tha—bilcool.' (What Dryden Sahib said was very true—'Only brave men deserve glorious women!') 'I am told,' she continued, 'there was an English lady on the field of Ferozeshah; that she went there disguised as a man on horseback, and followed her husband's regiment into action, and up to the muzzles of the guns, which they charged."
>
> (Lang 1858: 369-70)

The Rani's statement is another example of a Hindi punchline, which Lang believed in.

Dryden's lines are, however, different from Lang's 'quoting' of the same:

Happy, happy, happy pair,
None but the brave,
None but the brave,
None but the brave deserve the fair.[4]

The English woman who fought in the battle, mentioned by the Rani, is a matter of great interest and curiosity, but I haven't been able to find any documents to hint upon the identity of this woman. Of course, many Indian women had taken to the battlefield: Bibi Khem Kaur, for example, had a role to play in the Second Anglo Sikh War, but no Englishwoman is known to have fought on the battlefield. Had it been so, and had it been public knowledge—which it appears to be, for Augustus is told by a native Rani in the novel about it—it would have been much publicised.

It is probably a John Lang trick to please his English audiences, for apart from the action on the battlefield, what the writer does is primarily satirise both the military and the civil services of the East India Company. It could also be that he is alluding to the wife of Sir Robert Sale who fell at Moodkee in the First Afghan War[5]—Lang mentions his death when describing the battle of Moodkee.[6]

1n 1842, Lady Florentia Sale was with her husband Sir Robert Sale in Afghanistan. The British were trying to upstage the rule of Dost Mohammad, who had Russian allegiance; and were trying to plant Shah Shuja instead. The Afghans routed the British and forced them to retreat to Jalalabad. When a siege was laid on the British Army, Lady Sale had advised the British troops to fight their way through the siege to Bala Hissar, where they could be sure of getting provisions. This advice went unheeded; later the Duke of Wellington would remark that had Lady Sale been the Commander of the forces, the unfortunate events would never have chanced. Safe passage was offered to the defeated troops, but on the way the zealot tribes butchered many people, and many died of hunger and starvation. Lady Sale and her daughter Mrs Sturt dressed as men and rode on horses during this journey. Akbar Khan, one of the chieftains, offered to give shelter to families, women and children, and with them went Lady Sale. It was believed that he had taken these people for ransom, but by the lady's account, she was treated well. She refused to side with the British, and said that they were as much to blame for the war as the Afghans were. She wrote all this in a journal throughout this travail with the hope that she would publish it someday.[7] Upon publication in 1843,[8] it was a rage in Britain.

Sir Robert Sale having fallen at Moodkee, and Lang having heard stories about his wife's military acumen, probably decided to pay her a compliment by conflating the two incidents in his novel.

The Literary Gazette of 1858 provides a detailed review of *Will He Marry Her?* and gives us an insight into the contemporary critique of Lang's work. The reviewer gives away the story, much to the chagrin of the readers of the review at that time perhaps, because till the very end it is uncertain whether the marriage would take place. However, the moot interest is not in whether the marriage would take place, but in how the personalities in the novel go through their vicissitudes. At the heart of the story is the question of confluence of East and West, which is addressed in a very complicated manner. Like in Gabriel García Márquez's novel *Chronicle of a Death Foretold*[9]—in which everything is known from the beginning yet the reader wants to know why it happened, and what happened thereafter—we know in *Will He Marry Her?* that everyone is agreeable to the match between Augustus and Leonora, and yet despite her ardent love for him, she wants him to visit India before they get married. The reader is curious to know what is in the East that compels the heroine to put this condition fervently. Like the premise of *Chronicle of a Death Foretold* is laid down in the epigraph, a similar premise is set with the epigraph of Lang's novel with words from *Tasso's Lament* by Byron:

> *Yes Leonora, It shall be our fate,*
> *To be entwined for ever—but too late*

Doom looms over the love affair right from the start. Augustus Reckless falls in love with his new neighbour, Leonora Ornsbie, a dark-haired, dark-eyed beauty who is the cynosure of all eyes. Augustus proposing to her in their third meeting, but Leonora says she cannot marry him even though she loves him. This is the dialogue that commences between the lovers:

> 'Leonora, you distract me. You speak in parables and enigmas, which I cannot comprehend.'
>
> 'I regret that I cannot be more explicit…If it should please Heaven that we should ever meet in the land of my birth—in India—and if, after you have seen me there, in my own home, and all that I would there show to you, and all that I would there declare to you—if then you would say to me, 'Leonora, be mine,' most willingly would I consent.'
>
> 'I would follow you, Leonora, to the most remote corner of the earth…What can you have to show me that your lips cannot now describe? What to say to me in another land which you cannot mention in this?'
>
> 'Before our hands can be joined at any altar, you must visit another clime, and see another race of people. I am not worthy of that enterprise on your part. Forget me! It were better.'
>
> 'Forget thee, Leonora? Who that has ever seen thee and talked to thee, as I have, could forget thee? There is nothing you could divulge unto me that could erase from my heart the love I bear to you, Leonora.'
>
> 'Ah, no! It cannot be—unless it be in another land.'[10]

The above dialogue is very important to the novel, for both the lovers keep to their word. Reckless being reckless diverts his attentions to Edgar West's sister, then to Mrs North, and then turns to gambling towards the end—but nothing can erase from his heart the love he bears for Leonora. She, too, does not budge under any kind of pressure to dissolve her resolve, and remains steadfast in her love.

When Augustus tells Edgar West about his love and West asks him if he is happy, Augustus says that he is happy and he is not. To that, West replies, 'It is better to be unhappy in our love.'

> Successful love may sate[I] itself away—The wretched only are the faithful.
>
> For my part, Reckless, I should like to nurture in my heart a love as hopeless as that of Petrarch or of Tasso. I should like to love a woman utterly beyond my reach; but to whom, with my dying breath, I could utter such lines as these:
>
> ...No power in death can tear our names apart,
> As none in life could rend thee from my heart.
> Yes, Leonora! It shall be our fate
> To be entwined for ever—but too late![11]

The verses, as mentioned earlier, are from Byron's *Tasso's Lament*. The name Leonora has been chosen for Augustus's lover precisely because Lang knew Byron's works very well. In naming the protagonist Leonora, and in quoting these lines, the destiny of this love is fixed.

Another element of doom is added with Leonora gifting Augustus a ring, from which he must never part. The stone on the ring changes colour under different circumstances. Leonora tells Augustus that the price of the stone is worth a trifle, but that he should value it like his life. That there is something important and eerie connected with the ring is established right when it is gifted to the hero.

I 'sate' means 'to satisfy in excess'

From his proposal till their last meeting in England—well after 200 pages—Augustus continues his entreaties to Leonora to speak about her mysteries, and enlists the support of her 'sable friend' Baboo Zemindar, Leonora's father, and his own mother to persuade Leonora to drop her insistence. All this however only helps in strengthening her resolve that he must come to India.

On being entreated to look into Augustus's eye when he is courting her in England, Leonora declares: 'It is useless for me to look into your eyes, as it is for you to swear. Your eyes have not yet seen sufficient. England is not the world. So far as I am concerned, you are at present partially blind.'

Leonora is entreated by her father Colonel Ornsbie that if she and Augustus loved each other, they should get married right away. The father is more than keen to divulge to Augustus the reason why he must travel East. Leonora refuses to budge and says that he must go through the ordeal:

> 'Leonora, may I divulge to Mr. Reckless the reason why you wish him to journey to the East…I would do so, for your sake.'
>
> 'You do not—you cannot…If, after I have exhibited to Mr. Reckless a scene which he shall witness—that is to say, if he come to the East—if, after I have then told him the truth, which I will convey to him in four words…if then I observe in his features one look of horror,—I do not say surprise, remember, but horror,—if I observe one look of horror, I will not marry him.'[12]

The four words that Leonora is talking about are: 'She is my mother.'

The point of describing the ordeal of Leonora and Augustus's here is that the narrative builds up to a crescendo about the hero's inevitable journey to the East, and keeps the reader's attention undivided. Till Augustus reaches India, the novel is a page-turner. Lang could have done with better editing, for Augustus's pleadings are just too many and the plot hovers around his helplessness for a little too long. In hindsight, though, this builds the appetite for what is to come.

As we have seen, Lang engages with the issue of caste and colour in more than one work of his, and his understanding of the issues of Indian caste system was pretty clear. The four words, then, are 'She is my mother' referring to the native Rani who is 'black'.

At first, when Reckless comes to Leonora's home in India, he is welcomed by a 'black' girl, who somehow is very agreeable to him and the liking only grows with time. Next comes a 'black' boy whose face has been spoiled by small-pox. The next 'black' person the hero meets is an aged lady, and finally it is revealed to him that she is Leonora's mother.

Clearly writing for a British audience, he makes several characters of his works engage in dialogues to understand these matters, and through these he shows that caste is not to be confused with race in any way. In the previous chapter, we saw Lang, in 'Black and Blue', tells that Jehan was 'coal black'. He, however, clarifies to the reader that her white husband turned sufficiently brown by tanning to be considered an Indian; Lang also gives the example of two prince brothers—one of them black, and the other much fairer.

At another point, Lang writes that several of the natives are fairer than him. Lang makes these clarifications and yet creates obfuscations for the English reader in England whose imagination, it seems he believed, was caught in the warp of white–black dichotomy. One can conjecture that Lang, therefore, makes his strongest protagonists black—one, to deal with the limited imagination of his readership; two, to make very strong anti-racism statements; and three, to show how caste is very different from the ethnic race.

It is obvious that Lang was a man of his time: an ambitious writer, who knew his target audience and wanted to sell stories of the exotic East. He subverts the canon of 'Exotic East' through stratagems like these, by getting into the micro-view of his characters but in the end, conforms to what his reader wants. One almost gets the feeling of Lang's despondency in the way he ends his novels.

I, on the other hand, would venture to call his endings very clever; they are spoofs of the Victorian novel, almost mocking the readers' expectations from a narrative. And so, Augustus Reckless marries Leonora in the West after having visited the East, and after having had the knowledge of her 'sable' parentage.

However, minutes after the ceremony is concluded, shrieks are heard from a room, and there is pandemonium. It is learnt that Leonora had a fit of convulsion, and that the very fair and white girl turned 'black' within moments and lost her life. Room for ambiguity is left there too, for the doctor brother of Augustus thinks she has had an apoplectic fit, and cuts open a vein in her hand to cure her. He performs the surgery with the very instruments that he had gifted Augustus to always carry with him during war. All the three gifts, already mentioned, come to use, and all in life-and-death situations. The lawyer's gift—a brandy bottle, saves the life of a dying soldier, the cleric's gift—a book of Burial Service kept in the breast pocket of Augustus's jacket saves his life from a bullet; and the doctor's gift—the case of surgical instruments comes in use twice, once to save lives in the battlefield after all the provisions of the British had been stolen by Indians, and the next time, to save-kill Leonora.

This is how Lang describes the scene of Leonora feeling ill, and consequently dying:

> 'This—this—yes—this. Augustus! Augustus! This is death!' Those were the last words she uttered, sinking into an easy-chair, which was near the bed on which she died.
>
> The spirit had not taken its flight more than half an hour, when the body of Leonora became dark, and then darker and darker; and by the time that the limbs were rigid, and the flesh cold, it was as black as the blackest night! It was not

> the change of colour that accompanies rapid decomposition and decay. It was so different, that Doctor Reckless was led to believe that Leonora had been poisoned by some potent drug, and suggested that a surgeon might be sent for to assist him in making a post-mortem examination. He had never seen, he said, a case so extraordinary, nor had he heard of one.

Much to the surprise of the doctors, the now 'black' body of 'white' Leonora did not decompose even after three days. One is reminded of Gabriel García Márquez again, and of his novel *Of Love and Other Demons*[13] which opens with the exhuming of a grave to reveal a body that's still growing hair. The author claims in the prologue that this was a legend told to him by his grandmother.[14]

According to the *Literary Gazette* critic, *Will He Marry Her?* 'deals with characters and incidents which have no place in real life'. This seems to be a constant diatribe against Lang, for simulating verisimilitude, and departing from the true historical settings. Márquez's novels have been lauded and been circumscribed as 'magic-realism' by critics, for simulating the unreal that is so real. One sees shades of this unreal-realism, very deliberately contrived, in Lang's prose, which precedes the much-lauded modern genre by a century and a half.

To contrive 'white' Leonora to turn 'black as the blackest night' after death has two implications. The first one is what the reviewer of the *Literary Gazette* says, that 'the moral of the story is, that it is wicked for a white man to marry a half-caste woman'[15].

The other implication is that Lang laments the discrimination towards Anglo-Indians, which is the more plausible reading of this book. This is embodied in Augustus's quick death in the Second Anglo–Sikh War (1848–49) following Leonora's. Lang follows the historical events with precision, for in the Second Anglo–Sikh War, the British victors of the First War suffered huge reverses.

Like naming Leonora after Byron's character in *Tasso's Lament*, the choice of Anglo–Sikh wars as the setting for action is also premeditated, so that the hero can fall immediately after Leonora. We shall return to the subject of Lang's politics, as we intend to study John Lang's personality as much as his literary works; given that these two aspects, in Lang's case, constantly inform each other.

Augustus, who swoons over Leonora throughout the novel, is a confirmed racist. He calls Leonora's friend Baboo Zemindar 'your sable friend'—'sable' in 19th century was a pejorative term for 'black'; he dislikes the idea that the brilliant miniature likeness of Leonora has been made by a 'black' man Rooder Sein[II]; on seeing the 'black' siblings of Leonora he is perturbed and wishes they did not exist; he imagines that she is telling him a lie, for such a white offspring cannot be born of a black mother. Augustus is also man of prejudices. He always makes fun of his friend Edgar West for his short height, and thinks West is not fit enough to go into the army, or to fall in love. He is also classist, as he keeps pondering whether Leonora is of low birth and that is what she wants to reveal to him in India.

In comparison, Leonora who gets little space in the novel, stands tall and outshines him in every appearance they make together. She makes him adore her 'sable friend' to the extent that Augustus declares that he can do anything for that man; she praises the 'black' painter who made her portrait; she tolerates and forgives Augustus losing her portrait and his flirtations with other women; she tolerates his breaking his vows of not talking to anyone about her father and herself; and steadfastly remains resolute on all things she initially said. She is adored and desired by all. Leonora stands tall, and Augustus—despite his prejudices—is totally besotted and, willingly or unwillingly, does everything Leonora wants, and grows to like all that she likes.

II Lang has taken the name of the painter Rooder Sein from Raja Rooder Singh of Durbungha, who has already been mentioned in this chapter in the context of 'Black and Blue'. Rooder Singh was very dark in complexion, unlike his younger brother, Basdeo.

When going to India for the first time on board the ship *Hindoostan*, Augustus breaks the vow that he would not speak to anyone about Leonora or her father. He asks a couple of officers of the Bengal Army if they knew Colonel Ornsbie. He is told that Colonel is a very rich person, worth 25 lakh rupees and very eccentric, and that he did not have a family. When Augustus informs Captain Binfield of having met the Colonel's daughter, the captain asks if the daughter is dark—this is an insinuation of things that are to come later in the plot. Another officer, Major Cheywyn, also informs Augustus positively that Ornsbie had no family, and that he had never alluded to one either. Augustus finds all this mysterious and thinks that Leonora is a liar and a 'myth'. He decides to flirt with one Mrs North on the ship. In wandering around with Mrs North at the ports, Augustus loses the miniature portrait of Leonora, which later mysteriously appears at Leonora's house in India. Leonora knows the entire story, and has forgiven him for his curiosities and frivolities.

By the time Augustus meets Leonora at her home in India, it is clear that the Colonel has hidden his marriage and children from public view for 25 years. Leonora has grown up inside a house, hidden from public view, but she thinks that was the only prudent thing to do lest anyone should have said, 'There is black blood in her veins.'

The colonel, a valiant soldier and a successful businessman, has had to hide his marriage and the children of what Lady Reckless calls a 'curse'. Despite this, Leonora has grown up to be sensible, and without any complexes. The text clearly posits Leonora as the brightest character of them all. The novel, in this rather exaggerated plot, clearly makes a statement against the discrimination against Anglo-Indians, half-castes.

The Colonel's own love story, which is told at this point, further belittles the personality of the already racist and prejudiced Augustus. The Colonel was 23 years old then, and was acting as the Governor-General's agent at a native court:

> Here he was seen at the palace by a young girl, who became enamoured of him; and whenever he passed that portion of the building which she occupied, she would put her hand through the marble screen which concealed her from the view of those outside, and drop a flower. The young Lieutenant—such was then the Colonel's rank in the army—began to notice this, and to look regularly for the black hand dropping the flower, which he would pick up and carry away with him to his bungalow.[16]

The flower-dropping continues for five weeks, and the Colonel preserves all the flowers at his bungalow, and maintains a diary of what has been happening. One day, a piece of bamboo falls with the rose bud:

> That pretty little episode in Boccaccio's story of Sigismonda and Guiscardo instantly occurred to Lieutenant Ornsbie's mind; and taking up the piece of stick and the flower, he went straight to his abode...he proceeded to examine the piece of bamboo, and in it he found a ring, and a piece of paper, upon which was written, with gilt ink, and in Persian characters, one word—'MASHOOK,' which signifies 'my love.'[17]

Here the narrator says, 'There was a dash of romance in the character of young Ornsbie, and he was always a very adventurous person.' He had not seen the face of the owner of the 'black hand' and he did not know anything about her, but a series of notes started being exchanged between the two through a little hole in the wall. The notes, as Lang would put them, read like this:

> *Ornsbie: Kon? (Who?)*
> *Black Hand: Chhota Chyryea—pinjra mein (a little bird in a cage).*
> *Ornsbie: Araaiee denge.*[III]

III This should read *Urai denge*—'will make you fly' or *Azadi denge*—'will give you freedom.'

There are more elaborate correspondences in which the girl tells who she is and why she has been incarcerated, 'instead of being permitted to dwell with her relations in Gwalior'.

The young lieutenant goes on to marry his 'bird', and 'loved her as much as she loved him'. At this point, the narrator does not shower plaudits on the lieutenant who cast aside his racial prejudices for the sake of a lover he had not seen, but on the Rani:

> How fervent must be the love of a Hindoo woman—a Brahmin by caste—who sacrifices her religion for the sake of a man! It was not for the sake of her liberty—for to her imprisonment was no great punishment—that the Ranee left the palace: it was solely for the sake of her love that she longed to be free. … it was not until after the birth of Leonora—by which time the lieutenant had become rich—that her relations were aware of the facts—that she was still alive, and was the wife of a British officer; and, for their own sakes, they were anxious to conceal, rather than give publicity to, the truth, which, in their opinion, would have brought disgrace upon the royal house to which the Ranee belonged.[18]

Here the narrator chooses to not talk about the lieutenant's chivalry and romance, and his transgression as a white man marrying a black woman, but of the great sacrifice made by the woman in sacrificing her caste and marrying an 'infidel'. The Rani has three children, one white and two black, and the black ones are brought up as Hindus despite the fact that she has converted to Christianity. Her son has sympathies for the Marathas and harbours hopes of English defeat, despite his father being in the Bengal Army. The novel appears to be primarily about white people, but in several passages, the text clearly positions itself against the smugness of the West.

There seems to be some typological error in the text.

When she understands he is delaying their marriage because of her mixed parentage, she declines to marry him. When Augustus is leaving India, he gets a note from her to meet someone waiting in a palkie[IV] on his way. He hopes that it would be Leonora herself, but it turns out to be her black sister, Shereenee.

> 'Reckless was astounded at the wonderful resemblance which her features bore to those of Leonora…There could be no question that they were sisters (more than once Reckless had been sceptical on this point), and that both were daughters of the Colonel. Both of them had his brow and his chin...Sitting as Shereenee did—mute and motionless…the only difference between herself and her sister consisted, seemingly, in this, that one was White and the other Black.'[19]

Leonora turning black in death is intended to make the two sisters appear the same. The text clearly posits that the only difference between Leonora and Shereenee is that the former is white, and the latter is black. In Leonora turning black, Shereenee's position is redeemed, as well as an allusion is made to Leonora returning to her maternal origins rather than paternal.

The reversal of 19th century anthropological enterprise—in the narrator's stance of mentioning the black Rani's sacrificing her caste for her love, and stating that it was love and not incarceration that prompted her to flee; that it was the black, maternal side which was intent on hiding the marriage rather than the white paternal side—is one of the many subversions that this novel achieves, but does not stop at.

The novel problematises the caste system equally, and puts Leonora in 'cursed' position. The Colonel, after Leonora refused to marry Augustus in India, tells him that the young man should drop

IV Or Palki. A palanquin.

the idea of marrying his daughter. He says that if he were in Augustus's place, he himself would not have married her:

> 'My dear boy, listen to me! I have married a native lady of rank, and if I lived my life over again, I would do the same—that is to say, I have no reason, in a selfish point of view, to regret the step that I took. You have heard of our romantic history?'
>
> 'Yes, Colonel.'
>
> 'Well, my dear boy, if my wife had been a being of a mixed race, I would not have married her.'[20]

Even though the Colonel has been assimilated in the Indian caste system, and despite having married a black woman, he makes the difference clearly that she was a woman of high caste and rank, and that he himself would not have married someone of a mixed race. Leonora, then, does not have anyone for her cause—not her father, not her lover. It is only her black replica, Shereenee, her alter-ego, who never perturbs her.

The novel draws from various literary sources and scandals contemporary to Lang, but also draws inspiration from various instances in Lang's own life:

i. Margaret Wetter, Or the Tale of Marriage Without Divorce?

'He Does Marry Her' is the title of the penultimate chapter of *Will He Marry Her?* the novel. It should have rather been titled *Will He Be Able To Marry Her?* for the question is not about the 'will' of Augustus Reckless, as much as his destiny—whether destiny would acquiesce to get the lovers united. One suspects that there is a meta-joke inserted here by Lang, like he does in various works of his, alluding to his own personal circumstances.

Victor Crittenden contends that Lang's second wife, Margaret Wetter, whom he married in 1861, was an Anglo-Indian, a half-caste.[21] We now know that the divorce granted to Lang and Lucy was 'mensa et thoro', which did not grant either spouse a right to remarry. Despite this, Lang married Ms Wetter. The chapter title, therefore, is not to suggest that the circumstances of Leonora are founded upon those of Wetter, but that her persona probably is. The novel is a fictional tale that deals with one of the important issues that Lang dealt with throughout his stay in India—that of the confluence of East and West.

ii. Sable is Able, or the Critique of English Ignorance

Interestingly, Lang not only distributes deals with various aspects of his own personality by amongst characters of this novel, he also borrows from the people he knew. That Lang was impetuous, 'larrikin,' irreverent, is by now obvious. This impetuosity, he imparts to Reckless, who learns, never through books but by observation, hearing and through society of people. Reckless, though generally affable, is a racist. Leonora is his counterpoint who shows to him that the darkest of the people can be most accomplished and kind. Lang is critiquing the racism of the English people through this juxtaposition, but also probably dealing with his own demons.

The heroes of his novels love India, but the natives, though shown in a positive light, do not get much space, and are even slighted with stereotypes. It is difficult to clearly come to an understanding of Lang's own complex position on this issue. It is clear that the characters of novels offer different points of view, but difficult to fathom if the narrator is also playing another character for an audience, or if it is Lang's voice. In *Will He Marry Her?*, Lang is probably drawing out his own trajectory of how he would have come to India with racist prejudices, and how they got dissipated with mixing with society.

iii. Underwood Family, or Overcrowded Family

Lang's mother Elizabeth married Joseph Underwood after the death of her first husband. Underwood was a widower with four children when he married Elizabeth who had two children. She had six more children with Underwood.[22] That makes the number of step- and half-siblings to be 14.

The Reckless family is also huge. The novel begins with listing of the 14 Reckless children. Once Lang left Sydney to go study in England at the age of 22, he never really returned except for a brief period in 1841. He did not even return when his mother died. As such there were too many children in the family; and he, being a child from the first marriage, probably did not receive such paternal affection as he was wont to have. Despite the Underwoods being wealthy, the sheer number of dependants probably did not result in a very luxurious lifestyle. In *Will He Marry Her?*, Reckless's friend Dacre praises the former's family estate and worth, to which Reckless replies that he does not think £5000 amounts to much:

> 'My expectations!' exclaimed Augustus… '…are the mildest imaginable!…I am a younger son, sir; one of fourteen children, with a prospect of being, before I die, one of two-and twenty. After this disclosure, you will not think me a boaster when I inform you that my father has five thousand a-year; and that, although I do not say he is absolutely a poor man, still he is very far from being a rich one.'[23]

With Reckless saying that there would be 22 children before he died, Lang is probably taking a humorous dig at his stepfather.

iv. The Runaway Bride, or Hannah Harris

Lang has taken more than one reference in the novel straight from his family story. This is where we can see the workings of Lang as a writer—how he borrows from his experiences and weaves them seamlessly into his novels. In the novel, after Augustus and Edgar have shown great valour in the First Anglo–Sikh War, reports about them are published in British newspapers. This is, however, to the consternation of both—for in the case of Augustus, the newspapers print a story about an aunt of his, who had eloped with a married man. The brother of the man's wife challenged the eloper to a duel and killed him; and the girl committed suicide by stabbing herself in the heart. Reckless says on reading the newspaper:

> He has made my services a pretext for reminding the public of a horrible tragedy in our family. An aunt of mine ran away with a cousin of hers…—a Captain in the Coldstream Guards. Unfortunately, he was a married man…By this time—aye, long ago—the story was well forgotten...The present generation have now the benefit of it…it will form the subject of a controversy in most of the leading prints. Some man—some old fogy at his Club—will write to say that the lady in question was only a half-sister of Sir Charles Reckless. Another old fogy will contradict him…The conductors of some of the newspapers will not think or care one straw what tortures the Reckless family are enduring while this correspondence is going on, and greedily devoured by their readers, until they get tired of the subject. This is the penalty that my family has to pay for my being honourably mentioned in the despatches.[24]

Augustus's vivid speculations and conjecture regarding the press reminds one of today's press. Perhaps the press' spirit to gossip has not changed; it is just a geometrical progression through technology.

The story of Reckless family 'information' is inspired from that of his mother's sister, Hannah Harris. Hannah ran off with sea-Captain Thomas Ritchie, who worked on the ship Greyhound that traded between India and Australia. Hannah was underage and Ritchie was accused of having abducted her. He was found guilty, and had to pay a huge fine.[25]

According to Crittenden, Lang's stories have some foundation in facts, even if they sometimes have to be taken with a 'drop of salt water'.[26]

v. Saving a Child from Drops of Salt Water, or Lang's Own Child?

A Lang obituary tells a tale of his bravery where he jumped off a vessel once to save a child. Crittenden quotes from the obituary: 'Lang without thinking immediately dived overboard and quickly reached and supported the child. Lang had always been a strong swimmer from his earliest days at school and managed to keep himself and the child afloat for more than fifteen minutes in the tossing sea. The rescue boat was rowed by the crew towards what had become a very small blob in the ocean'[27]. The obituarist adds that Lang appeared to have suffered no ill consequences from the adventure, and that 'his wiry frame and natural vitality was still able to undergo feats of endurance without any noticeable ill effects'[28].

In *Will He Marry Her?* there is a scene enacted by a guest, Parry, at a party thrown by Augustus, where Parry says his voice is hoarse because that is how one would sound after having jumped into the sea to save a child.

> 'Never was in better voice in my life,' replied Parry; '...for you see the speech that I spoke was after the Stranger had jumped into the water to save the child; and it was only natural to suppose that he had taken cold, from the sudden chill.'[29]

This play, *The Stranger*, being used by Lang, obliquely referring to an incident in his life, gives rise to various speculations. A reference to this play itself is curious, since this minor German writer August von Koetzebue is placed along with Shakespeare, Byron, and Boccaccio who pervade the novel—and, therefore, one conjectures that this has an allusion to Lang's own incident of saving a child.

The novel is of 1858, and therefore, the incident of Lang saving a child would have to be before the novel—if Lang is in fact alluding to it. But, we know that Lang married Margaret Wetter in 1861. Crittenden contends that this child was illegitimate, though he does not cite his source, and that this was the child who Lang had saved, since one would not venture to save anyone else's child and put oneself in such danger.[30] Such an assumption that a man would save only his child is the matter of contriving a legend, but Crittenden perhaps finds support in the text of *The Stranger*, for in that obscure play the character saves the child because it is his.

There are too many variables to handle here, too much guesswork, but let us still proceed with it. If it was Lang's own child that he saved, and if it was on a voyage from England to India—and if the novel is after the incident—it would have to be 1854 when Lang returned from England to India for a brief while. This means that the child was born seven years before Lang married Wetter, which is unlikely.

Then it is someone else's child that Lang saved. Stretching the possibilities, he merely made up a story of himself saving a child with *The Stranger* in mind. Stretching possibilities further, we have seen three incidents made up by Lang that came true; then perhaps what appears in the novel is a premonition. The novel already has an incident that comes true in real life, about a book saving a man's life.

vi. A Marwari's Portrait, or The Botany Bay Trick Played upon Lala

We began this work with a conjecture that Lang was fond of liaising with aliases. He not just create aliases for himself, but aliases for others as well. This is one of the biggest pranks Lang played—which is about a portrait of a 'Marwari' banker becoming that of a now celebrated historical figure of the Mutiny of 1857.

Lang claimed to a friend that it was not his doing, but that the journalist did not care whose picture it was. There is, however, a little incident in *Will He Marry Her?*—the allusion of which only Lang's close friends would have understood. The incident is when Baboo Zemindar comes to meet Leonora for the first time, and she calls him Baboo. This is what transpires next:

> 'Baboo! Baboo, indeed!' said the Asiatic. 'Do you not know that I am a prince?—Prince Zemindar! Yes; I am a prince. You do not read the newspapers?'
>
> 'No.'
>
> 'I thought not. Yes! I am a prince of Royal blood; so one great journalist says. I will take his picture back to India, and show it to the Rajah of Burdwan; and I will give him (that paper man) a great present—a beautiful time-piece. The Prince Zemindar! Baboo, indeed!'—and the Asiatic laughed satirically for a brief while.

Here, Lang is conjecturing what would happen if Lala had come to meet Leonora. If we replace Baboo with Lala, it becomes, 'Lala! Lala, indeed. Do you not know I am Nana Sahib of Bhitoor? I am prince of Royal blood, so a great journalist says, and he has even printed my picture as the runaway Nana!'.

In my opinion, this is a coded joke, and would have given Lang a hearty laugh because he pranked three parties—Lala had suddenly become an unwilling celebrity like Baboo in the novel, Nana Sahib had been portrayed as a merchant which would be unpalatable for any nobleman, and the British journalists had been duped and proven stupid by some wayward tale concocted by Lang.

The other ramification of this outburst by Baboo is Lang mocking the British public for their exotic imagination: for imagining every Indian as a prince, which is what precisely happened when Lang easily passed off the picture of Lala as a prince.

vii. Botany Bay Tricks, or Trinity Treats Lang with Impunity

Lang began at Trinity College on 26 August 1837 as a pensioner—which means that he would have had to pay his own way through as a scholar. The sons of lords received a much more privileged treatment at Cambridge than commoners, and this would have irked Lang to no end, and perhaps made him resolve that he will call himself a 'gentleman' for the rest of his life. Lang makes a joke of this issue in *Will He Marry Her?* when the bed-maker Mrs Croppitt asks Augustus if he was a 'Hat Fellow-Commoner' or a 'Pensioner':

> 'Upon my honour, Mrs. Croppitt,' said Reckless, 'I cannot say exactly what I am. I am not, however, aware of being a pensioner; and if I am, I really don't know who has pensioned me, or for what services I have been pensioned. As for being a Hat Fellow-Commoner, I have not the faintest idea what it means.'[31]

Even though 'hat fellow-commoner' has the word commoner in it, it is reserved for nobility.[32]

In *Will He Marry Her?* Augustus takes on college authorities when he and his friend Edgar West are charged for attending a play and mixing with 'low actors and actresses'.

Lang, too, 'wrote English verse well but not wisely, and he brought himself into trouble with the heads of the college'[33]. In a letter, dated 11 August 1838, written to James Sheen Dowling,[V] his father, wrote he was glad that James had cut off all connections with Lang after Lang had been expelled from Trinity.[34] In his novels *Raymond* (1840) and *The Undergraduate* (1846), Lang's characters meet in the university and are up to some 'Botany Bay' trick or the other, which gets them in trouble with college authorities. The exact nature of Lang's offence at Trinity is not known.

V James Sheen Dowling was a judge in New South Wales and studied law with John Lang at Trinity

In Will He Marry Her?, Augustus and his friends, too, indulge in adventures, such as watching a play and being summoned about it, Augustus and Edgar West climbing into a burning building to save property, holding a mad supper party after which Mr Parry returns home black-faced with charcoal etc. In one instance, there are two students—one climbs on the shoulder of other and they put a cloak over themselves and pose as a ghost and scare fellow students. When they go to Edgar's room, he beats them up soundly, and Mrs Croppitt says he has the strength of a demon.

viii. Shakespeare of India, or Kalidasa of England?

Lang extends the debate of 'racial discrimination' to the realm of literature, and takes on the famous Macaulay's Minutes on Education of 1835, in which Macaulay had shown a very condescending view towards literature from the East.[35]

In a discussion between Augustus and Baboo Zemindaar about a Colonel Ornsbie's horse Ackbar (it was a real race horse in India by the way belonging to Colonel Felix)[36], Augustus says it seems sluggish, to which the Baboo replies:

> As the Persian poet very truly says, 'Who, to look at the shahma (an Indian bird), would suppose that he could sing so sweetly? Who, to look at the flamingo, would suppose his note so hideous? Who, to look at the painted skin of the adder, would fancy that he was more dangerous than the eel?'

Augustus replies quoting Shakespeare, and says that the poet makes one of his characters (Petruchio) say to another character (Catherine):

> What! Is the jay more precious than the lark,
> Because his feathers are more beautiful?

> Or is the adder better than the eel,
> Because his painted skin contents the eye?

The lines are from *Taming of the Shrew.*[37] Baboo is not impressed and says that the idea has been borrowed from poetry from the East:

> 'Humph!' said the Baboo, smiling, and approaching Augustus. 'What of that? Your great poet has treated the idea just as you treat the commodity of tea, and that of coffee, which you sweeten with sugar and colour with milk, just to suit the European palate and prejudice. All great poets must borrow from the great poets who preceded them. Admiration leads to imitation. I am now uttering the sentiments and quoting the words of a writer who lived and died before Europe was invented or born.'

Through Baboo Zemindar's statement, Lang clearly is sardonically replying to Macaulay and several others who were smug about Western literature without having read much of Indian or Persian literature.

In stating that 'all great poets must borrow from great poets that precede them', Lang is probably also hinting at Edgar Allan Poe, who he believed had just translated a Persian poem and passed it off as his most successful poem, *The Raven*. Lang is also joking at the English saying that Kalidasa was the Shakespeare of India, Kalidasa having preceded the English bard by several centuries.

ix. The Gift of an Orange, or the Annexation of a Princely State

While narrating the love affair between Paul Ornsbie and the woman-with-the-black hand, the narrator tells about the black girl dropping flowers for her 'mashook' through a hole in the wall. The symbolism of the flowers is immense—for Paul keeps each of them carefully; as is the symbolism of the short note she writes to him—*Chhota chyryea*—

pinjra mein (a little bird in a cage). These symbols are enough for Paul to stake his life and rescue the black Rani from her captivity:

> The natives are strange people, and often discourse symbolically, and a favourite means of conveying bribes is in fruit and in flowers. It was in an orange that Mrs. Clowman—'unbeknown' to her husband, of course, he being the Resident at Kubsow at the time—received her jewels from the Prime Minister of that corrupt native state, which, in consequence of its corruption, her husband wished to see 'annexed.' It was in a bunch of flowers that the earring of pearls came to the hands of the wife of the Governor-General's agent at Fidnepore—'unbeknown,' of course, to her husband, who was 'ready' (he said) to destroy himself when the facts became known.[38]

Several of such narratorial interventions in the novel are based on facts. Lang has changed the names of the people and the places, and one has not been able to trace the source of these scandals. Fidnepore, for example, is a twisting of the name 'Midnapore' in Bengal; Kusbow is a little tougher to decipher, but it sounds very like 'Lucknow'. Lucknow was the capital of Oude—one of the states to be annexed in 1856 under the 'Doctrine of Lapse' promulgated by Lord Dalhousie. I think my hunch about 'Kusbow' being Lucknow is right, for the resident in Lucknow at the time of annexation of Oude was Colonel Sleeman,[39]—the original for 'Clowman'—who was resident from 1849 to 1856 when he died. Sleeman is renowned in colonial history as having taken the menace of thugee[VI] head-on[40]; and the prime minister in question is Ali Naki Khan,[41] who was so close to the king, and powerful, that only he was allowed audience to the latter. Robert Minturn in his book

VI Thuggee/Thugee is the abstract noun form of the common noun thug, used to denote armed robbers who killed their victims before robbing them. Lang has also written about this cult. The British misunderstood this difference of noun forms in Hindi and employed 'thuggee' as a common noun for the thugs.

From New York to Delhi (1858)[42] opines that Ali Naki Khan was the chief instigator of the Mutiny.

But that is a matter of history that need not be delved into beyond the bare minimum to introduce these characters to the reader. As to the gift sent to Lady 'Clowman', there is nothing to be found. It is, however, common knowledge that Colonel Sleeman was opposed to the appointment of Khan as the Prime Minister, and this estranged Sleeman's relationship with the king, Wajid Ali Shah.[43] Perhaps the jewels inside the orange gifted by the prime minister to Sleeman/Clowman's wife were the reason for the colonel's vehement opposition. The resident of Kusbow/Lucknow was easy to locate since Oude was the epicentre of the revolt in 1857, but the gifts of Fidnepore/Midnapore mystery still eludes us, it having been a 'mofussil'[VII] station.

The only thing Lady Sleeman—the recipient of the valuable gift inside an orange—is remembered for is a line related by Colonel Sleeman in his book *Rambles and Recollections of an Indian Official*, which has been often quoted because it is one of the finest tributes to the Taj Mahal:

> I asked my wife, when she had gone over it, what she thought of the building.
>
> 'I cannot,' said she, 'tell you what I think, for I know not how to criticize such a building, but I can tell you what I feel. I would die to-morrow to have such another over me.'[44]

It is very interesting to note that Lang talks at length about Ali Naki Khan—who he spells as Ally Nucky Khan—and his associate Wuzzy Ally Khan in his *Wanderings in India*, but does not mention the gift inside the orange, which he saved to insert 'unbeknown' in his fictional work. Also, one tends to believe that as *Wanderings in India* is a post-Mutiny work, Lang steered clear of stating his obvious Indian

VII Mofussil: a small upcountry. In Urdu, it means a small town, away from main city.

alliances, lest the British reading public be offended. Another very pertinent example in this regard is that he talks about the case of Lala Jotee Persaud in the book, but does not state that he was the lawyer who won the case for him against East India Company.

x. The Curse of Rani's Ring, or the Genesis of the Moonstone

Coming back to *Will He Marry Her?*, one of the powerful symbols that silently pervades the novel is the ring that Leonora gifts Augustus. The importance of the ring first comes to the fore when Baboo Zemindar cannot take his eyes off Augustus's finger, and poor Augustus, in his flippancy, thinks that Baboo was probably a suitor of Leonora who had gifted him the ring. Finally, Baboo broaches the subject:

> 'Only fancy!' exclaimed the Baboo, taking the hand of Augustus, and glaring at his ring, 'only fancy seeing the Devil's Diamond! and on the finger of an Englishman, in London!!! I can scarcely believe my eyes. It would not surprise me now if I were to be shown the Koh-i-noor, out of the territories of Runjeet Singh.'
>
> 'Why is it called 'the Devil's Diamond,' Baboo?'
>
> 'I know not. But that is the name of that stone—the name by which it is known in history—the history of several native Courts—'SHYTAN KA HEERA;' which means—'THE DEVIL'S DIAMOND.'
>
> 'In this country the value of that stone would be very trifling: say in its best moments—its *brilliant* moments—not more than £20; and in its worst moments, nothing at all, or only the value of the gold which forms the setting. In India its value is incalculable—so incalculable, that I would not accept it as a gift, much as I covet it, if the condition were that I should wear it on my finger in the Upper Provinces of India, or even in the Lower Provinces. I never saw that ring till the other day,

> but I knew it instantly, from the wonderful description of it; and I had heard—often heard—that the possessor of it was Colonel Ornsbie; and often have I and others joked with him about it. But it was a subject *he* always turned away from—sometimes angrily. Does *he* know that you wear this ring?'

What transpires next is Baboo Zemindar taking his leave, but deciding to stay back at the Ornsbies' because a storm is approaching. When a perplexed Augustus remarks the weather is clear, Baboo says the stone on the ring has turned black which means portent for a storm. Baboo is even willing to wager his diamond ring against Augustus's ring. The storm hits within minutes.

Assuming Colonel Ornsbie didn't know Augustus was in possession of the ring, he meets the Colonel with his hand gloved. The Colonel, who had noticed the ring missing from Leonora's finger, asks Augustus about it. The Colonel then recounts the history of the ring and how it reached Leonora:

> I cannot say that it is not stolen property—for it has been stolen, like other jewels, and recovered, and stolen again, and recovered. Often and often has this happened. That ring, however, came into the possession of the person who gave it to Leonora honestly—that is to say, if an honest title to a chattel once stolen can be acquired by the last possessor. More than two hundred years have elapsed since that ring was last stolen. Several generations have passed away, and time has obliterated the crime which tainted the possession of those who last took it wrongfully.

The colonel gives Augustus 'a guard, or a case made of pure gold, which fits over and conceals the ring' and extracts a promise to always conceal the ring from everyone's gaze, save Leonora's, in India. Leonora also tells Augustus something about the mystery of the ring:

> This little stone is a Ladak pebble. Be very careful of it, if you value my love…it changes its colour frequently…These changes of colour are not sudden, but gradual. The history of this ring you may someday learn…is a very curious history. The intrinsic value… (is) nothing. But thousands and thousands of men have perished in consequence of the desire of one little man to become its possessor. Dear Augustus, it was in the search for this little stone—a search prompted by the purest curiosity—that the whereabouts of the most valuable jewel in the known world was discovered—a jewel for which Russia offered more than a million sterling…if I do not see it upon your finger when we meet in another land, I can never become your wife.

By saying 'thousands have perished' in its pursuit, it is insinuated that the stone is cursed. This is where the fatalism gets entrenched in the text—knowing that a curse surrounds the ring, the bearer still mustn't part with it. Fatalism is further grounded with Baboo Zemindar calling Leonora a fatalist—when she is not afraid in the face of a tempest.

'Shytan Ka Heera' or 'The Devil's Diamond' is probably Lang's own concoction but there are a few stones that seem to have been notorious for their curses. One of them that Leonora refers to, the one for which 'Russia offered more than a million sterling'—is The Orloff.

Madame Barrera tells in 1861: 'The Orloff, according to some accounts, formed one of the eyes of the idol Scheringham, in the temple of Brahma. The fame of these bright eyes having reached a certain French grenadier of Pondicherry, he deserted, adopted the religion and manners of the Brahmins, and subsequently succeeded in escaping with one of the coveted orbs. He sold the jewel to a sea captain for 50,000 francs; the sea-captain sold it to a Jew for 300,000; and an Armenian, named Shafrass, bought it for a much larger sum, and disposed it off to Count Orloff, for the Empress Catherine, for 450,000 roubles, and a grant of Russian nobility.'[45]

This could be the stone that inspired Lang for his Devil's Diamond. He, however, seems to be saying that people died in the pursuit of the latter and found the former. The term 'Shytan Ka Heera' or 'Devil's Diamond' is much more dramatic than 'The Orloff', and hence, could be the same stone he is talking about. With the stone fabled to have been stolen from the statue of a Hindu god, the plot for the curse is very much in place.

Stealing diamonds from Hindu deities was a commonplace discourse. India was the only known diamond field till very late—Brazil's fields were found in the 19th century—the sensational legends of purloining from Hindu gods' statues and thereby incurring their wrath would have been only too common. These legends, which would already have been in currency in India, got an international appeal with the burgeoning print media of the mid-19th century.

In *Will He Marry Her?* the stone belonged to the native Maratha Rani, who Paul Ornsbie married. Interestingly, India's biggest diamond mines were in Golkonda, a place that was controlled by the Marathas for a long time. Even though *The Literary Gazette* accuses Lang of wrongly reporting events, Lang knew his Indian affairs pretty well. Not only did he know the stories of these diamonds, he also knew that the Marathas possessed some of the fine diamonds. There is an incident of the early 19th century, reported from Sambalpur, where a Rani is supposed to get a diamond, but the Marathas exile her, and take possession of it. The story, told by a Dr Breton, and in a book about 'medico-topography', is recounted in *The Bengal Gazetteer*:

> A large diamond, weighing 672 grains had been found in the Mahanadi, and this the finders brought to the Rani. Unfortunately she was engaged in the funeral ceremonies of her mother-in-law, and before they were finished, the Maratha troops arrived and expelled her from the country. A treacherous servant betrayed the secret to Chandraji, the

> Maratha commandant, who offered to give the finders a village and Rs 1000 if they gave it up. When they claimed the reward, he stormed at them, saying that they had given him a stone instead of a diamond, and had them driven from his presence.[46]

Leonora calls the Marathas 'all cruel people', and says that if her own brother were to become a prince, he would be equally 'malicious and cruel'.

I have a feeling that the allusion to Maratha cruelty; the incarceration of Leonora's mother the native Rani, and other events, along with the cursed diamond, might have been borrowed by Lang from the above incident. It is interesting to see the stereotype of Maratha cruelty being perpetuated in the mid-19th century, as opposed to the image of the brave and patriotic Marathas in the 20th century. Given that the Mughals remained mere figureheads and the Marathas had gained control of vast territories by this time, they were an eyesore for the East India Company.

According to *The Eclectic Magazine* (1868), The Orloff is the inspiration for Wilkie Collins's *The Moonstone* (1868), a detective novel with a colonial Indian setting in which the cursed Moonstone was originally stolen from a Goddess' idol during the British attack at Serirangapatnam (1799).

Apart from being a classic in the genre of detective fiction, *The Moonstone* is laudable for its portrayal of Indians in a balanced and sympathetic light despite it being a post-Mutiny novel when most British writers, including Dickens, painted Indians in a dark light. At the end of *The Moonstone*, the natives acquiring the moonstone from the thief, and returning it to the temple where it originally belonged—is also a critique of the Empire, and also alludes to the British Crown wrongly detaining the Koh-i-noor.

Here comes the issue of yet another unacknowledged debt to John Lang. We have already seen how Wilkie Collins borrowed from Lang's

'Black and Blue' in the creation of a character who turns dark blue. Lang's *Will He Marry Her?* precedes *The Moonstone* by 10 years. If Collins knew Lang's 'Black and Blue', there is no reason he would not have known *Will He Marry Her?* which was first published in 1858. It remains an unacknowledged debt, in Collins never mentioning Lang as a source of inspiration, and, later, in the critics not being able to find this source or not mentioning it.

Coming back to 'Shytan Ka Heera' of Lang's novel, the stone wreaks havoc in the lives of its possessors. The doings of the ring are never juxtaposed directly with the narration of Leonora and Augustus' story, but the first possessor in the novel, the Rani has her face spoiled by smallpox. Colonel Ornsbie is cheated in his business and loses £80,000; Augustus journeys to the East in vain for Leonora; Leonora dies on the day of her marriage; Augustus dies soon after.

Baboo Zemindar tries to take the curse upon himself. He understands what the stone is capable of, and wants to salvage the situation for the couple. Reckless's salvation does indeed depend on removing the ring, which he does not. The cursed stone is the fulcrum of the narrative, and frames all events within its dark shadow.

The stone becomes a symbol for Leonora's fate, and Leonora a symbol for the fate of one who does not belong anywhere. Leonora's destiny is a critique of both the Empire and the caste-system in India. She cannot mix with the society of her land of birth, a land that she so ardently loves. She converses with the skies and birds. Leonora is a tribute to solipsistic genius as well as a lament at the destiny of such kind. Byron was one of the major literary influences on Lang, and several quotes from *Don Juan* and *Tasso's Lament* point out to Lang's fascination for solipsistic, wandering characters.

xi. Endings of Lang-u-age, or a Reader of Tragedies

Many or most of Lang's stories end in end of language for the protagonist, which is death. I use the phrase 'end of language' not just for the pun, but also because most of Lang's protagonists actually run out of language, of things to say at the end. Leonora knows she is cursed, her end has come, and there is nothing more to say than 'This is it'.

In 'The Mahomedan Mother', from *Wanderings in India*, too, a native lady is married to a British army officer; they beget a child and the husband dies. The child is given over to the white relatives of the deceased army officer, who do not know who his mother is. The mother waits by the roadside every day to catch one glimpse of the child. When the narrator has a meeting of the child and the mother contrived, the mother is overwhelmed with her oxymoronic emotion of joy and grief—joy of meeting her child, and grief that she cannot be with him or call him his own—and dies.

In 'Black and Blue', Francis Young meets a sudden and violent death—after having built a successful career in trade, he is simply hacked to pieces by thugs. His son, the black boy with blue eyes, simply vanishes in Europe after his travails as a wretched black boy seem to be over with him inheriting a huge fortune.

In the piece 'Marching', both the father and the mother of the orphan child have died violent deaths; and the child himself is left without language, he is in fits and convulsions when he is to be separated from his Afghan master, to be taken away by the deceased parents' relatives.

All these texts deal with the issue and fate of Anglo-Indians, and are in inter-textual dialogue with each other. In all the three short stories in *Wanderings in India*, the white father is dead, and this is symbolic; it is the beginning of an era of confluence, and yet the past haunts, and looms large. Lang uses all kinds of permutations of social stratification to engage with the destiny of half-castes. In 'Marching', the wife is white; in 'Black and Blue', the Muslim girl is from a very low caste, and in 'Mahomedan Mother' the lady is from the Muslim elite. In both the cases where the child is fair, his responsibility is taken by white people.

In 'Black and Blue', the black child's white father has given up everything English and lives as an Indian with Indian attire and language, for 'India he loved, England he despised'. The stories in *Wanderings in India* does not delve into the matter of how such a union of the Anglo and the Indian came about. It is only in *Will He Marry Her?* that the issue is dealt with at length; it is possible because Leonora is fair, because she is not the sable Shereenee. Lang had his restraints in writing for a white audience, but he achieves the object of undercutting his British reader's ideology with tremendous lament, sarcasm, and tragedy.

We have already seen that lines from Byron's *Tasso's Lament* form the epigraph of the novel, and that the book is a major influence in contriving the tragic fate of Leonora, in the very name chosen for her. Byron is mentioned in several other places in the book: in describing Leonora's eyes when Augustus meets her first—'She had such glorious eyes! so large, so soft, yet so full of fire! Byron's description of those handsome eyes of which he was so fond, seemed poor and weak to those who looked into Miss Ornsbie's'; in describing Augustus's rage when he and his friend are charged for participating in a play of 'low actors and actresses'—'...his eyes still glared wildly, and his chest heaved heavily', just like Byron graphically describes it in the *Shipwreck*—'The wind went down, but still the sea kept up'.

The trial scene, where Reckless and West have been charged with breaking college rules, and are condemned for severe censure, is peppered with various quotes from literary giants. When the Master, in his zeal, starts making personal remarks at West, the latter quotes from Cervantes, from a dialogue between Don Quixote and Sancho:

> Do not, Sancho, if you should have occasion to condemn a poor wretch, revile him with hard words. The law prescribes a certain punishment, and you have no right to augment it by abusing the culprit you are called upon to sentence.[47]

In the same college court, the Master has pronounced West expelled, and not yet pronounced a sentence on Reckless—for West doesn't have any lineage to boast of, while Reckless is the son of a Lord. At this point, Reckless becomes agitated, bolts the door from inside and exclaims that no one will exit before he has made his point. Reckless replying to the charge made against him quotes from Horace:

> The informant, in his statement, made use of the expression, 'low actors and actresses.'...Now...although I think it a very unseemly and improper thing to remind any man...of the meanness of his origin, nevertheless there are times when it would be equally improper to refrain from doing so. One of those times is the present, when a man who has sprung from the loins of a menial servant...dares to speak of a body of poor and honest people as 'low company,' and only because the stage happens to be their profession. 'Low company,' indeed! My father once told me if ever I met with a low fellow who prided himself, and presumed upon his wealth, or his learning, or his position, or whatever else, to fling our crest at him—
>
> Fortuna non mutat genus.[48]

The Latin phrase, translated, is 'fortune does not change nature' or 'dressing up a genre does not change it'. Reckless's speech has a double-edged sentiment. On the one hand, he is saying that his father advised him to utter this phrase when he meets a 'low fellow' who presumes upon his wealth, position or knowledge. This is clearly a classist sentiment where a man, despite his accomplishments, cannot hope to rise above his lot, for 'dressing up a genre does not change it'. On the other hand, this is in defence of 'actors' and, therefore, implies that though they may not be 'high born', they have their abilities, and nothing can take it away from them.

This conflict is one of the core dilemmas of Lang's life. He always liked to be called a 'gentleman' and included 'Barrister-at-law' with his name in his books, and made general remarks about natives, which is typical of the 19th century. On the other hand, he would argue court cases only for Indians, and would paint Indians in a sympathetic light in his works. This conflict emanates out of Lang's own position of being of convict origins—both his maternal grandfather and grandmother being convicts transported to Sydney, and the society of New South Wales in the mid-19th century deeply divided on the class lines between 'pure merinos[VIII]' and 'currency lads'. In political terms, this division was between Exclusivists—those who wanted all rights of authority vested in people of 'free origin'—and Emancipists—those who wanted to emancipate the people of convict origin from the stain of their forbearers' crimes. When Lang returned to Sydney after completing his education from Middle Temple, he obviously joined the Emancipists there. However, he left Sydney for India, where he would not talk about his Australian origins, and would have a curious position towards the natives—one that was a cross between sympathy, curiosity, breaking down of stereotypes about the East, and gross generalisation.

This is also where the irony is. The phrase quoted by Augustus also circumscribes Leonora's tragedy. Despite her qualities—her universally-praised beauty, sound knowledge acquired from self-education—her genre of 'half-caste' cannot be changed.

While Augustus quotes a part, West quotes the lines from Epode IV of Horace in full,[49] which when translated[IX] reads:

> Whatever discord obtains, through fate, between lamb
> And wolf, it's so with you and me,
> You whose sides are scarred by the Spanish lash, whose legs
> Are calloused by iron fetters.

VIII free people who had come to settle down in New South Wales, what is today Australia.

IX The translation is only of the lines quoted by Edgar West in the book.

Though you may strut around, so proud of your money,
Fortune can't alter your breeding.
As you measure the length of the Via Sacra
In a toga that's three yards wide,
Don't you see the unrestrained indignation,
On the faces of passers-by?[50]

Though these lines are directed in Lang's novel against the informant, they could well be used against Leonora, which is what her prime fear is—'unrestrained indignation on the faces of passers-by' when they get to know that she is of mixed parentage.

Another strong literary influence on Lang was that of the 14th century Italian writer, Giovanni Boccaccio. Lang rewrote one of the tales—*Federigo and His Falcon* from Boccaccio's *Decameron*[51]—as *Love's Last Sacrifice*[52]. The Falcon story is mentioned in *Will He Marry Her?*, as is another story from *Decameron—Ghismonda and Guiscardo*[53]. This story is also mentioned within the love story of Paul Ornsbie and the native Rani. When the Rani throws for him a bamboo stick with a cleft containing a letter, the narrator tells that the 'pretty little episode in Boccaccio's story of Sigismonda[X] and Guiscardo instantly occurred to Lieutenant Ornsbie's mind; and taking up the piece of stick and the flower he went straight to his abode...in it he found a ring, and a piece of paper upon which was written...one word—"MASHOOK," which signifies "my love".'[54]

Lang uses several of his literary influences as inspirations to contrive his plots: Leonora's name is taken from Byron's *Tasso's Lament*, another sub-plot involving Lady Reckless and Mr Brown is drawn from *Federigo and His Falcon*, and the manner in which Rani woos Paul is taken from Boccaccio's story of Ghismonda.[55]

Lang's plot involving the story of Paul Ornsbie and Rani follows the same trajectory as Boccaccio's, although in a complex way. The love

X Boccaccio's Ghismonda is 'renamed' as Sigismonda in *Will He Marry Her?* By John Lang.

interest of Paul is also nobility, and in a reversal of roles, it is not the white man hiding his 'sable' wife, but the other way around. The wife's family wants to hide her marriage with an 'infidel' Christian, and her non-European-looking children are brought up with Hindu values. In Boccaccio's story, too, it is the girl's fraternity which has problems with the union. In Lang's story, it is not quite a happy ending for the couple, for they get married, but the Colonel's family has to be hidden from the world's view, and the curse alights upon Leonora, who dies on the day of her marriage, and turns black as the blackest night. Lang follows the moot point of Boccaccio's narrator, in that Love is envied by Fortune, who brings 'a calamity, turning the joy of the two lovers into tears and sorrow'.

Tragedies loom large on Lang as a reader, and these get converted in tragedies of lovers in his writings. This is just one of the many ways to read into the psychology of Lang's literature. If one's propensity to read a certain genre of works, can be conjectured to be founded upon one's personal circumstances, this probably tells about the various heartburns that Lang himself went through, with a broken marriage, and a second illegitimate relationship.

Boccaccio, who wrote Decameron in the backdrop of the Great Plague of 1348, has little time for chastity. The plague becomes an allegory, insinuating that the society is plagued by medieval morality and the corruption of the churches. He pokes fun at crafty, hypocritical clerics and celebrates the power of passion to overcome obstacles and social divisions. *Decameron* is path-breaking for 14th century, and there are certain elements which are radical even for the modern day. No wonder then that Boccaccio would have appealed to Lang, who was also quite a subversive for his day.

Boccaccio and The Rani

On 4 August 1863, there appeared in *The Mofussilite* a story called 'Love's Last Sacrifice'. Crittenden republished it as a book by the same name in 2007 (Canberra, Mulini Press). It is a story about a Count who loves a married woman and she, realising this, stops entertaining him. The Count leaves his home, wanders away, and lives alone in the country with no means of subsistence but the vegetables he grows and the game that his falcon hunts for him. Several years later, the lady's husband is dead, and she has started living in the country. Destiny would make them meet again. Crittenden, in his introduction, says that he has not been able to trace the origin of the story. Lang, however, never has left a literary debt unacknowledged.

'Love's Last Sacrifice' is based on Boccaccio's 'Federigo and His Falcon' from *Decameron*[1]—Lang says this in, as many words, in *Ex-Wife*; in which Eva Merrydale writes stories to make a living. Perhaps, Lang had written this story and was contemplating its publication after he returned to India in 1859. We only know that he published it in 1863. This is what Eva Merrydale says about the story:

> I took for my subject the story in Boccaccio, which relates to the love of Federigo for Giovana—the story of the young nobleman who, having squandered all his wealth in giving entertainments to his lady-love (who rejects his suit) retires to a small farm, which he tills with his own hands, his only companion being a little falcon, by whose flights Federigo is supplied with game—and which falcon he subsequently sacrifices, to give a dinner to his lady-love, ignorant of the circumstance that she

> has come to crave the living bird for a dying child who fancied that the possession of the falcon would restore him to health. I anglicised the story, and laid the scene in this country. I called the story *Love's Last Sacrifice*, and gave it to Mathilde to submit, anonymously, to the conductor of the periodical in which the *Flights of Fancy* had appeared. To my intense joy, the paper was considered 'eligible,' and came out in the very next number that was issued. I scarcely know of which I was most proud—my first picture, that of a tobacconist's shop; or those sixteen pages of print, for which I received five bright sovereigns and two half-crowns. And what woman would *not* be proud to reflect that by her pen or paint-brush, or both combined, she could earn sufficient for the support of herself and her offspring? Several newspapers noticed *Love's Last Sacrifice* very favourably, and quoted several of the best scenes—that one especially of the struggle between Giovana's love for her child, and her own feelings when she consents to demand from the man whose proposals she has spurned, the falcon by which, in poverty, he was mainly supported.[2]

Lang points out to the pecuniary difficulties of a writer who lived by his pen. He also highlights the fact that it was very difficult for women to make a living out of writing.

We have seen that Boccaccio was one of the strongest literary influences on Lang. Bocaccio, in turn, was inspired by *The Arabian Nights*—which would have been in currency in 14th century. Several scholars conjecture that *The Arabian Nights* has taken influence from Chinese legends. It is noteworthy that the legend of 'monkey king' in China is loosely based on conflating of the legend of Hanuman (sans Ramayana) and the Buddhist tales that were carried to China by Huen-Tsang in the 7th century. The oral narrative was written by Wu Cheng-en and translated into English by Arthur Waley, and published in 1944 as *Monkey*.[3] In *The Arabian Nights*, there is a story in which a princess transmogrifies several times to fight a demon to save a 'Qalandar'. This has striking resemblances with the Chinese story in which the monkey king transmogrifies and takes on several forms to fight with Nath (based on the character of Meghnad perhaps).

Lang knew *The Arabian Nights* well, and alludes to it severally. He was particularly impressed by the story of 'Three Qalandars and the Five Women of Baghdad'.

Lang takes the name of his novel *Three Calendars, Or Too Much Alike* from this story of 'Three Qalandars and Five Women of Baghdad'.

In *Three Calendars, Or Too Much Alike* (1854), there are three men known as Calendars—they are not brothers, but look very much alike when they are in their Calendar attire. All the three men fall in love with the same girl, Jenny Dale, who has two other sisters. The girl also takes fancy to all the three. In a complicated plot, the third Calendar gets engaged to her but goes off to India, and so the second one marries her and the first one continues to flirt with her. Resolution is reached with much difficulty with the death of the husband, Jenny marrying the former fiancé, and the remaining Calendar being married to another Dale sister.

One can see the wit of Lang and strands of feminism in his work from the above account. In another novel, *Ex-Wife*, Lang's protagonist is a divorced lady who lives happily and self-sufficiently with her son and her maid Mathilde who, as an anti-class statement, is also her mentor, and has a young man Mr Penderfield as a tenant who she reforms and who proposes to her to marry him.

To spoof the institution of marriage in *Three Calendars, Or Too Much Alike* and to have a divorced woman who is independent in *Ex-Wife* are examples of Lang's revolutionary worldview—and we must keep in mind that he was writing primarily for a Victorian audience.

One of the most famous accounts of Lang is his presenting the case of the Rani of Jhansi to the British government, defending her right to rule Jhansi, which she had lost owing to the Doctrine of Lapse. The Rani had employed him because of his fame amongst the Indians but he lost the case quickly, probably because of his notoriety among the British.[4] A striking example of John Lang's amalgamations can be gauged from the following observation. This is what Lang says of the Rani in *Household Words*:

> She was…rather stout but not too stout. Her face must have been very handsome when she was younger and even now it had many charms…The eyes were particularly fine and the nose delicately shaped…

Let me compare this with the description of Jenny Dale in *The Three Calendars* (1854). The novel was serialised in *The Mofussilite* in 1847, but I have not yet chanced upon this version. If the serial is the sa me as the book of 1854, it is a premonition, for Jenny Dale is described thus:

> Jennette was not slim and yet she was not stout; she was not short, nor was she tall. Her face was loveliness itself...Amongst a thousand pair of eyes would those of Jenny Dale attract attention. Their expression had a sorrowful cast—and yet her lively laugh belied the thought that she could be unhappy...Had her eyes not been so bewitching, one would have praised her... delicately formed nose.[5]

Lang was summoned by the Rani of Jhansi to save her kingdom that was going to be annexed by the Doctrine of Lapse. The order had already been passed in 1854, and Lang was called to do something so that the annexation could be annulled. Apart from detailing his journey to Jhansi and the circumstances of the case, Lang also describes the Rani's person, which is the only description by anyone in English documentation, and thus has been oft-quoted. This is the paragraph of Lang which has appeared severally over the last century, and by which he is known to Indian, and even British, historians:

> I had heard from the vakeel that the Ranee was a very handsome woman, of about six or seven and twenty years of age, and I was very curious indeed to get a glimpse of her; and whether it was by accident, or by design on the Ranee's part, I know not, my curiosity was gratified. The curtain was drawn aside by the little boy, and I had a good view of the lady. It was only for a moment, it is true; still I saw her sufficiently to be able to describe her. She was a woman of about the middle size—rather stout, but not too stout. Her face must have been very handsome when she was younger, and even now it had many charms—though, according to my idea of beauty, it was too round. The expression also was very good, and very intelligent. The eyes were particularly fine, and the nose very delicately shaped. She was not very fair, though she was far from black. She had no ornaments, strange to say, upon her person, except a pair of gold ear-rings. Her dress was a plain white muslin, so fine in texture, and drawn about her in such a way, and so tightly, that the outline of her figure was plainly discernible—and a remarkably fine figure she had. What spoilt her was her voice, which was something between a whine and a croak. When the purdah was drawn aside, she was, or affected to be, very much annoyed; but presently she laughed, and good-humouredly expressed a hope that a sight of her had not lessened my sympathy with her sufferings nor prejudiced her cause.[6]

Lang is probably making up a tale—which he usually does while retelling it—in hinting that he flirted with the Rani:

> 'On the contrary,' I replied, 'if the Governor-General could only be as fortunate as I have been, and for even so brief a while, I feel quite sure that he would at once give Jhansi back again to be ruled over by its beautiful Queen.'
>
> She repaid this compliment, and the next ten minutes were devoted to an interchange of such matters. I told her that the whole world resounded with the praises of her beauty and the greatness of her intellect; and she told me that there was not a corner of the earth in which prayers for my welfare remained unsaid.[7]

This little passage has led to remarkable conflations and conjectures in popular culture—in fact, a television serial about the Rani of Jhansi, the lawyer and the Rani playing cricket, and he falling in love with her.

Lang was clearly boasting to his British readership. He tells about the various presents that the Rani gave him:

> The Ranee presented me with an elephant, a camel, an Arab, a pair of greyhounds of great swiftness, a quantity of silks and stuffs (the production of Jhansi), and a pair of Indian shawls. I accepted these things with great reluctance, but the financial minister entreated me to take them, insomuch as it would wound the Ranee's feelings if I refused. The Ranee also presented me with a portrait of herself, taken by a native, a Hindoo.[8]

This portrait of Rani 'by a Hindoo' has been the subject of discussion for historians for a long time, but it has never been discovered. As conjectured earlier, perhaps it hangs on some wall in Burma, for the descendants of Lang's son, Livingston Lang, fled Burma during the Second World War and left behind most of their property.

After Lang had failed in his initial attempts to get justice for the Rani, the Rani still reposed her faith in him, and he was retained as her counsel. We have seen earlier that Lang stayed in England from 1854–59 to further his literary career. However, the immediate reason to go to England in 1854 may have been to plead the case of the Rani in England. *Allen's Indian Mail* tells in 1854:

> Mr John Lang has been retained by the Jhansi Maharanee. He is said to have received a large retaining fee, and to have stipulated to visit England in the furtherance of the prosecution of his client's claims, if necessary. The old lady urges the right of an adopted son of the late Maharajah's to the succession to the annexed state. The Jhansi territory, we need scarcely remind our readers, was annexed to the British dominions in March last, by Lord Dalhousie.[9]

Let us now go to the case of Jotee Persaud, which Lang had won for him, and impressed thus by his prowess, the Rani had invited him.

The Curious Case of the Lala,

or the Furious Face of the Nana

Till now, Lala Jotee Persaud has made cameo appearances in this work, but he is a 'side-hero' capable of stealing the thunder. And hence, let us begin by questioning Lala in the manner we had asked questioned Lang at the beginning.

Lala Jotee Persaud, who are you? Are you (1810–1871)? Is that all? Can I tell you that you have invaded my imagination for the last four years? Can I tell you that, for you, I dropped all conventional research methodologies to adopt a methodology of rhyming names? At different points of time: Are you Wanted Dead or Alive? Are you a bone-collector? Are you the cause of nightmares for the John Company? Are you the best friend of John Lang? Are you Nana Sahib? Are you an incorrigible sycophant of the John Company? Are you not on talking terms with John Lang? Are you a 'Seikh Gooroo'? Are you the destroyer of the Mathura Observatory? Do you bake bread for the English at your own home? Do you know that your name figures even in a German encyclopaedia?

Lala Jotee Persaud is all this and much more.

Apart from being a bone-collector, baker of breads, and the 'prince of contractors', Lala is also a terrific director of theatre and an actor, who put up a play in the midst of the Mutiny of 1857 outside the Agra Fort, with murder and mayhem happening all around at that very moment.

Even in after-life, Lala keeps rendering his services and appears as a spirit to throw light on history, and give moral lessons. Such was Lala's spiritual power that even when every building in his locality—including a mosque—was razed to the ground, Lala's house remained unscathed, shining, and pristine white. None of this is a joke; all this is gleaned from credible documented sources. The bibliography involving Lala can rival that involving any tall figure of the 19th century.

Today's obviously unknown Lala was very well-known in his time; even 40 years after the court case that had saved his skin, and had made John Lang grin. From ear-to-ear, and from hemisphere-to-hemisphere. For, Rolf Boldrewood knew about it in Australia in the 1890s, and Englishmen obviously knew about it, unable to forget the humiliation that Lang had caused them.

Jotee Persaud would have been called Ayodhya Prasad, which was shortened to Jyoti Prasad for convenience of the English ear. This, however, did not help, for the British ear could not well discern the Indian sounds, and so we have a host of very interesting interpretations of Indian names in the 19th century. Hence, Ayodhya Prasad came to be known as Ajoodia Pershad, or Jotee Persaud, or Joti Persad, with the second of these names being the most in circulation in the 19th century. It is interesting to note that even now there are many people with the surname 'Persaud'—these families chose to keep the British interpretation for their posterity. Of course, it is common knowledge that names like 'Chattopadhyaya' became Chatterji and 'Bandopadhyaya' became Banerji with colonial intervention; but Prasad/Persaud paradigm is lesser known.

Let us have one more bit of preliminary background information before we embark on the story of the Lala and the Nana.

Lala is an honorific for a man, generally of a trading caste and with considerable wealth. Another famous man with the same honorific is Lala Lajpat Rai, who died of lathi blows while protesting against the Simon Commission. However, the stereotype attached with the title 'Lala' is generally the figure of a trading man with a pot belly, who is quite wealthy, and even more miserly. This stereotype is still in currency—as it was in the 19th century—which we get to know from William Forbes-Mitchell's account. However, the title of Lala had much more respectability in the 19th century. According to William Chambers, in his 1894 piece, 'Lala' is 'a Persian title given to gentlemen of position in Upper India, equivalent to the honorary title of Doctor, in English, LL.D'[1]. This idea would probably amuse a modern Indian reader. It is interesting that the word Lala, according to Chambers, is of Persian origin, for the word is also used as an endearment for a little child, as for a trader, in Awadhi language, which is quite free from Persian influence.

Now the honorific 'Nana' was used for a Maratha king or chieftain. Nana Sahib of Cawnpore (present-day Kanpur), who was the thorn for British side during the 1857 Mutiny. The stereotype attached with the word, then, is obviously the image of a man who is warrior-like. It is important to understand the two stereotypes, for they have a bearing on the story which is about to ensue.

Dear reader, let me introduce you to the Lala in John Lang's words:

> And presently a native gentleman walked, or rather limped (for he was lame of the right leg) into the room, and made a very graceful salaam, first to the Rajah and then to myself. He was rather short in stature, but very stoutly built, and about forty years of age. His eyes were full of intelligence and vigour, and his features regular and well-shapen. His manners were easy, affable, unassuming, and modest, and his attire as plain and quiet as possible.[2]

This description in *Wanderings in India* is from 1850, for the case against Jotee Persaud had not yet begun according to this account. From this estimation of Lang—that he was about 40 years old—the birth year of Lala also has been fixed. Lala, therefore, would have been born around 1810. He died in the year 1871,[3] seven years after Lang's death.

The destiny of Lang and Lala are intertwined in the decade of 1850–1860, and their roads cross quite often during this period, despite Lang having been away in England in the second half of the decade. Lala owed his freedom and fame to Lang, while Lang owed prosperity in his legal career to Lala. It must also be remarked that it is not just Lang by whose name Lala's name was known, but the other way around, too. Here is a sample from *Littell's Living Age* journal of 1853:

> John Lang, once of the *Mofussilite*, and noted in connection with Jotee Persaud, has begun a trashy Indian tale, *The Wetherbys, Father and Son*, appearing in *Fraser's Magazine*.[4]

Raja Lall Singh, or Not Constant Even to His Own Villainies

Lang's description of Lala is from the first time they met at the latter's home in Agra. Lang knew not Lala; the meeting was incidental, for Lang had gone to meet Raja Lall Singh, who was staying at Lala's house. Lall Singh was a famous traitor of the Anglo Sikh Wars (1845–46, and 1848–49). I use the term famous, for notoriety needs prejudice on some side against the accused, but Raja Lall Singh had betrayed both the Indian and the British sides. Lang resonates the same idea:

> Notwithstanding his previous character—that of a sensualist and faithless intriguer; one, indeed, who had not been constant even to his own villainies—I could not help liking his conversation, which was humorously enlivened with imitations of English officers with whom he had come in contact, and was entertaining to the last degree.[5]

At the time Lang meets Raja, the latter is a student of surgery in Agra, and Lang has been informed 'that the Raja was already a skilful operator, and could take off an arm or a leg with surprising dexterity'[6]. In the house is a table covered with surgical instruments. When Lang's sight is transfixed at a pair of swords in wooden scabbards covered with rich green velvet, Lall Singh tells him, 'These have performed some curious operations in their time; but never in a hospital. They have been used chiefly for taking off heads'.

Lang is further informed of the owners of the swords—made of Damascus steel—Dhyan Singh and Heera Singh, who were both assassinated. 'They are…are sharper than any of these knives or scalpels. I have sent a number of swords to England to have them made into surgical instruments.'[7]

Even though Lall Singh matter-of-factly tells of Heera Singh's assassination, he doesn't divulge his own role in that. Heera Singh was one of the many mentors of Lall Singh who were betrayed by him, which is why Lang uses the expression, 'not constant even to his own villainies'.

After the death of Runjeet Singh[I] in 1839, the Sikh empire became a hotbed of intrigues with the kingdom being passed in a passing-the-parcel manner till the British decided to take advantage of the situation.

Lall Singh entered the Sikh court as a treasury writer in 1832, and was promoted to the rank of Darogah-i-Toshkhana[II] in 1839. He slowly made his way up till his time came under Heera Singh, who gave him the military command of a few districts. Lall Singh rose on the ladder of intrigues, and in 1843, engineered the murder of Beli Ram (in whose place he had become the Darogah earlier, and who later became his benefactor) and Gurmukh Singh. This was done to please Heera Singh, who should have known that raw ambition doesn't ally itself to any one individual. When Maharani Jind Kaur turned against Heera Singh, Lall Singh lost no time in allying with her and her brother Jawahar Singh to have Heera Singh murdered. Lall Singh went on to become maharani's closest adviser.[8] In 1845, when her brother was assassinated, Lall Singh became the Wazir in his place. In 1845, the East India Company

I Popularly known as Sher-e-Punjab, Ranjit Singh built an empire covering the northwestern Indian subcontinent in early 19th century. He is also the first owner of the Koh-i-Noor diamond.

II This would roughly translate as 'inspector of the treasury' carried out a campaign against the Sikhs at Ferozepore, and nearly lost the battle, when Lall Singh once again switched sides and let out secret war plans to the British Army. This time he betrayed his queen, who was also rumoured to have been his lover.

Lall Singh was deposed from his post of Wazir at Lahore but his military command remained, and this gave him an opportunity to betray the Sikhs again. At the Battle of Sabhraon in early 1846, he is alleged to have given out maps of the Sikh entrenchments to Captain Nicholson. Gulab Singh and Lall Singh betrayed their own armies; and the former would be made the ruler of Kashmir, while the latter would serve as the first minister under the resident-ship of Colonel Henry Lawrence.[9] Lall Singh was ecstatic climbing up the ladder so fast, and decided to bring about the downfall of Gulab Singh as well. His letters were discovered by the British; Lall Singh was tried, convicted, and sent to Agra to on a pension where he met John Lang in 1850[III].

At the meeting, Lang is charmed by Lall Singh's anecdotes and broaches the subject of Jind Kaur, the Maharani of the Sikhs. The raja tells that she had worn the Koh-i-Noor diamond a thousand times in her bracelet, and that she was proud of being able to make men subservient to her. According to Lall Singh, Jind Kaur was not pretty but had 'eyes that could charm like those of a snake, and a voice sweeter than that of a bird'[10]. Lall Singh, however, dismisses the speculation that she had great power over Runjeet Singh, or that he himself had any relationship with her beyond political intrigues.

Most historians, however, contend that the relationship between Lall Singh and the Maharani was quite intimate. According to Dr Hari Ram Gupta, the Maharani and Lall Singh had a clandestine affair for a long time, but 'it developed into a scandal so much so that on March 24, 1844, the panchayat of the Sikh army in the open darbar demanded the surrender of Lall Singh'[11].

III Even though the year is not mentioned. The first meeting could only be in 1850, for this is the first time Lang meets Lala Jotee Persaud—in the year before the trial of Persaud in an Agra court.

In his story 'Mahomeddan Mother' in *Wanderings in India*, he wonders if the woman who sits by the road in Mussoorie in any weather waiting to catch a glimpse of her child is Rani Chunda (based on Jind Kaur).

Lall Singh tells Lang that the Maharani was a plaything of Runjeet Singh, but only she could calm him when he had the horrors:

> Runjeet Singh began life as a petty chieftain...He acquired a vast kingdom, and had the most powerful army that the East ever saw, or will see. Whilst he went on conquering, shedding blood, and plundering, he was easy in his mind; but, when he found that he had got as much as he could manage, he stopped; and then came his disquiet. His great fear then...and his chief *horror* was that the Koh-i-noor would be carried off—that diamond which Runjeet Singh stole, and which the Ranee has worn a thousand times as a bracelet. That diamond which is now in the crown of England.[12]

Raja shows Lang a portrait of Runjeet Singh made by a famous painter of Lahore and tells him that the great king was blinded in one eye by small-pox, but with the other, he could stare unblinkingly for hours.

Raja Lall Singh staying at Lala Jotee Persaud's house in Agra when he met Lang is curious, for Lala's head was wanted by Raja only 'a few years' prior to the moment mentioned.

Lala Jotee Persaud Wanted Dead for One Lakh, or Wanted Alive for Two Lakhs

The erstwhile Raja introduces Lala to Lang saying that he lives in the house of Lala:

> Only a few years ago, I offered a reward of a lac of rupees (ten thousand pounds) for his head, or two lacs to anyone who would bring him alive to my tent.[13]

Raja tells Lang that if Lala had been caught, it would have changed the affairs of the country, 'for this gentleman (Lala) was the contractor for the British army; and if I had got hold of him, the army could not have been supplied'[14].

This is a dubious claim, for Raja had already distinguished himself twice by betraying the Sikh army, and been awarded with the first-ministership of Lahore by the East India Company.

If Lala was secured alive, he could have been made to feed the Sikh armies instead, and at his own expense. This would also have paid the reward for his capture—therefore the bounty on his 'live' head was more than his 'dead' head. Lall Singh goes on to tell that several people did bring in 'cut heads'! 'This (the lakh rupee prize) was claimed by several who brought in heads, alleging that each was the head of Lala the contractor; but the attempted imposition was discovered, and the perpetrators were themselves decapitated.'[15]

Thus, quite a few heads rolled in pursuit of Jotee Persaud—of both the hunted and the hunters, while Persaud kept supplying provisions to the British. The hunters were hunted for their dishonesty (of which Lall Singh himself was a master), and the hunted were hunted in pursuit of a prize of a lakh rupees.

The more interesting time is when the Lala was 'wanted', yet again in 1857.

Nana Wanted, or Lala Haunted

Nana Sahib of Bithoor, was the scourge of the East India Company in 1857, and thus a fascinating figure for the British journalists. *The Illustrated London News*, which was hunting for a picture of Nana, called up all their British acquaintances regarding the same. There was no portrait of Nana available. Success eluded them till an artist reached John Lang. The story I am going to relate had been a secret for a long time; until William Forbes-Mitchell recounted it in his 1893 book *Reminiscences of the Great Mutiny: 1857–59*[16]. The following tale is gleaned from the account of Forbes-Mitchell.

Jotee Persaud, as stated, was a commissariat contractor for the East India Company's army throughout the second Anglo–Sikh War. When he presented his bill of three crore rupees, (Forbes-Mitchell has the amount wrong—it was 57 lakh rupees) the government blamed him of fraud and slapped a case against him. Lala sent a message to John Lang, who was Lala's barrister friend. The trial was held in December 1851 (Forbes-Mitchell has got the month wrong—the trial was held in April 1851), in the artillery mess in Meerut. Lang, who had taken six months to reach India on the ship *Nile*, cooled his heels in weariness and listened to the prosecution with a deadpan expression for days. Having done so, he began his cross examination:

> Everything went swimmingly with the prosecution till Mr Lang began his cross-examination of the witnesses, he having reserved his privilege till he heard the whole case for the prosecution. Directly the cross-examination commenced, the weakness of the Government case became apparent. I need not now recall how the commissary-general, the deputy commissary-general, and their assistants were made to contradict each other, and to contradict themselves out of their own mouths. Mr Lang, who appeared in court every day in his wig and gown, soon became a noted character in Meerut.[17]

The night before Lang was to sum up his defence, a few officers in the Artillery Mess asked Lang his opinion about the commission. Forbes-Mitchell tells:

> Not being a teetotaller, Mr Lang may have been at the time somewhat under the influence of 'John Exshaw' who was the

> ruling spirit in those days, and he replied that the whole batch, president and members, including the judge-advocate general, were a parcel of 'd---d soors'[IV].[18]

On hearing this opinion, several members of the audience challenged Lang if he could voice the same opinion in front of the jury, in the court. Lang accepted the challenge, a wager was laid, whereby every member involved deposited a sum of thousand rupees to an umpire. The following day, Lang made his address by 'pulling the evidence for the prosecution to shreds'. Forbes-Mitchell recounts the address, 'somewhat as follows—I can only give the purport':

> Gentlemen of the commission…I now place the dead carcass of this shameful case before you in all its naked deformity, and the more we stir it up the more it stinks! The only stink in my long experience that I can compare it to is the experience gained in the saloon of the *Nile* on my passage out to India the day after a pig was slaughtered. We had a pig's cheek at the head of the table [indicating the president of the commission]; we had a roast leg of pork on the right [pointing to another member]; we had a boiled leg, also pork, on the left [indicating a third member]'; and so on he went till he had apportioned out the whole carcass of the supposed pig amongst the members of the commission. Then, turning to the judge-advocate-general, who was a little man dressed in an elaborately frilled shirt, and his assistant, who was tall and thin, pointing to each in turn, Mr. Lang proceeded,—And for side-dishes we had chitterlings on one side, and sausages on the other. In brief, the whole saloon smelt of nothing but pork: and so it is, gentlemen, with this case. It is the Government of India who has ordered this trial. It is for the interest of that Government that my client should be

IV damned pigs

> convicted...In brief, the whole case against my client is nothing but pork, and a disgrace to the Government of India, and to the Honourable East India Company, who have sanctioned this trial, and who put every obstacle in my way to prevent my coming out to defend my client. I repeat my assertion that the case is a disgrace to the Honourable Company and the Government of India, and to every servant of that Government who has had any finger in the manufacture of this pork-pie.

The judge-advocate-general declared he felt ashamed to be connected with the case. The result was that Jotee Persaud was acquitted on all counts, and decreed to be entitled to his claims in full.

Lang had won the case and the bet.

Forbes-Mitchell recounted the events but did not check his dates rigorously as he was writing a memoir. The trial commenced at the end of March 1851 and lasted till 12 April, and is documented in various newspapers including *The Mofussilite, Delhi Gazette,* and *Allen's Indian Mail.* Lala was placed under house arrest sometime in September 1850; he obtained leave and went to Calcutta to file his suit for recovery of the money that East India Company owed him in October;[19] Lang was in Shimla, from where he appointed Wilby as the editor of his newspaper, *The Mofussilite.*[20]

Lang perhaps concocted the story of his journey aboard *Nile* because he had to make up the plot about calling the members of the jury pigs. Forbes-Mitchell tells that Lala Jotee Persaud was so impressed by Lang that he gave him an honorarium of three lakh rupees (equal to £30,000 in those days) in addition to his fees for the case. Lala gave Lang a portrait of himself painted by a native painter of great repute. Forbes-Mitchell says, 'The portrait was enshrined in a jewelled frame, worth another twenty-five thousand rupees.'[21]

Lang carried this portrait wherever he went 'to the day of his death'. as a good-luck charm.

During the Mutiny of 1857, there was a great demand in England for a picture of Nana Sahib, the 'arch-assassin of Cawnpore'. A journalist from *The Illustrated London News* went to Lang asking him if he had a picture of Nana Sahib. Forbes-Mitchell says that '...then, as now, all Indians were princes to the British public'. The journalist, who had come to Lang, assumed it was Nana Sahib portrayed in the picture—the one that Lang carried everywhere—for the frame of the portrait was bejewelled. Forbes-Mitchell writes:

> ...when he saw it he declared it was just the thing he wanted. Mr. Lang protested, pointing out that the picture no more resembled the Nana of Bithoor than it did her Gracious Majesty the Queen of England; that neither the dress nor the position of the person represented in the picture could pass in India for a Mahratta chief. The artist declared he did not care for people in India: he required the picture for the people of England. So he carried it off to the engraver, and in the next issue of *The Illustrated London News* the picture of Ajoodia Pershad[V], the commissariat contractor, appeared as that of the Nana Sahib.[22]

Forbes-Mitchell saw the portrait in December 1857, he does not recount the date. However, inquiries with *The Illustrated London News* confirm that the date of publication of the portrait was 26 September 1857. I am indebted to John Weedy of *The Illustrated London News* for sending me the page from the newspaper.

People who knew Nana said the picture did not resemble Nana in anyway. People who knew Jotee Persaud said that Nana resembled Jotee a lot! Lang lived in fear of Lala ever getting know that he was party to the faux pas:

V William Forbes-Mitchell calls Lala Jotee Persaud 'Ajoodia Pershad' throughout his recounting.

> When those in India who had known the Nana saw it, they declared it had no resemblance to him whatever, and those who had seen Ajoodia Pershad declared that the Nana was very like Ajoodia Pershad. But no one could understand how the Nana could ever have allowed himself to be painted in the dress of a Marwaree banker. To the day of his death John Lang was in mortal fear lest Ajoodia Pershad should ever come to hear how his picture had been allowed to figure as that of the arch-assassin of the Indian Mutiny.[23]

Meanwhile, the poor Lala helped the British again with provisions at the fort of Agra during the height of the Mutiny.

Nana, a martial man, passed off as a Lala—the stock image of Lala being that of a pot-bellied merchant—would have created quite a joke. Lang had recounted the tale to Forbes-Mitchell; Lang may well have made up that he had protested to the journalist that the picture was not of Nana. Lang may have, for the sake of this joke, very deliberately given the picture to the journalist. (see plate 6)

The article accompanying the picture tells that the picture has been sent by Major O' Gandini. However, there is no such Major recorded in the government gazettes. Neither does the name of such a person appear anywhere in the accounts of the Mutiny of 1857. Lang would obviously have wanted anonymity, and he was fond of aliases.

A year after the publication of Forbes-Mitchell's book, *The Saturday Review* expresses doubt about the Major as well, with a question mark:

> We happen to have a file of the *Illustrated London News* for 1857, and find there, in an issue of September, a gorgeous portrait of the so-called Nana. It was brought, the letterpress says, *by Major Gandini (?)* from India. To our thinking it is a compound of two or three typical natives made up to suit English notions.

> Sergeant Forbes-Mitchell's version may be true, in substance, all the same.[24]

There were several Americans who got killed at Kanpur during the Mutiny. A contemporary American ladies' magazine, also contends that the picture is not of Nana Sahib. The magazine perpetuates a set of stock Oriental images which, ironically, fits in with the stereotype of Lala:

> The name of the author of the Cawnpore massacre is, of course, well known.
>
> The picture of him here presented was drawn by Major O' Gandini...; but as it originally appeared, it was inaccurate representing him with flowing beard and long hair, whereas, like all the Mahratta people, to whom he (Nana) belonged, he was clean shaven in both head and chin, the moustache alone remaining. He was fat, with that unhealthy corpulence which marks the Eastern voluptuary, of sallow complexion, and middle height. He did not speak a word of English. His age at the time of massacre was about thirty-six years.[25]

Some scholars who have worked on John Lang have referred to this story (Victor Crittenden and Rick Hosking) by William Forbes-Mitchell, but no one has ever wondered who the engraver of *The Illustrated London News* was.

The engraver was none other than Henry Vizetelly, a friend of Lang's, and the one who published Lang's novel *Plot and Passion.* Vizetelly tells that the 'Indian mutiny which broke out in the summer... led to my making the acquaintance of John Lang, a smart and prolific contributor to the light literary publications of the day'[26]. In his memoir, Vizetelly writes that Lang had given him the portrait, and does not make any allusion to Lang having denied that it was the Nana's portrait:

> Nana Sahib was one of Lang's especial friends and had presented him with his portrait—a large oil-painting—for which he had sat to the European portrait painter to the King of Oude. This portrait Lang sent me for reproduction on a large scale in the 'Illustrated Times' and its publication excited a good deal of curiosity at that time.[27]

Vizetelly perhaps did not chance upon Forbes-Mitchell's work, or he would have written something about it. It is clear from Vizetelly's account that he was told by Lang the portrait was painted by a European portrait painter, and Nana Sahib himself presented the portrait to Lang. In *Wanderings in India*, Lang mentions of a portrait of Rani of Jhansi gifted to him by her; he does not refer to any portrait of Nana Sahib. The 'European portrait painter to the King of Oude' in question is Mr Beechey[VI]. Lang mentions Beechey in *Wanderings in India* as having painted portraits of Ally Nucky Khan, the prime minister of Wajid Ali Shah.[28] Beechey is not known to have drawn any portrait of Nana Sahib. Had he done so, the British people would have been able to procure it easily.

According to Forbes-Mitchell's account, Lang told him that a journalist from *The Illustrated London News* had come looking for Nana Sahib's picture, and assumed Jotee Persaud's portrait to be that of Nana's; and that Lang had told the journalist that the person in the picture resembled Nana only as much as he resembled the British queen. In Vizetelly's personal memoir he writes that Lang had sent Vizetelly the portrait with the above particulars already detailed.

VI Sir William Beechey (1753-1839) was a leading English portraitist and had the royal patronage. Beechey has notably painted portraits of Queen Charlotte, King George III, and Prince William Frederick, the Duke of Gloucester.

Clearly, Lang made up a story for Vizetelly about the European painter, as also about the painting being that of Nana Sahib. In the confessional story to Vizetelly, Lang makes it out to be a comedy of errors, and hides the story of his prank of passing off the Lala as Nana. Forbes-Mitchell, under an oath of secrecy to Lang, never mentioned the story to anyone till both Lang and Lala were dead for long. Lang had a spirit for such pranks, and his 'larrikin' nature keeps surfacing every now then

Vizetelly also tells about Lang's incorrigible alcoholism:

> Lang's literary career in England though brilliant in its way, was but brief. In a very few years he succumbed to an insatiable craving for champagne at all hours of the day and night, after this pleasant but insidious beverage had unstrung every nerve in his wiry frame.[29]

And so, Lala Jotee Persaud was 'Wanted Dead or Alive' twice. Once, as himself—dead for one lakh rupees, and alive for two lakh rupees. The second time, as Nana Sahib—dead or alive at any cost. Once wanted by the Sikh army; and the second time made 'WANTED' by his advocate.

Apart from being a much-wanted man, the Lala also holds the distinction of being a bone collector.

Bones In The Attic, or Gold That Made Lala Ecstatic

In the account given in *Wanderings in India*, while Lang and Raja Lall Singh discuss Runjeet Singh and his kingdom at Lala Jotee Persaud's house, a workman announces the discovery of another house under the earth while digging for the root of a vine-trellis and that 'in it had been found several gold and silver coins'. Here Raja Lall Singh tells Lang:

> This quarter of Agra was formerly inhabited by persons of the highest rank. Where we are now standing was, no doubt, once

> the site of a palace; and these walls are those of the ty-khana—a vault beneath the dwelling from which the light is excluded. In these dark places are usually perpetrated what you English call 'dark deeds'.[30]

Lang then rushes to Jatnee Bagh. According to Lang, 20 workmen commenced their labour to get to 'the bottom of the apartment in the ty-khana[VII]'. In the ty-khana, Lang finds a foot-wide ledge on the wall in the vault that was about six feet high from the floor (and carried up therefrom). 'This ledge, which was of brick and plaster, resembled a huge mantelpiece, which was continued from one end of the apartment to the other.'

To the narrator's/Lang's surprise and horror, he discovered that a human had been bricked into this wall. He describes the corpse as this: 'The skin was still upon the bones, which were covered with a costly dress of white muslin, spangled all over with gold; around the neck was a string of pearls; on the wrists and ankles were gold bangles, and on the feet were a pair of slippers, embroidered all over with silver wire or thread; such slippers as only Mahommedan women of rank or wealth can afford to wear. The body resembled a well-preserved mummy. The features were very distinct, and were those of a woman whose age could not at the time of her death have exceeded eighteen or nineteen years. The head was partially covered with the white dress. Long black hair was still clinging to the scalp, and was parted across the forehead and carried behind the ears.'[31]

Raja Lall Singh remarks that it might well have been a case of jealousy where the jealous husband punished her by entombing her alive. According to Lall Singh, the Hindus, as well as Muslims, punished their wives in that way. The narrator is shocked that the practice still was in vogue in the mid-19th century.

VII A dungeon-like vault under a dwelling to where no daylight enters, but where valuables are hidden.

Orders were given to the workmen to remove with great care the whole of the ledge. Four more bodies are found in what Lang describes as 'that awful spectacle'.

> One of the number (of skeletons) was a young man, who from his dress and the jewels on his finger-bones must have been a person of high rank; perhaps the lover of one, or both, of the young women; for he had been bricked up between two of them. The others were evidently those of confidential servants; old women, for they had grey hair. They possibly had been cognisant, or were supposed to be cognisant, of whatever offence the others had been deemed guilty.[32]

The bodies had been lying thus, Lang conjectures, for over a hundred and fifty years. The air has a speedy effect on them, and everything falls into a heap of dust. The jewellery, worth over a thousand pounds, is collected to be handed over to Lala Jotee Persaud.

Although a compelling account, it is difficult to establish its veracity. Lang was obviously writing to a British audience, and would have sold to them a set of stock Oriental images. Ruskin Bond, the Indian writer who discovered Lang, describes Lang as a *guppoo*; and Victor Crittenden, a biographer of Lang contends that Lang never told a good story without improving it. *Guppoo* is a Hindi word that is rather untranslatable, but the connotation is that of a teller of tales who would revel in making up stories and exaggerating them.

There is no reason to disbelieve Lang's account here but through such accounts, one sees the complexity and ambivalence of Lang's writings. On the one hand, Lang is bitterly critical of the British administration in India. On the other hand, he paints India as an esoteric land full of vaults and mesmerisers. Lang can be appropriated either way.

In a 2008 newspaper article, Brij Khandelwal wrote about the descendants of many of the houses of erstwhile royalty who were in a state of penury. According to Khandelwal, real estate developers are buying these properties, razing them to rubble, and constructing new buildings in their place. 'The Jat House and Jatnee Bagh are under threat, as are many other grand mansions of the city,' he wrote.[33]

In an interview, Khandelwal told me that Jatnee Bagh (Lala Jotee Persaud's house) was indeed a heritage structure, though not listed by any government agency for conservation: 'Now it is largely gone, market complexes have come up, and one by one all the structures within the Jatnee Bagh complex, which once used to be an industrial cluster of a Britisher Mr John, after whose name Jeoni Mandi was established, have been demolished. Only the name remains…Within the Jatnee Bagh industrial cluster, there once used to be a dozen industries which employed thousands of workers. Only the concrete chimneys remain as reminder of a bygone era.'[34]

The John mentioned here is certainly not John Lang, for Lang had died six years before Lala Jotee Persaud. The property belonged to A. John, who put up three mills known as John's Mills.[35] The huge garden-house seems to have gone into his possession soon after Lala's death. One would think that over a period of time, this place would have metamorphosed from John's to Jeoni, but the place was known by the name of Jeoni Mandi as far back as 1892, and it housed the National Book House then.[36]

Even now, the complex is home to the office of a newspaper, *Sainik*.[37] This newspaper appears to have been very active in the early 20th century, publishing nationalistic articles with great zeal. William Gould tells about the year 1930: '…in the week leading up to the 1930 Holi festival, the daily *Sainik*, run by Paliwal, ran a number of nationalistic articles based on Holi, one of which reported that Gandhi had undertaken to dye the bureaucracy with splashes of his blood; that now the people would play Holi as Lakshmana had played with Shurpanakha.'[38] This seems to be a rather violent image for the Messiah of non-violence.

Mosque Erased, Or Lala Praised, or, Jotee And Chuppatee, or The Making of a Roy Bahadoor

After winning the Lala's case, John Lang was carried by people on their shoulders in a procession. This was a symbolic victory over the tyrannical British rule for Indian people. Even after this, the Company delayed payments it owed to Lala, and this cause was taken up by Lang in *The Mofussilite* several times. However, Lala remained steadfastly loyal to the British Indian government, and bailed them out of trouble once more in 1857 by supplying victuals and provisions for the British at the Agra Fort that was besieged by the Indian mutineers.

The 'natives' who had attached so much importance to the case and made Jotee Persaud a symbol of their cause barely knew that Lala would want to have nothing to do with them. The 'mutineers' or the 'insurgents' applied to Lala to help them in 1857, but he instead reported the matter to the British authorities.

At this juncture, Jotee Persaud, to whom Company still owed a lot of money, offered them active help. He, along with Captain Chalmers, was instrumental in forming the ingenious Camel Troops. G. Dodd writes this in his account about 1857:

> ...Further to the northwest, the region around Delhi was nearly all in British hands, and the city itself wholly so—all the mutinous regiments being far away. The authorities, after Delhi had remained several months peacefully in their hands, resolved on the formation of a camel corps, under a peculiar system of organisation. It was completed by the end of March, by a native named Lala Jotee Pershaud, under the superintendence of Captain Chalmers, assistant commissary-general. The camels, 400 in number, were selected with great care, in the Bikaneer district. The drivers were armed each with a sword and fusil; and each camel was fitted to carry a European soldier

> if necessary. The drivers, equivalent to troopers or cavalry-men, were carefully selected from the natives of Rajpootana. The purpose in view was to form a corps of armed men capable of moving with great rapidity to any spot where their services might be urgently needed.[39]

Jotee Persaud even spread rumours in Agra about the defeat of the mutinying Indian troops to boost the morale of the British side that was nearly beaten at Agra. *The Annals of the Rebellion* published in 1859 reproduces the minutes of a meeting:

> There was no intimation given to Colonel Greathead, by any of the authorities, on the morning of the 10th, that the enemy were re-crossing. The city rumour to that effect, brought in by the **Seikh Gooroo Jotee Pershad**[VIII], Esree Pershad and other men whose loyalty has not been doubted, was unquestionably occasioned by the march through the town of Greathead's imposing column. The town's people never dreamt that the Dholepore rebels would have the audacity to run their heads against *such* a rock as that splendid force.

It is amusing to see the various names and attributions of Jotee Persaud. In this note he is called a 'Seikh Gooroo'. Jotee is called a Parsee banker in *The Spectator.*[40] Whether the British officers knew anything or not about who Jotee was, they certainly knew his name and where his loyalty rested. An August 1857 government memorandum elucidates how Jotee Persaud helped British campaign against mutineers in Agra, Aligarh and Hathras.[41]

The biggest help that Jotee Persaud rendered the British in 1857, however, was victualling the Agra Fort. There are scores of mid-19th century books remembering the services of 'Our friend Jotee'. John

VIII Emphasis mine

Lang himself tells in *Wanderings in India* that Agra could not have been held without the help of Lala. He points out to the whole context without naming himself as Lala's lawyer, bringing out the irony of the situation, that while Jotee's victory in the court case was seen as an emancipating agency for the Indians, it was Jotee who helped the British attain victory in Agra. Lang writes:

> The contractor, however, was eventually acquitted, and the Government paid the bill. But, to this day, the natives of India believe that the object of the Government was to cheat their creditor; while the officers, civil and military, are equally sanguine that it was 'the honour of the family' that led to the most extraordinary and protracted trial that ever was known in India, and which was emphatically denounced, by the press and public of every country in Europe, as absurd, unjust, and shameful. Nevertheless, Jotee Persaud cannot have harboured any revenge for the wrongs (involving disgrace and dishonour) which were heaped upon him; for it is he who has fed, for several months, the five thousand Christians during their incarceration in the fortress of Agra; and, amongst the number of civilians there shut up, is the gentleman who conducted the prosecution on the behalf of the Government, and who, in the execution of his duty, strove very hard indeed for a verdict of guilty! Without Jotee Persaud we could not have held Agra![42]

Jotee Persaud perhaps got his revenge by having at his mercy one of the jury members who wanted to incarcerate Lala. Perhaps the merchant did not give a thought to it. He, unlike Lang, was always pragmatic enough to think about his business rather than personal scores. He had become friends with Raja Lall Singh who had wanted him dead or alive; and he had made peace with the British who had wanted to see him in jail.

Lang was not in India during the Mutiny. It would have been very interesting to have had Lang's first-hand account of the matters. He might have written a few pieces, but it is not yet discernible to me which ones. The incumbent editor of *The Mofussilite* was bothered a lot by the mutineers, and he wrote an article in *Household Words* detailing the same. Lang, though critical of the East India Company—both its civil and military wings—somehow romanticised the British in the battlefield. All his novels set in India follow a formula: British man falls in love, has to go away in India, where there would be ample scenes to underscore Lang's point about the corruption in British Indian military and civil services. This would be followed by a war, which would be horrible, and there would be a general denouncing of the war, but the British soldiers would fight gallantly nonetheless.

Had Lang been in India in 1857, his mixed feelings would have been sorely tested.

Lang's relationship with the military was a curious one; and so was the military's relationship with the Lala. In 1851, most of the jury members were members of the army who had wanted to send the Lala to jail; and yet whenever they were in need, they turned to him. From this angle, this is a relationship of 'friend only in need'. In 1857, the British coffers were near-empty in Agra, and promissory notes were of little value. Most merchants and private bankers refused help. It was in this dire need that the British turned to the Lala again; but him helping them was also a matter of need. All the money the Lala had was British money; it would have been of no use if the John Company lost.

Robert Montgomery Martin, in his book *Our Indian Empire*, has a chapter on the 'Services of Lala Jotee Persaud'. Martin says that in May 1857, the 44th and 67th N.I regiments had been disarmed, and in ignominy, the soldiers had availed themselves 'permission to return home'. The Neemuch mutineers were in high spirits and marching towards Agra. Sir Patrick Grant, the acting commander-in-chief, in his memorandum had suggested that Akbar's Fort, built in 1570 could withstand any attack, and that the only way for the English to lose was if they were besieged and starved to surrender.

It is here that the Lala's crucial role comes. The British applied to various merchants and failed in procuring provisions. Their 'prince of contractors' came to the rescue. Martin tells:

> Provisions for six months had been secured, through the intervention of a famous commissariat contractor, Lala Jotee Persaud...when recourse was had to the Lala, whose previous most important services in the Sutlej campaign had been requited by an action for embezzlement. Happily for us, he had been acquitted, and the money due to him repaid at last. Perhaps, as a writer in the *Quarterly Review* suggests, 'he forgot our ingratitude in our justice.'[IX] The fact of his being an extensive proprietor of government paper, doubtless tended to make him desirous of the maintenance, or rather restoration, of British rule: but it is certain that he stood almost alone, loyal and friendly, in the midst of a disaffected population; never wavered even when our fortunes and exchequer were at the lowest, and continued to inform the authorities of the intelligence he received...at a time when Agra was the one remaining stronghold of the North-West Provinces, and stood 'surrounded, as it were, by a perfect sea of mutiny'[X].[43]

Thomas Frost, who wrote a book just after the Mutiny, wrote that '...our old friend Jotee Persaud has again shown himself the best commissariat officer in the world, by laying in, within thirty hours of receiving the order, stores and provisions to last 10,000 men for a month'[44].

IX Footnoted by Martin as 'Letter of one of the Agra garrison.—Times, April 4th, 1837.'

X Footnoted by Martin as 'See communication already quoted, made by Umballah correspondent to *the Times, Oct.* 26th, 1857.'

In such an hour of crisis for the British, Lala Jotee Persaud not only supplied food to the British, but also took care of their palette. If he had sublet the matter to someone else, the besieged white populace would have got 'chupatties' to eat, which they loathed. Jotee, therefore, had bread baked at his own house. Martin tells:

> Apprehensions were expressed by many persons regarding the consequences of the compression of so large and heterogeneous a multitude within the fort, at the worst season of the year; but the excellent arrangements made by Mr. Colvin, prevented much of the suffering which must otherwise have arisen. The want of bread was severely felt at Lucknow: women and children, the sick and the wounded, grew to loathe the sight of chupatties. But at Agra, after the battle, the first objects seen 'entering the gates, when the panic-stricken authorities ventured to open them wide enough to admit a mouse, were carts of bread, that the Lala [Jotee Persaud] had baked at his own house in the city, for the troops and people who were shut up[XI].[45]

When reading this book of Montogomery Martin, one is struck by his change of tone when he is talking about the mutineers. On the same page where he tells with great concern about women and children loathing the sight of chapattis, he matter-of-factly, almost in a celebratory tone, tells about the hanging of the natives:

> A body of troops was sent out to make a demonstration in the city; rows of gibbets were erected, and many natives hanged. The relatives or friends of the sufferers were at first allowed to take away the bodies: the permission was

XI Martin footnotes this as 'Letter from 'one of the late garrison at Agra.'—*Times*, April 4th, 1858.'

> rescinded because they were carried round the walls, decked with garlands of flowers, and reverenced as the relics of martyrs.[46]

Here, one is reminded of Lady Sale's journal mentioned in the chapter on *Will He Marry Her?* Lady Sale was reported having been held by Afghans for ransom during the Afghan War (1839–42) in which the whole of the British contingent was virtually wiped out. In her journal printed in 1853, not only did she refute the claim of her being kidnapped, but put the blame on the British as much as the Afghans for the gruesome war. One is also reminded of the recent comment of Sir V.S. Naipaul that men are better writers than women. In this case, Lady Sale seems to have been far more reasonable and better than Montgomery Martin.

After Agra had been restored to colonial rule, the British authorities once again tried to tighten the noose on Lala, albeit this time he had very strong support in the army that owed its success in great measure to him.

In 1858, the matter of supplies by Jotee Persaud came into question by Commissariat Committee of the House of Commons in Britain, and Lala like in 1851 was once again almost in the dock, but this time the military threw its weight behind him. Colonel McMurdo answered in Lala's defence. To the question if the native agents were remunerated, the colonel answered that there was no salary for them, but they were entitled to the profits. The committee put several uncomfortable questions like advertising a contract before giving it, and the issue of Jotee being masqueraded as merely an agent not supposed to make profits, while he was actually a contractor making huge profits. To all this, the colonel and his compatriots answered obstinately without an apology.[47]

An army officer writing a couple of decades after the Mutiny justified the military rallying behind Lala, for 'one Joti Persad with influence equal to the occasion was better than half-a-dozen Joti Persads of less ability and influence'[48]. The writer, however, says that Lala was, to a certainty, adept at plundering the government. The feeling about the great contractor remained a mixed one even in hindsight.

The military stood by the side of Jotee before the mutineers took hold of Agra, too, primarily because he was the only wealthy native friend on their side. It was military necessity to raze down several buildings to secure the Agra Fort. Jotee's new house stood in the way as well. Mark Thornhill tells the story of how important Lala was and how he was pampered by the John Company:

> The fort having been erected before the days of artillery was deficient in many of the modern requirements - among others, it had no glacis. On one side the town, on another side the ruins, came close up to the walls, while the ravines would afford shelter for any amount of assailants. Colonel Fraser had of late been very busy in remedying this defect, so far as it was capable of remedy. He had blown up the ruins, and sloped off the ravines, and now he proposed to demolish the houses. It was on this issue that dissensions arose.[49]

Thornhill tells that these houses were mud hovellings, and generally belonged to natives who were party to the Mutiny. The civil authorities, however, being generally opposed to the military, argued for the cause of the civilians. Everyone on the British side gradually got involved in the dispute, taking one side or the other. Finally, a solution was reached, with the government agreeing to pay compensation to those whose houses would be levelled. This, however, resulted in dissatisfaction on both the sides. The English people and the Christians grumbled because no favours had been shown to them, while the families of the mutineers were being paid handsomely. Those who got the compensation were distraught because the promissory notes would not mean anything in case the British lost—in short, it was waste paper. Out of need they sold these notes to wealthy merchants for whatever they could get, and they indeed got little. Of these merchants, our protagonist Lala may well have been one.

Another dispute arose because of an old mosque which Thornhill describes as 'very ugly, but large, massive and covering a great extent of the ground'. The Muslims petitioned to civil authorities who 'retained their partiality for the Mahommedans, and notwithstanding all that occurred and their belief'[50]. Thornhill tells that the military necessity was forgotten and there was political rallying. 'One party wanted the mosque destroyed because it was a mosque, the other party for that reason wanted to preserve it,' Thornhill writes.

What would be a nightmare for any government today that is even thinking of touching a religious place, seems to have been a rather easy affair in mid-19th century without ruffling too many feathers.

The engineers remained firm, since they contended that it was essential for the security of the Agra Fort, and decided to get a 'futwah' issued so that the demolition could be achieved without a fuss. Thornhill tells that the 'futwah' was procured on the precedent that Emperor Alamguire had pulled down a mosque that was sheltering the Marathas, and the doctors of law had sanctioned that Almighty would forgive this act since it was for the destruction of the enemies. This precedent, however, was no worthy precedent since this 'futwah' ensured that the rule of the 'infidel' Christians would continue. The 'futwah' was obtained nonetheless. The English were unhappy because they had to stoop down to the colonised man and let him decide the limits of the infidel ruler in matters of faith. The Muslims believed that the 'futwah' had been extorted; and Thornhill adds that the Cazee (Qazi) who had issued the 'futwah' himself encouraged this view.

Now comes the story of Jotee Persaud, whose new house was right next to the mosque. This episode, one deems it fit to quote ad verbatim:

> The demolition of the mosque was regarded as a defeat for those of the higher officials who had desired its preservation, and, as these were not at the time popular, their defeat gave satisfaction. They, however, had a consolation. The military favourite was Jotee Pershand, the Commissariat Contractor, and he had lately erected a very fine house in the suburb, and this, of course, would come down with the rest; and thus though Jotee Pershand had escaped arrest, he would suffer injury. In this expectation they were doomed to disappointment. The preliminary difficulties having been arranged, any army of workmen were let loose in the suburb. For some days they were concealed in a cloud of dust, out of which occasionally came sounds of explosions. When the dust cleared away, the mosque had gone, the suburb had gone, but to the indignation of the civil authorities the house of Jotee Pershand appeared as before—bright with fresh paint, white and triumphant.
>
> To the remonstrances made to them, the military, the story went, returned a very curt answer, to the effect that if the enemy approached the house would be destroyed, and that in the meanwhile it could remain as a reward to its owner for his good services; and with this unsatisfactory explanation the civil authorities had to rest content.[51]

And so, the mosque was razed. But the explosions did not even graze Jotee's pristine white house where bread was baked later on to save the starving population from chapattis. Jotee Persaud was suitably rewarded and he became a 'Roy Bahadoor'. The title, as an Indian reader would know, was bestowed on natives who were steadfastly loyal to the crown and rendered useful services to it.[52]

Lala was also rewarded with property in Gwalior for his services, and had a very positive opinion among the British populace by now. Malcom Lewin wrote in 1858:

> He it was who furnished the means which all others had refused; he it was that enabled the Government to confront the enemy.
>
> What reward Jotee Persaud will receive, for this second act of devotion to the British Government, is yet undecided. It is believed that the Indian Government has offered to confer on him certain confiscated lands in Gwalior, the title to which will probably hereafter become a question with the ruler of that state. It would be difficult to picture a case of deeper humiliation, than the one sustained by the British Government, at the hands of the noble minded man whose conduct is here referred to.[53]

That is roughly the end of Lala's story, but not quite. In the wireless age it is tough to imagine how the story of a court case would have remained in the imagination of people for a good 50 years, but it was so. Lala's ghost keeps appearing every now and then. Lang, had he lived longer, would have thoroughly enjoyed these stories, and perhaps written some himself, having had a great propensity for writing such stories.

The Sable Prince, or the White Interloper; or the Two Famous Cyclopaedia Men

When Lang and Lala first met, Lang was yet to taste professional success in the arena of law, and Lala was in dire straits. Within months of that, Lang became a household name as the white man capable of fighting injustice, and Lala became a symbol of the wronged nice man. In the times to come, both became the cause for each other's fame. Lang was known as the lawyer connected with the great contractor, and Lala was known as close to the editor of *The Mofussilite*, and the very incorrigible and successful lawyer.

In their first meeting, skeletons adorned with jewellery were discovered Lala's Jatnee Bagh house vault. The skeletons fell, and the gold went to Lala. This metaphorically became the fate of Lang and Lala as well. Lang kept troubling the British administration and became an eyesore for them. He took to heavy drinking, perhaps because of his personal problems—that might be too hackneyed a way of looking at it—Lang died young, at the age of 48. Lala, on the other hand, canonised as Roy Bahadoor and 'prince of contractors', continued to prosper.

After 1857, there are several references to Jotee Persaud, no longer as Lala, but with higher honorific such as 'Rao' and 'Roy Bahadoor'. He got involved in other small cases—like one against Emambaudi Begum[54]—but nothing matched the case in which Lang had been his lawyer. Lala's name appears in various social functions and other things as an important citizen: as a donor for schools in North Western Provinces,[55] as a dignitary invited at the laying of the foundation stone of Freemasons' Foundation in Lahore,[56] as an owner of huge properties, among others.

By 1863, the lawyer and Lala were no longer on good terms. We have already read about the court case in 1863 in which Lang's wife fought a case against friends of John Lang, Jotee Persaud and W.C. Hurry, for the payment for alimony on behalf of Lang. During the case, Mrs Lang's brother, Justice Peterson told the judge that 'Jotee Persaud told me that he was paying the money for the benefit of Mrs. Lang, because he could not trust her husband'[57].

Jotee Persaud who had once put his entire trust in the hands of Lang could not trust him any longer. One wonders what the reason might have been—there are no personal letters of either Lang or of Jotee Persaud to ascertain the problem correctly. It could well be that Lang's second marriage was not approved of by many, including Jotee.

Then there was the fact that the two men operated at different ends of the spectrum. Lang remained a bitter critic of the East India Company, and called himself an interloper—neither allied with the military, nor with the civil servants. On the other hand, Jotee Persaud was East India Company's pillar of steadfast support throughout their troubled times. Political differences could also have been the reason for estrangement in this friendship. It could also be that Lala did not take the prank about his portrait too lightly.

Whatever the case may have been, the two friends had fallen apart by 1863, a year before Lang died.

But between 1850 and 1860, the two men constantly hogged the limelight in the press. So known were these two, that their names were included in dictionaries to explain two terms related to them. The Hobson-Jobson Dictionary of Anglo-Indian terms, in its explanation of the word 'mofussil', added that Lang ran a very popular newspaper called *The Mofussilite.*[58]

Lala Jotee Persaud finds his name mentioned in an article by George Campbell about Indian castes and tribes. Campbell cites Jotee Persaud's name as a famous example of Khatree caste, and marks this caste as distinguished for producing prominent individuals:

> Small in number as they are, it is perfectly astonishing how prominent individuals of them have been in the history of different parts of India. Name a distinguished Hindoo and there seems to be a very great probability that he will turn out to be a Khatree. They were the brains and directing genius of the whole Sikh power, a very large proportion of Runjeet Singh's governors (he of Multan and others) were Khatrees, Akber's finance minister, Todar Mull, famous for the settlement of Bengal and other provinces, was a Khatree, Chandroo Lall, the notorious minister of the Nizam, was a Khatree, so was Jotee Pershad, the well known commissariat contractor of Agra. In Mogul times a Khatree was Governor of Badakshan, beyond the Himalayas, and many others might be named.[59]

The same entry appears in a German encyclopaedia titled *Archiv Für Anthropologie: Zeitschrift Für Naturgeschichte Und Urgeschichte Des*

Menschen (1870)[60]. Two years later, Matthew Sherring in his book about Indian castes and tribes improves upon this entry to highlight the importance of Jotee Persaud:

> The emperor Akbar's famous minister, Todar Mull, was a *Khatri*; and a relative of that man of undoubted energy, the great Commissioner Contractor of Agra, *Jotee* Parshad, lately informed me that he also is a *Khatri*.[61]

Upon Jotee Persaud's death in 1870, the newspaper *The Englishman* published an obituary which sums up the affinity the British press and the military had for the great contractor. The obituary also lashes out at the Civil Services for having wronged him:

> Lalla Jotee Pershad, the well-known and energetic Commissariat Contractor, long dead to the world, is now announced as having died his natural death—Jotee Pershad Rai Bahadoor, the persecuted and prosecuted of the Civil Service, for it was members of that service who, amazed at his wealth, could only account for it by ascribing its accumulation to corrupt practices. Colonel, now General, Ramsay, the chief of the Commissariat in the time of the Punjab campaigns, knew the Lalla's worth, and invested him with great powers, giving him, in fact, carte blanche authority to draw on any treasury he pleased. Jotee supplied the army in the field with carriage, forage, and cereals...In fact, Jotee Pershad, with an unlimited command of money at his disposal, accomplished in his department what Lord Napier of Magdala with the same power achieved in Abyssinia. It was even known that the Sikh forces, starving in their own country, were encamped at times over the pits of grain secured by Jotee Pershad.

What was Jotee Pershad's reward?...He himself, however, was chosen as the scapegoat, and Lord Dalhousie was with great difficulty prevailed upon to sanction his prosecution. It was supposed that great discoveries would be made of the peculation said to be rife in the Commissariat Department. Jotee Pershad was therefore brought to trial on a charge of making out false accounts, inasmuch as he had demanded pay in cut for the supply of a certain number of bullocks when he had actually supplied nothing like so many.

At the date of this prosecution the Lalla had sent in claims for fourteen or fifteen lakhs of rupees, as the balance of his account against Government; and it was admitted that some ten lakhs were really due to him. The great contractor...lost no time in retaining the services of the late Mr. John Lang, barrister-at-law, and editor of the Mofussilite in days gone past. The able defence made by that gentleman is still in the memories of all who take an interest in contemporary Indian history. His bold defiance of a Government, which was in his case plaintiff and prosecutor, judge and debtor; his famous simile of the whole being like the menu of a passenger ship, all pork together, roast and boiled, entrées and entremets, whatever the dishes might be called, they were all of one and the same thing, All Pork,—took the court by storm. The unanswerable defence, however, that the account between the parties was an open one, with a large balance admitted to be due to the defendant, and that the prosecutor could deduct any overcharge when he pleased, settled the question. Jotee was acquitted, but bitterly exclaimed, 'All the men who worked with me, and for whom I worked, have been rewarded—some with honours, some with pensions, and many with promotions. Look around you; what have I received in recognition of my services? A criminal prosecution!' The Lalla paid Mr. Lang two lakhs of rupees—one lakh in cash and

> one by bond, but all included in a settlement on his wife. True, he had to pay his clever counsel many a rupee in after years, which may possibly to make up the three lakhs mentioned by the *Delhi Gazette*…
>
> Jotee Pershad continued to reside at Agra, and had a glorious opportunity of avenging himself during the Mutinies. The civilians of Agra took refuge in the Fort, and amongst them were his actual prosecutors. The revenge he took was noble. He supplied the Fort with all sorts of food, as he had hitherto supplied the army, and was named Rai Bahadoor by a grateful Government. He has now passed away, the last of the great native Commissariat Contractors, and fortunate will the department be to meet with his equal on any future campaign, even should he acquire much wealth and make large profits.[62]

As we can see from this obituary notice, the pork incident—Lang comparing the case against Jotee Persaud with stale pork, as reported by William Forbes-Mitchell—actually took place. Every detail in Forbes-Mitchell's memoir stands corroborated; both the pork incident and the picture of Jotee Persaud being passed off as Nana Sahib's. However, a curious thing stands out in this obituary: part of the payment to Lang for the case was made through a bond included in the settlement on his wife. This sheds new light on Lang's life. Most researchers have assumed that Lucy separated from John Lang very early into his career in India, but it seems that she was with him till 1851, thirteen years into their married life, and nine years in their Indian life; or that at least they were on very good terms.

Also, it is naive to assume that Lala kept paying Lang because *The Delhi Gazette* had mentioned more money than had been paid. Lang continued to be a counsel for Lala, as well as carried out a crusade against the John Company in his newspaper for Lala's bills to be paid.

Jotee Persaud's legend does not end here. His ghost reappears several times, sometimes literally through the medium of William Lawrence.

Justice Summons Spirit, or Lala's Spirit Spits Fire

As we have established earlier, Justice Andrew Thomas Turton Peterson or A.T.T.P, brother of Lucy Lang, and a judge at Supreme Court in Calcutta for many years, became interested in 'Spiritualism'. He collaborated with William Lawrence, who was an uneducated 'sensitive', and made the latter a medium to communicate with the spirits. In his séances, he summoned various 'spirits'—right down from Pythagoras, Aristotle, Buddha, and Jesus to his contemporaries, who had passed away. Among the spirits who inhabited the body of the 'sensitive' William Lawrence, Lala Jotee Persaud was also one. The result was a book titled *Essays From the Unseen, Delivered Through the Mouth of W.L., a Sensitive, and Recorded by A.T.T.P.*[63]. Among the Oriental 'Controls', that is to say the 'Oriental' spirits that controlled the medium William Lawrence, there are several prominent figures. We shall however concern ourselves with just three—Henry Lawrence, Lala Jotee Persaud, and the Duke of Wellington, Arthur Wellesly.

Among these three, the first 'spirit' that A.T.T.P. summoned was Sir Henry Lawrence. Sir Lawrence had died in Lucknow in 1857, not on the battle-field but at his writing desk, when a shell hit him in the leg and exploded. The spirit of Sir Lawrence expressed its opinion that Lord Canning was not as good a diplomat as Lord Dalhousie; that if Sir Henry's own brother John Lawrence had been the governor-general, the position of the British would have been better etc. Sir Lawrence's spirit also talked about John Lang, Jotee Persaud and the famous trial. It also talked about *The Mofussilite* and *Friend of India* newspapers. When asked about Jotee, Sir Lawrence, the spirit, retorted, 'that old scoundrel, Jotee Persad!'[64].

The next to be summoned was Lala Jotee Persaud. The date recorded by A.T.T.P. is 14 December 1877—seven years after Lala's death. Before narrating what Lala, the spirit, told him, A.T.T.P. showers encomiums on the great contractor:

> Jotee Persad, the well-known Contractor and Army Supplier who fed and foraged the British forces during the Afghan, the Punjab, and the Sutlej Campaigns, was, I believe, a native of Cawnpoor[XII], in the north-west Provinces of India. Although the Government of India, in the hour of danger, were too glad of his services, they kept putting off, year after year, the payment of what they owed him; and when, at last, he sought redress in the old Supreme Court of Calcutta, the Government trumped up charges of fraud, and took criminal proceeding against him. He was taken from Calcutta by the police, to Agra, and passed from Thannh to Thannh, that is, from Police Station to Police Station, upwards of 800 miles, where the farce of a criminal charge (by a debtor, who could not, or would not, pay) was brought against him, for charging too much. It is useless to go through what occurred—he was acquitted at Agra, and came down to Calcutta, where he prosecuted his civil suit, and recovered an enormous sum of money. He was for many years a client of the Recorder of these Controls. He was a good and very charitable man, and much respected by most of the Europeans; although he was designated by one of the Controlling Spirits, Sir Henry Lawrence, as 'an old scoundrel.'[65]

When Lala's spirit was summoned, the medium W.L., before he was fully entranced, 'began singing out detached Hindustani words—'khitmutgar', 'khansameh' (the last word with a pronunciation I would defy any trickster to get up for the occasion), 'koee hyn',

XII A.T.T.P. spells modern-day Kanpur as Cawnpoor.

and other Hindustani words, and ended by emphasising the word 'griffin'.[66]

Once the medium passed into complete trance, the spirit of Jotee Persaud started speaking through the medium.

Jotee, the spirit, tells that he has with him a servant of Sir Wellesly who wants to tell that his master was impudent and a slave-driver, and that Europeans deliberatley do not do any work themselves and burden their servants unnecessarily and incessantly.

At this point, A.T.T.P. draws the reader's attention to the word 'griffin', which he says is 'wonderfully connected with something that followed with another Control'.

The 'another Control', was the spirit of Arthur Wellesly who was nicknamed Griffin—this was apparently unknown. A.T.T.P., in the chapter about Wellesly's (the control/spirit) visit, tells that he has been included to show the power of the 'Spiritual Aura'. Jotee's aura had attracted that of the old 'khansamah', whose aura in turn had attracted that of Wellesly, his master. Sir Wellesly is of an era before A.T.T.P. and his lot. He was involved in the battle against Tipu Sultan at Srirangapatnam at the end of 18th century, as well as in the battle of Waterloo. The spirit tells A.T.T.P. that he was known as 'Griffin'[67] amongst Indian celebrities. This, A.T.T.P. tells, is the proof that spirits were actually communicating with him. The tongue twisting Hindustani words pronounced by the uneducated Englishman W.L., because Wellesly's servant was communicating with him, is also proof of the same.

Coming back to the spirit of Jotee Persaud, it asks Peterson, 'How are you getting on, P—?', to which A.T.T.P. answers that he is doing well, but that Henry Lawrence had visited and expressed not so sound an opinion of Jotee. A.T.T.P writes about the great Lala's retort:

> So, Sir Henry Lawrence has not as favorable an opinion of me as of an effeminate, idle, vicious, rind unruly pale-face. A

> good many of your white-faces are well worthy of the name of Griffin. How easily they forget the industrious habits of their forefathers, and settle down into a state of idleness.... You are one of the very few who understand some of the high-minded natives of India. Some of the pale-faces would deny us to possess even human feelings. They termed my countrymen walking liars—creatures in their hearts only fit to be spurned. These feelings are not only those of the Superiors, but they are faithfully copied by those in subordinate stations in the military ranks. They, too, must have their lacqueys[XIII] to clean their arms and brush up their uniforms and groom their horses. Jotee had the audacity to say to one of these (I am referring to an officer) it would have been much better if, instead of forgetting their English habits, they had clung to them, and learned all the advantages to be got from early-rising, and performing for themselves duties they would have done in England...
>
> Sir H. Lawrence may call Jotee scoundrel, but the same Spirit that burned in him burned in me—love of country—he for honor of his country, I for love of mine. He served his faithfully; I did mine. He would have reached high honors, fame, and wealth, had not his career been shortened. I, by the merciful allowance of the same mind and will that governed us both, was permitted to obtain, if not name and fame, at all events wealth, which I freely spent as I freely made.[68]

It is interesting to see Lala's spirit say that he was as much of service to his country as Sir Lawrence was to his. If the country is the same, it is not an issue, but if their countries are different then Lala and Lord Lawrence have to be on opposite sides—which they were not. Even if all this be considered rambles of Peterson himself, by that his 'fiction' here is a powerful critique of racism in British India. Sir Henry

XIII The sense of 'lacquey' in 19th century is both a male servant, and a sycophant.

Lawrence, the spirit, called A.T.T.P. 'a forward man', and perhaps A.T.T.P. is insinuating that he, having spent many years in India, understands India better than most white men, and that he is above racial prejudices.

A.T.T.P. then asked Jotee, the spirit, or the control whether he had any contracts for Lucknow before the Mutiny. He said:

> No old Jotee was not in favor then, but when the Mutiny did take place, they were courting old Jotee, and promising him everything; all back claims were to be paid, and no questions to be asked.[69]

A.T.T.P. then brought up the issue of John Lang: 'I then asked him about J. L.—and his family, of whom he spoke in terms of great gratitude and affection.'[70]

It is interesting to see that both Henry Lawrence, the control and Jotee Persaud, the control, spoke about John Lang, but A.T.T.P. shies away from detailing what they said. The relationship between Lang and A.T.T.P. would also have been strained, with Lucy having a very strained relationship with Lang. From these accounts, it seems that A.T.T.P. was a good friend of Lang's in earlier days and remembers the times fondly, though with mixed feelings.

Lala's spirit, before leaving the body of William Lawrence, uttered the following words:

> Put what I am going to say down in black and white—that spiritual happiness decreases as worldly wishes gain ascendancy, when ambitions continually fill the soul, when its hopes are continually in action. The very wealth I left was a source of unhappiness to me, and that is why strange incidences stir up. If the experiences of others, as well as myself, were dependent on further consummations of their desires on earth, then would

> their state spiritually be a miserable one; but our happiness increases continually by furthering the well-being of others, and not opposing them—Jotee's lesson.[71]

This was Jotee Persaud's spirit and his moral lesson in 1877. Jotee's legend does not end here either. His ghost appears again, and this time with the ghost of Akbar.

Akbar's Ghost, or Lala and the Lantern

Various stories about the Mutiny of 1857 kept appearing in books and journals for a long time. One of these tales appeared in *The Chamber's Journal* in 1894. The writer is difficult to ascertain since most journals did not attribute stories to anyone. The tale in *The Chamber's Journal* is called 'Romantic Tales of Indian War: Blockade of Agra in 1857'.[72] The writer of this tale was, in all probability, an armyman, since according to the account, the writer had gone to visit the Agra Fort with a few army officers.

The story is about Mutiny in Agra in 1857. The writer tells that when the Mutiny reared its head 'and the cry arose on all sides, 'Feringhee ke Raj hogaya' (the rule of the foreigner is over), the fort of Agra was without victuals of any sort'[73]. He goes on to tell how the British Raj was in dire straits with Indian soldiers of the Kotah regiment mutinying and killing most of the European officers on 5 July 1857.

The British committed the same mistake as was made in Lucknow in trying to fight the mutineers at Chinhut, with the result that 141 British soldiers were killed, including Captain D'Oyly. Every European rushed to the fort to save his life, with the result that the prisoners and 'budmashes[XIV]' broke loose and joined the mutineers. In the middle of this murder and mayhem was heard the roaring sound of what sounded like an apparoaching cavalcade from the direction of Sikandara, where the tomb of Emperor Akbar is. The writer tells that

XIV Scoundrels, criminals.

the story from this point has been narrated to him by Rahim Buksh, a 'moonshee':

> Above all this dreadful din, the trumpeting of elephants, the neighing of horses, and the beating of drums—in brief, the noise of the advance of a great host—was distinctly heard approaching the main gate of the fort, which was securely barred, with drawbridges raised. The sentries stood on their posts paralysed with fear at the sound of the great commotion as it came nearer and nearer, till at length the cavalcade appeared to be advancing over the raised drawbridge and through the closely-barred massive gates, without the least delay or opposition. The Europeans heard the noise, but did not see the figures of the cavalcade; yet the noise was sufficient to paralyse them.[74]

One daring Sikh soldier by the name of Jawhir Singh gathered courage and challenged the party:

> 'Kis ke Sowaree hain?' (Whose cavalcade comes?) The reply was instantly given in three languages at once, Urdoo, Punjabi, and English: 'The cavalcade of Akbar, King of kings, whose palace is in Paradise; come back to his throne on earth to give strength and power and wisdom to the English. Fear not, Jawhir Singh; the rule of the English is not over, for Allah has given them the kingdom, and no power which shall rise up against them shall prosper. Allah Hu Akbar—God alone is great.[75]

The sentry, in spite of his fear, replied, 'Advance, Akbar Badsha. All is well'. At this point, according to Rahim Buksh the sentry Jawhir Singh saw a huge elephant with tusks more than two yards long knelt and an old man, 'his eyes shining like carbuncles, with a glistening white moustache, just like the pictures of Akbar Badsha so common about Agra', descended and in a commanding but sweet and pleasant voice said:

> I am Akbar, King of kings. Prostrate thyself, and repeat after me, and say: 'God is one God. He is the Eternal God. He begeteth not, neither is He begotten. And there is not any one like unto Him'. In the name of the Most Merciful, arise, go, and be circumcised, and assume the name of Abd'allah Rahmen (a follower of God, the Most Merciful, a common name for all converts to Mohammedanism)...[76]

The great emperor having commanded the brave Sikh soldier to get circumcised and become a 'believer' thus, asks him to go and proclaim that the rule of the British would not end even though they are 'sore pressed', for 'Allah had given them the kingdom'. The emperor, for the veracity of this prediction, swears upon the Holy Koran. He also predicts the death of the lieutenant governor John Colvin:

> As for John Colvin, Bahadur (Valiant or Mighty), bear good tidings to him of mercy and an honourable reward. For, verily, sixty-six days hence he shall join me in Paradise; and within the compass of one moon from the date on which he shall be carried to his rest, his people shall no longer need my protection. Till then, I and my retinue shall guard this fortress. Amen! Allah Hu Akbar.

Saying this, the emperor remounted his elephant and went. From this day till 10 October 1857, when General Greathead was able to finally secure Agra for the British, the apparition kept appearing. Whenever challenged by a sentry, the reply was the same:

> The cavalcade of Akbar, the guardian of this fortress, passes and the sentry was always compelled to reply, in spite of himself: 'Pass, Akbar Badsha. All is well'.[77]

In this tale of Rahim Buksh, however, only the 'believers' could see the emperor, for the European sentries heard the noise but did not see anything. The writer tells that Buksh could not explain how in the middle of rioting Abd'allah Rahman, the converted Sikh, got to the great mosque which was outside the fort. But he got outside and to the mosque somehow, 'and long before the cock crew, he had proclaimed the vision to every follower of the Prophet in the city of Agra'.

Rahim Buksh's tale now introduces Lala Jotee Persaud:

> And on peeping through a chink in the wicket of the main gate at daybreak the following morning, the first thing the European sentries saw was about a score of carts, on the opposite side of the drawbridge, loaded with bread fresh from the ovens, which Lalla Jotee Pershand had baked at his own house in the city after hearing the proclamation of the vision of Akbar Badsha. And within the next few days, the Lalla (a Persian title given to gentlemen of position in Upper India, equivalent to the honorary title of Doctor, in English, LL.D.), Jotee Pershand, had poured sufficient provisions into the fort to victual the garrison for a siege of more than six months' duration, accepting payment in supply bills bearing five per cent interest.

We already know how Lala had stood by the British when no Indian merchant was willing to—that all this had anything to do with Akbar, one knew not, but one knows now.

According to Rahim Buksh, the premonition of the emperor came true, the 'Raj' was restored to the British, and John Colvin died to exhaustion and anxiety on 9 September, exactly 66 days after the first vision of Akbar within the revolution of another moon from the date of his funeral—the blockade of Agra was raised, and the garrison relieved.

The writer tells that he remembered the story very well, but never had the opportunity to verify it. The occasion arose when he visited Agra Fort in 1893 in the company of a few army officers. The party asked the old maulvi who was acting as their guide if he had heard of this story. The maulvi said that he had not just heard it, but that he was an eyewitness to the entire proceedings, and that he could vouch for every word of it.

At this point, the writer has a theory. He says that it could have been a 'pious fraud performed by someone possessed of a magic-lantern, an instrument which was not so well known in India in 1857 as in 1893'[78].

The picture (plate no.) is the frontispiece from a book written by 'A Mere Phantom' in 1866, and it is called *The Magic Lantern, How to Buy and How to Use It.* (see plate 7) *Also, How to Raise a Ghost.* The chapter on 'The Ghost' describes how the lantern is used to raise an apparition:

> The frontispiece so clearly shows the conditions necessary to be observed in this, the modern method of raising a ghost, that a verbal description is almost unnecessary. It will be seen that the spectators are placed in a distant and for the most part elevated portion of an assembly room, which is darkened. In front of these is a stage, upon which actors are engaged.
>
> The spectators regard both as living actors, while in reality one is but 'the shadow of a dream,' and 'coming like a shadow, so departs.' The *real* 'woman in white' stands *under* the stage, concealed from the spectators by the usual board near the orchestra; the Magic Lantern, illuminated by the oxyhydrogen light, directs its beams full upon her figure, the reflection of which appears as far behind the inclined plate of glass as the real

> figure is in front. The living actor on the stage, notwithstanding his expressive attitude of surprise, really *sees nothing*, and is simply staring at a portion of space where he has been previously instructed 'the apparition comes,' the spectators alone being so situated that they 'take false shadows for true substances'.
>
> It will thus be seen that the peculiar feature of the exhibition consists in associating living actors with those which are merely visionary, and in so sustaining the illusion that no distinguishable difference shall appear to the spectators until the requirements of the scene necessitate the vanishing of the spectre. The disappearance or 'vanishing' of the Ghost is produced by simply turning off the light either suddenly or gradually, according to circumstances.[79]

The magic lantern was invented by one Kircher about the middle of the 17th century, and it was of great use to magicians who could baffle the spectators with their spectres. A manual on 'Parlour Magic' in 1858 tells that 'as a vehicle of amusement, it contributes in no small degree…to the hilarity of a party in a long winter's night; and as a means by which lectures on astronomy can be elucidated, it arrests the attention of graver spectators'.[80]

To come back to the tale in *The Chamber's Journal*, the writer suggests that the apparition of Akbar may have been raised by none other than Lala Jotee Persaud, 'who was known to have held about a million and a half sterling in Company's paper, the whole of which he would have lost if the rule of the British had been over thrown'[81].

One knows that John Lang was fond of ghosts, and that he read too much Shakespeare. That his fancies would rub on to Lala is difficult to imagine. The writer's imagination seems to be a little too farfetched—to set up a whole apparatus in front of the fort, and then to act out a little skit in front of the fort gate posing as Akbar. One can almost imagine it to be a sequel to the Nana's-picture-story. Jotee Persaud, in knowledge that everyone thinks that he looks like Nana Sahib, decided that he must play the role of a monarch. Inspired by the literary and theatrical stories he has heard from John Lang, he dons the clothes of Akbar Badsha, calls for a magic lantern and appears as the great emperor to the eyes of the soldiers. In that case, a bigger performance has not been performed in the entire history of theatre.

In the middle of rioting and many important immediate concerns, it is difficult to imagine such a stellar performance having taken place.

The writer tells that he is informed that the story is related either in a biography of Mr John Colvin, or some other work about the Mutiny in Agra in 1857, but that he has never seen any such work.

However, his informant positively assures him that 'he read the story in some book in the Public Library of Melbourne. Be that as it may, I have no doubt that the reported vision did the British good service in the dark days of 1857, as also did the great comet of September 1858'[82].

Yours truly, too, had some curious things to read at a Public Library in Melbourne. This, however, concerned Dr John McArthur and Margaret Thomas, a famous 19th century sculptor and writer. I had been researching about Alice Richman who was a friend of Margaret Thomas. Dr John McArthur, who I had never met, had left a set of documents at Melrose Historical Society (South Australia), which included a print of my blog wondering about the relation between Thomas and Richman. I took the contact details of Dr McArthur, but received no replies, whereupon I went in person to his house in Melbourne. The bell was not answered. I then went to the Victoria State Library and opened an encyclopaedia which had an entry that said that Dr John McArthur, in his unpublished manuscript, tells that Margaret Thomas was actually Margaret Cook and had changed her surname on a whim. I presume Dr McArthur is dead, but I'm still hunting for his unpublished manuscript.

Whether people saw Akbar's ghost or not is not the matter here. The matter is that they believed it, and we know of at least two 'eyewitnesses'—Rahim Buksh, the 'moonshee', and the 'maulvi'. If seeing is believing, the converse also holds true perhaps. I have gone through John Colvin's biography, but the matter of Akbar's ghost does not come up in that book. Also, another curious thing reported is that the ghost was visible only to Muslims and not to unbelievers. This explanation rules out the question of testimonies of European soldiers.

Rumours had a very important role to play in the War of 1857, a fact that most readers would be acquainted with. It was rumoured that that greased cartridges were being introduced in the army, and this would defile the religion of both Muslims and Hindus, as the grease would contain fat of both pig and beef. Another rumour in currency was that the 'hundred-year rule' theory which espoused that the English had gained ground in 1757 with victory at Battle of Plassey, and their rule would end in 1857. Another rumour was reported in Lang's newspaper *The Mofussilite* in February 1857, just prior to the revolution/mutiny. The newspaper reported that 'small baked cakes of atta have been distributed through the chowkeydars of certain districts in North Western Provinces for some unknown purpose'[83].

It now appears that the British ladies could not stand the sight of 'chupatties' during their incarceration in the Agra Fort, because unconsciously they knew that these 'baked cakes of atta' had been the symbol of the revolution, and of their nemesis.

In a letter dated 5 March 1857, Major W.C. Erskine tells C.B. Thornhill, officiating secretary to the Government of India about this mysterious symbol, and tells that there has been much discussion about this, but it has been viewed as a harmless gesture with Hindus conducting this ritual to propitiate the Lord Vishnu. He also tells about a placard in Madras exhorting Hindus to drive away the unbelievers who had lost all sense of justice. The major tells that the situation was one of 'lull before the storm', for the newspapers had reported in

January and February that the country was 'profoundly tranquil'. The major also tells about an incident in Lucknow where a maulvi had exhorted both Muslims and Hindus to rise to the occasion, or perish. A scuffle ensued with armed men in which Lieutenant Thomas and four sepoys were wounded.[84]

It is curious how the British barely got a whiff of the rumours that were doing rounds, and without telegrams or a clearly organised system, the Indian soldiers were able to co-ordinate their movements and wage this war against the British government. One is reminded of John Steinbeck's 1947 novel *The Pearl*[85] where Kino, the fisherman, chances upon a pearl and sees in it a chance to improve his life. Before Kino reaches the city to sell the pearl, the news has travelled ahead of him through talks over fences, even though he has not breathed a word about it. The narrator tells that that the city is like an animal, that it has got a nervous system of its own through which news travels.

Lala Jotee Persaud seems to have known this system pretty well, and the writer of the Romantic Tale about the War may not be too much off the mark when he says that Jotee may have played this 'pious fraud'. The magic-lantern was probably not used, neither probably did the vision of Akbar appear, but a rumour was spread. It was believed, endorsed, and believed so fervently—because of the invocation of the Koran, the story of the circumcision and conversion of the Sikh soldier—that those who believed it started thinking that they had seen it. Government records show that Jotee had definitely been party to spreading a rumour that the mutinying soldiers were retreating. He used the same strategy as did the mutineers, to make rumours a device to demoralise the opponents, and encourage the sagging hopes of the Indian soldiers on the British side. That said, it adds another dimension to Lala's personality who, till now, seems to have been just a wily merchant. That this rumour turned into a legend, and entered into folklore to be remembered almost four decades later by a maulvi who claimed to be an eyewitness, is a counterpoint to the idea of history as verifiable and citeable all the time.

The writer is unable to pin his source down to any written source except the version of an informant who had read the story in a 'public library in Melbourne'. Neither have I been able to find out any other source that documents this story.

I, however, am positive that I have known the story very well. The vision was for the 'believers' and not for the 'infidels', and therefore, the lore also passed down through folklore rather than documented sources. It is interesting to see that while the British people in India wrote reams and reams about everything—from politics, personal memoirs, and very detailed ethnographies to descriptions of nature—the unlettered Indian majority had its own way to discourse through its oral traditions.

This is the story of Lala Jotee Persaud, who in modern history books finds mentions in citations in history of Indian banking, or in the story of Nana Sahib, but never as someone around whom a story can be woven. Lang's case is perhaps more unfortunate. In relating the various incidents related to Lala, we did not focus on 1851, which merits a more detailed discussion because it became a metaphor of resistance as well as of corruption in the governance of the East India Company.

Lala and Gwala, or Lang and Slang, or Lang Plays Portia

If the reader has noticed, Lala never speaks except as a spirit or a control, to A.T.T.P. Even that consolation can be taken away, for the modern reader could suspect that it is A.T.T.P. speaking. In every other case, one has heard the Lala being spoken about or spoken to. One writer, however, records a comment of Lala, and his comment sums up the corruption and the red-tape that existed in the bureaucracy of British India. One almost gets the idea that the context is quite contemporary:

> We long ago read a very instructive little story on this point, Jotee Pershad, the famous Commissariat Contractor, once described our modern system as that of a man who had cowherd for his fine milch cow. Thinking the Gwalla made profit from the cow's food, he got another to superintend him. The cow grew thin, he got a third Gwalla on higher wages to superintend the second, and the cow died of starvation. Now said he—the native contractor is like the first Gwalla; he makes his profit, but the cow thrives. But you appoint a European over him, he makes his profit too, and then you put a Sahib over him, and he must also have his profit, and then you wonder that you have long bills and bad work. The Moral is obvious.[86]

The context here is a discussion in the House of Commons in 1865, whereby the *Bootan Blue Book* was ordered to be published. The speaker is Mr Eden, who is criticising Colonel Balfour for cutting down the military departments below the size of efficiency:

> There is no doubt that Colonel Balfour cut down the different Military Departments below the limits of efficiency, and therefore of the economy. Our Commissariat so lamentably failed in this last campaign, that it proved itself nearly equal to the Home one. While Government is so lavish in superintendence, it is stingy and parsimonious in all other outlay. It prefers a lean, half-starved Cerebrus with three heads, to a sturdy, well mastiff one.[87]

Things do not seem to have changed between 1851 and 1865, or for that matter now, in Indian governance. The 'gwalla' metaphor pretty much sums up the way in which hierarchies operated in British Indian administration. The case against Lala in 1851 opened up a can of worms, and the accusations hurled at him ricocheted back at the government, exposing gaping holes in its fabric of finance and governance. The case was so important that a whole book titled *The Trial of Lalla Jotee Pershad and Others: Reported for the Delhi Gazette*[88] was published about it. Save for the *Delhi Gazette*, the government's action was condemned by the press all over India. It is also remarkable that there was a constant war between the editor of *Delhi Gazette* and the editor of *The Mofussilite*, John Lang. Many of the early issues of *The Mofussilite* are filled with editorial columns replying caustically to the editor of its 'contemporary'.

Lest we forget, a mention must be made of the way Lang defended Lala Jotee Persaud. He seems to have gathered all his facilities together—he was sharp, witty, quick, incisive, did not mind use of invective, and did not forget to quote lines from his favourite author, which he unfailingly does in all his literary works. As we have already seen, he compared the case with the carcass of a stale pork-pie.

To begin with, Lang's position was like that of Portia in Shakespeare's *The Merchant of Venice*, with Lala facing a certain defeat, for it was him against East India Company in a court of the East India Company, facing charges on 23 counts.[89] Like Portia, Lang comes out victorious in the end, setting an unprecedented example of the company losing on home turf, and does not forget to quote Shakespeare. There was an important point in the case which hinged upon a person, Chotah Lall, being a government servant. It so turned out that Chotah was an employee in pay of Jotee Persaud. Lang said:

> Had I been conducting this trial in the Supreme Court of India, I should have come to issue with my opponent on one point at a very early stage. Had he been unable to prove that Chotah Lall was a servant of the Government, he would have abandoned the case in despair. Here are decisions bearing immediately on the subject...I have ransacked every legal work...to see if there is any precedent...but my labours have been crowned with

> indifferent success. It is true that I do remember something of the kind; but I question, Sir, whether you could receive it as an authority in a Criminal Trial. Mr Shakespeare in his play called *The Twelfth Night* gives us the following scene:-
>
> Viola — My duty, Madam, your most humble servant!
>
> Olivia — What is your name?
>
> Viola — Cesario is your servant's name, fair princess.
>
> Olivia — My servant, sir! You are servant with Count Orsino, youth.
>
> Viola — And he is yours — and his must needs be yours. Your servant's servant, is your servant madam.
>
> Now, Sir, this may be most unexceptionable poetry; but very indifferent Law, and worse Reason.[90]

The prosecution's case hinged on the fact that Chotah Lall was a government servant. He, in fact, was Jotee's servant. Jotee was government's servant, being a commissariat contractor. Therefore, the allusion to the above scene. Lang was at his rhetorical best in this case, and would have enjoyed every moment of it.

Let us go back to the first meeting between Lang and Lala, when Lang had gone to meet Raja Lal Singh at Lala's house in Agra. It is in this very first meeting that Lal Singh acquaints Lang with Lala's woes that the government had not paid him the money for his services in the Afghan war and the Anglo-Sikh wars. Lala said that the government owed him 57 lakh of rupees, and that it had threatened to sue him in one of its own courts, 'for an attempt to make an overcharge of forty thousand rupees, or four thousand pounds'[91].

Lall Singh knowing the principles of tyrannical governance well, ironically says that the government should convict him for making so large a claim.

Lang says in this account in *Wanderings in India* that in this opinion, Raja was wrong (meaning that Raja was right in hinting that the government would prosecute him), for Lala was informed that he was, to all intents and purposes, a prisoner and must not leave Agra.

The natives believed that the government was denying the contractor's just demands, but Lala was the first one to deny this assertion and declare:

> …'the prosecution arose out of the circumstance of the Commissary-General being a near relative of the Governor-General of India; that a civilian in power had a quarrel with the Commissary-General, and had represented, semi-officially, that great frauds had been committed, and there could be no question that the heads of the departments were cognisant of such frauds; that the Governor-General, anxious that the honour of a member of his ancient family should be cleared up, had determined upon a strict investigation; and that the civilian in question suggested the public prosecution of the contractor as the speediest and most satisfactory means of arriving at the result!'[92]

Lang says that such was the opinion of many officers of the government, civil and military. Lang goes on to tell that the contractor was acquitted, and had come to the aid of the British again when they were very hard pressed at Agra in 1857.

Interestingly, in *Wanderings In India,* Lang keeps the account about Jotee Persaud very short, and does not state the fact that he was the lawyer who had fought the case. He also does not take sides, which he had done so ardently, and pursued the matter of payment to the Lala by the government in his newspaper for several years after the case.

While the case was on, he was excited enough to write a libellous passage in *The Mofussilite* and land in jail. Lang has compressed the story to him meeting Lala, Lala getting incarcerated, and thereafter a quick statement that Lala was acquitted in the case. When Lang got to know from Lala that the government intended to prosecute him, he advised him to file a counter-suit to recover his money. The idea was that the government would get intimidated and would not thus prosecute Lala, and hence reach an out-of-court settlement.

Wanderings in India was published in 1859 after the Mutiny of 1857, and Lang would have wanted to be cautious to a British reading public. However, given that Jotee Persaud was in great favour with the British people at that time, this caution was unnecessary. Lang could well have flaunted that if he had not saved Lala in 1851, the British Army would not have got his help in 1857. It may also be that by this time, the two were not on as good terms as they were previously. Also, it is difficult to understand Lang's position about the Mutiny. Although he certainly was cashing on the demand for stories about the protagonists of this war, and he puts in a line here and there about 'native avarice', he does not condemn Nana Sahib or Tatya Tope as rest of the writers and the British press were wont to.

Six months before the commencement of the case against Lala, this is what the *Delhi Gazette* reported:

> Jotee Pershaud we have heard, has offered to cry 'quits' with the Government, if they forego the criminal prosecution against him. The proposal was, we are [assured, deliberately forwarded to the Governor-General, it is needless to say with what result.] The *Mofussilite* declares that either Jotee Pershaud shall have his money and freedom, and reparation for the insults 'and injuries which have been heaped upon him, or Parliament shall have a new Indian grievance, which it will never hear the last of.[93]

Lang's words proved to be prophetic, and the matter became a very important one. After the case was decided, the matter was even brought up in the House of Lords for detailed discussion. Disregarding Lang's challenge, the government went ahead with the prosecution, and Lang became Jotee's guarantor. Jotee sought leave and went to Calcutta, and filed his suit for the recovery of 57 lakh rupees. An arrest warrant was issued against him and he was brought back to Agra. It seems some of Lang's property also was seized, and this is what probably infuriated Lang more than anything else.

A February 1851 article of the *Delhi Gazette* jibes at Lang saying that he is trying to play the martyr. The newspaper reports that Lang's 'breeches' were captured. One cannot quite fathom if 'breeches' entails any other sense than it usually does, and it sounds like a farce if it entails its usual sense:

> …Nor is there a whit more of foundation for the assertion, that an attachment was issued against the press at Meerut, on account of the bail given by Mr. Lang. The magistrate of Agra wrote two letters to the magistrate of Meerut. The first requested that property to the value of Rs. 20,000 might be seized, without specifying any particulars, and the second contained a request, that the press might, on no account, be touched, even though the full amount could not otherwise be levied. The efforts of Mr. Lang to incur the honour of martyrdom were not quite successful, but along with his client he suffers in fiction, and endures undeserved woes. When his breeches were captured at Agra, the police acted under written orders not to take anything that might inconvenience him or prevent him going about as usual. Jotee wanted to pay the money for him, but no, he would be a victim. It was pleasant, and he liked it.

It has already been established that the *Delhi Gazette* was always opposed to John Lang, and although it recognised that Lang suffered along with Jotee, it insinuated that Lang was just politicking and trying to gain sympathy. *The Hurkaru* newspaper of Calcutta, however, suggested that Lang's property had been taken illegally.

> An action is to be brought in the Supreme Court here to test the effect of the new Magistrates' Protection Act in screening Mr. Martin Gubbins from the proper consequences of his illegal seizure of Mr. Lang's *property;* and if, as is possible, the Court decides in favour *of the* magistrate, the matter is to be carried before the Privy Council.[94]

The matter was gathering heat and the whole of the commissariat—with which Jotee was attached—came under the scanner. *The Hurkaru* reported that 'a commission has been appointed to make the most complete investigation into the whole organization of the Commissariat.'[95] The government decided on a complete overhaul of the commissariat, and introduce a 'root-and-branch' system. *Delhi Gazette* said that this was a welcome decision and that the halcyon days of the likes of Lala were over.[96]

The case generated so much interest that many Indian newspapers of 1851 are filled with its details, and discussion pertaining to it. I have mostly used *Allen's Indian Mail* as my source, for the journal did a constant follow up of the case. Lang's newspaper, *The Mofussilite*, has been obviously perused, besides its arch rival the *Delhi Gazette;* and some other newspapers like *The Englishman* and *The Hurkaru.* The trial was to commence in February but the defence asked for more time. The prosecution had lined up 200 witnesses to ensure that Jotee could not escape. The charges were summed up by the *Delhi Gazette* as follows:

> Jotee Pershad, Chote Lal, his Agra agent, Shunkurdoss, his Loodiana agent, and Harilal Mahajun of Agra, were committed

> for trial on the 8th instant in three several cases. Jotee Pershad is arraigned on about twenty-three charges, of obtaining money under false pretences, fraud, and subordination of perjury. These trials do not include the cases of Bareilly and Bijnore, which are separately under preparation by Mr. Wylly, joint-magistrate of Bareilly.[97]

The trial of Jotee Persaud and his accomplices commenced in Agra on 27 March, before Mr S.S. Brown, civil and sessions judge. The jury consisted of Messrs. J.P. Ledlie, W. Johnson, A.M. Wollaston, and J.L. Smith, East-Indians, and Baboo Shama Churn, Sudder Ameen of Muttra, native. 'For the prosecution, Mr. Wylie, C.S; for the defence, Mr. J. Lang, barrister of the Supreme Court.'[98]

Lang asked for a 'mookhtiar's services' to help him in the examination of some natives. The Court intimated that the mode of procedure ought to be understood. There could be no departure from the ordinary usage of the Court. There could be no pleading except what must form matter of record. Oral pleading itself must be taken down.[99]

This matter has been singled out because the legacy of 'everything on record' still continues. It is a bane of the Indian legal system even today, and the strength of the red-tape-mired bureaucracy, as also a means to find loopholes; thereby corroborating the Derridian idea that there's no centre in a text, that the meaning lies somewhere in the gaps.

That opinion aside, the matter has also been singled out because an important writer and thinker of the 19th century, a Brit Sir George Campbell, wrote about why everything is written down in India:

> In India all business is conducted in writing to an extent quite beyond anything known in this country, even in our most important courts of record. There is more official writing and recording in a case of petty theft in an Indian police office than in

> the gravest case in Westminster Hall. All petitions, statements, applications of every description, are filed in writing…all orders and instructions of every kind are formally written and signed. This is much facilitated by the cheapness of the labour of clerks and the facility and brevity of the Persian character. It is also rendered necessary by the incorrectness, vagueness, and talent for speaking hyperbolically of the natives. There is no getting them to make exact statements till they see their words put down in writing; and, moreover, where there is no press, no reporters, and a jealously centralizing system, a minute record is necessary for future reference, to show exactly what has been done, and on what grounds. I have seen it somewhere stated that the same peculiarity exists in Russian courts, perhaps for similar reasons.[100]

In the reasons cited by Campbell—brevity of Persian script, cheapness of labour, native talent for speaking hyperbolically, and a jealously centralizing system—sans the Persian script and the hyperbolic speech, which can be contested, the other two reasons perhaps hold true even now in various spheres, not just legal.

Coming back to the case, the prosecutor said that Jotee Persaud was a very wealthy and an influential man, and that the natives in the commissariat of the government were all his dependents. The prosecutor pointed out to the curious fact that the witnesses called on by the defence were mostly British officers from the army who had come to vouch for Lala's character. He said that the presence of English gentlemen in district courts was infrequent, and insinuated that 'connection of private interest existed between the accused and these witnesses'. The prosecutor alleged that the machinations of the accused 'have been of a peculiarly daring character; for they have not scrupled to use the names of English officers as the supporters and defenders of the man and the system. His friends and advisers have even presumed, perhaps unwisely, to threaten officers of the military and civil services who could not protect or who dared to attack him.'[101]

Having thus rhetorically built his platform, Mr Wylie then pressed the charges. In summary, Jotee was accused of having obtained false receipts in Persian character from Mahesh Doss for hiring bullocks, and had made Doss acknowledge these false receipts to Captain Davidson. Various other charges were corollaries of this main charge. Wylie also pointed out that it had been misrepresented that the criminal charges against Lala had been framed, after he had filed his civil suit for the recovery of his money from the government.

The actual case started on the 1 April, the first four days having been spent in noting objections and amending charges. Lang made ample use of this case in his later fictional works to show how slow, salubrious, and farcical the British Indian legal system was.

The details of the case, as commence, have been gleaned from various issues of the *Delhi Gazette* of 1851.

The witnesses called upon by the prosecution included both commissariat officers and natives associated with Lala. The officers testified in good terms of Lala's 'character'. Several native witnesses, however, were declared by the court unworthy of credit since they had changed their testimonies. Mahesh Doss said certain things to establish facts against the government, and then confessed that he had sworn falsely, and changed his statement. Lang took objection to this, and the court said that the witness's credibility was in question. Another witness, Bhowannee, an old man, said in his first statement that he had indeed supplied the bullocks, and retracted in his second statement. Bhowannee later stood by his first statement, and denied having said the second one at all.

Yet another hole appeared in the prosecution's argument, with Captain Davidson's statement being recorded in England, and the defence thus having no chance to question him. Lang stated that the whole case should be quashed for its irregularities and be reserved for judgement. On the first day, Lang also said that the governor-general had merely called for a report regarding the irregularities of the commissariat, and that the court had no authority to try Lala. Mr Wylie produced documents from the governor-general's office that showed orders of this prosecution. Lang also raised objections to copies being produced instead of original receipts and certificates.

With the perjury of the witnesses and sensing that the case was his, Lang was on fire, and he declared that the 'guts of the case went out with the witnesses'. The jury was called for a majority vote, and the opinion was divided among them. Mr Ledlie, however, concurred that he would call for an acquittal *instanter*, for if the counsel (for defence) abandoned the case at this point, could they convict?

The next morning, Lang asked the court again to quash the proceedings, and was refused. He then asked time to prepare, but the court said that the case had already taken up a lot of time and a lot of the court's business was at a standstill because of this case. The next day, Lang asked permission for all his witnesses to be admitted, and stated that he would examine only two of them, though the rest of them were open for questioning by the prosecution. The two witnesses called by Lang were Major Ramsey and Brigadier Parsons, C.B., who gave the very highest 'character for ability and energy' to Lala, besides a handsome testimonial from Lord Gough. Lang also presented a warm-hearted letter from the late Sir Dudley Hill. Before the witnesses were brought, the court asked Lang to proceed with his defence.

Here is an account of Lang's defence from the *Delhi Gazette*. A huge audience had been amassed both in person, and those waiting to read about the case in the newspapers. The stage was set, and with the demolition of the prosecution, all that Lang needed to do was to give a stellar performance, which he did. The *Delhi Gazette* reported it as this:

> Mr. Lang commenced, by declaiming against the hardship of being forced to plead on a case with such voluminous evidence,

> absolutely without time even to read it once over…all he could do was to note a few remarks on a bit of paper. All his previous technical objections stood good; not one had been answered. He laughed at the constitution of the jury…the machinery of the trial was remarkable,—a Company's court—a Company's judge,—a Company's prosecutor, and a Company's jury…the evidence on record was worthless,—documents filed were unattested, and most of that given orally and noted by the judge was a mass of utter nonsense, made up of belief and supposition of witnesses…Next he met the assumption on a vital point, that Choteh Lal was a servant of Government, on which point the 'fraud' depended. There were precedents which ruled that a man in his position (paid by Jotee Persaud) was a private agent; there was no better authority than 'Mr. Shakespeare' to make him out a public servant (quoting 'Twelfth-Night'), where Viola claims to be Olivia's servant, because servant to Orsino, her servitor in love—good poetry, but bad law! Next adverting to the prosecutor's allusion to the wealth of the defendant, he observed that it was an old imputation against the Company that they, when it suited them, accused people of crime and convicted them of wealth:—here the charge was 'fraud,' the object 'wealth.' As to the case itself, he was like a clergyman called in to console a corpse,—its life was gone. He then analyzed the evidence, pointing out how much of it was gone; all the life was gone, and yet the case moved like a galvanized dead body; he inveighed bitterly and sarcastically at being forced to defend such a case…

And so, there was Lang, using all his legal, literary, journalistic, and caustic prowess to defend Lala—quoting from Burke and Shakespeare, calling the case a dead galvanised body, a stale pork-pie etc. The prosecutor asked permission to react, but the judge did not allow him that, the jury retired and returned with a verdict of 'not guilty'. William Forbes-Mitchell added in his memoir that the judge-advocate-general said that he was ashamed to have been associated with the case.

The Delhi Gazette reported that 'The monster trial terminated on the 11th April, by the *acquittal* of Jotee Persaud and the other two defendants,—a result which seemed to afford much satisfaction to a great crowd, chiefly natives, within and without the court'.

The Delhi Gazette was pro-government, and bitterly anti-Lang, and carried out a series of articles to show that it was a case of not 'not guilty' but of 'not proven guilty'. Depositions were made by an informer in 1849 that great frauds had been committed by the commissariat, but Captain Ramsay, deputy commissary general, contended that the informer's 'character' could not be relied upon. Lt. Colonel Mactier, on the contrary, opined that Lala Jotee Persaud's word about the informer's character could not be relied upon.

Lang knew that Lieutenant Colonel Mactier was the cause of all this trouble, and he also dug up his history. This would get Lang into trouble very soon after the case.

Mactier gave the case a life, inquiry was instituted, and magistrates at various levels found that there had been frauds. Finally, with the approval of the governor-general, a letter was issued in July 1850 to prosecute the Lala.[102]

This is when Lang would have first met the Lala. *Delhi Gazette* tells that the Lala went with Lang to Calcutta in September to file a civil suit for the recovery of the money. The journal's argument is that this counter-suit filed by Jotee to reach an out-of-court settlement insinuates that he was not guiltless. *Allen's Indian Mail* records the time of filing of suit by Lala in Calcutta as 3 October, with 'a notice of proceedings for the recovery of the balance due to him amounting to Rs. 57,79,239, with interest.'[103]

Lala, after winning this case, dropped his charges against the government in order to be in their good books, and confident now that his balance sum would be paid. While on the one hand there was general condemnation of the East India Company, some newspapers, while enjoining in such condemnation, tried to redeem the situation by stating that the case proved one point—that the jury was fair. *Friend of India* wrote:

> In one of the most important suits in which the Government has been engaged for many years, the Government has been defeated in its own courts…this fact at least is established beyond all farther question, that the judges are not affected by the fear of removal, and that they have the solid substance, however they may want the shadow, of judicial independence.'[104]

The *Madras Athanaeum* expressed its unhappiness over the exuberance shown by the natives after winning the case. Lang was also chastised for being ungentlemanly in his speeches:

> The speech of Jotee Persaud's counsel is very generally condemned here for its flippant, jesting, unbecoming style, unworthy altogether of the gravity of the subject and occasion. It was also grossly insulting to both judge and jury, and such as no barrister would have been allowed to proceed with by any judge in any of her Majesty's courts. It should also be observed, that the frantic paeans of victory in which Jotee Persaud's friends have indulged, since his acquittal, are somewhat more exuberant than the pretended cause warrants. The Scotch verdict of 'not proven' would have suited the case better than that of 'not guilty,' and would doubtless have been the one delivered had the form of the court allowed of it… In fact, as has been well remarked, Mr. Lang chiefly relied upon 'the merit' of his client, in not being a bigger rascal than the prosecutor would make him out to be.[105]

The 'Chara Ghotala' is not an ingenious modern trick after all, it has a legacy.

Allen's Indian Mail of 17 June 1850 wrote a coded open letter to Lang with a literary allusion from Smollett. The convoluted yet brilliant metaphor shows how Lang pulled off this masterstroke. In today's parlance, this metaphor would probably be replaced with theorization using Marshall McLuhan's *Medium is Massage*. The journal says:

> SMOLLETT, in the Proem[XV] to one of his novels, introduces an author encouraging a bookseller to publish a libel he had written, by assuring him that, if he should be prosecuted for it and flogged at a cart's tail, his fortune would be made. He might have added, as a further encouragement, that, if the prosecution failed, his prospects would have been brighter still.
>
> The break-down of the prosecution in the case of the great Indian commissariat contractor, Lala Jotee Persaud, must have exalted that personage far above his most sanguine hopes; it has insured to him all his vast gains; it has spread the hue of honesty over all his deeds; it has exhibited him in the light of a victim of unjust and vindictive persecution, and diffused his fame over the Western as well as the Eastern world.

These are some of the replies of the English Language Press to Lang's defence of Lala. There seem to have been a lot of grey areas, and despite Lang's stupefying performance at the court, the matter was not what either parties made it out to be. The British government certainly was not justified in prosecuting with zeal a man who had helped it in times of need. Lala, on the other hand, seems to have had a field day, along with many officers in the hierarchy, in charging money for 'paper bullocks'. Lang himself puts the matter succinctly in *Wanderings in India* with his use of the word 'believe':

XV 'proem' is 'preface' from Latin '*prooemium*' which means 'introduction'

> But, to this day, the natives of India believe that the object of the Government was to cheat their creditor; while the officers, civil and military, are equally sanguine that it was 'the honour of the family' that led to the most extraordinary and protracted trial that ever was known in India.[106]

Lang does not tell about his own 'belief' in this chronicle. The hint through the phrase 'the honour of the family' is at Governor-General Dalhousie—that one of his close relatives was a high official in the commissariat and he wanted his name cleared, and therefore ordered the trial.

Malcolm Lewin—who was a bitter critic of the East India Company and wrote several books attacking its policies, compared the case of Lala Jotee Persaud and the Nawab of Oude, Wajid Ali Shah, and said that the Company's policy was that of use and throw in both the cases. Like Jotee Persaud, the Nawab had come to the aid of the Company by giving it his armies and lands when it needed them the most. The result was annexation of Oude. Lewin contends that if the Supreme Court had not stood between Jotee Persaud and his ruin, the Company would have added yet another scalp to its vault.[107]

The din of the case created furore in England, and the matter was taken up by Lord Ellenborough, the former governor-general, and who John Lang had christened Lord 'Elephantborough'.

Lala's Victory at Lord's, or Lord Elephantborough Trumpets

The *Earl of Ellenborough*, in the House of Lords censured the government of India for having instituted a trial against Lala Jotee Persaud. He dwelt upon the 'gentlemanlike manners of the Lala, upon the services he had rendered in the Gwalior and Punjab campaigns, and blamed the Indian Government…especially since he had commenced a civil suit in the Supreme Court, where the frauds, if true, would have come out: though the noble Earl thought this proceeding ill-advised on the part of the Lala.[108] In unequivocal terms, the lord condemned such a noble native having been caused such harassment by the government.

Lord Broughton came to the defence of the government, and said that it was known clearly by now that Lala had filed his civil suit after the criminal charges were pressed against him. Lord Broughton quoted from Dalhousie's reply that Lala had offered to give up the names of departmental officers, if he was made a government witness. He further added that Dalhousie, at such an instance, was even more keen to go with the case to know the workings of the commissariat—if it was corrupt, names would come up and it would help clean the system; if Lala was innocent, he would get insight into why there was such a delay in the payment. Broughton contended that the government had no option but to go with the trial.

The British press in general did not like Lord Ellenborough's move, and contended that Lala may have had the right to his acquittal, but the government was fair in having pressed the charges.

That is the story of Lala who was 'Wanted Dead or Alive' by the Sikh army; who supplied provisions to the British Army; who was one of the founding members of Delhi Bank; who was jailed by the British government who was bailed out of trouble by John Lang; whose story created unprecedented uproar in the British press; who went to the aid of the British again in 1857; whose picture was passed off as Nana Sahib's by Lang; who spread rumours about retreat of mutineers and about Akbar's ghost ordaining maintenance of British rule; who destroyed many heritage buildings for building materials during 1857; who baked bread because English women did not like chapatis; who was awarded royal land in Gwalior along with the title of Roy Bahadoor; and whose spirit was summoned by Judge Peterson the Spiritualist.

With this victory, Lala's star was on the ascendant, and it was reported that he had gone to Shimla to dine with the governor-general[109]. The cause of the nemesis of the Indian government, Mr Lang, however, would be in deep trouble very soon.

My Friend's Wife, or Lang You're Wanted

or Coward Colonel Crushes Lala's Counsel, or Australian Barrister Behind Bars in Austria

This chapter's title takes its inspiration from John Lang's novel *My Friend's Wife,* Or *York You're Wanted* (1859).[1] 'My' in 'my friend's wife' in this chapter's title alludes to Lala Jotee Persaud, the friend is John Lang, the wife is Lucy Lang. This is the story of the Lala acting as a benefactor for his friend's wife.

As we read earlier, Lucy Lang filed a case against William Cobb Hurry and the Lala in 1863, for the recovery of her alimony from her estranged husband, John Lang.[2] This is curious as any case of alimony would have to be fought against the husband, and not his friends.

In 1851, after Lang had won the case for the Lala, *The Delhi Gazette* had reported that the Lala had paid Lang three lakh rupees for his service. Upon the death of the Lala in 1870, an obituary notice about him tells that the Lala had actually paid Lang two lakh rupees:

> The Lalla paid Mr. Lang two lakhs of rupees—one lakh in cash and one by bond, but all included in a settlement on his wife. True, he had to pay his clever counsel many a rupee in after years, which may possibly make up the three lakhs mentioned by the *Delhi Gazette*.[3]

It is interesting to see the idea of the 'clever counsel' being paid 'many a rupee', but this probably was not because *The Delhi Gazette* had mentioned three lakhs, but because the Lala remained a client of Lang.

What is interesting here is that the payment for the case was 'included in a settlement on his wife'. This means that John and Lucy Lang were probably still together in 1851. Victor Crittenden contends that they separated very early, after being together in India for just a little time. The above-mentioned obituary refutes the assumption. Even if they were separated, the couple were on very good terms. For, the payment in bond included in a settlement on his wife could not have been Lala's idea, for Lala barely knew Lang then. It, then, was definitely Lang's desire that the payment be made through such a stratagem.

It is for the settlement of this bond that Lucy fought the case in 1863 against Mr Hurry and the Lala. During the case hearing, Lucy's brother Andrew Peterson testified to the judge that 'Jotee Persaud told me that he was paying the money for the benefit of Mrs. Lang, because he could not trust her husband'.

It is an irony that 12 years after the case, Lala was paying the same money to Mrs Lang because 'he could not trust' John Lang. And thence, the honorarium obtained by Lang in 1851 was settled in 1863 upon his first wife Lucy and their children—Aimee (Lang/Riccardi), William Bland Lang, Lucy (Lang/Burlamacchi/Manzi) and Margaret (Lang/?).

Now, let's look at the second part of the first half of the title, 'Lang, you're wanted'. We have seen how Indians indulged in exuberant celebrations on Lala Jotee Persaud's victory in 1851.[4] The East India Company was irked at its humiliating defeat and its condemnation in the House of Lords, and was determined to be avenged. There was a report in the *Lahore Chronicle* that 'further proceedings were threatened by the civil authorities, and that the Lala was about to betake himself to Calcutta, there to reside for the rest of his days under the aegis of the Supreme Court'[5]. A letter received by *Allen's Indian Mail* said that the Lala had gone to Simla to obtain an interview with the Governor-General.[6]

Lang, on the other hand, was determined to show the East India Company some more of his mettle as a lawyer. He took magistrate Martin Gubbins to court for the illegal seizure of various goods and chattels. According to *Allen's Indian Mail*, 'The defence was grounded on the recently-passed Act for the protection of judicial officers; but the Chief Justice (who is said to have been the framer of that Act) decided that it did not give impunity to the magistrate on the mere assertion of his belief that he had jurisdiction…Judgement was given for plaintiff, damages fifty rupees, reserving certain points of law for future decision'[7].

This case was decided on 6 August 1851. Lang's second victory would be short lived, for the East India Company was now determined to rein him in.

Once Lang had won the case, he decided to write a few invectives against Colonel Mactier, who during the case against the Lala had insisted that the Lala was not completely faultless, even though the informer was of 'suspect character'.

In the report of the defence published by *Agra Messenger*, and later in *The Mofussilite* on 18 April 1851, the speech of defence contained an extra line than what Lang had spoken. Mactier sued Lang for libel in the Supreme Court of Calcutta for this extra line:

> The Military Board has not a high character for liberality, but such were its sentiments; one member alone of that Board, a person distinguished for cowardice at Kotah, Col. Mactier (belonging to some regiment of light cavalry, I forget its number at present), differed from the rest, and became the sole parent of that disgraceful mischief.[8]

There are two accusations that Lang made in this 'libel': one, that Mactier had shown cowardice on the battlefield, and two, that he solely was responsible for heaping misery on Lala Jotee Persaud by insisting on going ahead with the case of fraud against the latter.

Lang was right on both the counts.

The Colonel had indeed acted with cowardice during the Kotah campaign of 1821, 30 years preceding the time of this libel case against

Lang. Lang, with his many military connections and correspondents, would have found out about the colonel, or may be the story was well-known. However, there are just two documented sources for this, and they are of a much later date than the demise of Lang. It took four years of sleuthing to know about Colonel Mactier, and finally it yielded fruit. A note on Henry Rede/Reade in *A Record of the Redes of Barton Court*… tells that:

> The major in command, together with Henry J. Reade, rode in advance of the troop. When within fifty yards of the enemy, an officer in the rear rank, Lieut. Mactier, suddenly gave the order to retire, with the result that two officers at the front (Edward Jervoise Ridge and Henry Jonathan Reade, qq.v.), deserted by their men, rode alone to meet inevitable death. Mactier's interest with E.I.C.[I] being strong, he escaped with reprimand…A court of Enquiry which was ordered by the C.D. in June 1825, was not held owing to the absence in England of many witnesses.[9]

The same note is copied in the entry under 'William Mactier' in Hodson's *List of the Officers of the Bengal Army, 1758–1834.*[10] This book lists Mactier's services as follows:

> Services : Barasat C.C. 81 mos. Cadet d.d. 4th N.C. 1811. Posted Cornet to 4th N.C. 1813. Leave s.c. 6 mos. to sea 4 July 1817. Third Mahratta War 1818; Cornet 4th N.C. Intr. & Qmr. 4th L.C. 10 Apr. 1819 till 29 June 1824. Operations in Kotah 1821; Mangrol (? w.); Lieut. 4th L.C.[II] Leave u.p.a. to.Calcutta 19 Apr. till 14 Dec. 1822. Leave s.c. 12 mos. to N.S.W. 3 May 1823 till 16 Apr. 1826. Fur. s.c. 4 June 1826 till 14 May 1831…[11]

It is the words in bold that concern us here. It can be seen that

I E.I.C. is East India Company

II There is footnote appended at this point in the entry which details the act of Mactier's cowardice.

immediately after the Kotah war, Mactier went for a very long leave—first to Calcutta, then to, interestingly, New South Wales, and then to an unknown destination. Mactier resurfaces in action only in 1834, thirteen years after he had left two of his fellow officers to die in the battlefield. The issue of this leave was also brought forward by Lang in court. The entry in Hodson's book also tells that Mactier got promoted in 1824 to the rank of captain. This means that he got promoted while his case of cowardice was still sub-judice. The entry also tells that William Mactier was the brother of Anthony Mactier, head commander, Court of Requests, Bengal. These points corroborate the footnote to the entry that tells that Mactier escaped because of his influence with the East India Company.

During the case against the Lala, Lang confronted Mactier, who was a jury member:

> Now, Col. Mactier, you were present at the action of Kotah, and have you no remembrance of a Lieut. Mactier, on that occasion, showing the white feather, ordering threes about, when it was not at all necessary? in fact, he ran away?[12]

Cross-examination was not allowed to Lang.

Edward Jervoise Ridge was a major in the Kotah campaign, and did sustain severe injuries. An account of the Kotah war published in an obituary notice upon the death of Ridge in 1833, also mentions the two killed officers.[13]

It is interesting to note that the other slain officer, Henry Jonathan Reade, was an elder brother of Charles Reade who had collaborated with Tom Taylor as a co-author for several plays. Lang had suggested the plot about Fouche and his cohorts to Charles Reade and Tom Taylor so that they could write a play about it.[14]

Charles Reade had never seen his unfortunate brother Henry, and two other elder brothers for all three had died in India while he was still a little child. Reade's biographer Malcolm Elwin tells this about the large family and its misfortunes:

> She (Charles's mother) bore a numerous family, of whom ten lived to maturity—seven sons and three daughters. There was necessarily considerable disparity in the ages of her children, so that when Charles Reade, her youngest child was born on the 8th of June 1814, his eldest brother was seventeen and about to enter the service of the East India Company. Charles never knew his three eldest brothers, for John Thurlow died in India when he was thirty, the second, George Edward, died there when his youngest brother was an infant, and the third Henry Jonathan, when he was only seven.[15]

The tombs of these two slain officers, Lieutenants Reade and Clarke, still exist in Kota, Rajasthan.[16]

Mactier was infuriated as the 'libel' was published in two newspapers. Mr Newmarch, on the request of Mactier, wrote a letter to Lang asking him to apologise to the colonel in a frank and unqualified manner, whereupon he would forgive him and not pursue the matter. Lang replied with these words:

> Gentlemen…I am pained to think that Col. Mactier should have been so exceedingly ill-advised… and I have to request you will not write to me any more on this subject.[17]

The die was cast, and a case against John Lang was filed by Mactier. There was a delay in the case because the prosecution wanted to bring the editor of *The Mofussilite*, G.R. Wilby, to Calcutta. A report in the newspaper criticised the government for this act, for Lang had already filed an affidavit that he had sold the newspaper many months previous to Lala Jotee Persaud's trial. The intention of the prosecution was obviously to cause as much damage to Lang as possible. *The Mofussilite* wrote:

> If we complain of the hardship of dragging men nine hundred miles away from their business to give evidence before this Court we shall be told by the Company's defenders, that is our own fault in resisting that paternal jurisdiction which they wish to extend over us. We reply that so far from defending, we have steadily exposed the absurdities of the English system of law; but that abuses being easily removable do not constitute sufficient reason for depriving British subjects of their birthright.[18]

The writer, quite obviously John Lang himself, expounded on how this kind of arbitrary governance would stifle the freedom of the press:

> It is that a proceeding of this kind puts a weapon into the hands of any malicious person to oppress others. He has only to watch an opportunity, and on the publication of anything which he can allege to be libellous, subpoena the whole establishment of a person whom he wishes to injure.[19]

Meanwhile, the *Delhi Gazette* reported in June that Lang had passed on the proprietorship of *The Mofussilite* to Lala Jotee Persaud, who would employ a new editor.[20] The proprietorship was given by Lang to Mr Gibbons many months previously, and this news report of *Delhi Gazette* seems to have been a rumour meant to undermine Lang's position in the case since Jotee Persaud was his client, and him becoming the proprietor would insinuate that Lang controlled the newspaper through a remote-control technique.

The case of libel commenced in the Supreme Court of Calcutta on 19 August 1851. Mr Morton, with Mr Welsh, appeared for the prosecution; Mr Lang supported his own case, assisted by Mr Bell.

Mr Morton said that a few months previously, Lang had defended Jotee Persaud in a court at Agra. He said that in his defence speech for Jotee, Lang had not uttered the libellous passage, which he wrote or caused to be written in *Mofussilite*, the newspaper of which he was the proprietor. The prosecutor added that the passage had cast cruel aspersions on Mactier's character. About Kotah, Morton merely said that Mactier was involved in the Kotah campaign of 1821, and that the distinctions earned by Mactier were evidence of his honourable character, and that the libeller ought to be punished.

G.R. Wilby told the court that previously he was the editor of *The Hurkaru*, and that he assumed the office of the editor of *The Mofussilite* in August 1850. He said that Lang never interfered with the editorial work, nor did he write for the paper during the period beginning from August 1850 till the end of the trial of Jotee Persaud in April 1851. Wilby also added that Lang had positively distanced himself from the newspaper, and also, that he received payments not from Lang but from Mr Gibbons, who conducted the business of the paper in the absence of Lang. Wilby also added that while he had been subpoenaed to produce notes and proofs of Lang's speech, he did not have any notes as it was not a custom of the newspaper to preserve such proofs. He also could not say for certain if the defence speech had been published first in *The Mofussilite* or if it had been copied from *Agra Messenger.* He, however, stated that on 17 April—the day before the libel was printed—Mr Lang was at the printer. This last statement would become a clinching evidence against Lang.

Mr Newmarch, who had written to Lang on Mactier's behalf, told the court that another person, Mr J. Spankie, had been subpoenaed, but couldn't appear in court due to illness. Newmarch told the court that Lang, after the conclusion of the Jotee Persaud case, had told Spankie:

> It is a pity I forgot to allude to Col. Mactier's cowardice in my speech for the defence; but it is no matter, as it will be made all right in my published speech.

It is of note that Spankie himself did not make this statement—not even in writing—to the court; Newmarch used as evidence the memory of his eavesdropping of the Lang and Spankie's conversation.

John Lang himself then addressed the court. He contended there was not sufficient evidence to send the case to the jury; the whole matter was founded on inference. As for the indictment, the first count alleged that he was the proprietor of a newspaper called *The Mofussilite*; but it did not allege that he published the speech in question as the proprietor of *The Mofussilite*, nor that Colonel Mactier was libelled in his character as a soldier. These points Lang thought most material. He contended there was nothing in the words of the libel themselves unexplained that could render this an offence punishable by law. He raised another objection that the newspaper had been admitted as evidence against him, and not the original transcript.

The prosecutor argued that the circumstantial evidence against Lang formed *prima facie* evidence, and the judge concurred.

Lang then, addressing the jury, said that had he been in England, he would not have been facing his current predicament, as there was an Act in the English constitution which dealt with such cases very differently—that in cases of libel, the character of the both the libeller and the libelled were taken into account. According to that Act, the libelled person has to clear his name with regard to the libel written against him. Lang therefore expressed his desire to question Mactier, but was prevented by the judge.

Lang in his defence said that his proprietorship could not be proved by Wilby's statement. Lang also questioned as to why Wilby, who could tell nothing, was brought down to Calcutta instead of Gibbons, the proprietor. He also added that even if he were proved to be proprietor, in England, only the editor and the publisher were charged, and not the proprietor. Lang also pointed out that after the case of Jotee Persaud newspaper reports had made slanderous remarks against himself (Lang). Such reports were likely to operate to his prejudice, and doubtless were spread in order to bias the minds of people on his trial.

Lang emphasised the fact that the so-called libel was published first in the *Agra Messenger* and that *The Mofussilite* report was merely a copy.

At this time in the court, Lang was at his impetuous and passionate best; one can gauge Lang's rhetorical capabilities and sharp tongue from *Allen's Indian Mail's* account of the last part of Lang's defence:

> He (Lang) saw many military officers in court, who knew him well, and who could say that he had erased from the Army List many rogues, rascals, cowards, and rapscallions; but, at the same time, he was the last person in the world to cast aspersions upon the character of an innocent man. How many officers of high standing, who had been hidden by the cloud of disfavour, had he assisted, and by his means dispelled the cloud that enveloped them! After a few further remarks, he left his fate entirely in the hands of the jury, declining to call any witnesses.

Lang's passion, which had won him the Jotee Persaud case, became his nemesis in his own case. Had been a little less passionate, and cross-examined witnesses, primarily Wilby; or if he had insisted that the proprietor of *The Mofussilite*, Mr Gibbons, be presented in the court, he would, perhaps, have been saved. Lang is also quite right in his statement about the military that he had stood by them. In all his novels that are set in India, while Lang is critical of the decadence in the army, , when it comes to the battle-field, he paints quite a romantic picture of the British Indian Army's valour.

Lang's defence was quite strong, as the reader can discern. Even though Wilby's statement put Lang at the printer's office the day before the libellous report was published, or that Newmarch's overheard conversation between Spankie and Lang only point a finger at Lang. In legal terms, these do not mean much to prove Lang had a hand in the publishing of the libellous report.

Sir Arthur Buller, the judge, in summing up, told the jury they had three points to consider: firstly, whether the words in question amounted to libel; secondly, whether they related to Colonel Mactier; and, thirdly, whether, supposing the first two points proved to their satisfaction, the defendant was guilty of the publication. He also read the definition of a criminal libel, as given by Hawkins: 'A malicious defamation, expressed either in printing or writing, and tending either to blacken the memory of one that is dead, or the reputation of one that is alive, and expose him to public ridicule, hatred, or contempt.'

He then left the case in the hands of the jury, who returned with the verdict of 'guilty'.

On 23 August 1851, Lang moved for a new trial. In the fresh case, he listed multiple reasons for unfair judgement. All of Lang's objections were overruled, and Justice Buller pronounced Lang guilty of the offence of libel. He said that people utter slanderous words in moments of excitement, but in this case, it was a premeditated act on the part of Lang, that the subject was not a matter of public gossip, and it had been forgotten for 30 years. The judge also said that Lang had carried out this attack because Mactier had ordered further inquiry into Lala Jotee Persaud's case. The judge added that the intention was also to prevent a public servant to perform his duties properly. The judge said it would be ridiculous to suppose that the passage against Mactier was written for public benefit. The judge then pronounced the sentence:

> The sentence of the Court is, that you be imprisoned in the common jail of Calcutta for the space of two calendar months;

> that you do pay a fine of one thousand rupees to her Majesty the Queen, and that you be further imprisoned until that sum be paid.[21]

The section of the press—the one that Lang alleged had been slandering him ever since his victory in the John Company's case against Jotee Persaud—took Lang's defeat in the libel case as their own victory and vindication. *The Hurkaru* wrote summarising the case:

> ...And mark the affectation and artful semblance which this precious paragraph exhibits. In speaking of Col. Mactier's *status,* the words used are, 'Belonging to some regiment of light cavalry, *of which I forget the number at present!*' This is manifestly intended to convey the idea that the brilliant speaker was hurried away by the intensity of his feelings, and poured forth his crushing philippics in the heat of Demosthenic eloquence and argument…Alas in prosaic pitiful contrast, now comes out the damning fact,—proved and admitted,—that the whole was a subsequent concoction,—an unprecedented compound of audacity and folly. Those who heard the defendant's address to the jury declare it the most miserable exhibition ever witnessed within the walls of the Supreme Court…one confused incoherent rant, bald and disjointed in language, and utterly puerile in argument.[22]

And so, Mr Lang went to jail in Calcutta in 1851. Lala Jotee Persaud was saved by Lang from the clutches of the East India Company; the same Lala later became friends with the said company and was given high honours, but Lang, who targeted the company's policies, got targeted in return, as part of the company policy.

The John Lang who, haunted by the fact of convict origins, had carefully cultivated the image of a 'gentleman' in India and Britain, landed in jail himself. His term in jail, however, helped strengthen Lang's resolve and ambition; from hereon, he would take very seriously his career both as a journalist and a novelist. Till the end of his life he would speak jestingly about the libel issue—that he had been imprisoned for *Agra Messenger's* crime.[23]

Lang Runs Optimist, or British Press Calls Him Pessimist

While Lang waited in Calcutta for Wilby, for the trial to begin, he started a new newspaper called *The Optimist*.[24]

Lang, at this point of time, seems to have been in a really bad mood—one can see a virtual war declared by Lang against East India Company, based on the articles of *The Optimist*. Lang wrote an article against Sir Charles Napier; and Major McMurdo, the lord's son-in-law, wrote to *Delhi Gazette*, verbally horsewhipping 'a notorious buffoon of the name of Lang'.[25] *The Englishman* stated that the editor of the paper (Lang) had changed his mind some half-dozen times in half as many years regarding the character of Sir Napiers.[26]

The Optimist replied very briefly to Major McMurdo's offensive letter, '"McMurdo is not a bad fellow; but, as everybody knows, a great ass"—*Napier*'.

This new newspaper of Lang reported about various excesses of East India Company. In one of its issues, *The Optimist* alleged that an army officer had committed homicide:

> A letter from Wuzeerabad mentions that an artillery officer, travelling in Cashmere, was talking to a young female in the bazaar, when a sepoy, in the service of the Maharajah came up, and interrupted the discourse. The officer struck the sepoy a blow, and killed him. We abstain from mentioning the officer's name at present, though we do not doubt the truth of what we have above stated.[27]

How Lang manoeuvred to print this is a matter of curiosity, for he was still in jail when this news report was published on 1 October 1851. The report mentions the source to be a letter; this implies that Lang managed to evade censorship of the correspondences he carried out from the jail. *The Lahore Chronicle* tried to repair the damage by publishing a contrary report, saying that Captain Hungerfort had seen two of his servants, 'a seepahee and a bheestee' misbehaving with a 'koolee' and that they on being reprimanded had attacked and nearly killed him. The seepahee (soldier) of the Maharaja's regiment was returned to his master's services, and one day had been found dead.[28]

It is quite obvious from *The Lahore Chronicle's* reply that the soldier had indeed died, and the 'explanatory' story insinuates a cover up—as was norm in those days.

The Mofussilite, with Gibbons as proprietor and Wilby as editor, paid its compliments to the editor of *The Optimist*:

> *The Optimist* of the 6th instant is a remarkably good number. Like John Bunyan in Bedford jail our contemporary's wits do not appear to grow rusty in confinement.[29]

The Optimist stopped getting published in October 1851. This is the time Lang got out of jail and returned to Meerut. It is unfortunate that there is no prison diary or known account of Lang's stint in jail.

After returning to Meerut, Lang bought back *The Mofussilite* from Gibbons and resumed his editorial career. Lang wrote caustically about the government not having paid Jotee Persaud his dues. Here is a sample of one such article written by Lang:

> The Government have ordered the payment of some 14 Lacs of rupees to be made to Lalla Jotee Persaud, in part

> payment of his account. It is a great pity that Government is not amenable (like a poor Subaltern) to a Military Court of Request. We should advise the Lalla to sue them therein, take out an execution general, sell the pictures of Louis XVI and Marie Antoinette, the frowsy furniture in Government House, and then the various effects which are scattered about Fort William and Calcutta.[30]

This is Lang at his typically caustic best with a ready wit. This is the kind of writing that had made *The Mofussilite* both famous and notorious. Lang continues the said article like this:

> ...There is no pretext to avoid payment, that the Government has not resorted to…Lacs and lacs of rupees have been struck off the Bill on mere suspicion of 'overcharge'...If the government were to act with only decent liberality, they would pay Lallah Jotee Persaud 59 Lac rupees...the man whose exertions our operations much depended on is 'fobbed off'...The writer of this article once suggested that Jotee Persaud forego all claim to a sum only £11,000 which Major Bygrave had cut out of the claim—and his reply was—'I would give the Government double the amount if they wanted it; but if I forgo this it will be construed into an admission that I have cheated them!' Such is the man whom the Government of India is not, seemingly ashamed to haggle!

The Jotee Persaud case continued to hog headlines till the end of 1853 in various newspapers, and his account had not been settled till 1857, when ironically the Lala came to the aid of the British again.

The Friend of India newspaper reported on 18 December 1851 that Lala Jotee Persaud was going to hire Mr Morton, 'the most eminent barrister of Calcutta'. If this were to be true, it would be a great irony, for it was this same Morton who was the prosecutor in the case that got Lang a stay in Calcutta jail.

The information about Morton becoming Jotee's counsel, however, seems to have been a rumour, for Lang was engaged with Jotee's affairs for a long time after the famous trial. One cannot, however, rule out some substance being to this rumour—Jotee Persaud would have have had the desire to gradually distance himself from Lang, who was avowedly against the East India Company.

As seen the pro-establishment press loathed Lang. In his literary career his destiny was no different. His biting sarcasm against the ills of East India Company found its way into fiction, too; this was one of the reasons why he was ignored or slandered by the white press. An issue of the *Calcutta Review* played upon his having had been the editor of *The Optimist* while in true nature being a real pessimist. The journal, in an article about Anglo-Indian writing, said:

> Foremost among our Indian pessimists is the quondam[III] Editor of 'The Optimist'. Mr. Lang was a successful journalist in this country, and at home has proved himself to possess some dramatic power and narrative skill…But the pictures given of Indian Society in Mr. Lang's works do far 'more credit to his head than his heart.' The tale which appeared serially in 'Fraser's Magazine' some years ago under the title of 'The Wetherbys', was completely constructed on the hospital-scheme above referred to; the whole of the characters being…selected from the rogues and drabs whom the author may have known or met during the course of an Indian career…However this may be, we cannot allow that such a book presents a fair specimen of the constitution of Indian Society. A later work—'Will He Marry Her?'—is free from this objection…but it is inferior in construction, in probability, in every point of literary execution,

III erstwhile

> that it can hardly be looked to as an antidote to the Venom of 'The Wetherbys.'

The Wetherbys, arguably the most satirical of Lang's novels, was published during this 'venomous' phase, in 1853, when the East India Company was determined to become a bane for Lang, and vice versa. Just after getting out of jail in 1852, Lang began writing a sequel to *The Wetherbys*, called *My Furlough by Robert Wetherby*[31] (1854). Even though the first novel was already written, probably before the trial of Jotee Persaud, it was published in 1853 in *Fraser's Magazine*, and later as a novel.

'The Indians' referred to in the above review does not mean the actual Indians, lest the reader get confused. In the 19th century, Indians were always referred to as 'natives'. Ironically, *Will He Marry Her?* which is cast aside as novel of inferior construction in the above review, occupies a large bulk of this research for its ideological stand of framing its narrative against class and racism. *The Wetherbys* is accused of picking from the English society, 'rogues and drabs'. That the English writers chose to depict only wretchedness, calumny and perjury amongst natives is not taken as a 'depiction' but as 'real' for most reviewers of this time. John Lang, with a few other writers like Arnold and Malcolm Lewin, thus became the doppelganger of the painters of the East.

That, then, was the reward for John Lang for winning the case of Jotee Persaud, and for calling Colonel Mactier a coward—a stint in prison. The money earned from the Jotee Persaud case was to be settled upon Lang's wife; and when the time for settlement came, Jotee Persaud said he could not trust Lang. Mactier's cowardice had resulted in the death of two young officers, but instead of him, it was Lang who ended up being incarcerated.

This was not the only time Lang went to jail. The next time was in Vienna, during his third 'British' phase—the last one when he stayed in England for five years to further his literary career and become as famous as Dickens, which he was unable to. The account of Lang's second jail journey comes from one of his own short pieces, 'An Experience of Austria'.

Barrister of Australia, or Behind the Bars in Austria

The account 'An Experience of Austria' appears in Charles Dickens's journal *Household Words* in 1857.[32] Until the publication of Anne Lohrli's book, *Household Words: A Weekly Journal 1850–1859*,[33] most of the articles in the *Household Words* had been unattributed. Lohrli's book provides a whole list of Lang's works in *Household Words*.[34] Besides that, I have perused the correspondences between John Earnshaw—who did a lot of fundamental research about Lang—and Leslie C. Staples, of *The Dickensian*.[35]

Crittenden gives a background to the article about Lang's Austrian experience, expounding the political situation of Europe during mid-19th century:

> This article (Lang's story) presents us with a view into conditions in Vienna, the capital city of Imperial Austria in the 1850s. In 1848, the Hungarians had revolted and declared a short-lived republic. The eighteen-year-old Franz Joseph of the House of Hapsburg became Emperor. The Chancellor Prince von Metternich who had dominated the countries of Europe since the fall of Napoleon lost his position…1848 had been a dramatic year for the monarchs of mainland Europe…By 1854, things had settled down but there had emerged a rivalry between Austria and Prussia for dominance over independent German states.[36]

This is how Lang begins his story:

> ON the tenth of December, eighteen hundred and fifty-four, I entered the Austrian capital, and took up my abode at a

> certain hotel. I had no particular business in Vienna. My object was to amuse myself; and, at my leisure, see the many works of art of which the imperial city can boast. My name, reader, is Jenkins—Alfred Jenkins. My passport, according to the regulation, was deposited with the police, and I was presented in lieu thereof with a pass, or permission to remain one month; this pass was renewable, provided the authorities had no objection.[37]

In the story, on the third day of his arrival in Vienna, Alfred Jenkins asks the kellner for *The Lloyd* newspaper; the kellner tells him it was banned for writing against the Emperor of Prussia. Jenkins is then advised by his friend to be careful about what he speaks, for there is a man lurking in a corner who only listens, and opens his mouth only to eat.

Lang thus sets the tone for the story right away. His protagonist Jenkins is in Austria, and is in trouble for speaking about the freedom of press. In the evening, Jenkins asks for newspapers again—this time for the *Times* and the *Daily News*; he is told that both the papers are banned. The kellner says, 'When an English paper says anything bad, there comes a telegraphic message from London, and when that paper comes to the frontier it is seized and burnt.'[38] Jenkins receives a letter from Brussels which requires him to answer several questions through telegraph. Jenkins goes to the telegraph office and sends the following reply:

> Number One: Frazer's Magazine, October, one thousand eight hundred and fifty-two.—Number Two: One thousand eight hundred and forty-eight.—Number Three: Let it stand as written.—Number Four : Send no money till you hear from me.[39]

The next day an officer comes and informs Jenkins that he is to appear at the police station at 2 am. At the police station, Jenkins is made to wait; he and starts walking up and down since he cannot stand for long. The officer, annoyed, utters 'something like Donnerwetter!'. Jenkins is quizzed at length about his purpose of visiting Austria, and finally asked why he corresponds in cipher. Jenkins is astounded at this, but the officer, unfazed mentions the telegraph he had sent out the previous night:

> 'There!' exclaimed the official, triumphantly. 'There ! Yes! Forty-eight!…What business has an Englishman with Forty-eight?'
>
> I began to inform the official that they were replies to certain questions forwarded to me by a literary friend in Brussels. I told him that the first question concerned the date in which a certain article had appeared in an English periodical—an article to which my friend desired to make immediate reference; that the second question referred to the year in which a new edition of a certain work had been published; that the third question was about a sentence that my friend wished to alter in a work of mine, the proof sheets of which he was then correcting; and the fourth question was simply this—Should he, my friend, remit me from Brussels, or from London, (to which last-mentioned place he was about to proceed), a sum of money I had left in his hands.[40]

Jenkins thinks he has answered the questions to the officer's satisfaction, but he is too far off the point in assuming this:

> …the official did not listen to one word of it. He had made up his mind that I had come to Vienna as the agent of all the exiles in England; and that I was, therefore, a dangerous character in the Austrian capital.
>
> 'You are then a literary man?'

> 'Yes.'
>
> 'I thought so. Well, I must see your papers.'
>
> 'I trust I may be spared the indignity of having my papers searched.'
>
> 'Indignity! What indignity! Many correspondents of English journals have had their papers searched in Vienna…'[41]

The officer who accompanies Jenkins to his apartment tells him that he had been shown kind treatment because of a treaty between England and Austria, or else it would have been rough for him. The papers in Jenkin's apartments are then checked:

> The first was a letter from a late Indian Brigadier-General… It was dated Ramnugger, and was posted just before the fatal charge in which he fell. Over the superscription of this letter were several words in Persian character, signifying that 'the postage had not been paid in camp, and was payable on delivery.' There was also on the superscription, a few words in Bengalee, written by the Baboo in the Meerut Post-office. These words signified my name and address, and were intended as a guide to the native postman, who could not read English. This letter was put aside. The next document…was a letter from my mother…I now became acquainted with the fact, that the officer was able to read our language; for, after he had got through the first page, he remarked, 'this is nothing,' and handed me the letter. A Grand Lodge manuscript certificate now caught his eye, and he opened it out. He was not a Freemason, and had never seen a piece of parchment of the like character. He asked me what it was; I told him. Nevertheless, he put it aside with the Brigadier's letter. The fourth document that came to his hand was a letter from a German gentleman, holding an office in the Prussian Embassy in London. In that letter he had facetiously alluded to

> my intended visit to Vienna, and recommended me to take care that they did not lock me up. No sooner did I see the officer take that epistle in his hand, than I felt it was all over with me, and I dare say I turned pale. Albeit, I laughed heartily, for the whole affair struck me as something comical. My laughter, however, was soon changed to gravity, when I beheld the officer put back the papers into my desk—lock it…and request me to 'come along.'

I have dwelt upon the contents in Jenkin's desk at length, for a purpose—which is that we get valuable insights into Lang's life from these letters. The story may be a little fictionalised but it is quite clear that Lang, for the most part of this story, is speaking from his own experience. The battle which Lang refers to here is the Second Anglo-Sikh War (1848–49), about which Lang wrote extensively in *The Mofussilite*. The officer who Lang is referring to is Brigadier General Cureton, who died in the battle of Ramnugger, as did his son. A reference can be found to the brigadier alluded to by Lang in *The Literary Gazette:*

> Major Christie, with many of his gunners, was cut down on horseback. The approach of the Goorchurras was so sudden that this lamented officer had not drawn his sword from its scabbard when he received the first wound…Many an officer and man, overturned by the cavalry, were trampled on the ground…Young Cureton, a Lieutenant in the 14th Dragoons, son of the distinguished sabreur of that name, was killed in this affair. His horse, it is said, ran away with him, and carried him into the hostile ranks. It will be remembered that Brigadier-General Cureton sustained a mortal wound some few days before, at the cavalry skirmish of Ramnugger—the opening scene of the second Seikh war.[42]

What is interesting is that the address on the letter found among Jenkins' belongings, was in 'Bengalee, written by the Baboo in the Meerut Post-office'. Meerut is in the heart of North India, and not a place where Bengali can be understood even verbally. This shows how the Bengali community got early hold on government jobs during British Raj. Since Calcutta was the capital of British India, the Bengalis were the first to learn English as well as seek government jobs. Also noteworthy is that even the British used the Persian script for their official work, with words to the effect of 'postage not paid' written in Urdu on the letter.

Jenkins is taken to prison on charge of spying. Jenkins here tells that he knows the British ambassador and his son personally, but that the former is ill and the latter is away, and he would bide his time till the son returns. It was characteristic of Lang, like Jenkins, to drop names of highly placed officials as his friends.

Jenkins tells that he had read of a morning newspaper journalist being in a Vienna prison in 1852, and prepares himself to be herded with 'felons', to sleep on stone plank, and to have 'black bread and water', and in the worst case perhaps undergo the punishment called *Spiessrutben-laufen*. He describes it thus:

> An avenue of soldiers is formed. Each soldier holds in his hand a sort of knout—peculiar to Austria, I believe. The knout is formed of three leather straps, attached to a wooden handle. At the end of each strap is a bullet pierced with two spikes, crossways. The prisoner passes through the avenue, and each soldier gives him a blow. The length of the avenue, and the number of times the prisoner has to pass through it, is determined by the character of the offence which has been committed.[43]

However, Jenkins is not subjected to *Spiessrutben-laufen* or anything remotely like that. He is allowed to order food from outside, as well as to have a bottle of *Hockheimer* from the hotel. It is, of course, typical Lang, to be found together with alcohol. Jenkins tells that he was in the least worried because he was not guilty of anything, and that he passed the second day in prison in 'excellent' spirits. He is confident also because he had left a note for the ambassador's son that he would be found at a place where he would be 'at home'. Jenkins tells that his attendant had grown to like him in these two days, and told him confidentially that his papers had been forwarded to Brussels for inquiry since the intercepted telegraphic message was addressed to a gentleman in Brussels. Lang has made Jenkins a very cool and composed character who is barely concerned about his incarceration. On the third day, Jenkins tells that he was smoking and thinking when the officer who had behaved so rudely with him a few days ago came in, looking embarrassed.

In the dialogue that ensues between Jenkins and the officer, Lang's satirical wit manifests itself in its usual form:

> 'You will forgive my stupidity? It is proverbial that the English are as generous as they are brave.'
>
> 'Yes. I will forgive you,' I replied. 'But on one condition.'
>
> 'Which is?'
>
> 'That you never visit England.'
>
> 'Why that condition ?'
>
> 'I will cause you to be received by the English draymen, and you may have heard how reckless a race they are.' I said this jocularly.[44]

This is the story of Lang's incarceration in Vienna. Perhaps under the pen of another English writer of the 19th century, the matter would have received a different treatment; perhaps, there would have been a lot of gall and outrage. This is one of the hallmarks of Lang's writing—his ability to show ready wit. Through his satirical form, Lang has dealt with very serious issues concerning mid-19th century Europe (temporality or location is quite pointless when it comes to these issues)—that of press censorship, of suspicion towards men of letters, and of extreme torture in prisons. The writing style of Lang was an extension of Lang's personality—witty, (over)confident, excitable when fighting, calm and composed after a matter had been decided—for or against his cause. We have already seen it in the libel case, that Lang, after having argued the case for himself, refused to call any witnesses and resigned his fate to the decision of the jury. And that personality is what talks through the narrator of the Austrian story who says:

> To tell the real truth, I regarded my wrongs as a mere adventure; of which the reminiscence, in after life, would be—at all events—amusing.

If the name of the protagonist of this story, Alfred Jenkins, is to be anagramitised, one of the anagrams is 'Lank Finds Jeer'. One wonders if Lang, the alias-o-philiac, was also fond of anagrams, for the phrase fits the story perfectly well—Lang found himself jailed through an amusing suspicion, and found it a reason for one of his witty and jeering writings. The reader would interject that 'Lank' is not 'Lang', but I argue that Alfred Jengins would be a jarring, a fictional surname.

It was his status as a writer that mattered most to Lang, and stories from his life were also stories—good stories to be written down. Even about the Mactier case, Lang used to jest about his imprisonment—that he was jailed for the *Agra Messenger's* crime. Lang was the protagonist of most of his stories with his personality and events from his life strewn through his novels. One wonders if many of Lang's adventures were for the sake of writing a good story afterwards. That is the predicament of many writers—that they write about what they live, but they also start living what they write.

And so, Lang journeyed to the jail twice: in 1851 for libellously calling Colonel Mactier a coward, and in 1854 on charges of telegraphic spying.

But amidst the suspicious charges of spying, the Austrian policeman came across a curious document found among Jenkins' personal belongings, the Grand Lodge manuscript certificate.

Free Mason, or the Man Who Had No Tension

The Grand Lodge manuscript certificate refers to Freemasonry, an esoteric cult of obscure origins in Scotland and Ireland in the 16th and 17th centuries. The cult originated in 'Grand Lodge', under which rubric all denominations are known now. By the 19th century, Freemasonry was a force to reckon with. Interestingly, several Indians were also a part of this cult, even though Indians, in Bengal, were initially forbidden from joining. This distinction was done away with in 1872, with 'Brother' P.C. Dutt joining the cult. In other parts of India, this discrimination did not exist. Famous Indians such as Swami Vivekananda, Motilal Nehru, C. Rajagopalachari and Fakhruddin Ali Ahmad are also known to have joined the ranks of Freemasons.[45] The central preoccupations of the cult are charitable work, moral uprightness (requiring a belief in a Supreme Being), and development of fraternal friendship.

Freemasonry primarily uses symbolism of medieval tools of masonry, a compass and a square. By appending 'free' to 'mason', the idea is that of a speculative building rather than a literal one—that is to say, the philosophical and the moral building of society. There are several symbols and rituals associated with Freemasons. Freemasonry uses the metaphors of operative stonemasons' implements, against the allegorical backdrop of the building of King Solomon's Temple, 'a system of morality veiled in allegory and illustrated by symbols'[46]. Initially, it was essential for members to believe in a deity, but this clause was removed by Grande Oriente de France in late 19th century, which led to many atheists also joining the denomination. The two types of Lodges, therefore, are not in 'regular amity', most believing in a belief in deity, some not. John Lang, however, would have been a part of the deity or Bible-believing denomination, for in India, the Lodges were under the, of course Scottish and English Lodges.

This background is important to understand Lang's religious belief. As already seen in 'An Experience of Austria', Lang's autobiographical protagonist was carrying a Grand Lodge certificate. It is a matter of conjecture—but we shall believe in the existence of the Masonic certificate as well. Also, a cult is not a religion, and people can join it and leave it.

I do not know of Lang's involvement with the cult, since I haven't found any newspaper reports regarding this matter. However, there is a report of Lala Jotee Persaud invited as a dignitary to a ceremony of laying the foundation stone of Freemasons' Foundation in Lahore in 1859.[47]

Lala Jotee Persaud perhaps went because of his connection with Lang, or may be in his own right after having been made a Roy Bahadoor, we do not know.

As we have seen throughout this work, Lang had a great interest in curiosities and knowledge systems. He had interests in phrenology, mesmerism, esoteric texts of the East, besides the usual interests in art and rising technology. Perhaps it was the philosophical core of Freemasonry that appealed to Lang the most—the one of a philosophic, speculative building. In terms of Freemasonic symbology, I would argue that Lang interpreted it in his own way and made it resonate with his existing worldviews. He believed in compassing the world—physically, through his wanderings across India and Europe, and mentally, through his diverse interests. He also interpreted the idea of 'free mason' literally, and his career if observed closely, is that of a free mason—someone who is engaged in building fraternities and values, and is fighting a corrupt system, but who is free from cares. He starts from Calcutta as a lawyer; moves to Meerut to start a journalistic career and gives a pause to his legal career; sells off his newspaper to fight the case of Jotee Persaud; starts another newspaper from Calcutta when in jail; buys his old newspaper back; takes a leave from everything and goes to England for six years to write books; comes back to India where he thinks he belongs; and ends his days there.

In this sense, he was a mason, and quite free a mason. In an ossified sense of the conventions of the cult, he probably would not fit in.

There are evidences—apart from the Masonic certificate of Jenkins and Jotee Persaud's attendance of a function in Lahore—to show that Lang had dealings with Freemasonry. The evidences come from his newspaper *The Mofussilite* and his novels. These evidences do not prove anything. However, the insinuation of Lang's connection with the cult, through them, becomes stronger.

In Lang's obituary notice in *The Mofussilite*, many of his friends are mentioned. Among them are Henry M. Elliott and Henry W. Torrens. In a book of collection of Torrens's work,[48] J. Hume draws attention to comparisons that had been made in an 1854 article in *The Mofussilite* between these Elliott and Torrens. The writer of the article in *The Mofussilite* is obviously Lang:

> Mr. Elliot and Mr. Torrens were singularly alike in essentials, though in some matters they were peculiarly dissimilar. Both were endowed with great natural abilities, and both had made the most of the superior education which they had the good fortune to receive. Both entered the Civil Service together… they were both scholars…they were both distinguished for their knowledge of Persian and Oordoo: they were both passionately fond of the stage, and, at Meerut, guided, in their day, all the theatrical arrangements; they were both high Masons, and endeared themselves to all with whom they came in contact; they were both addicted to writing for the Press,

> and for generations to come their names in this country will not be forgotten.[49]

The shared interests between these two men were Lang's interests, too—Persian and Urdu, theatre, and writing for the press. The fourth interest mentioned is Masonry. That an affiliation to a cult is specifically mentioned hints that Lang also had a shared interest.

Another article in *The Mofussilite* in 1849 reports that Sir Charles Napier attended a meeting of Masons in Simla, where he spoke of his long-standing connection with the cult, and said that no one owed more to Masonry than he did. Sir Napier told why he was so indebted to Masonry:

> I was once a prisoner, without a hope of being even exchanged, and expected to be sent to Verdun, to which fortress in France all prisoners were consigned; for at this time the two Governments of France and England were so exasperated against each other, that their anger fell on individuals, and there was no exchange of prisoners. A man who was taken, lost all chance…In this state of despair and misery…It came into my head that I was a Mason, and I contrived to poke out a Brother. He was a French Officer…for like a good and honourable Brother he managed to send a letter for me to England—by no means an easy matter in those days…it was at this time an extremely dangerous and hazardous undertaking for a French Officer—but my honest and good Brother did it for me, and within three months my family knew that I was alive.[50]

We have seen earlier that in *The Optimist*, Lang wrote articles against Sir Charles Napier, but *Allen's Indian Mail* alleged that Lang's opinion about Napier had changed half a dozen times. It is perhaps due to Napier's Masonic connection that Lang was ambivalent about him.

Also, the article about Napier's Masonic speech is complimentary in its entirety.

There are the allusions to Lang's affiliation with Freemasonry in his writings. In his 1856 novel *Captain MacDonald, Or Haps and Mishaps at the Capias Castle*, the captain has fortified his castle to fend off Jewish bailiffs to whom he and his friends owe money. (see plate 1) Within this fort, is also Alice, who is the beloved of Hector, who arrives in the disguise of a parson and amuses the party with his jokes. Among one of his jokes is a Masonic joke. In Masonic fraternity, everyone is known by the honorific of 'Brother'. The joke is self-explanatory:

> It reminds me, good sir, of a mistake made by the Earl of—, who, at a masonic dinner, addressed His Royal Highness as 'Brother Prince of Wales.' 'Brother Guelph, if you like,' said the Prince; 'but, as you well know, we cannot bear a brother near the throne.'[51]

The protagonist of *Ex-Wife*, Sir George Merrydale, who is as avid an alcoholic as Lang himself, asks Ms Johnson:

> Don't you remember what quantities of table-beer I used to drink at the Hall sometimes of a morning after I had been to the Freemasons' Lodge overnight?[52]

I have delved into the matter of Lang's Freemason affiliation because earlier scholarships about Lang, that of John Earnshaw and Victor Crittenden, harp on the matter of his being a Jew. A believer of Judaism can as well be a Freemason, but this aspect about Lang's life has never previously been broached. Crittenden dwells on the idea that Lang had Jewish heritage and that he did his best to conceal this identity. In Lang's writings or writings about him, there are no hints of him being religious in any way.

Then there is the matter of the title of this chapter, 'My Friend's Wife, Or Lang You're Wanted'. This has been taken from the title of one of Lang's 1859 novels—*My Friend's Wife, Or York You're Wanted*. This is a novel—a racy one at that—which was one of the four published during the last two years of Lang's stay in England.

Admirer of Mrs Bink, or Exasperated to the Brink

My Friend's Wife, Or York You're Wanted is a railway novel and a ship novel, a start-to-finish novel, which despite its plotless-ness, is eminently readable for its wit, and its twists and turns. Many of Lang's novels were sold as railway novels, for their fast-paced action and dialogue; this one perfectly fits the bill. The plot of this novel is that a young lieutenant, York, is returning to England after having fought in the War of 1857 in India. He is infatuated by a Civil Servant's wife who, with her three children and an ayah[IV], is also aboard the same ship. The entire hundred-page novel is about how deeply infatuated York is with Mrs Bink, and how she uses this situation to her advantage by exploiting the young man throughout the journey.

A major constituency of Lang's readership was female, and this is reflected in Lang's complete attention to female protagonists in his last novels. From the novel's plot, it seems that he was risking this constituency, but quite on the contrary, he was feeding into the popular sentiment among women that several married women were wont to exploit young and unmarried men. This is not the first time Lang mentions this situation—rather it is one of his standard formulas. In *The Wetherbys,* the young Wetherby romances on a ship a lady whose husband is an old man of great influence in Calcutta, and whom she has married because of this reason. Wetherby, despite his decadent lifestyle in the army quickly rises in ranks because the lady influences her husband to get Wetherby promoted. In *Will He Marry Her?*, Augustus Reckless, who is perplexed by the mysteries

IV An Indian au pair, a nanny.

surrounding his beloved Leonora, has a ship romance with a woman of similar description as in *The Wetherbys*. When he reaches India, she and her husband are constantly invited to the governor-general's parties because Augustus happens to be on the governor-general's staff. A very similar sub-plot is found in *The Three Calendars* as well. This is the first time, however, that this becomes the main plot of a Lang novel.

Lang seems to have taken great pleasure in observing these ship romances—perhaps he was party to some as well. Given that the journey between England and India took anywhere between three and six months, such events were only too common. Lang's own mother had journeyed to England after the death of her husband Walter Lang, and had married Joseph Underwood on board a ship.

In *My Friend's Wife*, Lang reverse his standard plot sequence—here instead of from England, a voyage begins from India—and sans all the other Lang-esque twists. Lang could not do without bringing the Indian connection and use of Hindustani words; he puts these words into the mouths of Mrs Bink's children, who have been brought up by an Indian ayah. It is mostly Hindustani expletives that these children, Alfred and Georgina, mouth:

> Both were as naughty and as self-willed as are the majority of children brought up in India, and tended by slaves for servants. One of the mildest of Alfred's threats (in Hindustanee) was to break every bone in my body, and give it to the crows to eat while Georgina, whenever I requested her to be quiet, invariably said, *'Choop! Hum toomara nak kat-dalega!'* ('Hold your tongue! I will cut your nose off!') But what recked I of their abuse—I, who loved and kissed them for their mother's sake! Numberless were the pleasantries I had to endure from the old lieutenant and others, while keeping out of danger these mercurial little beings, who flew about the deck in

> opposite directions like two little birds, delighting, seemingly, in the trouble they gave me.[53]

This is roughly the plot of the entire novel—the two children troubling York, and the old lieutenant Bloomfield exasperating him with his tricks and stories, and he enduring it all for Mrs Bink's sake. The expression that Lang uses for the children brought up in India should not be taken as his condescending attitude towards India. By 'naughty and self-willed' he means only as much, and the children, though a great nuisance for York, begin liking him and vice versa. Lang was writing for an English audience and kept their prejudices in mind, while undermining them through his plot.

The novel does not veer away from its title at all. 'My Friend's Wife' remains the friend's wife, for all the trouble York takes for her, and she is quite thankless about the ordeal he has had to go through. The other half of the title, 'York, You're Wanted', is what forms the bulk of the action—York is forever wanted by Mrs Bink for this or that sundry job:

> She sent for me on all occasions when *I* was absent from her side, and there was not a moment when I might not expect to be interrupted. It mattered not whether I was playing at whist, ecarte, or vingt-un—reading, writing, or talking. The ayah would be sure to come to me, and say, '*Mem sahib salaam diya*' ('The mem sahib sends her salaam.') My name suggested a vulgar saying, which was continually bawled out to me by some person or other—'York! You're wanted!' Such is the vanity of some men, circumstanced as I was, that I would have suffered any amount of badinage and inconvenience rather than have removed the impression that got abroad in the ship, namely, that Mrs. Bink was in love with me! I knew she liked me; but as for love—bah! I have since become perfectly satisfied that she

> was the most selfish woman in the world. She loved herself, and she loved her children, but beyond that her heart was incapable of either affection or gratitude.[54]

As the above passage suggests, the protagonist has been named York to include the popular 19th century phrase, 'York, you're wanted'. It is characteristic of Lang never to leave a literary debt unmentioned. He borrows characters from his favourite literary works and does not fail to allude to his source, unlike his contemporary Tom Taylor. 'York you're wanted' seems to have been a very popular phrase in early andmid-19th century England, and there are various sources for it. One sense is of the absence of the right man from the right place, and comes from Frederick Marryat's novel *Newton Forster*. In that, Captain Carrington has become the captain of a ship without having gone through the rigours of cadetship, and is ill-suited for his job. Things go askew and there is announcement for the Captain all over the ship, on loudspeaker, through whispers: 'York. You're Wanted'.[55] Lang, of course, alludes to this debt to Marryat, and York mentions him as one of the authors whose collection he is carrying on the ship.

The phrase also occurs in the same sense *The Slave*, a musical drama by Thomas Morton as mentioned above:[56]

> Miss Von Frump: Well, nephew, have you been looking out a tomb for me?[57]
>
> Fogrum: No, dear Aunt, but I've been looking out a husband for you—my dear York, you're wanted.—Act II. Sc. 4.

There is also a comic song written by P.P. Phillips, entitled 'York, you're Wanted'.[58]

This phrase was in great currency in the 1830s among the creditors of the Duke of York. J.J. Reed tells about this origin of the phrase in a letter to the editor of *Lippinscott* magazine:

> I was in London from 1827 to 1834, and remember having frequently heard the expression, though not directly applied to the duke. It was, however, directly applied to his memory in several facetious ways on the occasion of erecting the granite column called the 'Duke of York's Column', at the top of the flight of steps leading from Waterloo Place to St. James's Park, which took place somewhere about 1830, as well as I can recollect, but I will not be positive at the point. The duke died in 1827, deeply in debt, and one of the current jokes of the day was that his friends had placed him at the top of the column to keep him out of the reach of his creditors, who might, therefore, shout out 'York, you're wanted' until they were tired.[59]

The phrase, then, was very much in currency in the mid-19th century, and Lang used this as a title to catch the attention of the reader. When this novel was published in 1859, there was a surfeit of works about the Mutiny. Lang always wishing to stand out and not be a part of the herd, did not write any work exclusively pertaining to the events of 1857. When this novel opens, the protagonist declares that he has been a part of the action of 1857, but he would rather not relate anything from the war:

> I am a lieutenant in one of Her Majesty's regiments of foot, and have just returned to England after a long service in India. I have nothing to tell about the mutiny or the battles in which I was engaged…I am not disappointed or annoyed at what has been done or undone, with respect to prize money; I do not grumble at the amount of compensation I am to receive for the loss of my 'little all' in Meerut. I have not the faintest animosity towards the general officer who commanded the force to which I was attached, for not provisionally investing me with the Victoria Cross.[60]

Lang's newspaper, *The Mofussilite*, of course, reported the events of 1857, and he was well aware of the facts thereof. The issues which the lieutenant brings up in these short passages are important ones—there was immense plundering in Delhi after it was won by the British, and there was a lot of acrimony between the English parties about the distribution of the 'prize money'. Like in many other places, Lang insinuates nepotism in the army which results in medals for some, and ignominy for some.

As has been stated earlier, the plot of the *My Friend's Wife* comprises of Mrs Bink asking York for favours, and he falling into trouble with most of the people on board the ship because of her vanity. Lang would have observed his fellow travellers on each of his numerous journeys and reserved the funny ones for this novel. The portrayal of life aboard a ship is vivid with its numerous difficulties. The novel can also be read as a travelogue with descriptions of various places—Madras, Ceylon, Aden, Suez, Malta—and the hot air of Red Sea which cause great inconvenience to the passengers, the fear of small-pox spreading on the ship, are some of the most entertaining piece of writing.

One amusing sub-plots of the novel is an old navy Lieutenant Bloomfield, who is a rival to York for Mrs Bink's attentions. Bloomfield mingles in the society of Mrs Bink but does not take any pains in getting anything done for her, albeit he scores points over York all the time by promising tall. Bloomfield has a story to tell from the days he was the in command of the ship 'Jasper' on every occasion, and York is always exasperated by these stories and never cares to complete any of Bloomfield's tales for the reader. At the beginning of the novel, after Mr Bink has, to the great delight of York, requested him to take care of his wife and children on board the ship, York decides to begin his flirtations by getting a seat near Mrs Bink. He, however, discovers that the seats for repasts had already been decided and that Bloomfield would be sitting next to the lady. York tries to impress Bloomfield by listening to the grievances of his job, and suggesting that he should write to *The Times* about his grievances. Bloomfield says that there is no point in writing a letter to the editor, for, 'Those who read 'em, never heed 'em; Those who do not, never see'd 'em'[61].

This verse is representative of many such verses that are strewn across Lang's works—witty, humorous, easy-flowing. This is also a detached critique of the newspaper trade from an insider. In *Ex-Wife*, a young couple has eloped and rented Mrs Grey's apartments. Mrs Grey sees an advertisement offering a prize for apprehending the couple and wonders if they have read it, but then thinks that a young couple in love would have nothing to do with the drab advertisements and news in the newspapers.

York supplicates to Bloomfield that he should give up his seat for him, since he has been entrusted to take care of Mr Bink's family. Bloomfield declares that he would think about the matter only after he has seen the lady despite the assurances of York that she is plain looking:

> The whole of my affections, sir, ever since I was fifteen, have been divided between the service and the sex. By the side of a pretty and conversationable lady I always feel in heaven. Oh, no! I cannot promise, but I'll see about it, as the independent voter always says to the candidate, on the first time of asking.[62]

It is typical of Lang to use political or legal examples in matters of heart. In *Plot and Passion*, one of Marie St. Cyr's suitors supplicates to her friend to appeal on his behalf, but the latter refuses saying that his situation was like that of a third party in a court-martial, and therefore he would not like to intervene.

In *My Friend's Wife*, Bloomfield refuses York the favour and thus commences their comical rivalry.

At another instance in *My Friend's Wife*, during their rivalry for Mrs Bink's affections, the old lieutenant announces that he once sailed on the same ship as William IV when he was the Duke of Clarence. The lieutenant made friends with duke, and was invited by the latter to his house whenever he was 'in town'. Bloomfield subsequently paid a visit to the duke. The tale of the singing mouse commences here:

> Whilst we were talking and sipping our Madeira, I heard, in an adjoining room, what I thought was a lady's voice, singing some of the airs out of the 'Beggar's Opera. 'That's very pretty,' said I. 'Very,' said the Duke, laughing. 'How charmingly she sings, to be sure,' said I. 'It does not happen to be a *she*' said the Duke. 'What!' said I; 'do you mean to say that it is not the voice of a female?' 'I do,' said the Duke. 'What man in this world could sing like that?' I asked. 'But, it is not a man,' said the Duke. 'Then *what* is it?' said I. 'It is a mouse!' said the Duke; 'a male mouse!' I thought, of course, that he was joking, for he liked a bit of fun now and then, as well as you and I, York. But presently he satisfied me that he was in earnest. Opening the door which separated the rooms, he told me to follow him. I did so. In we went, and sure enough there was a mouse, in a large cage, made of solid gold wire, singing away as gaily as a lark. I was never so astonished in the whole course of my life. If I had not seen it, I could not have believed it. The whole of *Polly's* songs did that mouse sing; every word distinctly pronounced, and every note as perfect as could be. I asked the Duke where he got that mouse, and he told me that it was caught in the Haymarket Theatre. It seems that the mouse was so struck with Mrs. Jordan's singing, that whenever she went to rehearsal he would come out of his hole and listen, till at last he took to imitate her. On one occasion Mrs. Jordan was unable to attend rehearsal, but the company went on without her, omitting the part of

> Polly. The mouse, unable to understand this, and to control himself, leaves his hole, runs upon the stage, and strikes up, sir. The manager had a trap baited with a small musical box, and into that trap went the mouse, and was caught. The manager, out of compliment to His Royal Highness, presented him with the little animal, cage and all. On his next voyage the Duke took the mouse to sea with him, and hung up the cage in his cabin. But the poor little thing did not live very long. It died on the South American station; and the Duke, who assured me that as the sight of the empty cage almost maddened him, and as he was rather in want of money at the time, he parted with it to a Jew, at Bahia, for the worth of its mere weight in gold—£95. The wire was not heavy, but the frame-work was tolerably massive.[63]

I quoted the entire story of the singing mouse for its intrinsic entertaining value, and to show the kind of tales Lang conjured up. More than that, the utterance of this story through Bloomfield is a joke practised by Lang upon several Victorian writers, himself included. Seafaring people, when they used to go back home, were in great demand for tales of their voyages, and they very often concocted tales of the Bloomfield variety to entertain their audiences, as well as to increase their own worth in the society's collective eyes. Lang himself tells such tales. For example, in a tale in *Wanderings in India*, a snake understands the music played by an undertaker at a graveyard. In another story in *Wanderings...*, a Baron picks up a flower from a grave. The Baron tells Lang that on that night 'the door of my room was opened; and in glided, noiselessly, a pale spectral figure, clad in a white robe, and wearing a garland of flowers. It was the figure of a young girl, and the face was angelic. With motionless eyes and outstretched hand she approached my couch, and in a plaintive voice asked me: 'Why has thou robbed the Dead? Why hast thou taken that flower which a faithful lover threw upon my last resting place on earth?[64].

Such stories were in great demand at taverns and in travellers' circles, and even amongst readers of journals. This was how a multitude of ghost stories came to be prevalent in the 19th century. The tales told by travellers with all the hyperbole created a whole exotic image of the East. Another matter of importance regarding Lang here is the influence of Boccaccio's *Decameron;* and *Arabian Nights* on his writing. Like these two cycles of tales that have layers of stories within stories, Lang, despite superficially keeping the structure of comedy of manners, makes his characters mouthpieces to tell fantastic tales.

At the end of the mouse story, the lieutenant tells York that he had fabricated the whole story for the audience but that he would tell another story that he knew was entirely true. He again tells a story of William IV, when he was a lieutenant and travelling on a ship. When the duke got ready to disembark at a port where the ship stopped for refuelling, his commanding officer told him that he could not disembark for he had not sought permission from his superior either in writing or verbally. Exasperated, the duke changed back to his uniform, asked for permission—and with an intention to show the officer his position, said that he hoped he would have the right to royal honours when he disembarked. The commanding officer made such a pomp and show of it that the entire island gathered around the duke, who had wished that he would quietly be able to go around and partake of the pleasures. This act the commanding officer repeated several times, till the duke learnt his lesson and requested him not to reveal his royal identity. When the duke was crowned a king, he invited the officer, and on seeing him, forgot all protocol and hollered at him if he remembered those days.

Lang had extensively read biographies about celebrities of his time and before, and he uses these side stories very often in his novels. This is a short novel, and he does not digress much.

Lang cannot write without mentioning a court martial in any of his novels. It is almost compulsive, whatever the nature of the story of the novel in question. If we include court scenes as well, perhaps no work of Lang would escape the rubric. Lang was fascinated by the legal profession. The court scenes invariably are farcical in all of Lang's writings; they show his knowledge as well as contempt for the legal system of his time. In *My Friend's Wife*, Lang contrives to frame the pinnacle of all his farcical court scenes. The background to it is this: in the novel, Mrs Bink requests York to accommodate her son Alfred in his room at night, for her room is very hot. That night, Alfred has a bad dream and he wakes up and wails out loud. Every passenger on the ship has in some way or the other been bothered by Alfred during the journey, and some of them decide to lodge a formal complaint with the captain of the ship. Among this number is an elderly colonel, who had been much vexed by Alfred and Georgina having entered his cabin and spilling his shaving water into his boots, and spoiling one of his wigs with a scissor. According to York, when the 'hearing' begins, there are 17 people on one side of the table to press charges against him, and he on the other side. Fourteen of these men are in uniform. Here, Lang deliberately creates the scene of a court-martial yes, "here" can go to show the banality of the institution. York says, 'charges upon which I was arraigned were read out by Captain Bulke', and were as follows:

> 1st. That he, the said Lieutenant Charles Staunton York, of H.M.'s—Regiment of Foot, did, on the night of the 6th instant, take into his cabin (No. 129) a little boy, named Alfred Halliday Bink, he, the said Lieutenant Charles Staunton York, well knowing the wakeful and troublesome disposition of the said little boy, with the intent to disturb all the passengers and officers of the ship in the vicinity of cabin No. 129—such being contrary to the rides of good society, and unworthy the position of an officer in Her Majesty's service.
>
> 2nd. With having, when the said little boy, mentioned in the first charge, had awakened from their slumbers all the

> passengers and officers of the ship whose cabins were in the vicinity of cabin No. 129, used no effort to soothe, solace, or quiet the said little boy; but, on the contrary thereof, permitted the said little boy to scream until three bells in the middle watch—such being contrary, &c, &c.[65]

According to York, the narrator, whenever such a complaint is made on board a ship, this is the nature of the investigation. York pleads 'not guilty', and the trial commences. The colonel gives his evidence against York in the most 'offensive manner possible' and York decides to get even with him. York enquires of the colonel if he had not complained about him earlier; and the colonel replies that he had indeed complained when York had suffered the children to enter the colonel's cabin and pour shaving water into his boots. York then questions him about the wig, at which the colonel becomes fidgety because he affected the idea of having black hair, and never admitted to wearing a wig:

> 'Did you say nothing about your wig (in the former complaint)?'
>
> 'Wig, sir?' (The old colonel laboured under the delusion that no one suspected that his black hair was false.)
>
> 'Yes, wig.'
>
> 'I decline to answer that question.' (Laughter from the ladies' cabins, in which the majority of the court was compelled to join.)
>
> 'Do you, or do you not, wear a wig? On your word and honour as an officer and gentleman, did those jetty locks grow on your own head?' (Renewed laughter from the ladies and the members of the court.) Bulke laughed so heartily, and seemed to enjoy the joke so much, I forgave him all his past offensive conduct—especially as he said to the colonel, 'I think, sir, you must answer the prisoner's question.' At the word ' prisoner' he appeared to be choking. I, of course, looked as gravely as possible.

> 'What *is* the question?'said the colonel.
>
> I repeated it.
>
> 'Yes!' was the reply. 'It is not a wig. The hair is my own.' (Loud laughter from the ladies' cabins, and shouts from every member of the court.) Bulke threw down his pen, for he could not write down the colonel's reply, and placing his head on the table, his whole body seemed violently convulsed. I, too, was forced to laugh at the idea of the old colonel's vanity so getting the better of him that it prompted him, on his word and honour as a gentleman, to state that which was so palpably untrue.
>
> Lieutenant Bloomfield, who was a member of the court, and sat opposite, suggested that to clear the matter up, Lieutenant Jameson, who sat next to the colonel, should be allowed to have a pull at the hair; and Lieutenant Jameson, having coincided in that opinion, made a movement of his hand towards the colonel's head, whereupon the old officer sprang up and roared out:—'If you dare to put a finger upon me, sir, I will place you under an arrest!' (Roars of laughter.)[66]

This is just one of the examples of Lang's satirical jibes, and indulgence in fun, while writing. The case continued, other witnesses were examined, and lieutenant Bloomfield told one of his many 'Jasper' stories—that once on board the Jasper, there was a man in love who kept singing love poetry, and that he had placed him under arrest for so disturbing his passengers. Bloomfield tells that he intended to have the poet-officer tried at a court-martial, 'but, by Jove, the admiral told me to release the lad immediately, and hinted that if the Admiralty came to hear of it, it would be all cock-a-hoop with my commission'[67].

To this Bulke, the judge for the case, replies: 'Well if it is decided that that little boy is to howl in (cabin) 129, I will set my three big musical boxes going, all at the same time, and keep them wound up till daylight does appear. And if anybody gets a wink of sleep till those boxes are stopped, all I can say is, they are welcome to it.'[68]

Lang makes the reader have a hearty laugh at the cost of the mock-trial. In *Wanderings In India*, too, Lang narrates the story of a court-martial…and the case drags on for a month with adjournments; the story ends with Lang announcing he has attended several of these courts-martial and they were all of similar character.

Whenever he can, Lang does not fail to take a dig at the colonial officers. Mrs Bink has no money to make purchases at Malta because her husband had left her with just a few sovereigns for use on board the ship. She had assumed that she could shop anywhere and that the bills would be sent to her husband:

> She had, of course, bills on his agents for hundreds of pounds, payable at sight, but these were not negotiable on board ship, or even at Malta, for no one there knew anything of Bink, or of his means. Mrs. Bink seemed amazed when I delicately hinted as much to her. She fancied that the whole world had judicial and other cognizance of such a place as India, and, therefore, that everybody must know that her husband—Edward Chiceley Edmonstone Colebrooke Crushington Bink—was the civil and sessions judge of Humdrumabad, in the Upper Provinces of the Bengal Presidency.[69]

No such place exists as Humdrumabad—as the name itself suggests—it has been inserted along with the long-drawn name of Bink to jibe at the vanity of civil services officers in colonial India.

At the close of the novel, Lang turns his pen against clerics, and the official practice of attesting the most sundry document. Mrs Bink's brother-in-law—a pastor described as a cadaverous man wearing all black—comes to receive her, whereupon she bids York a very cold bye. The cleric asks York if Mrs Bink owes him anything, upon which York feels hurt, but names a sum. The clergyman withdraws for a conference with Mrs Bink to verify the sum, and then asks York to write a receipt for him. A few days later, there is an advertisement in a newspaper urging York to apply to a certain church for a huge benefit. York undertakes a long journey only to find it is the same man who had advertised. The reverend asks him if he had sold Mrs Bink a very unbecoming dress. York tells that he had bought a 'Bournose' at Alexandria for his sister, but when Mrs Bink took a fancy to it, he had gifted it to her. To this, the reverend says, '…for persons whose tastes lead them to attend balls, such a garment would be an invaluable possession but for a lady whose relations and friends regard such assemblies as ungodly, the case is very different.'[70]

Rev. Bink then asks York what the premium would be for holding the dress for a month. Much amused, York says it would be 20 shillings; which the reverend haggles down to 15 after quoting the market prices of interest, and then again draws out a receipt and sells a revenue stamp to York since he is not carrying it. York returns home to a waiting mother who thinks he has inherited a huge fortune, and hands her over the fifteen shillings, which are returned by his sister to Mrs Bink saying that York just intended to amuse himself by asking for interest.

This entire episode on surface seems like an apparently harmless story; but Lang, through his jokes and witty narrative, does not let up his crusade against the conservative Victorian society, red-tapism, the bane of unnecessary paperwork, and general corruption and shallowness in society. *My Friend's Wife, Or York You're Wanted*, thus, above all, is about the power equations in man-woman relationships, and Lang shows astutely how women can beat patriarchy at its own game. This does not in any way indict Lang of any misogynistic tendencies, for most of his works have women as central and very powerful characters. He, however, wanted to offer a counter-point that feminism—of course the term 'feminism' is from a much later time—cannot be an overarching narrative, that man-woman relationships are too fluid to be subsumed by a singular kind of narrative, that it needed diverse treatments from experience.

Just take into consideration York's musings as Mrs Bink alights from the ship at the end of the voyage. York, who has helped Mrs Bink in every way on the ship and has received carrots and sticks in return, is desperate and even more fondly in love with her. He says:

> And (heaven forgive me!) what would I not have given could I have received authentic information of Bink's death—so sure was I that 'dear Laura' would have accepted the offer of marriage I should have made her. She had seemed, since we left Alexandria, so fond of me, and looked at me so tenderly, that had she been a widow with six children instead of three, I would have gone down upon my knees and have sworn to be unto her a loving husband, and a most affectionate step-father to her little offspring.[71]

The passage proves that York is prepared to be a husband to Laura even if she were a widow with six children instead of three. The novel—it would generally go unnoticed to a reader—closes the same way it opens. York expresses his fancy at the beginning of the novel, too, that if Mrs Bink had been a widow how happy he would be:

> 'Whenever my eyes met her lovely hazel orbs, my heart fluttered like a little bird in a schoolboy's hand; and when she opened her pretty little red lips, showed her white teeth, and spoke to me, the sound of her voice quite enraptured me. Had she been a widow, I would have 'proposed' to her—for she was a woman of good birth, and her manners were extremely ladylike and gentle with all (save Bink, with whom she was brusque and off-handed).'[72]

Lang seems to have had a fancy for widows, especially those with children; this is quite a curious revelation about his personal life, yet shrouded in great mystery.

Is She a Widow? or Window to Lang's Heart

My Friend's Wife is not the only instance in Lang's works where the protagonist desires to be the husband of a widow. In this novel, the sentiment is laced because Mrs Bink is actually not a widow, only York wishes so, because he is already in love with her, and desired her to be a widow so that York can marry her.

In Lang's novel *Too Clever By Half*, Sam Freeport takes fancy to a widow. The courtship is faster than a whirlwind—just page long—within which Freeport proposes to the 'monstrously fine woman', and yet, Lang's wit carries off the library courtship with parenthetical finesse:

> The following morning various excursions were in progress. Some were for visiting a curious rock, some miles distant; others rode on horseback to the nearest town—and young Wrexton shouldered his gun and roamed round the woods for the purpose of getting a pheasant or two. But Sam declared he had a severe headache, and therefore preferred lounging about the library, and reclining on a couch. The truth was this: the widow, at breakfast, refused to join any party, and Sam stayed at home [he was 'at home' everywhere] in the hope of having a quiet chat with her. And he succeeded in his design; for as he reclined on a couch in the library, when the house was deserted by its inmates, the door was opened, and the lady walked up to one of the shelves, and took down a book, without observing Freeport (of course) and without being observed, as she fancied. Sam arose and approached her; but when he spoke, the book fell, she uttered a faint shriek, turned

> round, and expressed her surprise. No woman but an actress could have done it half so well.[73]

The irony and the brevity of the remark in the parenthesis is the hallmark of Lang's wit, and another example of Lang's keen observations and insight regarding romantic affairs.

The narrator here says, 'Freeport admired the widow excessively, and for her personal attractions, notwithstanding she was some years older than himself, would he have married her, had he been a man of fortune; but...all his wealth was in his waistcoat pocket.'

One of the reasons why Lang was rejected by the critics was because he was very 'forward'. We have seen that a critic had said of *Will He Marry Her?* that the love scenes must be protested against, 'for they are tremendous'[74]. In *Too Clever By Half*, too, the 'love making' (the term used in 19th century for serenading) is 'tremendous' with the widow quickly and easily reciprocating Freeport's advances:

> Freeport's attentions became 'marked,' and it was very clear that the widow was glad to receive them. One moonlight night, the visitors strolled upon the lawn in front of the house. After walking for a short time, Sam led the lady of his love away from the party, and down the avenue, towards the gate. She looked round several tunes, as though she dreaded to go so far away; but Sam walked on, talking in the most impressive manner, and bidding her not to be alarmed, and assuring her there were no ghosts or goblins.
>
> The widow sighed, and so did Sam.[75]

Sighing is a sure sign of love in Lang's works. In *Love's Last Sacrifice*[76] Alberighi falls in love with a married woman, Giovanna. She is aware of the attentions he is showering on her but becomes sure that he loves her when he sighs:

> One night it became manifest to Giovanna that she was beloved by Marquis of Salusso. It was not his discourse that led to the discovery, nor was it any alteration in his manner. His looks and his sighs betrayed the secret he had so long concealed from the world in which he moved.[77]

Similarly, in *Plot and Passion*, because 'Disque' or Jerome, the writer of pamphlets against Napoleon's regime, sighs, his sister discovers that he is in love with Marie.

Lang, who is witty and sarcastic—while writing about political matters which are always juxtaposed with matters of the heart—is also subtle and touching when writing about relationships and courtships. Lang's forte was to write about relationships between men and women, and this situation perhaps arose from his own failed first marriage, and subsequent marriage with Margaret Wetter. He was also a very social man who heard stories from friends and took inspiration from their lives. It was Lang's mainstay to delve into the psychologies of love-stricken people and what made them fall in love. Fouche, in *Plot and Passion*, soliloquises a lot about the nature of men and women; while the narrator of *Forger's Wife* tells why Emily refused three nice gentlemen but chose to fall in love with an impetuous and dubious man who appeared reticent towards her.

As to the issue of widows, we have two examples—one from *My Friend's Wife, Or York You're Wanted*, and another from *Too Clever By Half, Or The Harroways*—where the protagonist has the desire to marry a widow. Another example is in *The Secret Police, Or Plot and Passion*, where attraction and widowhood are intrinsically intertwined. Fouche, the head of the secret service in Napoleon's kingdom, has to find out about the anonymous writer (actually pseudonymous—he calls himself 'Disque') of pamphlets against the incumbent regime. His spy network is called 'Cohorte Cytherean' and comprises of young, beautiful girls who make suspects fall in love with them to elicit information. Marie

St. Cyr is appointed by Fouche to trap Jerome Legrange alias Disque. Fouche thinks that widows are more desirable by men, more so if they have a child, and so Marie assumes the name of Countess de Calmet, a widow with a child. Countess de Calmet and her brother travel with an English gentleman on their way to England to find Jerome, but the gentleman falls in love with the supposed countess, and goes raving mad and dies by the end of the novel. Jerome alias Disque also falls in love with the supposed widow, despite him not having bestowed his heart to anyone before that. In fact, Marie St. Cyr, who has assumed the false identity of a widow, is actually a widow. Another woman in Fouche's 'cohort', Louise Duval, is also a widow. The most attractive and sensuous women in Napoleon's employ, in Lang's version, are widows. Following is the description of Duval in the novel:

> Louise Duval was a German by birth. She was not strictly handsome, but then she had a very distinguished face, with an expression so fascinating that it rarely failed in charming her beholder. And her figure was so superb—and her manners so bewitching and seemingly artless; her voice so sweet in song and conversation; her knowledge of music so extensive and profound; her memory, touching all matters connected with literature, art, and history, so acute and so accurate—it is scarcely to be wondered that the number of her admirers almost equalled those of Marie St. Cyr—the more especially when the reader is informed that Louise Duval spoke English, Italian, and Spanish, as fluently and almost as accurately as she spoke French and German. Louise Duval was also a widow.[78]

I have quoted the description of Louise Duval to show the narrative strategy employed by Lang—a long list of accomplishments and evidences of great beauty, followed by and juxtaposed with 'Louise Duval was also a widow'. The 'also' in the statement, connecting

Duval with Marie, is an emphatic statement of the narrator about the desirability of widows. Colonel Cartouche, who is an informer of Fouche, and who reveals the identity of Disque as Jerome to him, also tells Fouche that he had proposed to Jerome's mother after she had become a widow.[79]

In *Three Calendars*, the first Calendar to whom Jenny was engaged initially, finally marries her after many travails, only after she becomes the second Calendar's widow. In *Love's Last Sacrifice*, the Marquis of Salusso gets united with Giovana after she has become a widow.

The narrator of *Wanderings in India*, which is Lang himself—since the wanderings are claimed by Lang as his own experiences—takes great fancy to a woman in Mussoorie, who keeps waiting by the roadside to catch a glimpse of her child. At first, Lang thinks she is Rani Chunda of the defeated Punjab province pining for her child, Duleep Singh; but it later turns out that she is the widow of a friend of the narrator himself.

In *Will He Marry Her?* when Augustus is told by Leonora that she cannot marry him unless he has met her and heard her in India, he goes insane thinking about the mystery surrounding his beloved. One of the thoughts that cross his mind are:

> What can it be? She cannot be a widow—with a young child, perhaps, in India? No, no! It cannot be that; and if it were, I would marry her![80]

Someone who reads just one or two books by Lang might ignore this a point of no import—that the character of a widow is intrinsic to the plot, or the fascination of a protagonist for a widow is a passing statement. However, one who peruses several works of Lang is likely to be struck by this fact.

There is no evidence within the texts that any of the characters offer for this fascination, except in Chapter 5 of the 1856 serialised edition of *Plot and Passion.*[V] The 1859 publication edition does not contain this chapter. Fouche tells Marie St. Cyr that she is to leave for England (from France) with Lord Brenton, as a widow and with a child. Marie is startled about the additional burden of the child:

> (Marie): 'But why should I be burdened with a child?'
>
> (Fouche): Burdened? You will not be burdened. The nurse will look after it. Yes, take the child. It will give your appearance an additional interest. Besides there is something so tremendously real and imposing in a beautiful and well-dressed child. Widows with one or two children are thought a great deal more than those who have not any, I assure you.
>
> (Marie): Well, just as you please. In your judgement I have ever reposed the most implicit confidence.[81] (Lang 2008 (1856): 25)

That the matter of interest in widows is put in the mouth of Fouche is of importance because Fouche, though the villain of the novel, is a schemer, thinker, and astute observer of people. In my opinion, Lang has put many of his thoughts about society in soliloquies of Fouche. Also, that which Marie reposes 'implicit' confidence in Fouche's judgement, highlights the point of Lang's own interest. No further explanation is offered by Fouche than appearance of 'an additional interest', and 'widows with children are thought a great deal more than those who have not any'.

The second statement is perhaps because a widow with a child wasn't considered as erroneous or wanton. To argue this point through

V The 1859 Ward and Lock edition of the novel does not carry this matter. However, a longer version that was published in *The Mofussilite* in 1856 has it. Chapter 5 of *The Mofussilite* text is missing in the later edition. Victor Crittenden contends that in the edition published by him in 2008 the omission was made because the chapter contained characters of British Prime Minister, and Fouche conversing with Napoleon – "making it sound like a dramatic international plot." Crittenden also thinks that the character of Lord Brenton in the novel was probably too close to a real British Lord. Henry Vizetelly, the publisher, in the light of these matters, perhaps decided to remove these volatile matters.

an example, there was a scandal in 1850, wherein Captain Richardson, a professor of Hindu College, was much hounded for having sheltered a young widow under his roof. He was shifted from department to department, and then his resignation was demanded.[82]

Yet another dimension to the matter is that there were too many English widows in India, with all the wars that the East India Company was involved in. More than the wars, as Lang suggests in *The Wetherbys*, it was cholera and other diseases that killed men (but that would include women, too). In a very interesting episode in *The Wetherbys*, the narrator tells that widows married shortly after the death of their husbands, for if they did not marry, they would not be allowed to remain within the barracks. In this episode of the novel, several men go missing and are presumed dead; their wives remarry, and the missing/dead husbands return, resulting in great confusion and duels.[83]

There's yet another dimension to the matter. Several young girls came to India to be married to rich and established but much older men. To take examples from Lang's works, Robert Wetherby had a smooth sail in India because he had flirted with a lady on his passage to India on board a ship, and the young lady whose husband was much older, helped him get plush positions. In the same novel, Baxter, who is 70 years old, marries a 17-year-old girl.[84] In *Will He Marry Her?*, Augustus Reckless flirts on board the ship on his passage to India, again with a young lady with an old rich husband, and gets favours from her in India.

These various contexts perhaps created a state of flux in the British Indian social situation—on the one hand, there were scandals about keeping a widow at home; on the other, there were many young women who got widowed due to the deaths of their husbands in the army; then there would have been young widows because certain young girls married very old men for want of money and social respectability attached with their husbands' position.

To add to this context, I shall suffer the reader the introduction of an 1853 journal by Mrs Colin Mackenzie, who spent several years in British Indian society and came up with a book called *Life in the Mission, the Camp and the Zenana; or Six Years in India*. Mackenzie's work is an interesting addition to the corpus of books written by British women in colonial India, for it is quite critical of the British institutions, both civil and military. She criticises the racist attitude of the British towards Indians among several other things, but says that young men who come to India are far better off than men who remain in England, for in India they are given huge responsibilities as soon as they come here. She, however, does not have the same opinion of young women:

> But if the gentlemen in India are above the home average, the ladies are certainly below it. Young men constantly make inferior marriages; and girls, after having been deprived of a mother's care half their lives, are brought out and married far too young—before their education (if they have had any) is finished, or their minds formed; and before they have enjoyed what, in the present deficient system, *is* often the best part of a girl's training—the advantage of intercourse with really good society. They have thus no standard of manners or taste, by which to test the manners of those among whom they are thrown; they probably marry under eighteen, often under sixteen, and adopt the strangest phraseology from their husbands and their husbands' friends. It is common to hear ladies speaking not only of their husbands by their surnames (a thing unpardonable, except of a peer), but of other gentlemen in the same manner; talking of 'our kit,' and using such terms as 'jolly,' 'pluck,' 'a cool thing,'[VI] 'lots,' 'rows,' and 'no end of things!' I think the wives of military men are worse in this respect than those of civilians.[85]

Mrs Mackenzie, however, holds a different view of women who have lived long enough in India:

VI It is interesting to see that 'a cool thing'—which is considered a late 20th century teenage phrase—was very much in vogue in the mid-19th century.

> I really think the ladies in India are much less extravagant than their husbands; and often the best thing a man can do to get out of debt, is to take unto himself a wife. I have been quite touched by the self-denial and exertions of women (accustomed before their marriage to every comfort), in order to avoid incurring debt, or from an honourable desire to liquidate those already incurred by their husbands.[86]

Now, to combine all these contexts and opinions together—young women came out to India very early and were shallow; ladies who had spent time in India were pragmatic and economical; there were several young widows because of deaths in the army and also because young girls married very old men.

If all this held in general, we have a case for Lang. A widow with a child would not raise many eyebrows when a man is having an affair with her because she is a mother; and a widow would have gone through the travails, would know Indian society well, and would not be dismissive of Indian people or things, unlike the young girls who had just come out to India. Lang, who was deeply attached to India and decidedly an intellectual, would desire the society of a mature lady who could partake in his thoughts rather than just flirt. These, perhaps, would have been Lang's reasons. Of course, this is purely conjectural, since nothing is known about Lang's personal life apart from his two marriages, and separation from his first wife sometime in the 1850s. From various descriptions by Lang himself and his propensity to mix with a lot of people hints that he would have had romantic interests.

One wonders if this idea of Lang also had roots in the Indian 'native' situation. Given that the affairs in Indian society were quite the opposite of that in British society in India, that young widows had to look forward to a life of stigma and wretchedness, Lang would have been irked by the situation.

The rebel in him, the underdog in him which so often manifested itself would have wanted to do something about it, but could only eventually find manifestation in writing—a fantasy that the wretched of the society are the most desired. He would have taken his revenge on the social stigmas through his writing. Perhaps he did like some young Indian widow.

It is noteworthy that there were reforms in the air during this period—there are reports of Indian widows remarrying in the 1850s; it was mere tokenism though, for I have been able to find just two reports, one from 1852[87] and another from 1857[88]. Perhaps it would interest the reader to know that my grandmother was a widow with a child when my grandfather married her in 1940. He, however, had read no John Lang to get this idea, for he never learnt English—this act was a symbol of resistance—despite having been an accomplished doctor.

Lang's mother was also a widow with two children—John Lang included—when Joseph Underwood married her. This, perhaps, explains the situation of Lang in an Oedipal manner. This psychological reading, however, floats upon oxymoronic waters, for the Oedipal object of seeing the father dead had already been achieved literally with the death of Walter Lang. The foster father would then become the next rival, and the Oedipal fantasy would play out in all of Lang's works.

The fascination for widow with a child could be, above all these conjectures, purely a whim of Lang, or rather, a conviction.

We began with the issue of fascination for 'widow with children' with York's desire to marry Mrs Bink. There are two other novels that have 'wife' in their titles—and they are both representative works of Lang in different sense.

The Tale of Two Wives,

or Ex-Wife and Forger's Wife or Lang Returns Home, or 'India He Loved, England He Despised'

We now come to the two wives of John Lang—'ex-wife' Lucy Lang nee Peterson, and 'forger's wife' Margaret Lang nee Wetter. 'Forger's wife' because Lang's divorce from Lucy was *divorce mensa et thoro* which did not allow him to remarry. Lang eventually married again in 1861. The chapter shall also discuss Lang's two novels which form the second part of the title—*Ex-Wife* and *Forger's Wife.*

In a Hurry, or a Flurry of Novels

Lang wrote three novels with the word 'wife' in title—*The Forger's Wife* (1853), *My Friend's Wife, Or York You're Wanted* (1859), and *Ex-Wife* (1859). *The Forger's Wife* was first a serial in *Fraser's Magazine* in 1853; then a serial in *The Mofussilite* in 1855; and then published as a book by Ward and Lock in 1855. There are other editions of the book where the title changes, though with the same intent—*Assigned to His Wife, Or, The Adventures of George Flower, the Celebrated Detective;* and *The Convict's Wife: A True Tale of Early Australia.* The latter two titles were published in New South Wales, and therefore, emphasise the story of convicts and detective rather than the wife. In England, of course, the titles with 'wife' would generate interest amongst the large female readership.

My Friend's Wife was first published as a serial in *The Mofussilite* in 1859, and then as a book by Ward and Lock in the same year. *Ex-Wife* was first published in *The Mofussilite* in 1856 as a serial titled *Passages in The Life of a Divorcee by Herself.* It was later published as the book, *Ex-Wife*, by Routledge in 1858. The other 1858 novel *Will He Marry Her?* could well have been titled 'Will She Be His Wife?', for the story revolves around Leonara's repeated refusals to marry Augustus.

The years 1858 and 1859 are practically the last two years of Lang's career as a novelist. During these two years, six of Lang's books were published—apart from the three mentioned; the other three were a new edition of *Wanderings in India*, [parts of it having had been published earlier in *Household Words* (1853 and 1857) and in *The Mofussilite* (1859)]; *Plot and Passion* (1859),[1] and *Botany Bay or True Tales of the Early Days of Australia* (1859).[2] *Botany Bay* had already been published as 'sketches' in *Household Words* (1853 onwards), and as a series in *Welcome Guest* (1859). This work went into many editions and still gets published because of Australian interest in it. It is by this book that Lang is primarily known in Australia. Other early editions were *Clever Criminals: Recollections of Botany Bay* (1871),[3] and *Fisher's Ghost: And Other Stories of the Early Days of Australia* (1920).[4]

By 1859, Lang had lived in England for five years. He left England for Calcutta on the 27 August 1859.[5] His newspaper's subscription had gone down—editors after him had not been able to match his wit and gall. The editor at this time, Sidney Landor Blanchard, had left the job, which also necessitated Lang's return.[6] Once back, Lang resumed his editorship of *The Mofussilite,* and published some translations of Persian poems of Sadi of Shiraz. Victor Crittenden tells that Lang referred to himself as leading a quiet life in his Tusculum, and that 'Tusculum was a harking back to the retirement of Cicero from active involvement in political life and a plan to concentrate on literature'.[7] The idea of Tusculum once again underscores Lang's Latin scholarship.

Lang's mother died in Sydney in 1858, but he could not attend her funeral. With his mother's passing away in Sydney, and with the success of *Botany Bay,* Lang perhaps became nostalgic about his youth in Australia and published some writings about Australia. Among these were J.C. Carleton's poem 'The Song of Australia'[8], which Crittenden tells, is still well known for 'its lilting tone and enraptured first lines':

'This is a land where summer skies are gleaming with a thousand dyes.' In 1860, Lang started writing another serial called *The Detective* in his newspaper, but its publication ceased when it reached chapter 14. There was an announcement in the newspaper that the rest of the book had been lost:

> We regret to inform our readers that a large portion (some 22 chapters) of the MS of *The Detective* is missing and that unless we can find it...we shall be compelled to write it over again.[9]

In this novel, a man's promised bride goes missing, and it is rumoured that she has married a nobleman. The hero takes help of a detective, and learns techniques of investigation from him, and becomes a detective himself. It is unfortunate that the manuscript was lost, for detective novels became very popular in the late 19th century. Crittenden contends that perhaps the manuscript was never written beyond Chapter 14, that perhaps Lang made up an excuse for his readers.[10] Or, perhaps 'John Exshaw', the leading 'spirit' of the day did not let Lang complete the novel. This could well be true, for one can construe haste in most of the endings of Lang's novels.

For example, after creating a complicated plot in *Three Calendars*—wherein Jenny Dale likes all the Three Calendars, who look alike in the Calendar dress; and gets engaged to the First Calendar, but gets married to the Second Calendar, while the Third Calendar continues to flirt with her—Lang collapses the maze suddenly. He kills off the Second Calendar, calls the First Calendar back to England from India to marry Jenny.

This is just one of the examples of the haste that Lang shows towards the end of his novels. Lang was at his best when he wrote short works, but had taken to writing longer works by 1859—*Ex-Wife* and *Will He Marry Her?* both being over 400 pages—for long works and multi-volume novels were in demand at this time.

Lang also started publishing his older works in book form, and advertised in *The Mofussilite* that *The Wetherbys* could be purchased for two rupees by applying to the printer.[11]

In the summer of 1861, Lang went to Mussoorie, and married Margaret Wetter. Mussoorie appears in many of Lang's works, for he often frequented the hill station when the heat in the plains became unbearable. Lang now had a wife to look after their bungalow in Meerut, which was often trespassed. Lang inserted a notice in *The Mofussilite* 'complaining about people taking a shortcut through his grounds'.[12]

There is a vivid description of Mussoorie in 'Himalayan Club' in *Wanderings in India*. In his chronicle, Lang tells that Mussoorie, along with Simla, was the hub of fashion and scandal. Most army officers took 'sick-leave' to relax at Mussoorie, where, in Lang's account, they led a life of great indulgence drinking, gambling, playing billiards, and having affairs with wives of officers who were absent. Lang's 'Himalayan Club' is one of his wittiest works. Lang alludes to Mussoorie being a place for scandal in *My Friend's Wife*, in which Mr Bink keeps his wife always in good humour lest she retire to Mussoorie:

> The post-nuptial and lover-like attentions of Bink towards his 'own beloved Laura,' as he called her in company, were generally attributed to a fear that if he relaxed...she would insist on spending the summer at that charming, but dangerous place, Mussoorie, whilst he was toiling in the plains. Mrs. Bink was not a flirt exactly; but she liked exceedingly to be admired.[13]

Lang, who had published six books in 1858–59, seems very distracted in the last five years of his life. There are several poems in *The Mofussilite* that are signed under his name or his aliases: 'Anette' by J.L. Meerut,[14] for example. However, there are no new novels that appear as serials, except *The Detective*, and *Ellen Wareham* in 1862. Lang's interest in Napoleonic France is resurrected in the latter novel. Ellen is an

Englishwoman whose husband goes to France for some work and gets arrested there because Napoleon has decided to put all Englishmen behind bars. The missing husband, subsequently, is then presumed to be dead. Ellen remarries and has a child from her new marriage. The first husband returns and sues Ellen for bigamy.

Lang, of course, seldom wrote a novel without a court scene in it. He delineates the problems that women had to face vis-à-vis legal procedures. In *Ex-Wife*, Eva is sued by her husband for having been unfaithful to him but she cannot appear in court; instead, her supposed paramour has to appear in her defence. The supposed paramour, Mr Stoneycombe, actually fancies being a paramour and jeopardises her case. In a way, *Ellen Wareham* is a counter-point to *Ex-Wife*, where in despite the fact that the wife is legally divorced from the husband, she does not remarry and knows that one day, her estranged husband George Merrydale will come back.

In the usual Lang way of solving a complicated plot, in the end, the first husband of Ellen Wareham dies. The novel *Ellen Wareham* looks complete with the death of the first husband but in *The Mofussilite*, the last episode had the postscript of 'To be continued…'.

Even after the denouement in a novel, Lang generally added a chapter or two, touching on the fate of more characters, other than the principal ones. In *Ex-Wife*, there are thirty-odd pages after George Merrydale returns. Even in a short novel like *My Friend's Wife*, the novel lingers on after Mrs Bink has said a cold goodbye to York. An announcement appeared in *The Mofussilite* in late 1862 that Mr William Grant would be the editor, and that all cheques would be signed by him.[15] Lang's health was failing and he did not complete the novel.

In 1863, John Lang wrote in *The Mofussilite* under his own name, an article titled 'We've All Our Little Weaknesses, Or Reminiscences of Sporting'. The article is in first person, like several stories of Lang, and may have autobiographical information but it cannot be said for certain. In it, he wrote that he liked hunting but the number of injuries and falls sustained in the pursuit far outweighed the pleasures.[16]

In his long career with *The Mofussilite*, Lang translated a lot of Persian literature—right from the beginning in 1845, when he translated *Goolistan*, which was later followed by the poetry of Sadi of Shiraz. In 1863, he translated a Persian poem which he titled 'Death of Hossein'. Other short stories written by Lang and printed in *The Mofussilite* in 1863—which are some of Lang's best works—are 'Love's Last Sacrifice, A Tale of the 15th Century', 'Saville' and 'Mr Flax'.

Apart from these short pieces, Lang engaged himself in reprinting his older works. In 1861 he republished *Mazarine*, one of his earliest novels, which appeared in *The Mofussilite* in 1845 as authored by 'Old Trinity'.[17] In the 1861 serial, there appeared a preface which is an apology for republishing a 'boy novel'.[18]

Lang claims in the preface that his later novels have had their 'run', which was quite so with Lang's novels being advertised in most books of the mid-19th century. Given that Lang says here that the novel was written 20 years prior to republication, the date of writing of this novel would be around 1841.

Mazarine is yet another novel where the heroine is a stronger and a more vividly drawn out character than the hero. Anne Mazarine, the wife of Mr. Mazarine is an intelligent woman who finds herself without any occupation after her marriage. She does not find the marriage intellectually stimulating, and elopes with another man. Another interesting aspect of the novel is that the narrator of the story is also in love with Anne, but reveals it only towards the end of the story.

This 'boy novel' can be grouped together with other 'boy novels' written by Lang in the 1840s—*Raymond* published in *Blackwood's Edinburgh Magazine* in 1840; *The Legends of Australia: Charles Frederick Howard* published in 1842 by James Tegg; *Lucy Cooper* published in *Sharpe's London Magazine* in 1846[19]; and *Passages in Life of an Undergraduate* in *The Mofussilite* in 1847. Along with these, there

THE MOFUSSILITE. 51

Literature, &c.

[*Original.*]

MAZARINE.

BY "OLD TRINITY."

CHAPTER 2.

Our stay at Heidelburg was not prolonged more than ten days. There were exception to be sure, but the generality of the students were a low set of people, with souls nothing above tobacco pipes, and bad beer. They were noisy, and boisterous in their conversation, quarrelsome, and uncouth—and entertained an idea that, because in a moment of great excitement, they would go out, and cut each other to pieces with sabres, they were consequently, the bravest fellows on the face of the earth.—Nor was their linen the cleanest, and they used to carry copper coin in their pockets, to pay their losings at dominoes, or any other such game in which they might be unfortunaet. This style of thing disgusted us extremely, but our disgust was accompanied by a pleasurable feeling,—called up by the comparison,—that of an increased affection for our own ALMA MATER.—After leaving Heidelburg we went to Baden Baden, where we were pigioned at *Roulette* and driven to the shores of Albion, rather) prematurely. From the day we parted on board the Steam Boat, till we returned to College, we saw nothing of Mazarine. He kept, it seemed, following in the wake of the Lindsays, as far he could, with decency, and on his return to England, proposed to the lovely Anne.

Mazarine was worth some £ 700 a year on his becoming of age, and he had other expectations from an uncle—who was a Rector, and one talked of as likely to succeed to the first vacant Bishoprick—*provided the Ministry kept in*: for as it is with the ermine, so is it with the mitre—the fittest man for preferment is he whose polititics give a flavour to his pretensions. Major Lindsay was as poor as a man in his position could well be

My acquaintance, however, with Mazarine was not interrupted by this change which had come over him. He kept in the rooms below me, and whenever I happened to be alone, invariably came up to have a quiet gossip.—Indeed we saw more of each other after our return, than formerly—and the great liking I had for the man was strengthened, if not encreased.—The death of a near relative compelled me to quit the University, and go to the West Indies, where I remained for a year. On returning I found Mazarine married,—and living very comfortably, though not extravagantly, in a house he had rented at Norwood. Our acquaintance was renewed, and I used to dine with them, probably three times in every month. Mrs. Mazarine was certainly a fine woman: queenly, and commanding.—And she had such a pretty voice for conversation; one might listen to it for ever, and not grow tired.—Mazarine loved her with all his heart and soul—nay, he idolized her—and always appeared to me to be thinking how he could make her most happy. To the extent of his means, he gratified her most childish whims, and fancies, and it was solely with the hope of adding to her comforts and pleasures, that he resolved on being called to the bar, and thereby fitted, for some appointment which he knew his interest might obtain for him.—Mazarine was, as I have before stated him to be, "a clever man"—but his abilities were entitled to no greater share of commendation than this expression conveys;—while his wife had a very superior order of intellect. She was quick, beyond anything I have seen in her sex, and her knowledge of character and general matters seemed intuitive, rather than acquired. Her wit was of the quiet order,—but her satire was as keen as the edge of a razor. Like the lightning, it seemed to wither whatever it struck upon—and even in her most playful moods, she could impart a rancour sufficient to disturb the stoutest heart. Vain, to a degree, she cared not at whose expense she gained admiration,—and I have seen her on many occasions wound—and that deeply—the feelings of her own and her husband's best friends, for

cally in gold, caught my eye. The driver poked his fore finger at me so temptingly, I raised my hand by instinct as it were, and not being a proud man, I clambered up to the box.

I soon reached Mazarine's house, where I was informed that "Master had gone down to see the Rector, who was very ill, and would'nt be back for two, or three days, but Missus was in the drawing room."

I did'nt wish to see Mrs. Mazarine, for she had said some cruel things to me when I last dined with them, but as I was there, I thought I might as well pay my *formal* respects, and therefore, suffered myself to be ushered into her august presence. She received me with marked kindness—and expressed how glad she was to see me—

"The Rector is ill, I am sorry to hear." said I after the usual compliments.

"Yes—but why should you be sorry? For my part I hope he may die—and then we shall be better off." She replied.

I was not unprepared for such a speech, for I *knew* the woman.

"And Mazarine has gone to see him?" I observed.

"Yes—to see an old stupid uncle, who does not give us a shilling in a year, he leaves me here, all alone "I hope when you get married, Mr. Maxwell, you'll not behave so to your poor wife."

She will be well off if I do not leave her, more than Mazarine leaves you Mrs. Mazarine." said I.

"Perhaps not—you may be so excessively disagreeable that your absence may be a luxury," and here the lady laughed good humouredly at me.

"Thank you—for the compliment." I rejoined.

"Why did'nt you dine here last Saturday? I am very angry with you, for sending an excuse.—We had a dreadfully stupid dinner party—fearful bores—just the kind of people I detest—and you, unkind one, were not here to help me out."

"I was very unwell I assure you, or nothing would have more delighted me. Did you ever know me before make an excuse?"

Mazarine is one of Lang's early novels, serialized in his newspaper in 1845. It was republished in 1861. Like many of Lang's women characters, the female protagonist of this novel too is rebellious.

were a series of sketches called *Jack Weatherly by His Brother Geoffery* published in *The Mofussilite* in August 1845.

The sketches stopped midway to give way to *Mazarine.* Crittenden contends that *Raymond* is autobiographical, and Lang relives his childhood as well as his college life through this novel, even though it is set entirely in England. Crittenden, in his biography of Lang, has tried to reconstruct Lang's childhood largely through the scenes and events depicted in *Raymond*. *The Legends of Australia* being Lang's work is conjectural, since Lang never claimed it. John Earnshaw argues through evidences related to publishers, in *Biblionews* of April 1958, that this was Lang's work. One evidence from within Lang's corpus of works is that the plot of *Frederick Charles Howard* has parallels with the plot of *Forger's Wife,* for in the latter work, the wife goes to Australia in search of her husband who is a convict, and is assisted in this search by a young impetuous man. Another literary evidence from the book is that it begins with a line from Shakespeare, as do many works of Lang which have Shakespearean or Byronic epigraphs.

The above-mentioned novels of Lang are all short works and show Lang's acumen as a writer, but the work from which Lang gets a hold on his writing as well as the publishing market is *The Wetherbys.* Lang often returned to subjects he had dealt with in earlier novels, and he creates the university scene of *Raymond,* and *Passages in the Life of An Undergraduate* again in *Will He Marry Her?*

After *Mazarine* appeared as a serial in 1861, *The Undergraduate*—which had appeared as a serial called *Passages in the Life of an Undergraduate* in 1847—was again serialised in *The Mofussilite* in 1862. At the end of this serial, Lang wrote, 'Go little book from this my solitude, I cast thee on the waters. Go thy ways. John Lang.'[20] After *The Undergraduate*; *Raymond* was republished as a serial in *The Mofussilite.* It seems, from these activities, that Lang was wrapping up, and claiming authorship of his earlier works for posterity.

Unfortunately, 1862 onward, his health seems to have been on the wane. However, he would not have expected an end in 1864, neither would anyone else have, for he had recovered many times from illnesses. This is stated by Lang's obituarist in *The Mofussilite.*[21]

Apart from these literary activities, and various changes in the management of the newspaper, nothing much is known about the last years of Lang's life. Not much is known about Margaret Wetter, either. It is an irony that not much is known about the women in Lang's life, for as a novelist, most of his protagonists are women.

Two Wives, or Two Lives

Two lives, not because the two wives caused each other consternation—for the temporal difference between the two marriages is 23 years—

but because Lang lived most of his life as a single man. In various accounts by his friends, one does not find any mention of his wife or a lover. Victor Crittenden contends that he perhaps had a mistress or mistresses:

> We know that from early in his Indian experience John Lang lived as a 'single' man. That is not to say he did not have a mistress...but there is no record of one. Lang remained on friendly terms with Lucy's brother Andrew Petersen who some years later assisted in defending Lang in a court case in India.[22]

The assumption of Crittenden regarding 'not to say he did not have a mistress' is perhaps founded on the idea that Lang's protagonists are women, and he gives lengthy descriptions of women's beauty in his works. The point is well taken, but contrariwise, given Lang's ambition as a writer and journalist, and his alcoholism, he seems also to have been a loner who spent long stretches in solitude. Contradictions are a part of the Lang lore, and it is also evident that he liked going to parties, and was a teller of tales at these parties. To me, it appears that mixing with society was a need for Lang, to imbibe tales, to be able to tell tales. Given that none of his friends knew much about his personal life, shows that he did draw boundaries. After telling tales and hearing tales, he would perhaps withdraw to his chambers to smoke, drink, write, and read some Latin and Persian, and imbibe some Bocaccio, Shakespeare, and Byron—the three writers who seem to have loomed large over the writings and life of Lang.

After comparison of Lang's works with his life, one can conjecture that he had modelled himself after Byron. He liked to wander, to gather tales, to be irreverent.

These pictures (see plate 10) appeared in the 4 October, 1845 edition of *The Mofussilite*. Both the pictures have been signed 'Scrooge'. The sense of 'Scrooge' as a miserly man was imminent in 19th century, from a famous Christmas carol about this character. It is interesting to note that Dickens wrote a book based on this Christmas carol in 1846, entitled *A Christmas Carol in Prose: The Chimes; the Cricket on the Hearth*[23]. Perhaps these are self-portraits of Lang signed under this pseudonym, perhaps they are not—it is difficult to tell, but Lang never uses the alias of Scrooge again. Perhaps, it was a friend of Lang's who used this pseudonym.

The picture (plate no.) on top bears the date '1843' and has a header, 'Mofussilite'. Mofussilite, apart from being the title of Lang's newspaper, was his 'alias' on several occasions. *Too Clever By Half* was first published in 1853 with the author's name as 'The Mofussilite'. There is a reference to Lang in *Tait's Magazine* as John Mofussilite Lang in an interesting episode regarding Edgar Allen Poe. *Too Clever By Half* has numerous engravings and they are signed by 'M', which could stand for Mofussilite.

The second picture (plate no.) is also by 'Scrooge', and perhaps is a sketch of John and Lucy Lang in their 'happier times'. There are no known portraits either of John Lang or of his wife Lucy. Crittenden, in an essay about *Mazarine,* reproduced this picture with the subtitle 'Mrs Mazarine and one of her admirers'.[24] The picture does not have any connection with *Mazarine*; Crittenden has used it because the image perhaps suits the plot of *Mazarine.*

John Lang married Lucy Peterson in 1839. We come to know from the papers of James Dowling—an Australian friend and student who was with Lang during Lang's Cambridge days—that Lang broke a leg in one of the hunting expeditions and was compensated by destiny with a bride, who was the daughter of the host.[25] Lang perhaps made a joke out of the accident, and impressed Lucy with his scholarship and ready wit.

Lucy Peterson was the daughter of Henry Peterson, gentleman of Wakefield. Lucy was at this time aged 21.[26] The wedding took place on 2 February 1839, and among the witnesses was Lucy's brother Andrew Thomas Turton Peterson.

Crittenden considers *Raymond* an autobiographical novel and reconstructs a lot of Lang's youth with the help of this book. In the novel, the protagonist writes to his mother telling her of his debts and his love interest, and his resolve to make a new start. Lang perhaps was deeply in love, or perhaps pragmatic enough to think that he could not let go of this opportunity to marry a gentleman's daughter. To reconstruct through the narrative of *Raymond*, this is how the couple commenced their married life:

> He took a small cheap and retired cottage at West-End near Hampstead. From this period the young couple's domestic career was one of unclouded happiness. They dwelt in comparative retirement with all the comforts, and some of the luxuries of life at their command...His original passion for study—especially the classics of Greece and Rome...came back on Raymond's mind with all the freshness and ardour of a first love, refining and elevating his character; but alas tending also to unfit him for active intercourse with the practical, hard-working world...he devoted hours to a translation...which he had selected as his opus magnum—his first great literary undertaking: at noon, provided the weather permitted, he would stroll about the neighbourhood with Julia, listening delighted to her arch sallies and the merry music of her voice: and the day would be closed with conversation, or a song or two at the piano.

Eva in *Ex-Wife*—from a novel written 15 years after *Raymond*—has similar qualities; she translates from German and French to earn a living, writes stories, sketches, gives piano lessons.

If we look at the marriage certificate, Lang's age there appears as 21; but he was 23 in 1839. His father Walter Lang mentioned as 'Late captain in the army' was just a sailor and merchant. Lang, in trying to cultivate his image as a gentleman, perhaps thought that gentlemen went to the army and did not take up trading.

In May 1841, Lang was called to the Bar, and he departed for Sydney on June 13, aboard the ship *Lady Kennaway* with his wife and daughter Aimee, who was born within a year of the marriage. Even though Lang was married and had a child already by the time he returned to Sydney, his friend Dowling was suspicious of his 'character'. He wrote a letter to his family on 30 June 1841, in which he said:

> I cannot say much for Lang; he leaves by no means a good character in England, neither for gentlemanly conduct or sobriety. But judge him for yourself. Unless much altered on the passage out, I should be very sorry indeed to her of him being very often at Brougham Place. Put no wrong construction of my motive in saying this: I do it out of strict regard and affection for my sisters.[27]

This epistle throws some light on why John and Lucy Lang would have separated. Perhaps Lang continued to show interest in women outside his marriage. This letter may also be misleading, for Dowling and his family had a decided class prejudice, and Lang was looked down upon by them. On 2 May 1840, Dowling wrote a letter, saying:

> Young Lang proceeds to the colony next year; he has become a steady fellow and studies very closely with a special pleader of some note; he is very sanguine of 'what he will do,' and I have no doubt you will find him a clever fellow, but somewhat troublesome. His family connections will somewhat mar his fortune; they will be stumbling blocks in his path.[28]

The letter of 1841 which says that 'he leaves by no means a good character' is contradicted by the earlier letter which says that 'he has become a steady fellow'. The issue of 'family connections' clearly shows the social attitude as well as Dowling's prejudice. In the 1841 letter, Dowling is almost jealous of Lang having married a 'lady-like person':

> He has married, as I am informed, a very ladylike person, but I am afraid she is not aware of her husband's connections in the Colony, or she would not be so intent on going there.[29]

Dowling's father Sir James Dowling did not sympathise with John Lang when he was expelled from Cambridge for one of his pranks. He wrote in a letter to his son, dated 11 August 1838:

> I am concerned to hear of Mr Lang, of whom I know nothing…I have always understood here he was a little scampish. I am glad you have made up your mind to cut him...His expulsion from Cambridge will doubtless affect his call to the Bar, as it ought.[30]

In a letter written just a few days later, Sir James again implores his son to have nothing to do with Lang:

> So Mr Lang has been expelled from college for his tricks, Botany Bay tricks, not gentlemanly tricks...I advise you to have nothing to do with him, for if you do, when you both come out he will be a constant annoyance to you.[31]

This goes on to show how deeply rooted the class divisions were in the British Empire. Class difference could have been a reason for the separation of the couple; in my opinion, this theory does not hold. Lucy travelled with Lang to India as well, and they had four children before they separated. The time of separation could be anywhere between 1845 and 1854, for the fourth child, Margaret, was born in October 1844, and Lang went to England for five years in 1854. Lang's mother's family in Australia was very wealthy and well-known, with his foster father being a whaler and a trader on the seas, and the owner of huge property in Ashfield Park in Sydney. Lang, however, never mentioned Joseph Underwood as his father, and concocted an identity of an army man for his deceased merchant father as well. In most of Lang's novels, the bitter class struggle of England is depicted vividly. Lang, though, is at sea in these narratives, struggling with his own emotions. For his readers, he was a 'gentleman'.

Therefore, in *Will He Marry Her?* when Edgar West—who is of 'good birth' but of fallen pecuniary circumstances—is abused by a bully in Trinity College; John Chayworth comes to his rescue and counter-abuses the bully by saying, 'You whose father blackened my uncle's boots...'. The episode of Augustus delivering a passionate speech, criticizing the difference in punishments meted out to Edgar and Augustus, is a veiled attack on the class system, where the protagonist representing Lang is shown to be a gentleman, but one who is self-critical of his own position. In *Ex-Wife*, too, Lady Eva Merrydale—who is bailed out of her troubles by her maid Mathilde and becomes literally dependant on her—is conscious of her class and keeps the equation of a lady and her maid intact with the alibi that the maid would feel offended by the prospect of equality. However, Eva is acutely conscious of her debt to Mathilde and chastises her brother when he says he would call the maid. The entire novel is a critique of class hierarchy and hypocrisy.

This, then, is the complicated position of Lang about class system—that he would pose as a gentleman, that his protagonists would be gentlemen who would look down upon the humble-born, but the narrative of the novel would proceed to show these gentlemen as decadent, imprudent, and vain, and destiny would teach them a lesson or two. Sir George Merrydale and his wife Eva have to go through such a lesson for 12 years—the entire length of the novel—in *Ex-Wife.* The self-positioning of Lang is that he is a gentleman by contrivance of destiny, by circumstance, by birth—but that by thought and action, he is critical of such divisions and distinctions, and his heart lies with the struggles of the 'humble born'.

Like Lang's, Lucy's family, too, had colonial connections; this would have been a common thread of discussion between their family members. Lucy's great-grandfather had settled in America and come back to England. Colin Roderick writes:

> Lucy Peterson's great-grandfather, Henry Peterson, was the son of-an American colonist who had settled at Middleton in the tiny province of Delaware. Henry Peterson came back... to Settle at Wakefield in Yorkshire in 1786...the evidence faintly suggests that their ancestors may have been among the Swedish settlers who first occupied the country lying south of the Delaware River...it suggests that he was loyal to the British cause and that after the signing of the 1783 treaty of independence he left the United States before Delaware signed the ratification of the Federal constitution in 1787.[32]

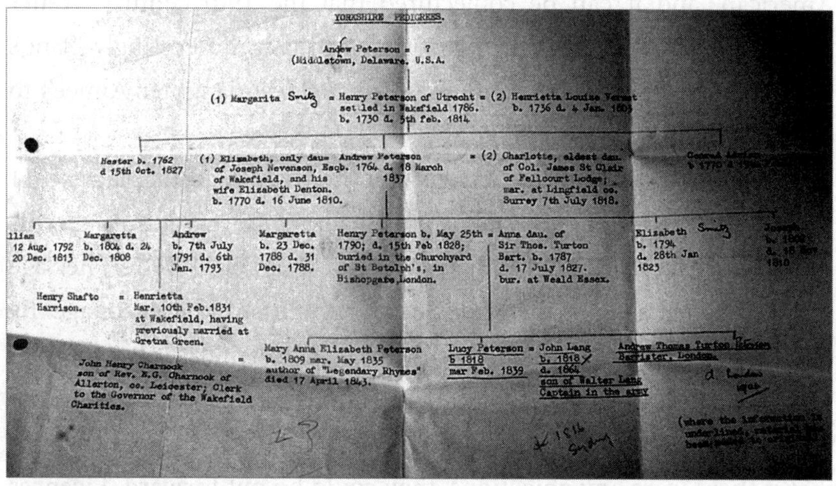

YORKSHIRE PEDIGREES.

Andew Peterson = ?
(Middletown, Delaware. U.S.A.

(1) Margarita Smitz = Henry Peterson of Utrecht = (2) Henrietta Louise Vermet
settled in Wakefield 1786.
b. 1730 d. 5th feb. 1814
b. 1736 d. 4 Jan. 1803

Hester b. 1762
d 15th Oct. 1827

(1) Elizabeth, only dau= of Joseph Nevenson, Esqb. of Wakefield, and his wife Elizabeth Denton. b. 1770 d. 16 June 1810.

Andrew Peterson 1764 d. 18 March 1837

= (2) Charlotte, eldest dau. of Col. James St Clair of Fellcourt Lodge; mar. at Lingfield co. Surrey 7th July 1818.

...lliam 12 Aug. 1792 20 Dec. 1813

Margaretta b. 1804 d. 24 Dec. 1808

Andrew b. 7th July 1791 d. 6th Jan. 1793

Margaretta b. 23 Dec. 1788 d. 31 Dec. 1788.

Henry Peterson b. May 25th 1790; d. 15th Feb 1828; buried in the Churchyard of St Botolph's, in Bishopgate, London.

= Anna dau. of Sir Thos. Turton Bart. b. 1787 d. 17 July 1827. bur. at Weald Essex.

Elizabeth Smitz b. 1794 d. 28th Jan 1823

Henry Shafto Harrison. = Henrietta Mar. 10th Feb.1831 at Wakefield, having previously married at Gretna Green.

John Henry Charnock son of Rev. N.G. Charnock of Allerton, co. Leicester; Clerk to the Governor of the Wakefield Charities.

= Mary Anna Elizabeth Peterson b. 1809 mar. May 1835 author of "Legendary Rhymes" died 17 April 1843.

Lucy Peterson b 1818 mar Feb. 1839 = John Lang b. 1818 d. 1864 son of Walter Lang Captain in the army

Andrew Thomas Turton Harden Barrister, London.

The family tree of Lucy Peterson

Another fact of interest is one of Lucy's sisters, Mary, who was an authoress. The book *Legendary Rhymes* (1843)[33] is attested under her married name, Mary Anna Elizabeth Charnock. Mary, who was nine years elder to Lucy Lang, died young at the age of 34. This could have been one of the deaths that made Lang mention death so often in his literary works. *Legendary Rhymes* was published posthumously, and Mary's husband John Charnock wrote a preface saying that had Mary lived longer, she would have flourished as a writer. Even though the title says 'rhymes', these are long poems about historical subjects ranging from the ruins of the Roman Empire, through an imaginary meeting of Chaucer and Petrarch, to Princess Victoria.[34] Also mentioned are Petersons in Brussels. This shows that the Peterson family was spread over continental Europe. The continental connections of the family could also explain why Lucy was living in Italy, and how her two elder daughters got married into Italian noble families.

The second marriage of Lang was with Margaret Wetter. Crittenden contends that Wetter is not a common British surname, and that Wetter could have been an Indian Christian or part Indian.

The surname 'Wetter', however, appears in several texts, especially American, and it can be conjectured that the 19th century Wetter surname could have been half-British, or British. Interestingly, Lang's second marriage is in the same year as his eldest daughter Aimee's to Conte Adolfo Riccardi in Italy.

The marriage certificate tells us that the wedding took place on 11 May 1861. It is difficult to establish much about Margaret through this certificate, except that her father's name is Paul Peter Wetter; her age is not specified as both the bride and the groom are shown 'of age'. By our calculation, Lang was 45 at this time. The certificate also shows it was 'by license'. By banns would have entailed an announcement that would be followed by a three-week interim before the marriage, so that if there were any objections, they could be put forward. Licences were obtained on payment, and generally taken if a couple intended to marry quickly, or away from their home parish. It was also seen as a status symbol. Residence at the time of marriage is Landour (in Mussoorie) for both the bride and the groom, showing that Lang regularly resided in Landour in the summer months.

George Carmichael Smyth, Lang's witness in the marriage, is an important figure of 19th century British India. He was commander of 3rd Bengal Light Cavalry during the Mutiny of 1857.[35]

George Smyth was also a writer of army matters and history, and wrote two books—*A History of the Reigning Family of Lahore: With Some Account of the Jummoo Rajahs, the Seik Soldiers and Their Sirdars*,[36] and *Secret History of the Khalsa Durbar*. There were many army men who contributed to *The Mofussilite*, and the intelligence of the newspaper regarding Sikh matters was impeccable. Smyth may have been one of the contributors to Lang's newspaper in the run-up to Anglo-Sikh wars during the decade of 1840s. The book about Lahore was reviewed by *The Mofussilite*, which expressed the opinion that the book was well written, and with a 'decidedly independent tone'. Gianeshwar Khurana[37] tells that *The Mofussilite* did cite Smyth as one of its sources for intelligence about Punjab. He also tells that Smyth knew neither Punjabi nor Persian, but knew the importance of indigenous sources and employed natives for the purpose.

Smyth, who retired as major-general, was the last of ten children of James C. Smyth, Physician Extraordinary to King George III[38].

The witness on Margaret Wetter's side I.C.C. Gray M.G. also seems to have been a prominent man in the British Indian Army. He was on the board of Delhi and London Bank, and there is a reference to him proposing a motion to recover the losses of the bank in *The Bankers' Magazine and Journal of the Money Market* of 1870.[39]

The priest who officiated the Lang-Wetter marriage is also a well-known clergyman of 19th century India. He was an assistant chaplain in Lucknow in 1852[40] (he is referred to as Milward R. Burge M.A.), and chaplain at Dinapore during the Mutiny.[41]

Thus, this wedding occurred under the presence of influential people of their time. It is unfortunate that we still cannot glean anything about Margaret Wetter.

Let us now turn to the two novels, *The Forger's Wife,* and *Ex-Wife.*

Ex-Wife has already been discussed periodically in this work. It is one of the few 'long' novels by Lang, and practically his last; *The Detective*, in 1861, and *Ellen Wareham*, in 1862,) appeared only as serials in *The Mofussilite* and never as books.

Ex-Wife could be called a proto-feminist text, with the novel having been written in the first-person voice of a divorced lady, Eva Merrydale, and with his plot majorly constructed around the lives of Eva and Mathilde, her former maid. *Ex-Wife* also uses the meta-narrative or the frame narrative technique of Boccaccio's *Decameron* and the tale of *The Arabian Nights*. Through this technique, several stories are told by travellers who come to Mathilde's shop.

The summary of the plot is this: lord meets lady, they get married. Lord suspects lady, divorces her. The said lady lives with her maid, depending on the latter, and makes her living writing and doing sundry jobs. The said lord regrets having done what he did, and wanders around the world in a ship called *Wanderer.* By the time he returns, he is haggard and his wife's once pretty face is freckled with small-pox. Redemption comes, but only after death, despair and going through fire.

Lord George Merrydale had been in the army; it remains Lang's ploy to satirise the army of the British Empire, for Lord Merrydale says that 'the members of gentry barely did anything noteworthy, but that their presence was necessary for the commoners to get inspired.[42] The lord is wayward in his ways, and is known to visit an actress named Isabel Morton. Later in the novel, when the lord has to get rid of this actress, it is suggested by Mathilde that he should lay the condition that she would not act in the future. The actress rejects this idea outright and leaves the lord, asking him 'to go to the devil'[43]. This is one of the many instances in the novel of women with strong personalities.

When the wife, Eva Merrydale, gets suspicious of Merrydale's wayward ways, she mildly flirts with Mr. Stoneycombe, who tells her about her husband's infidelity and proposes that they elope. Eva, however, spurns Stoneycombe's advances. The servants spy Eva wandering with Stoneycombe in parks, and they start gossiping. Merrydale gets a whiff of this chatter, and takes Eva to court for divorce. George knows that Eva is innocent, and he is well aware of his own wayward ways, but he takes Eva to court because he is more concerned about market chatter.

Eva is not allowed to appear personally to defend herself in the court. She has to be defended by the man with whom she is alleged to have 'criminal familiarity'. Stoneycombe wants to marry Eva, and he is rich; thus, he willingly loses the case. The long description of the court case again shows how well-versed Lang was with legal matters. Lang's account of the case is a scathing critique of the contemporary British legal system, which denied to women even the right of defending themselves. After the case, Eva starts living with her maid Mathilde. Eva's name is too blemished for her to appear in public. She sits at home knitting, sewing, sketching pictures; and these wares are sold by Mathilde—who has set up a shop at the front of the house. There is a small room just behind the shop so that Eva can see people and sketch them, and hear Mathilde conversing with people. Mathilde is Eva's window to the world.

The novel is a strong statement against class, where the lords and ladies are kept afloat by the commoners. Later in the novel, when Eva lets out her house for tenants, a couple stays at her house, who she recognises as fish merchants from whom her servants used to buy fish. She is astounded to discover that the couple has exquisite taste in literature and music. Using several sub-plots like these, Lang has continually challenged the class system and the smugness of the gentry throughout the novel.

Mathilde marries a man named Clatter, who is employed as a royal courier on the continent. He loses his job, and becomes decadent, gambling and wasting himself away. He starts abusing Mathilde and extorting money from her. He is even able to extort money out of her creditors. This is, again, a critique of British law that almost made a man the master of his wife—for all that belonged to her, he could claim as his right. Mathilde is exasperated and says, 'the laws of this land are only for men' and that 'getting beaten is not enough to get a divorce' Once a burglar enters Eva's house, and when she has to depose as a witness in this case, the lawyer insinuates that the thief and Eva were having an affair, that things went sour, therefore the complaint.

Lang engages with the issue of divorce severally. He had not been able to get a divorce from his wife Lucy, even though they had been separated for a long time. One must credit Lang for not bringing his personal prejudices on this matter, for he entirely sides with women as victimised by law. There are numerous literary allusions in the novel as is the case with most of Lang's novels. Mathilde knows literature and history, having overheard her masters' conversations—Penderfield is a scholar, Eva is a writer, George is an avid reader, and Shortning is a theatre man. In short, all characters are capable of holding literary conversations. There are references to 'Sancho and the Duchess'; a farcical play 'Force of Example'; Koetzebue's play *The Stranger*, which we have also seen mentioned in another Lang novel; Friedrich Halm's *Griseldis*; Ovid; the novel *Violet the Danseuse*, which is conjectured to be a Lang novel but of which there is no concrete proof; a Thomas Hood poem; Horace; Giovanni Boccaccio; *Arabian Nights*; and Pope and his views on grief—among several others. Lang also highlights, through *Ex-Wife*, how difficult it was for a divorced woman to make a living for herself. Eva sews, knits, draws sketches, learns photography, writes for magazines, translates, gives music lessons and lessons in classics and languages, rents her house for tenants, cooks for them, et al. Her son learns the art of carpentry. Lang also returns to the topic of the difficulty of a writer if he or she is not from the gentry. Eva earns less because she doesn't have a title or a surname to add to her name.

With its frame narrative, this novel is a warehouse of information, as also interesting for its construction of intricate plots.

The other novel, *Forger's Wife*, published in 1855, is an Australian classic. It depicts the 19th century Australian life in vivid detail, and draws from the lives of convicts and ex-convicts. The enterprise of bushranging, or bounty-hunting, is brought out very evocatively. The novel is noteworthy for packing in a lot of issues in a very short space with dexterity. Lang also engages in discussion about love and marriage through his various characters.

In the preface to the 1855 edition, Lang claims that the novel is based on true incidents, and that the letters written by the unfortunate heroine 'came into the possession of the author some sixteen years ago, and it was from these letters that the idea of her sufferings was gleaned'.

This is the plot of the novel: a gentleman meets a lady in England and marries her. During their honeymoon days, Captain Harcourt showers Emily Orford with love and spends extravagantly. It turns out, however, that it is not his own money; he had forged a cheque. He is transported to New South Wales. Emily is convinced that her husband is innocent, and decides to get justice for him, and thus, travels to Sydney. No one is ready to shelter a convict's wife; there are lecherous eyes on the prowl. She manages to find another convict who was transported on the same ship as her husband, and entreats him to find about Harcourt's whereabouts. In Sydney, convicts were mostly assigned as workmen on free people's estates. It turns out that Harcourt has run away from his master, and now has a prize of five pounds for his capture. Harcourt's friend meets him and promises to reunite him with his wife, but has ulterior plans running beneath the benign veneer.

The friend contacts George Flower, the famous 'thief-taker', to get a share in the prize but Flower is not interested. Flower looks into the history of Harcourt, and upon finding that the latter had been a forger, says that forgers were useless and did not have the heart to kill, and therefore, the prize on their heads would never be big.

This is an interesting comment. Runaway convicts were allowed to ripen as dreaded criminals—with a big sum on their head—before they were harvested by 'thief takers'. At last, Flower arrests Harcourt at Emily's house, but is moved upon seeing Emily. This is a rare moment when Lang shows fraternal love in a man-woman relationship. Flower, in Emily, is reminded of his sister, who had been dishonoured by a rogue—to avenge which, Flower had killed the rogue and had been sentenced to be transported to New South Wales. In Sydney, by catching runaway convicts, he became a free man, and then a policeman. Flower then gets Harcourt assigned to himself; and after thrashing him soundly, gets him employed with an attorney as a note-taker. Harcourt tries to get assigned to his own wife, so that he can stop living in Flower's dread. Emily manages to prevail upon Flower to have her husband assigned to her, which he does, despite several warnings of that would be her undoing. Harcourt returns to his old ways and cheats on his wife. One of the police magistrates, Mr Brade, takes fancy to Emily; and upon learning that that Flower is her protector, determines to get him out of the way. He connives to send Flower on a bounty-hunt, but the latter is reluctant, out of concern for Emily's safety. Once Flower takes off for the bush, after Brade insinuates the former has lost his courage, the novel starts parallel narratives—Flower's adventure, and Brade's lusty advances towards Emily. As Brade knows that Harcourt just cares for money and alcohol, he invites Mr and Mrs Harcourt to his house; while Harcourt vanishes to drown in cups, Brade molests Emily. She is helpless, for her husband is both a convict and a spineless man.

These episodes are too bold for an 1850s novel.

While Emily suffers thus, George Flower mingles in the society of dreaded convicts. This is the best part of the novel—the description of the life of convicts in the bush. Take for example what happens in the novel: Flower thinks he himself will become one of them if he did not hurry his mission. He takes their head Millighan to a secluded spot and has a long conversation, typical of bush literature. Flower asks Millighan what if he met George Flower in a secluded spot like this; to which Millighan says that he would invite him to a fair fight. Flower reveals his true identity, and invites Millighan to 'draw'—the convention of drawing pistols, walking 12 paces each, turning, and shooting. Both the men turn but do not shoot, for Flower has great regard for Millighan, who finally shoots, but misses Flower. He in turn finishes Millighan in a single shot. Millighan had requested Flower to leave his body to be devoured by eagles, which Flower does after shedding tears. Millighan's faithful dog does not leave, and dies with his master.

Passages like these are important in the construction of early Australian identity and values. Even a runaway brigand, like Millighan, has high values, and even though Flower is a mercenary 'thief-taker', he has great regard for courage.

Flower returns to Sydney with the rest of his prisoners, and also gets a wife on his way. On his return, he is enraged to hear about Brade's designs: Emily tells him that Brade has invited her and her husband, and had sent a carriage for her, for Harcourt would come later. Flower says that he will 'cut off' Brade's throat; and he does indeed hold him by the throat. Harcourt again forges a cheque, is imprisoned, tries to run away, is caught, and becomes a dreaded convict. Flower, who has retired from police and become a businessman, takes upon himself to kill Harcourt, for Emily would not go back to her parents 'as long as that man lives'. Flower kills Harcourt. Flower's character is based upon the character of Israel Chapman, a Jewish convict-turned-bushranger. Grace Karskens of UNSW has written an interesting history of Chapman in her essay 'Resurrecting Chapman'.[44] *The Forger's Wife* is a prototype of later police and detective novels, and even today's reader, much removed from the context of the novel, would enjoy it for its plot and dialogue construction. Thus, in a manner, Lang was not of his times—and definitely not liked by his times. His works were ahead of his time, and yet time itself seems to have forgotten him.

Ahead of His Times,

or No One Will Write Rhymes For You Mr Lang

Lang had foreseen Google.

In *Ex-Wife,* when Eva Merrydale looked up 'Eva Merrydale + Divorced by Husband for Criminal Familiarity With Another Man' on her search engine, there were 114,227 results for the query:

> Heaven knows, I have had a surfeit of publicity. I made a calculation last week, the result of which was that my name has appeared in type no less than one hundred and fourteen thousand two hundred and seventy times in various papers! In one column alone of the Times, it was printed one hundred and seven times.[1]

The context is that Eva's brother says that he will whip the hide of the lawyer who had tried to defame her, and she says that she did not want to attract any publicity, for after her divorce on the charge that she had cheated on him, the press had constantly been engaged in raking up the issue for several years. Through the exaggerated figures of 114,227 and 107 times in *Times* alone, Lang is clearly lampooning the British media.

Lang had a sour relation with the British media, for his anti-Raj novels were called 'hospital-scene' by the press—that is, depicting the dregs of the society rather than real representation. The pro-establishment Indian newspapers like the *Delhi Gazette* were even more hostile towards him. If one reads the issues of the first year of *The Mofussilite,* there is a column virtually in every edition where Lang is replying to 'our contemporary' (editor of *Delhi Gazette* with acerbic phrases). Peter

Stanley tells that 'the Mofussilite edited by John Lang, (regarded by Rose as a dangerous radical) excited the minds of the men'[2].

Lang had his own share of jokes at the cost of the British press and the English press of India. We have seen how he passed off the picture of pot-bellied Lala Jotee Persaud as that of the royal Nana Sahib in *The Illustrated London News* in 1857. Curiously paralleling the Indian caste system where the Kshatriyas (Nana) looked down upon Khatris (Lala), the British class system also had the gentry looking down upon the mercantile class.

We have also seen how a stray comment by him in 1855 about Edgar Allan Poe's poem 'The Raven'—that it was a translation of a Persian original—had British media churning columns about this matter defending Poe. It is interesting to note that neither Lang spoke about the matter ever again, nor did Poe write a defence. Only a Persian scholar can verify the claim of Lang. His calling the jury at Jotee Persaud's case in 1851 was clearly a strategy to hog the limelight, to be remembered for his audacity for ages to come.

In another case related with sensationalism, Lang and journalism, Henry George Keene tells a very interesting story about the Gorham case in his book entitled *A Servant of John Company*:

> Dissatisfied with London openings, he (Lang) came out to India when Hardinge was Governor-General, married a Miss Peterson, and tried his fortune at the bar of Calcutta Courts. Not succeeding at once, he accepted an engagement as editor of a new journal to be founded at Meerut, under the title of The Mofussilite, and by the time under notice was an established journalist and social celebrity in all the Upper Provinces. His paper enjoyed the distinction of producing the most laconic leading article on record; it appeared in 1850, when England was in one of her periodic flurries about a West of England clergyman, named Gorham, whom Bishop Philpotts, of Exeter,

> refused to induct into his living, on the allegation of unsound doctrine. The matter was heard in the Queen's Bench, and carried thence into the Privy Council, where the Archbishop of Canterbury expressed himself in favour of Mr. Gorham; the Bishop of Exeter excommunicated his Primate, and all England rang with the controversy.[3]

Lang, known to be a gifted writer of witty prose, was called upon from Meerut by his printer Gibbons and editor Wilby to write on the Gorham case. Keene continues:

> It was during this excitement that Lang was, one morning, called upon to write a 'leader' on the prevailing topic. He was of convivial habits, and his matutinal headache often led to short paragraphs and most unblushing excuses.[4]

Keene's euphemism, 'he was of convivial habits, and his matutinal headache' converts to 20th century as 'he used to party till late, because of which he was hungover in the morning'. On this occasion, called upon to write about the Gorham case, this is how unabashed Lang was. The entire article consisted of these words:

> 'THE GORHAM CASE.'
> 'D--n[I] the Gorham Case.'[5]

Keene tells that 'Readers were convulsed'. He goes on to says that *The Mofussilite* was a favourite of people, as he also tells about yet another alias of Lang:

> There is little admirable in the incident, but it is perhaps worth recording, if only as a sample of the liberty allowed to a general

I 'Damn the Gorham Case'

> favourite by the Anglo-Indian public, and the ease with which that public was amused. It may be added that this briefest of 'leaders' was popularly attributed to Mr F.F.Courtenay, Private Secretary to Lord Dalhousie. It was in all probability a mere piece of petulance due to importunities from the printer.[6]

Lang claims in *Wanderings in India* that he is an 'interloper' who does not belong to either the civil side or the military side of the British establishment in India. However, he had friends aplenty in both due to his 'convivial habits' and, in fact, most of the subscribers of his newspaper were military men. *The Reports of the Committees* of 1853 told that 'in 1848 the "Mofussilite" printed a list of all its subscribers, from which it appeared that four-fifths of these were members of the public service'.[7]

Lang's newspaper was for the members of public service thus, and it thrived on scandals related to them. Lang can indeed be viewed as the father of Indian tabloid journalism. The tabloid, of course, had its equivalent of what is now known as 'Page 3', but it was very different—in that it was very literary, with an overdose of Lang's Latin, Boccaccios and Byrons. *The Mofussilite*'s military intelligence was impeccable, owing to the number of friends Lang had in the military. An army officer, Mr Campbell, wrote under the name nom-de-guerre of 'Economist' in *The Mofussilite* regarding army intelligence and Punjab. Campbell knew more than the government did, and his articles were perused by the government in preparing strategies for Anglo-Sikh wars of the 1840s.[8] *The Mofussilite* thus became a much subscribed-to newspaper. Laurie, writing about Anglo-Indians, comments, 'The Mofussilite, when edited by its founder, John Lang, attained very high positions in the newspaper literature'[9].

So intimate was the relation of *The Mofussilite* with the military that during the Mutiny of 1857, it was printed from inside the Agra Fort. A writer writing about the Mutiny tells in 1858:

> The printing presses of the 'Mofussilite' newspaper were also secured in the fort; and the journal was printed under the same roof with the whole of its local subscribers.[10]

Being so close to the military, Lang shared a love-hate relationship with it. He took its establishment by the horns in the Jotee Persaud case and mocked it. In his novels he constantly criticised the military for its policies. However, whenever it came to war scenes, his novels painted a chivalrous picture of the British army. In the Anglo-Sikh wars, there were quite a few cowards attested in official gazettes, but Lang does not allude to any of them—including Mactier, who also fought the battles in the two wars.

Another joke that Lang played on the establishment and the pro-establishment newspapers is told by Lang himself in *Wanderings in India*. It's more of Lang taking on the establishment through innovative means where he could not do it himself, and shows his rebellious streak and the kind of resentment he had for the rule of the East India Company. Lang writes:

> There was a native newspaper published at Meerut, called the *Jam-i-Jumsheed,* which title signifies a bowl or glass, into which if you look, you will see what transpires the whole world.[11]

Lang is witty while telling stories about himself. In translating the name of the native newspaper, he is grounding the fact that this newspaper told stories that were otherwise untold. He goes on to write that the editor of this newspaper was skilled in English, as in Urdu—the language of his newspaper—and that this editor was a native 'moonshee', and was also employed in the printing press of an English newspaper published from Meerut. Lang has named the Urdu newspaper, and translated the meaning of its name, but not mentioned the name of the English newspaper. The newspaper, in my opinion, is

The Mofussilite and the printing press in question is The Mofussilite Press. Lang further writes:

> Having constant access to the desks of the compositors, this press moonshee acquired knowledge of every item of news furnished by European as well as native correspondents, and of this knowledge he failed not to avail himself. This, however, was but a small evil, comparatively. Unknown to the conductor of the Meerut paper, a much greater evil arose from the publication of the native print. Availing himself of such sources of information, its editor seized the views of his employer—views intended only for European eyes, and gave his own version of them to his readers in the Hindoostanee language; and, what was equally mischievous, he published quantities of matter which the conductor of the Meerut paper thought proper to suppress after it was set up in type.[12]

After this, Lang mock-sympathises with the imaginary English editor whose stories were pilfered by the native 'moonshee', the 'Oordoo' editor. He tells that the English editor did not publish a certain piece of news because his friends advised him against it. Lang goes on to translate what was printed in *Jam-i-Jumsheed* (since Lang was a good translator from Urdu to English). In this way, Lang apparently sympathises with the cause of the establishment, apparently tells of the moonshee's mischief. Lang says:

> These were the morsels in which the native editor took most delight A single instance will suffice. The following appeared in the leading columns of the *Jam-i-Jumsheed*, the facts having been kept out of the columns of the Meerut paper, at the instance of the friends of the gentleman who was guilty of the indiscretion :—

> An act of retributive justice has just been committed by the worthy magistrate of this district. It was supposed that an escaped convict from the jail was secreted in a village about four miles distant from this cantonment. In the dead of the night, the magistrate, at the head of a large body of police, visited the village, aroused the inhabitants from their slumbers, and demanded the culprit. The villagers denied any knowledge of him. The magistrate, with characteristic kindness and consideration, gave them half-an-hour to make up their minds. At the expiration of that time, as the culprit was not produced, he set fire to the village. In those flames, which illuminated the country for miles round, thirteen lives were sacrificed; namely, those of three men, four women, and six children. One of the unfortunate women was in labour at the time. Some malicious natives in the neighbourhood of Meerut give out that the Sahib has been notoriously mad for several years past. Let us hope, however, that the Lieutenant-Governor will not heed such insinuations, but after complimenting the magistrate on his vigour and his zeal, appoint him to the first judgeship that may become vacant. No less than six hundred persons are, by this fire, rendered homeless beggars. But what of that? Must justice be obstructed?
>
> It remains for us to add that the escaped convict of whom the magistrate was in search, has been in Oude for the past month, and that no notice of this affair will appear in any of the papers printed in English and edited by the Sahib Logue. Those gentlemen are far too modest to make known the manifest blessings which arise out of British rule in India.[13]

It is clear that Lang leaked all the news that he could not print in his paper to native newspapers so that acts of injustice towards Indians came to light. In this way, he continued to remain popular with the civil and military authorities, while also undertaking his act of rebellion.

And so, Lang attacked the government through his own newspaper in ways he could; and when he could not, he employed native 'moonshees' to pass on such news to Urdu newspapers—while his newspaper continued to flourish.

We have earlier seen from an article in *Courier* of 1853 that Lang was worth around £50,000. There are insinuations, however, that he was carefree and squandered away as fast as he earned.

Henry George Keene, in another book, again writes about the Gorham case and the Jotee Persaud case, but clarifies, 'Many anecdotes of Lang were in circulation at the time; but their repetition might lead to scandal and wounded feeling'[14].

One only wishes that Keene had not held his tongue and told about more anecdotes.

A couple of more anecdotes, though, will suffice to tell how 'happening' Lang's life was. There was a court-martial case in Simla between Lang and Lieutenant Rose, where Lang had charged the lieutenant of having falsely stated that Lang was intoxicated and dressed in shooting-coat. The lieutenant did not know that he had walked into the territory of a belligerent lawyer. Even without going into the particulars of the case, the reader would be amiss to not believe that Lang was intoxicated indeed. Lang had threatened the lieutenant with manhandling and the army man, afraid of John Lang, had applied for bodyguards. This is another matter Lang would have laughed at all his life, for having scared a lieutenant out of his wits. We deem it apt to reproduce the entire court proceedings for the comedy in it:

Case of Lang V Rose

Court Martial

Lieutenant Hugh Rose, 3rd 2V. J., Deputy Assistant Quarter Master General.

Tried by General Court Martial at Simla, 2nd August 1850.

Charge.—For conduct highly unbecoming an Officer and a Gentleman, in the following instances:

1st. In having, at Simla, on the evening of the 24th of June 1850, falsely stated in the hearing of several persons, that at a ball which had been recently given at Simla, Mr. John Lang, editor of the Mofussilite newspaper, was intoxicated, and dressed in a shooting coat.

2nd. In having, on the same occasion, when contradicted by an Officer present, taken no measures to establish his own veracity, and to relieve himself of the imputation of falsehood conveyed in that contradiction.

3rd. In having, at Simla, on the 29th of June 1850, when he received a letter of that date from Mr. Lang, couched in very offensive terms, accusing him of falsehood in his assertions made on the 24th of the month, and threatening him with personal chastisement, taken no steps to disprove to the proper Military Authorities the gross accusations made against him in that letter, and instead of so doing, having on the 1st of July 1850, sworn the peace against Mr. Lang in the Civil Court at Simla.

4th. In having, at Simla, on the 1st of July 1850, applied to the Civil power to provide him with an escort of police on his way to the Court, to protect him from the violence of Mr. Lang, and in having availed himself of such escort in proceeding to the Court; he being an armed military man; his conduct herein displaying a want of spirit unbecoming in an Officer in the Army.

5th. In having, in a statement, dated Simla, 3rd July 1850, made for the information of His Excellency the Commander in Chief, falsely represented that all he had said on the 24th of June 1850, regarding Mr. Lang, was, that when the ladies were going away (from the ball) Mr. Lang came down in a shooting coat whitened with the wall.

Finding.—On the 1st instance of the charge, not guilty, as, though the Court are of opinion that Lieutenant Rose did make the statement as alleged in the charge, they do not consider that it was falsely made; 2nd instance, not guilty, 3rd instance, guilty, 4th instance, guilty, and 5th instance, not guilty.

And the Court are further of opinion, that such conduct as contained in the two instances of the charge of which they have found him guilty, is unbecoming an Officer; but the Court acquit him of the remainder of the charge.

Sentence.—To be severely reprimanded in such terms as His Excellency the Commander in Chief may be pleased to direct.—*Approved and confirmed.*

Remarks by His Excellency the Commander in Chief.—Lieutenant Rose has been acquitted of *three* charges, and found guilty on *two.* He is sentenced to be severely reprimanded.

The most severe, but at the same time the most just, that I can give to Lieutenant Rose, appears to me to be a summary of his own conduct as regards the two charges on which he has been found guilty.

Proved to have been grossly insulted and threatened with *personal castigation,* by a Gentleman, whose physical powers Lieutenant Rose publicly declared to be inferior to his own, he took no one of those simple measures which it becomes a British Officer to do, when grossly insulted.

Among the steps which Lieutenant Rose ought to have taken, there were two so obvious as hardly to need being pointed out. They offended neither Military nor Civil law, and were in accordance with common sense.

The one was for Lieutenant Rose *immediately* to have called upon the head of his department with Mr. Lang's letter in his hand, and declared his readiness to meet and disprove all assertions to the prejudice of his character, in any way that the

Commander in Chief should direct. This Lieutenant Rose did not do till after he had adopted, and felt the result of, that line of conduct for which he stands condemned by the Court. It was then too late! It then became a mockery.

The other step which Lieutenant Rose might have taken was still more simple, more becoming, more efficacious, one perfectly justified by law, and by the conventional rules of society. It was to have applied his boasted superior physical strength to the defence of his person and his honor.

As Lieutenant Rose has been acquitted by the Court of having given just cause for Mr. Lang's insulting letter, this last mode of proceeding must have met with the approbation of all honorable men.

Lieutenant Rose is said to have been ill-advised. This may have been so, but he must take the responsibility of having acted by that bad advice, and of having failed, in the most simple of all possible cases, to do that which, in the opinion of all honest men, was the proper mode for him to have maintained the integrity of his own character as a British Officer.—*Head Quarters, 16th August* 1850.

Lieutenant Rose was released from arrest, but was not directed to resume his duties as Deputy Assistant Quarter Master General.'[15]

That was Lang bullying a lieutenant and the lieutenant applying for physical protection. The reader must not assume that Lang was a burly, hefty man—according to Henry Vizetelly, Lang was of a 'wiry frame'[16] especially his love for smoking and alcohol had contributed to it.

Lang's wiry frame was once manhandled in the court of an Indian Raja. In 1846, a newspaper in Australia reported Lang's attendance in the court of an Indian king, where he thought that the plaintiff was not presenting his case properly and offered his services as a barrister. 'The Indian plaintiff was so furious at this interruption, he picked up Lang bodily and threw him into the gathering. Lang was unhurt except, perhaps, his dignity, and threatened to sue the Indian. His interference was not always appreciated'[17].

However, it turns out the plaintiff was not Indian, but circus-man Della Case from Mauritius, the man credited with bringing circus to Sydney in 1840.[1] Later in his travels, he would also come to India and get the opportunity to throw Lang like a projectile, for the latter's audacity for giving the former English lessons in a Bengal court:

> The papers last week alluded to a scuffle between Mr Lang the barrister, the editor of the Mofussilite, and Signor Dalle Case, at the Doorga poojah nautches at the house of Rajan Radhakantu Deb. *The Hurakuru* of this morning places the affair in its true light, and exonerates Mr. Lang from all censure.It appears he had been invited to the platform by the Rajah himself, that the Signor approached the Rajah, and addressed him in broken English, when Mr Lang offered his assistance to interpret his address, on which the big and muscular Dalle Case seized him by the collar, and hurled him among the crowd. The affair is likely to end in a prosecution for assault

Vizetelly tells, among other things, that '...some millionaire Begum had presented him with £10,000 for successfully pleading her suit against the John Company'[18], This little wayward statement, which would have been told to him by Lang, had me hunting for four years to authenticate its veracity, but I have been unable to find a connection between any Begum and Lang.

Vizetelly is not confusing with Rani of Jhansi, for he clearly tells that owing to the success in the Begum's case and Jotee Persaud case, the Rani had summoned him.

Henry George Keene in his book *A Servant of John Company*, while telling about the Gorham case, 'believes' that Lang was 'Australian'. Lang did not reveal his Australian identity—in most history books, he is attested as 'English'. We have variously seen Lang hiding his convict origins. His maternal grandfather John Harris was a First Fleet Convict who had been transported for stealing eight silver spoons.[19] He went on to become one of the first policemen of Sydney.

There is a debate about Lang's Jewish heritage. It is supposed that John Harris was a Jew. However, the grandmother is not known at all, except that her name may have been Mary Green—a name that does not indicate Jewishness generally. Judaism being a matrilineal religion, the assumption falls *ab initio*. However, John Harris has been claimed as a Jew by Bergman and Rabbi Levi in their work *Australian Genesis: Jewish Convicts and Settlers, 1788-1860* (1974). There was a furious debate between Rabbi Levi and Laurence Halloran—a descendant of Elizabeth Underwood (Lang's mother)—about this issue.

Whatever be the matter, in my opinion, it does not have a bearing on Lang, who was barely religious. I met Rabbi Levi in Melbourne in November 2010, and was introduced at the synagogue as an Indian friend who was researching about the 'great Jewish ancestor'. When I asked Rabbi Levi about the caustic correspondences between him and Halloran, he chuckled, 'I was young then'.

While we have discussed Lang's family severally, we have not been introduced to his siblings. There has also been the speculation that Lang might have been an illegitimate child, for he was born on 19 December 1816, some 264 days after the death of his father Walter Lang—who died at the age of 27. Colin Roderick says:

> The circumstances of his birth and his mother's conduct not very long afterwards have not failed to arouse suspicion that Walter Lang's fatherhood of this boy may have been a legal fiction.[20]

Victor Crittenden disagrees with this view but not does not cite a reason why.[21]

We know that Elizabeth Lang went on to marry Joseph Underwood after a ship-romance on the way to England from Sydney. Underwood was a widower who already had four children, and Elizabeth had two. John Lang's elder brother, also Walter Lang, died at the age of 21, on 4 January 1835.[22] Elizabeth had several children with Joseph. Here is a quick list of the Underwood children from Liz Parkinson's book *The Underwoods: Lock, Stock and Barrel*[23]:

RICHARD UNDERWOOD
Richard is the first known child born to Joseph and his first wife Charlotte. Richard made his arrival in 1801—probably before his parents were married on 22 December 1801 at St. Dunstan's Stepney.

THOMAS JAMES UNDERWOOD
Joseph and Charlotte's second son, Thomas, was born in Bristol, the UK, in about 1803, according to his death certificate.

MARY ANNE UNDERWOOD
Mary Anne was born in Sydney, to Charlotte and Joseph, on 26 August 1808, and baptised five days later. She was educated by governesses, and probably had a close relationship with her father—she was his only surviving daughter until Elizabeth's birth in 1822.

JAMES WILLIAM and JOSEPH TREMAYNE UNDERWOOD (The 1st)
On 17 May 1810, Charlotte had twin boys called James William and Joseph Tremayne, who were baptised in a private ceremony the following day. Young Joseph didn't survive, and was buried on the 19 of May.

FREDERICK JOSEPH UNDERWOOD
Fred was the first child born to Joseph and Elizabeth Underwood (nee

Lang, previously Harris). He was born in England on 12 June 1820, and baptised in Sydney (St. Philips) on 14 March 1821.

ELIZABETH HENRIETTA UNDERWOOD and the HALLORANS
Elizabeth was the second child born to Joseph and Elizabeth on 14 August 1822. She was baptised on 15 September 1822 at St. Phillips. She married Henry Halloran, who was a poet. There would probably have been some correspondence between Henry and John Lang, both sharing literary interests—and Elizabeth being Lang's half-sister.

CHARLOTTE MARIA UNDERWOOD and the WANTS
Charlotte was the third child and second daughter born to Elizabeth and Joseph Underwood. She was born on 29 April 1825. On 4 July 1849 she married John Armand Cladan Want. Their marriage registration says they both came from the parish of Ashfield, the Underwood estate.

JULIA SARAH UNDERWOOD and the WILKINSONS
Julia was born on 15 November 1827, and on 12 February 1851 she married Thomas Hattam Wilkinson.

MATILDA SOPHIA UNDERWOOD and the HOLLINWORTHS
Matilda was born on 20 June 1830, and she was 17 years old when, she married Edwin William Hollinworth on 3 November 1846.

JOSEPH TREMAYNE UNDERWOOD (The second)
Joseph and Elizabeth's youngest son was born on 30 June 1833, exactly two months before his father died.

With the addition of the two Lang children, there were 12 children in the Underwood Household. Lang was number six—the impetuous but gifted boy in the middle. Being in the middle and lost in the sea of children, Lang was determined to shine, and shine he did.

Lang, who died on 20 August 1864, is buried in Camel's Back Cemetery in Mussoorie. Let's now look closely through a few obituaries to Lang, as obituaries are quite useful research tools, especially when it comes to a life lived. Crittenden attributes the obituary published in Lang's own newspaper, *The Mofussilite*, to William Grant; there is no evidence of this, except that Grant was the editor of *The Mofussilite* at that time. Grant may well have asked a close of friend of Lang to write the obituary. The obituary was printed on 26 August 1864:

> At Mussoorie, on the 20th of August, at half-past ten o'clock in the morning, the spirit of John Lang...The sad fact will excite deepest sorrow…; for, with all his human frailties, John Lang was a man to be truly loved.
>
> Hundreds of his friends in England, in Australia, and in India, will, on reading these lines, deplore, with heartful grief, the loss of one of Nature's most gifted sons—a man truly remarkable for the highest qualities of human intellectuality.

The writer goes on to gives a very important piece of information—that Lang had 'strange powers of vitality' which had made him recover from bad situations in the past:

> On the 12th of May last he left Meerut, for change of air to the Hills. On the 20th of June he was attacked with bronchitis. From this attack he had almost recovered; but its effects had gradually induced extreme debility and lassitude, which appear to have been the immediate cause of his death. In spite of his sufferings, very anxious hopes were entertained of his ultimate recovery—the more confidently because those around him, well know, from former experiences, his strange powers of endurance and vitality.

> His best and dearest friends, however, seemed unable, (perhaps because unwilling), to accept the fact of his approaching dissolution. Although he was extremely enfeebled, and the ardour and vivacity of his mind unquestionably subdued, yet the ravages of the disease had failed to produce great changes in that remarkable countenance;—and it was only a sudden crisis at last occurred, and he sank into a placid swoon, that all doubt as to his real condition was removed. His cares and pains were then at an end; and, as the rays of the morning sun, gliding the Himalayan heights around, shone broadly into his apartment, John Lang expired painlessly.
>
> He died pressing the hand of a friend. He died with those around him, who, in the tenderness of deep love and friendship, reverently closed his eyes in death.

The writer does not say who the friend is. Perhaps it is Margaret Wetter, but she would have been mentioned as wife.

> For ever that great spirit is still, for ever rests that gigantic intellect which evoked a pleasurable smile whenever it was uttered and which ensured to its owner a heartfelt welcome everywhere.
>
> Singularly calm and expressive was his countenance in death. So pure and passionless, as if the mind were freed from all its earthly dress. So placid and contemplative; as if the great spirit animated the image of what was once the delight of a wide circle of friends; and yet something was wanting there, which in its absences, bespoke the sad reality. Insensibly did the words of his favourite poet recur to the memory, in all the distinctness of their awful beauty; insensibly the gazer repeated those matchless lines of pathos, deploring—
>
> 'Greece, but living Greece no more.'

These lines are by Lang's favourite poet, Byron, from the poem 'Giaour'.

> Those who looked upon the features of John Lang in death, could not but be struck by the remarkable beauty of that lofty forehead which painters in Europe have admired with ecstasy.
>
> They could but fondly mourn as they looked for the last time, on:
>
> 'That sad shrouded eye
> That fires not, wins not, weeps not now.'

> The following is a brief outline of John Lang's career:
> He was born in Australia, on the 19th December 1817. He was the posthumous child of Captain Lang, Military Secretary to General Lauchlin Macquarie, Governor of New South Wales. He was educated by Doctor Blande, and gained gold medals and other honours at Sydney College.

We now know that 'Captain Lang' was an identity made up by Lang to present his merchant father appear a gentleman. Lang did indeed get a gold medal.

> In 1829, he entered the Navy, and, on board the Warspite line-of-battle ship, he went to South America and many other parts of the world.

This battle-of-line-ship is in probability another piece of fiction Lang conjured out of his fancy. Both his father and foster-father were seafaring merchants, and he may have travelled on sea, but battle ship is improbable. According to Earnshaw, the muster of Warspite does not have the name Lang or Underwood between 1829 and 1833.[24] He contends that the writer believed Lang, that he was on the ship, and looked up where the ship had been, and put that place down in his writing. The obituary continues thus:

> In 1837, he was sent to England to finish his education at Trinity College, Cambridge. During his first year there he gained a Scholarship. He afterwards distinguished himself, in his own peculiar way, by writing a quaint Litany, which was condemned as blasphemous, and for which he was rusticated for a time. He was, however, afterwards, permitted to finish his terms. On leaving Cambridge, he became pupil of Mr (now Judge) Whiteman.

This writing of 'quaint litany' we have seen from a letter of James Sheen Dowling as well. What exactly it was, is unknown. Lang's heroes in three novels—*Raymond, Undergraduate* and *Will He Marry Her?* get into trouble similarly in their college life.

> He was called to the Bar on the 20th May 1840, and was one of the most brilliant men of his day at the Temple.
>
> At the early age of twenty-three or twenty-four he went as Attorney General to Australia. He retained the appointment but a short time, and came to India in 1842.

The business of attorney-general is also a Lang-concocted fiction. Lang, in fact, left Sydney on a sour note with opposition from Exclusivists obviously; from Emancipists as well, for he—in his impetuosity—had said that the colony was not yet ready for self-rule.

> He practised at the Bar in Calcutta until 1845. After this his health began to give way, he acceded to the proposal of Colonel Pugh, and started the Mofussilite newspaper in the Upper Provinces.

> The periodical was first the property of shareholders; after a few years, however, Mr Lang bought up all the shares, and in 1849, he became its sole proprietor and Editor.
>
> Before the famous trial of the state prisoner Moolraj, which occurred at Mooltan, he was asked by the Government if he would plead as Counsel for the accused. He offered to do so for two lakh of rupees. He was invited to accept one lakh instead, but he politely declined the offer, remarking, in his private correspondence on the subject, to the Secretaries of the Government, that he was 'a Professional Barrister at Law, and not a catsmeat-man' who might be beaten down from his original charges!

This could be one of the anecdotes that Keene was insinuating at. This, in my opinion, is fact, for Lang was brash and quite sure of himself.

> In 1850, he gained, for Lalla Jotee Pershaud, his celebrated lawsuit against the Government. For this single success he received the magnificent fee of two lakhs of rupees. The manly fearlessness of Mr Lang's speech on this occasion...Lord Brougham in the 'House of Lords'.

The date given here is wrong. The case was in 1851. Here, we finally are sure Lang had not gone to England and rushed back to India to fight Lala's case. That rushing back story might have again be cooked by Lang while narrating it to William Forbes-Mitchell to add spice to the pork-pie story.

> In 1852, he went to England where he remained only about a year. During that time he wrote in 'Fraser's Magazine'—'The Forger's Wife' and 'The Wetherbys, Father and Son'. He also republished, from the columns of the 'Mofussilite' his two

> novels —'Too Clever By Half' and 'Too Much Alike or the Three Calendars'.

The date of this England journey is suspect. It could be 1853 or 1852.

> At the same time, he produced a play called 'Plot and Passion' which excited great interest and had a very prolonged run. This production of his pen was pruned and revised by Tom Taylor; and Douglas Jerrold, without being aware of the fact.—with his usual felicity used to say; the 'passion' is unmistakably Lang's, the 'plot' I'll let Tom have as a present.'

Douglas Jerrold is unmistakably right, as we have seen in a lengthy discussion about Tom Taylor.

> On the 19th December 1853, he again embarked for India. Shortly afterwards the Ranee of Jhansee sent her minister to him inviting him to come and plead a cause for her. He went accordingly, and received, as an acknowledgement for the favour, one thousand guineas in a purse, besides shawls, dresses, golden ornaments, &c. On his journey back from Jhansi he contracted 'jungle fever,' which had a disastrous effect on his health, and from he himself used to say, he never altogether recovered.

Lang does not mention the 'jungle fever' in his account about Rani of Jhansi in *Wanderings in India.* Perhaps he did not want to reduce the flavour of the story in which he had written about him flirting with the Rani and receipt of costly gifts by adding 'jungle fever' to it.

> In July 1854 he again embarked for England. His health was then so bad, that, in various quarters, he was reported dead; and he used to say that it afforded him very great amusement

> to read the story of his own virtues and frailties as they were facetiously set down by the Journalists of the day.

I have looked for these 'stories of his virtue' but not been able to find them. This, however, matches with the obituary writer's claim that friends had hoped Lang would recover like he always did.

> From 1854 until 1859, he remained in England and devoted himself to literary labors. During that time he wrote the 'Ex Wife,'—'Will He Marry Her?'—'The Secret Police'—'York You're Wanted, or Wife'—and 'Captain MacDonald or Capias Castle.' He also produced in Household Words,'—'Recollections of Botany Bay' and 'Wanderings in India.' The latter was written at the request of Mr Charles Dickens.

We have seen earlier that Dickens needed an India specialist, and Lang was the man. Dickens had high regard for Lang but it does not appear in any Dickens scholarship.

> He contributed frequently to the 'Times,' the 'Globe' and other leading periodicals; besides throwing off, with scarcely an effort, volumes of Poetry of no mean standard. In 1855, he went on the Continent, and travelled over Italy, Austria, Saxony, Prussia, Belgium, France, Switzerland, and Germany.
>
> On the 17th August 1859, he again embarked for India. On the passage out an episode occurred which beautifully proved John Lang's high spirited courage and magnanimity.
>
> A child dropped overboard. Without a moment's hesitation Lang plunged into the deep after the helpless little thing, seized the child and fondly supported it for more than a quarter of an hour in a marvellous way, when a boat reached him and both lives were saved! Such true manly valour as this requires not a

> word of comment. It was, however only on par with the usual generous impulses of John Lang's great heart.

This incident is quite shadowy by now. This may have been yet another John Lang tale to impress his friends. Contrariwise, this is yet another premonition on the part of Lang.

> From 1859 until 1864 he remained at Meerut, conducting the 'Mofussilite' and, as he used to say, enjoyed quiet existence in his little Tusculum there. He had pet animals about him,—favourite servants, and many an admiring friend:—and happy were the days and many were the scenes, when at his hospitable board, those who knew him and understood him, delighted to look at his genial eye and listen to his marvellous powers of conversation. There was not a subject he could not take up with graceful case. His wit was ever ready. His marvellous memory continually flashed forth appropriate illustrations from the ancient classics. His appreciation of the beautiful was delightfully conspicuous; and, withal, there was a solidity about his friendship, which defied all restraint. Perhaps no trait of his character was more remarkable than this. 'Never mind,' he used to say to his friends, 'never mind what you do, or what you say, or what you write, I'll pull you through thick and thin!' He was thus ever displaying, in quaint ways, the confidence of gigantic intellect and the unselfishness of a truly kind heart. Many remarkable and well known persons were his private friends. In England—Father Prout, Tom Taylor, Robert Brough, Gilbert Becket, Mrs Gaskell, Douglas Jerrold, Albert Smith, the Kelleys, The Keans, Bon Webster, Madame Celeste, Paul Bedford etc.

This is a very vivid and encompassing characterisation of Lang, and shows the kind of private man he was.

In India his friends were innumerable:—Dean Lushington, Jackson, Torrens, Elliott, Sir William Mansfield, Courtenay, the Thackwells, Fitzroy Somerset, Edmonstone, Wingfield, Whelor, J.O.B. Saunders, Sir Mordant Wells, Fred. Cooper, Robert Spankie, and many, many more. His favourite writers were,—Voltaire, Volney, Shakespeare, Fielding, Sterne, Canning, Pope, Goldsmith, &c.

He was continually quoting, with a beaming eye, from Juvenal, Persius, and Horace. It may not be generally known that he was one of the best Persian scholars, that ever came to India. He was remarkable as an amateur actor. Mercutio was his favourite character, with whom he often humorously exclaimed, in a manner which can only be appreciated by those who really knew him:—'If you ask for me to-morrow, you shall find me a grave man!'

His love of children and of flowers was very beautiful. He had an excellent musical ear. His talents were marvellously excursive. His memory perfectly wonderful; its natural power enabling him to dispense with the usual drudgery of study and reference. More remarkable than all, perhaps, was his shrewd common sense—his unerring judgement and his accurate knowledge of Law. ...his powers of vituperation and withering sarcasm. At the same time, the readiness with which he extended the hand of friendship to an antagonist, the frankness with which he acknowledged an error, and the efforts he made to repair it, unmistakably indicated the innate goodness of his heart, whilst they were accompanied by a winning fascination of manner which was irresistible.

His unselfishness did not forsake him even in the last days of his illness and suffering.

He had been removed for more careful treatment, from a public hotel, to the residence of his medical attendant. The

> house being a very large one, contained, at one extremity an apartment in which was proposed a public Ball should be given. He was informed of the fact, and asked if he thought the music would disturb him. His immediate and characteristic reply was:—'God forbid that any human enjoyment should be put a stop to, on my account.'
>
> It was always his wish that a good post mortem examination should be made of his body. This was accordingly acted up to, and revealed the striking fact that his brain weighed eight ounces less than the average, in the human adult.
>
> It appears, however, that it was peculiarly notable on account of the excess of 'grey or cortical substance' so called, to which the physiologist has traced the seat of thought and intelligence.
>
> John Lang now sleeps peacefully in a mountain grave, far from the scene of his earthly cares and intellectual triumphs. The world's loftiest mountains now cast their broad and silent shadows over the sacred spot, which will often be visited with respect by stranger and with deep emotion by his friends.
>
> Buried with him, and on his breast, lies the New Testament in Greek—whilst a deep and touching solemnity was conveyed to the heart of the mourner by a few 'forget me nots' which were seen on the pall as it was slowly conveyed to its last resting place,—humble flowers quietly deposited there by a friendly hand, and silently expressive of the last wishes of the departed.
>
> Ye! who have traced the Pilgrim in the scene
> Which is his last, if in your memories dwell
> A thought which once was his, if on ye swell
> A single recollection, not in rain
> He wore his sandal sheen, and scallop shell

Crittenden has attached importance to getting buried with the New Testament. He says it is to hide his Jewish identity even in death. I think this idea far-fetched. We have seen that the issue of Jewishness of grandfather of Lang itself is suspect.

That was the obituary of the home paper. The one in *Allen's Indian Mail* had a different tone, which shows the attitude of British press towards Lang. The excerpts included here are more about the opinions about Lang that were in currency. Following are the excerpts from the obituary. It is not a continuous text:

> British India has been glorified by the deeds of many great statesmen and heroic and skilful generals, but her list of eminent *literati* is comparatively short. Aman, therefore, of literary fame, or even of literary notoriety, cannot pass that bourne whence no traveller returns without calling forth something beyond the common obituary record in a country like British India, in which an author of any pretension is still a *ram avis.*
>
> His various novels...are all printed in a cheap form for railway reading; so that travellers in every part of the kingdom who have cast their eyes over the bookstalls are all more or less familiar with the name of the author and the titles of his works, even when they may not have read a page of their interiors.
>
> Though a very sharp and clever man undoubtedly, we are inclined to think he never had any real liking or peculiar fitness for his profession, which demands a steadiness of purpose, and a closeness of application to dry details, which were not amongst his characteristic qualities. We give no credit to the story that Lord Dalhousie was 'so extremely partial to him' that his lordship expressed a desire to recommend Mr. Lang for an Indian judgeship; and the friend who narrates this anecdote admits that the idle free life which Mr. Lang had led unfitted him for such an appointment. It is added that he had the impudence to ask his lordship of what particular offence he had been guilty that so degrading an offer should be thrust upon him.

Another story of a similar character, and equally apocryphal, is told of him. When the State prisoner Moolraj Mooltan was prosecuted, the Government, it is said, asked him to plead for the accused; he demanded a fee of two lakhs. The Government offered one lakh. Mr. Lang declined it, adding that he was a professional barrister-at-law, and not a *cats-meat-man,* who might be beaten down in his charges. These were, perhaps, mere after-dinner anecdotes from Mr. Lang's own lips. There is not always truth in wine.

Mr. Lang felt himself more at home when he deserted the bar for the press, and became editor of the *Mofussilile.* Here he was eminently successful. His articles were spicy and piquant, and personal and powerful. He purchased the *Mofussilite,* and soon made the paper a valuable property; but it is said that latterly he so neglected it, and left the editorial department so much to feebler hands, that its subscription list was reduced from 2,000 to 200. His contributors were quite as venomous and personal as himself, but they had no share of his ready wit and freshness and force of style.

Mr. Lang was once punished for a malignant libel by a heavy fine and a month's imprisonment in the Calcutta jail. His most partial friends must admit that he was a bad-natured writer, but he is said to have been a good-natured man, though passionate and impulsive, and always getting into awkward scrapes and personal disputes, in which he was generally in the wrong, because he was rash and reckless; and if he was very warm-hearted, he was, also, very hot-headed. We never heard of but one success of his at the bar, and that was the famous case of Lalla Jotee Persaud, the Government commissariat contractor. The Government, unwilling to pay his heavy bill for supplies, had the meanness to attempt to evade the debt by charging the Lalla with fraud and conspiracy. The case was a simple and easy one, and Mr. Lang undertook and carried it through with complete success. The Government was compelled to settle the account against it, and the grateful Lalla Jotee Persaud presented Mr. Lang with a fee of two lacs of rupees.

Mr. Lang's novels are light and amusing, excellent railway reading, but they give him no station in the literature of his country. But for a sort of brilliant flippancy, and for gay and easy humour, and forcible satire, and pungent personality, his editorial writings were unrivalled in British India.

The immediate cause of his death was an attack of bronchitis, but he had long been reduced to a skeleton, and, latterly could not write an article or undergo any physical effort without stimulants, and pouring gurrahs of cold water on his head. At a *post mortem* examination (which Mr. Lang had himself desired in the event of his death), the fact was elicited that his brain, though healthy, was nine ounces less in weight than the average weight of the brains of ordinary men. This fact is curious, for John Lang, though he may not have been a man of genius, was, unquestionably, a man of very remarkable powers and great readiness and versatility of mind. He was not, however, what some of his admirers describe him to have been, 'a man of gigantic intellect.' He seems, with all his failings, to have been very warmly beloved by many intimate friends, and though he had obtained by his fierce personalities, when he had the editorial pen in his hands, the character of a most unamiable writer, he is said, in private life, to have been a warm-hearted and generous companion—

'The best-natured man with the worst-natured muse.'

It would be unjust to his memory if we were to pass over the anecdote of his having plunged into the sea on his passage out to India to save a little child that had fallen overboard. He saved the child's life, but not without great risk to his own, for he was

> a quarter of an hour in the water, and was not, as we have heard, a good swimmer.

Given that Lang was not a good swimmer, if the saving of the child was a premonition in his two novels of 1858 and 1859 respectively, Lang was indeed a clairvoyant. If not, he made a good story out of an episode in *The Stranger.*

This is the culmination of my research into John Lang. However, I must mention that this research started with the hunt for Alice Richman. It was in December 2006 that I stumbled upon the grave of Alice Richman in the Pune University gardens, also known as Alice Garden. The epitaph on the grave is haunting, with the following inscription: 'Born at Melrose, South Australia, November 23, 1856. Died at this very spot, of cholera, in January 1886'.

Something about Alice was very fascinating; I became determined, nay, obsessed with her, or as a famous song says, 'Who the F*** is Alice'. On this matter, too, I have written a lengthy paper, but perhaps not in the scope of this work. However, I must mention an interesting part of it. There are several campus legends around Alice, as there always are campus legends. One says that she was in love with an Indian man and they could not marry, and so she committed suicide. There are ghost stories saying she roams around the campus at night in white robes.

The newspaper *The Indian Express* reports on urban legends in a column. In one issue, it tries to delve into the question of 'Who is Alice Richman?'. The city edition of 13 April, 2007 has this to say about Alice:

> One version has it that Alice Richman, daughter of a prominent British official, committed suicide post an unfulfilled love story, and now roams the graves at night in a translucent white fabric. According to the PRO of the university, Gangadhar Jangamwal, who rubbishes all the rumours, the story traces back to Jan 14, 1882. He says, '26-year-old Alice, daughter of former British

> governor Richman was horse riding in the garden, when she fell down and died.'[25]

Love stories are always made, their invention is almost a necessity, and their mythification an inevitability. However, the horse story is rather startling. I have a hypothesis to offer for the origin of the horse tale. *Bulletin*, that reported the death of Oliver, has two intriguing tales reported as well on the same day.[26] Kate Blakeney, daughter of the Deputy Registrar General of Queensland, was riding on a quiet horse, which started galloping, and the lady threw herself off the horse and dashed against a tree and died. The other horse death must be quoted ad verbatim:

> Ebenezar OLIVER, champion light-weight wrestler of New South Wales, is dead. He went from Sydney to Illawarra to act as referee in a wrestling match, and while under the influence of liqueur, saw a horse tied up to the Cricketer's Arms and galloped it furiously round a corner. The animal fell and threw him violently. He died later in the hospital, insensible.

These reports got mixed up by the teller of tales in Pune, or were deliberately exaggerated to give Alice more mysterious colours. When a story passes down, it does transform itself. And the horse-account is really not an aberration; when I, myself, saw Alice's epitaph and read it, I memorised something else, something more sensational that was posted on a blog. The construction of history is fascinating indeed, and the written word is not quite independent of the spoken word, sensational imaginations, or flawed memories.

It was in search of this Alice Richman that I started looking up various Australians in the 19th century and stumbled upon John Lang. The first story I read of his was 'Black and Blue', and I knew this was my calling.

Now let's come to the second half of the title of this chapter 'No One Will Write Rhymes for You Mr Lang'—there is a third unsaid part which is 'But I Will'.

So, here is a poem dedicated to Alice Richman and John Lang:

If die I will
Which I will not
It's my will
That I be given a grave
So that a hundred and fifty years later
Some wanderer
Spots an old wanderer,
Not at his best;
Ignominiously
At rest.

Like I spotted Alice.
The stupid epitaphist
Behaves like a typist
And doesn't mention
If her cheeks were like rose
But says she was born at Melrose.
Died in 1882 at this very spot.
Died of cholera.
They never write that
On soldiers' graves.
A poet says she died four years before
The epitaphist wrote his choleric prose
About dates and Melrose.
Poor Alice Richman.
Graves do lie
Or else how would Keats'

Name be writ in water
Or is it why they say
Stone-wash!

Alice's ghost refuses to tell anymore
But hangs around
And takes me to Landour's ghosts
Hills, thunder, rain, dark nights
Perfect to raise a toast
To the ghost
Of a Mofussilite.

The young barrister ran away from Sydney
As if drunk upon the verses of Sir Philip Sidney
And his huge desyre.
The gale of the sea done
He had to the face the ire
Of the raj babus
And see gaol and dungeon
For he shook them a little
With his words and letters.
Cicero he wanted to be
And barely knew fetters.
The Rani of Jhansi gifted him with her portrait
For he unsuccessfully defended her sealed fate.

Once he saved a child
From the seas wild
But the seas of time
Have quite drowned the man
And the name is indeed
Writ on water.

He could not become Dickens
But his poetry about Jenny Dale
And her name all around in the gale
Tells a very old tale
Of love.

He lies in Camel's Back cemetery
Camels store water on their back.
Alice and John did not know each other
But their graves do.

End Notes and References

Stories Forgotten, or Lying in the Cold

1. Lang, John. *Too Clever by Half, Or The Harroways.* A serial in *The Mofussilite.* 1848.
2. Lang, John. *The Wetherbys, Or Chapters of Indian Experience.* London: Chapman and Hall, 1853.
3. Lang, John.*The Secret Police or Plot and Passion.* London: Ward and Lock, 1859.
4. Lang, John. *My Friend's Wife or York You're Wanted.* London: Ward and Lock, 1859.
5. Lang, John. *Botany Bay or True Tales of the Early Days of Australia.* London: W. Tegg, 1859.
6. Lang, John. *Captain Macdonald, Or Haps and Mishaps at Capias Castle.* London: Ward and Lock, 1858.
7. Lang, John. *Captain Macdonald, Or Bailiffs Outwitted.* London: Ward and Lock, 1860.
8. Lang, John. *Wanderings in India.* London: Routledge, 1859.

Tom Taylor, or Sartor Resartus

1. Purnell, Thomas. *Dramatists of the Present Day.* Chapman and Hall, 1871. p95
2. Ibid. p136-137
3. France, Peter. *The Oxford Guide to Literature in English Translation.* Oxford University Press, 2000. p1.b.4
4. Planche, James Robinson. *Recollections and Reflections: A Professional Autobiography.* De Capo Press, 1978. p246-247
5. Novello, J Alfredo. *The Musical World.* Volume 31. 1853. p675
6. Tolles, Winton. *Tom Taylor and The Victorian Drama.* New York: Columbia University Press, 1940.

The Death of Abe Lincoln

1. G.E.M. 'The Plays of Tom Taylor'. *The New York Times.* 18 July 1880.
2. Anon. "Punch (1841-1992; 1996-2002)". As retrieved from http://www.bodley.ox.ac.uk/dept/ scwmss/projects/disraeli/punchstoryboard.html, as viewed on 12.05.2011
3. Edmund Clarence Stedman, ed. (1833–1908). *A Victorian Anthology, 1837–1895.* 1895. The tribute poem can be read in Appendix 1. This was considered the "famous recantation" by Tom Taylor.

4. Tsiokos, Kosta. 'Abe Lincoln's Final Sockdologising Moment.' http://www.populationstatistic.com/archives/2009/02/12/abe-lincolns-sockdologising-final-moment/ as viewed on 12 May, 2011
5. Vowell, Sarah. *Assassination Vacation.* New York: Simon and Schuster, 2005. p46
6. Ashford, Ken. 'You Sockdologising Old Man Trap' on the internet blog (http://ken_ashford.typepad.com/blog/2007/08/you-sockdologiz.html. 03.08.2007). As viewed on 12 May, 2011.

What Shaw Saw, or The Seed Planted

1. Laurence, Dan H. ed. *Bernard Shaw Theatrics: Selected Correspondence of Bernard Shaw.* University of Toronto Press, 2005.
2. Laurence, *Bernard Shaw Theatrics.* p12. Cited in this book from: Roy Nash. 'The Theatre Today and Yesterday according to Bernard Shaw', Manchester Evening News, 6 December 1938; I&R 382-3; DHL; Theatrics xii
3. Gibbs, Anthony Matthews. *A Bernard Shaw Chronology.* Palgrave Macmillan, 2001. p25.

The Book That Saved a Life

1. Library of Congress. 'The Book That Saved A Life' (Text and Video). As viewed on the website (http://www.youtube.com/watch?v=TnZlEFL-1iU). 13.05.2011
2. Wynn, Debra. 'Traffics and Re-discoveries: Rudyard Kipling Collections at the Library of Congress'. Paper presented at the Kipling Society Conference, Kent, 7–8 September, 2007. Available online at (http://www.kipling.org.uk/rg_kent_wynn.htm), as viewed on 13 May, 2011
3. 'The Book That Saved a Life' (Video). It can be viewed online at (http://www.youtube.com/watch?v=TnZlEFL-1iU) as viewed on 13 May, 2011
4. Original correspondence between Kipling and Maurice Hammoneau and his son Jean Hammoneau concerning the affair at the Library of Congress under the title: *How 'Kim' saved the life of a French soldier: a remarkable series of autograph letters of Rudyard Kipling, with the soldier's Croix de Guerre, 1918-1933.* (LOC Ref#2007566938). The library also possesses the actual French 389-page paperback edition of *Kim* that saved Hammoneau's life, (LOC Ref 2007581430)
5. Kipling, Rudyard. *Kim.* Maccmillan & Co. Ltd, 1901.
6. Dir. Saville, Victor. *Rudyard Kipling's Kim.* MGM, 1950.
7. Dir. Saville, Victor. 'Official trailer of 'Kim'. MGM, 1950. As viewed on (http://www.youtube.com/watch?v=b5hqKsMyPsk&feature=related) on 24 May, 2011

8. Ed. Kemp, Sandra and Lewis, Lisa. *Writings on Writing - Rudyard Kipling.* Cambridge University Press. 1996
9. Wynn, 'Traffics and Re-discoveries: Rudyard Kipling Collections at the Library of Congress.' Available online at (http://www.kipling.org.uk/rg_kent_wynn.htm), as viewed on 13 May, 2011
10. The words in the bracket are mine. John Lang's authorship of *Plot and Passion*, however, is acknowledged by other writers who have written about Kipling having acted in this play.
11. Ed. Littell, Eliakim and Robert S. Littell, *The Living Age.* Making of America Project. Littell, Son & Company, 1856.
12. Moore-Gilbert, BJ. *Kipling and 'Orientalism'.* London: Croom Helm, 1986. p23-24
13. Bristow, Joseph. *Empire Boys: Adventures In A Man's World.* Harper Collins Academic, 1991.
14. Lang, John. *Will He Marry Her?* London: Routledge, 1858.

The Story of Isaacs

1. The details about FM Crawford are gleaned from "Major Pond's *Reminscenes*" recounted in the following book: Harkins, Edward Francis. *Little Pilgrimages Among The Men Who Have Written Famous Books.* L. C. Page & Company, 1901. Pp 169-180
2. Ibid.
3. Ibid. p173
4. Crawford, Francis Marion. *Mr Isaacs: A Tale of Modern India.* London: Macmillan, 1882. p19
5. Joshi, Priya. *In Another Country: Colonialism, Culture, and the English Novel in India.* Columbia University Press, 2002. p125
6. Forbes-Mitchell, William. *Remiscences of The Great Mutiny.* Calcutta, 1893. p73
7. Vizetelly, Henry. *Glances Back Through Seventy Years. Volume II.* London: Kegan Paul, Trench Trubner and Co Ltd, 1893. p7
8. Ramsay, Lieutenant Colonel Balcarres D. Wardlaw. *Rough Recollections of Military Service and Society. Volume I.* Edinburgh and London: William Blackwood and Sons, 1882. p123-124.

The Italian Connexion

1. Burlamacchi, L. Marchesa. *Luca Della Robbia.* London: George Bell and Sons, 1900.
2. Ed. Francis, J. *The Athenæum: a journal of literature, science, the fine arts, the music and the drama. London, 1901.*

3. Hyett, Francis A. *Florence, Her History and Art to the Fall of the Republic.* London: Metheun, 1903. p397
4. Roderick, Colin and John Earnshaw. 'John Lang: First Australian-born Novelist' *Journal and Proccedings of Royal Australian Historical Society. Vol 49, Part 2.* Sydney: 1963. p130
5. Allen, WH. *Allen's Indian Mail.* 1863. p535
6. 'Divorce a mensa et thoro' from Lectric Law Library's Lexicon. As viewed on (http://www.lectlaw.com/def/a122.htm). Viewed on 05 June, 2011
7. Roderick, Colin and John Earnshaw. 'John Lang: First Australian-born Novelist' *Journal and Proccedings of Royal Australian Historical Society. Vol 49, Part 2.* Sydney: 1963. P 130
8. *The Indian Mail: A Monthly Register for British and Foreign India, China, and Australasia.* 1844. Print. p625
9. Roderick, Colin and John Earnshaw. 'John Lang: First Australian-born Novelist' *Journal and Proccedings of Royal Australian Historical Society. Vol 49, Part 2.* Sydney: 1963. p114
10. *Allen's Indian Mail.* October 20, 1864. p833
11. 'Crimean Heroes' *Illustrated London News.* 12 April, 1856
12. Lalumia, M.P. *Realism and Politics in Victorian Art of the Crimean War.* UMI Research Press, 1984. Print.
13. *The Mofussilite,* 26 August, 1864.
14. Lang, John. 'Himalayan Club.' (ed. Charles Dickens) *Household Words: A Weekly Journal.* Bradbury and Evans, 1857. Print. p268
15. See Roderick, Colin and John Earnshaw. 'John Lang: First Australian-born Novelist' *Journal and Proccedings of Royal Australian Historical Society. Vol 49, Part 2.* Sydney: 1963. p107
16. Lang, John. *The Ex-Wife.* London: Routledge, 1859. Print. p330
17. Ibid.
18. Lang, John. 'The Keranees'. *The Welcome Guest.* 1860. Print.pp35-37
19. Roderick, Colin and John Earnshaw. 'John Lang: First Australian-born Novelist' *Journal and Proccedings of Royal Australian Historical Society. Vol 49, Part 2.* Sydney: 1963. p112
20. Parkinson, Liz. *The Underwoods: Lock, Stock and Barrel.* Sydney: Lady Lizard, 1989.
21. Ruvigny, Melville H.(Melville Henry Massue, and Marquis de Ruvigny). *The Nobilities Of Europe.* London: Melville and Company, 1910. P228
22. Brewer, E Cobham. *Dictionary of Phrase and Fable.* 1898.
23. Burke, Sir Bernard. *Genealogical and Heraldic History of the Landed Gentry. Volume I.* London: Shaw, 1937. p533

24. 1905. Count Riccardi-Cubitt (123,421 [HO 45/10311/123421]) Petitioner's wife was the heiress of the ancient and famous Florentine family of Riccardi and in 1902 the title was specially granted by the King of Italy to petitioner. Limitation—to petitioner and his wife only. Submitted by H.O. without recommendation.
25. 'Count Thomas Riccardi-Cubitt' in 'Royal Styles and Titles'. *UK National Archives.* (http://www.heraldica.org/topics/britain/TNA/HO_45_10192_358070.htm) As viewed on 10 October, 2010
26. 'Monique Riccardi-Cubitt'. Web. (http://www.arcadiamundi.eu/index_en.html) As viewed on 10 October, 2010
27. Ibid.
28. 'Count Riccardi Thomas Cubitt'. Web. (http://www.dodingtonfamily.org/Individuals/i119.htm), as viewed on 23 November, 2010
29. Marquis of Ruvigny. *The Plantagenet Roll of the Blood Royal: The Mortimer-Percy Volume.* London, 1911
30. Riccardi-Cubitt, Vera and Sydney Smith (S.J.). *The Pearl of Great Price.* Washbourne: R&T, 1913.
31. *Flight International: Volume 9, Issue 2.* United Service and Royal Aero Club (Great Britain), Royal Aero Club of the United Kingdom, 1917. p1177
32. The London Gazette. June 2, 1944. p2552
33. http://thepeerage.com/p34835.htm (As viewed on 25 May, 2011)

The citations within the quote are:

i) Charles Mosley, editor, *Burke's Peerage, Baronetage & Knightage, 107th edition, 3 volumes* (Wilmington, Delaware, U.S.A.: Burke's Peerage (Genealogical Books) Ltd, 2003), volume 1, page 1069. Hereinafter cited as *Burke's Peerage and Baronetage, 107th edition.*

ii) Charles Mosley, *Burke's Peerage and Baronetage, 107th edition.*

iii) Charles Mosley, *Burke's Peerage and Baronetage, 107th edition,* volume 2, p1069.

34. Bracketed explanation mine
35. http://www.arcadiamundi.eu/index_en.html (As viewed on 30 May, 2011)
36. Ibid.
37. E-mail from Countess Monique Riccardi-Cubitt, 15 May, 2011.
38. Ibid. 18 May, 2011.
39. Ibid 25 May, 2011.
40. Ibid 29 May, 2011
41. James Dowling Papers. Mitchell Library, Sydney. C194

42. This is mentioned in his obituary in *The Mofussilite*
43. See Chapter 15, 'My Friend's Wife, Or Lang You're Wanted' for a detailed account of how Lang went to the jail in Calcutta.
44. Ibid.
45. That Lang knew French and German is told by Victor Crittenden in an interview at Canberra, May 2010. Eva Merrydale in the novel *Ex-Wife* translates German and French manuscripts. The literary activities of Eva in this novel follow Lang's own trajectory.
46. That Lang knew Greek, I am conjecturing through a character in *Ex-Wife,* Mr Penderfield who gives Greek lessons to Merrydale Stair.
47. Lang, John. Wanderings in India. London: Routledge, 1859.p103
48. See Roderick, Colin and John Earnshaw. 'John Lang: First Australian-born Novelist' *Journal and Proccedings of Royal Australian Historical Society. Vol 49, Part 2.* Sydney: 1963. p110.
49. Ibid.

William Cobb Hurry, or the Skull Smuggler

1. T. Taylor, T. *History of the Rectory Manor.* Wakefield, 1886 Cited in Roderick, Colin and John Earnshaw. 'John Lang: First Australian-born Novelist' *Journal and Proccedings of Royal Australian Historical Society. Vol 49, Part 2.* Sydney: 1963. 113
2. Rollo DD Massey quoted in auctioneer's brochure, *Peterson's Tower, Tower Lodge, Hollywood Cottage and Hollywood.* Lymingston: Jackson and Masters, 1957. Pp1-2
3. Ibid.
4. *Public Dinner at Calcutta to Mr. A.T.T. Peterson.* Printed at the Baptist Mission Press, 1863. Print.
5. Chapman, J. *Diarrhœa and Cholera.* Trübner and Co., 1866. Print. p227
6. Ibid.
7. Ibid. p228
8. Ibid. p229
9. Esadaile, James. *Mesmerism in India, and its Practical Application in Surgery and Medicine.* London, 1846.
10. *The Mofussilite,* 9 August 1845, p22
11. *The Mofussilite,* 23 August 1845, p63
12. *The Mofussilite, 2* August 1845. p6
13. A more detailed account of the case is there in the chapter about Lala Jotee Persaud.

14. Lang, John. *Wanderings in India*. London: Routledge, 1859
15. Lang, John. Wanderings in India. London: Routledge, 1859. Pp343
16. Lang, John. *Wanderings in India*. London: Routledge, 1859. Pp343-44
17. Ibid.
18. This fact is detailed in the chapter about Lala Jotee Persaud.
19. Lang, John. *Wanderings in India*. London: Routledge, 1859. 347
20. See Fanon, Frantz: Towards the African Revolution. London: Penguin, 1970
21. Lang, John. *Ex-Wife*. Routledge, 1859. 93
22. See Hoare, Philip. *England's Lost Eden: Adventures in a Victorian Utopia*. Fourth Estate, 2005. Print.
23. Peterson, Andrew Thomas Turton. *Essays from the Unseen, Delivered through the Mouth of W.L., a Sensitive, and Recorded by A.T.T.P.* London: J.Burns, 1885. Print.
24. See Hoare, Philip. *England's Lost Eden: Adventures in a Victorian Utopia*. Fourth Estate, 2005. Print.
25. PP346-371
26. Vay, B.L. *Eccentric Britain, 2nd: The Bradt Guide to Britain's Follies and Foibles*. Bradt Travel Guides, 2005. Print. 231.
27. Palmer, C.J. *The Perlustration of Great Yarmouth, with Gorleston and Southtown*. G. Nall, 1874. Print. 439
28. Agricultural, and Horticultural Society of India. *Transactions of the Agricultural and Horticultural Society of India*. Reprinted at Baptist Mission Press, 1839. Print.p46-50
29. Mehrotra, S.R. *The Emergence of the Indian National Congress*. Vikas Publications, 1971. Print. 11
30. Hurry-Houghton, T., and M. Hurry-Houghton. *Memorials of the Family of Hurry of Great Yarmouth, Norfolk, and of America, Australia, and South Africa*. C. Tinling, 1926. Print. 48
31. *Asiatic Journal and Monthly Miscellany*. Wm. H. Allen & Co., 1835. Print.p73
32. Lang. John. 'Inundation in Bengal'. (Ed Charles Dickens.) *Household Words*. Berh. Tauchnitz. 1853. Print.p12
33. Lang, John. Wanderings in India. London Routlege. 1859. 342.
34. See *Asiatic Journal and Monthly Miscellany*. Wm. H. Allen & Co., 1835. Print. pp65-75
35. Lang, John. Wanderings in India. London Routledge. 1859, p343.
36. See Sprod, Dan. Alexander Pearce of Macquarie Harbour. Hobart: Cat & Fiddle Press, 1977, pp123-29

37. *The Australian.* October, 1827.
38. See Cooter, R. *The Cultural Meaning of Popular Science: Phrenology and the Organization of Consent in Nineteenth-Century Britain.* Cambridge University Press, 1984. Print.
39. See Ruth Richardson, Death, Dissection and the Destitute, Routledge and Kegan Paul, London, 1988.
40. Lang, John. Wanderings In India. London. Routledge. 1859. p273.
41. Ibid. p273.
42. Ibid. p272.
43. Ibid. p273
44. Lang, John. *Will He Marry Her?* London. Routledge. 1858. Pp83-84
45. Ibid. Pp84-86
46. Ibid. p86
47. This is evident in the numerous quotations that fly easily in a Lang novel. This fact is stated by Lang's obituarist also in *The Mofussilite* of 26 August, 1864
48. *The Mofussilite.* 26 August, 1864
49. After the Act of 1752 was passed, riots broke out in Tyburn, London, against surgeons over the dissection of the bodies of hanged convicts.
50. Linebaugh, P. 'Introduction'. *The London Hanged: Crime and Civil Society in the Eighteenth Century.* Verso, 2003. Print. XIX

Fisher Dead Is More Powerful Than Fisher Alive

1. The Sydney Gazette and New South Wales Advertiser
2. Lohrli, A., and H. words. *Household Words: A Weekly Journal, 1850-1859, Conducted by Charles Dickens: Table of Contents, List of Contributors and Their Contributions, Based on the Household Words Office Book in the Morris L. Parrish Collection of Victorian Novelists, Princeton.* University of Toronto Press, 1973. Print. 337-338
3. Lang, J. *Botany Bay, or, True Tales of Early Australia.* J. Walch, 1859. Print.
4. Lang, J. *Fisher's Ghost: And Other Stories of the Early Days of Australia.* E.W. Cole, 1920. Print.
5. http://www.fishersghost.com.au (as visited on 31 May, 2011). The website now has been revamped an the poem can now be found here: https://www.campbelltown.nsw.gov.au/FishersGhost/History/PoemTheLegendofFishersGhost
6. Lang, John. *Fisher's Ghost and Other Stories.* (1859) Melbourne: EW Cole, 1920. p20

7. Bulwer, E.L. *Eugene Aram: A Tale*. Tauchnit, 1842. Print.
8. Hood, T., and W. Harvey. *The Dream of Eugene Aram, the Murderer*. Tilt, 1831. Print.
9. Lang, A. *The Valet's Tragedy, and Other Studies, by Andrew Lang*. Longmans, Green and Co., 1903. Print.
10. Lang, A. *The Valet's Tragedy, and Other Studies, by Andrew Lang*. Longmans, Green and Co., 1903. Print. 258
11. Martin, Montogomery. *History of British Colonies. Vol IV.* pp303-304
12. Roderick, Colin and John Earnshaw. 'John Lang: First Australian-born Novelist' *Journal and Proccedings of Royal Australian Historical Society. Vol 49, Part 2.* Sydney: 1963. p125
13. Lang, A. *The Valet's Tragedy, and Other Studies, by Andrew Lang*. Longmans, Green and Co., 1903. Print. p262
14. Ibid. p270
15. Rusden, G.W. *History of Australia, by G. W. Rusden*. Chapman and Hall, 1883. Print. pp44-45
16. Suttor, W.H., Australian Stories Retold, and, Sketches of Country Life. Bathurst [N.S.W.], 1887. Print. p16
17. See Lang, A. *The Valet's Tragedy, and Other Studies, by Andrew Lang*. Longmans, Green and Co., 1903. Print. p272
18. Lang, John. *Fisher's Ghost and Other Stories* (1859). Melbourne: EW Cole, 1920. p23

Poe's Woes, or Ravens, Roosters and Pigs

1. Poe, E.A. *The Raven, and Other Poems*. Wiley & Putnam, 1846. Print.
2. Poe, E.A. *The Poetical Works of Edgar Allan Poe with a Notice by J. Hannay*. 1856. Print. P48
3. Poe, EA. 'The Philosophy of Composition'. *Graham's Magazine*. Philadelphia, April 1846
4. Tait, W. *Tait's Edinburgh Magazine*. 1855. Print.p34
5. Hake, T. *The Life and Letters of Theodore Watts Dunton*. Kessinger Publishing, LLC, 2005. Print. 298
6. James Sheen Dowling papers. Mitchell Library, Sydney. C194
7. *Notes and Queries*. September 17, 1864. 224
8. Lang, John. *Wanderings in India*. Routledge, 1859. 103
9. The Mofussilite, 26 August, 1864.
10. Lang, John. Wanderings in India. Routledge, 1859. 97
11. Palmer, EA. *The Poetical Works of Beha-Ed-Din Zoheir, of Egypt*. With a

Metrical English Translation, Notes, and Introduction, by E. H. Palmer, M.A., Lord Almoner's Reader and Professor of Arabic, Cambridge. Cambridge: University Press. 1877.

12. *The Saturday Review. Vol 43.* Pp 737-79
13. Lang, John. *Ex-Wife*. London: Routledge, 1859. 348
14. Lang, John. *Wanderings in India*. Routledge, 1859. Pp 350-51
15. Dowling Papers. Mitchell Library, Sydney. C194
16. Roderick, Colin and John Earnshaw. 'John Lang: First Australian-born Novelist' *Journal and Proccedings of Royal Australian Historical Society. Vol 49, Part 2.* Sydney: 1963. P 110
17. Dowling papers, Mitchell Library. C194. Cited in Ibid. 111
18. *The Mofussilite.* 27 September, 1845. Article by 'London Correspondent of *Glasgow Argus*
19. *The Mofussilite.* 27 September, 1845. Article taken from *Louisville Journal*
20. Article from *The Mofussilite* cited in *Allen's Indian Mail,* September 3, 1858
21. *The Mofussilite.* 2 August, 1845. Article taken from *Examiner*

Undeclared Cards on Dickens's Table

1. See Nayder, L. *Unequal Partners: Charles Dickens, Wilkie Collins, and Victorian Authorship*. Cornell University Press, 2002. Print. pp1-2
2. Dickens, C. *The Mystery of Edwin Drood.* Chapman and Hall, 1870. Print.
3. Dickens, C. *A Tale of Two Cities: With a Critical and Biographical Profile of Charles Dickens.* Franklin Watts, 1859. Print.
4. See Nayder, L. *Unequal Partners: Charles Dickens, Wilkie Collins, and Victorian Authorship*. Cornell University Press, 2002. Print. 198-99
5. *The Courier.* 28 November, 1853. Article taken from *Empire.*
6. Lohrli, A., and H. words. *Household Words: A Weekly Journal, 1850-1859, Conducted by Charles Dickens:Table of Contents, List of Contributors and Their Contributions, Based on the Household Words Office Book in the Morris L. Parrish Collection of Victorian Novelists, Princeton.* University of Toronto Press, 1973. Print. 337
7. See Chapter 'My Friend's Wife, Or Lang You're Wanted'
8. Halkett, S., and J. Laing. *Dictionary of Anonymous and Pseudonymous Literature of Great Britain.* William Paterson, 1882. Print.
9. Lang, John. *The Secret Police, or Plot and Passion.* Ward and Lock, 1859. Print.
10. See Chapter 'Tale of Two Wives' for a copy of the marriage certificate of John and Lucy Lang

11. Lang, John. *The Secret Police, or Plot and Passion*. Ward and Lock, 1859. p28
12. Perkins, F.B., and H. Taine. *Charles Dickens: A Sketch of His Life and Works*. G. P. Putnam & Sons, 1870. Print. p156
13. Ibid. 158
14. Collins, Wilkie. *Poor Miss Finch: A Novel. With Illustrations*. Harper & Brothers, 1872. Print.
15. Household Words, (Vol XIV, 4 October 1856, p276-82)
16. Wanderings In India. (1859, pp59-83)
17. Watson, T., and D.F. Condie. *Lectures on the Principles and Practice of Physic Delivered at King's College, London*. Lea and Blanchard, 1855. Print.
18. Nayder, Lilian. 'Blue Like Me' in ed. Bachman, M.K., and D.R. Cox. *Reality's Dark Light: The Sensational Wilkie Collins*. University of Tennessee Press, 2003. Print. 278
19. *Wanderings in India*. P59
20. Ibid.
21. Ibid.
22. Ibid. 62
23. Ibid.
24. Byron, G.G.B. *The Corsair, A Tale*. Printed for John Murray by Thomas Davison, 1814. Print.
25. Wanderings in India. 65
26. See Duyker, Edward and Coralie Younger. *Molly and the Rajah: Race, Romance and the Raj*. Sylvania, N.S.W: Australian Mauritian Press, 1991.
27. Wanderings in India. Page 65.
28. See Foucault, M. *Madness and Civilization: A History of Insanity in the Age of Reason*. Taylor and Francis, 2001. Print.
29. Ibid
30. Wanderings in India. 69.
31. Wanderings in India. p314
32. Lang, John. *Dresden China*. (1863) Canberra: Mulini Press, 2008. p12
33. Lang, *Wanderings in India*. p144
34. Lang, *Dresden China*.
35. Luther, U.M., and M. Raza. *Historical Routes of North West Indian Subcontinent, Lahore to Delhi, 1550s-1850s A.D.: Network Analysis through DNA-Micro Methodology*. Sagar Publications, 1990. Print.
36. Wanderings in India. 72
37. Ibid. 73

38. Ibid. 74
39. Ibid. 79
40. Nayder, Lilian. 'Blue Like Me' in ed. Bachman, M.K., and D.R. Cox. *Reality's Dark Light: The Sensational Wilkie Collins*. University of Tennessee Press, 2003. Print. 278
41. Ibid.

Will He Marry Her? or Will She Marry Him?

1. Lang, John. *Will He Marry Her?* London: Routledge, 1858.
2. Caxton, Pisistratus (Sir Edward Bulwer Lytton). *What Will He Do With It?* Leipzig: Bernhard Tauchnitz, 1857.
3. *Town Talk*. Volume I. H. Tuck, 1859. 176
4. Dryden, John. 'Alexander's Feast, Or The Power Of Music: A Song In Honour of St. Cecilia's Day, 1697'. In Carpenter, F.I. *English Lyric Poetry, 1500-1700*. Books for Libraries Press, 1906. 256
5. Macaulay, J. *Stirring Stories of Peace and War, by Sea and Land*. Hodder and Stoughton, 1885. 106
6. Lang, *Will He Marry Her?* p341-345
7. All information about Lady Sale has been gleaned from: Crosland, N., and M.B. Foster. *Memorable Women: The Story of Their Lives*. Ticknor and Fields, 1854. Pp323-355. See also: 'Foreword' Sale, F., et al. *A Journal of the First Afghan War*. Oxford University Press, 2002.
8. Sale, Florentia. *A Journal of the First Afghan War*. Hamden, Connecticut: Archon Books, 1843.
9. Márquez, G.G. *Chronicle of a Death Foretold*. Ballantine Books, 1992.
10. Lang, John. Will He Marry Her? 1858. p59-60
11. Ibid. p77
12. Ibid. p212-213
13. Márquez, Gabriel Garcia. Trans. E. Grossman trans. *Of Love and Other Demons*. 1995.
14. Solanet, Mariana. *García Márquez for Beginners*. New York: Writers and Readers, 2001
15. Lang, *Will He Marry Her?* p448
16. Ibid. p326
17. Ibid.
18. Ibid. p329
19. Ibid. p394

20. Ibid. p387
21. Crittenden says this in an interview with Amit Ranjan. Canberra, May 2010.
22. See Roderick, Colin and John Earnshaw. 'John Lang: First Australian-born Novelist' *Journal and Proceedings of Royal Australian Historical Society. Vol 49, Part 2.* Sydney: 1963. p105
23. Lang, *Will He Marry Her?* p11-12
24. Ibid. p398-99
25. Crittenden, Victor. *John Lang: Australia's Larrikin Writer.* Canberra: Mulini Press, 2005. p14
26. Ibid. p18
27. Ibid p194
28. Ibid.
29. Lang, *Will He Marry Her?* p89-90
30. Crittenden says this in an interview with Amit Ranjan. Canberra, May 2010.
31. Lang, *Will He Marry Her?* p16
32. See Hall, B.H. *A Collection of College Words and Customs.* Echo Library, 2006. Print. p147
33. James Dowling Papers. Mitchell Library, Sydney. C194
34. James Dowling Papers cited in Roderick, Colin and John Earnshaw. 'John Lang: First Australian-born Novelist' *Journal and Proccedings of Royal Australian Historical Society. Vol 49, Part 2.* Sydney: 1963. p111
35. See Jayapalan, N. *History of Education in India.* Atlantic Publishers and Distributors, 2005. Print. p47
36. See *Allen's Indian Mail.* 1851. p196
37. Shakespeare, W. *The Taming of the Shrew.* Cambridge Univ. Press, 1953. Print. P139
38. Lang, *Will He Marry Her?* p326
39. It is a well-known fact in modern Indian history that Colonel Sleeman was the Resident at Lucknow 1849-1856. Sleeman died in 1856, in office. His appointment is recorded, among other places, an annotated edition of his recollections. His appointment was five years after the publication of this book in 1844: Sleeman, William. *Rambles and Recollections of an Indian Official.* (Revised, Annotated edition by Vincent A Smith) London: Humphrey Milford, 1915.
40. See Boehmer, E., and S. Morton. *Terror and the Postcolonial.* Wiley-Blackwell, 2009. p184
41. *The Westminster Review.* J. Chapman, 1859. p272.
42. Minturn, Robert B. *From New York to Delhi.* London: Longman and Co. 1858.

43. Studies, Institute of Historical. *The Quarterly Review of Historical Studies.* Calcutta: Institute of Historical Studies, 1963. p41
44. Sleeman, William. *Rambles and Recollections of an Indian Official.* (Revised, Annotated edition by Vincent A Smith) London: Humphrey Milford, 1915. Chapter 51.
45. Madame De Barrera. *Gems and Jewels from The Earliest Ages Down to the Present Time.* Bentley. 1861, Cited in Agnew, J.H., and W.H. Bidwell. *The Eclectic Magazine: Foreign Literature.* Leavitt, Trow & Co., 1861. P64
46. P.Breton. 'Medico-Topography of the Ceded Provinces, South West Frontier'. 1826.
47. Lang, *Will He Marry Her?* p123
48. Ibid. p128
49. Ibid.
50. Kline, A.S. 'Horace: The Epodes And Carmen Saeculare'. Electronic resource, 2005.(http://www.poetryintranslation.com/PITBR/Latin/HoraceEpodesAndCarmenSaeculare.htm#_Toc98670071), viewed on 30 May, 2011
51. Boccaccio, Giovanni. (trans. G.H. McWilliam) *Decameron.* Harmondsworth, 1972.
52. Lang, John. *Love's Last Sacrifice: A Tale of the 15th Century.* Canberra: Mulini Press, 2007. (*Mofussilite.* Meerut, 4 August 1863)
53. Boccaccio, G. (trans. J.M. Rigg.) *The Decameron.* Digireads, 2010.
54. Lang, Will He Marry Her? p326
55. Boccaccio, trans. Riggs. p166

Boccacio and The Rani

1. Boccacio, Giovanni. (tr. G.H. McWilliam) *Decameron.* Harmondsworth, 1972. (1371)
2. Lang, John. *Ex-Wife.* London: Routledge, 1859. p203
3. Wu, C. and A. Waley. *Monkey: From the Chinese by Arthur Waley.* Allen, 1944.
4. Lebra-Chapman, Joyce. *The Rani of Jhansi.* Honolulu: University of Hawaii Press, 1986.
5. Lang, John. *The Three Calendars.* London: Ward Lock, 1854. p6
6. Lang, John. *Wanderings in India.* London: Ward & Lock. p93-94
7. Ibid. p94
8. Ibid. p95
9. Allen's Indian Mail, 1854. p354

The Curious Case of the Lala

1. Chambers, W., and R. Chambers. 'Romantic Tales of Indian War.' *Chamber's Journal of Popular Literature, Science and Arts.* W & R Chambers, 1894. Print. p717
2. The above account is from John Lang's *Wanderings In India* (1859). Pp 188-89.
3. Irving, J. The Annals of Our Time [1837 to 1868]. [with] 1871 To. 1871. Print. p904
4. Littell, E., and R.S. Littell. Littell's Living Age. T.H. Carter & Co., 1853. Print. p41
5. Lang, John. *Wanderings in India.* London: Routledge, 1859. p186
6. Ibid.
7. Ibid. p188
8. The facts in this paragraph are taken from 'Raja Lal Singh: Traitor of the British Army', on the website http://www.allaboutsikhs.com/1800/lal-singh-raja.html. These facts resonate through various British records as well.
9. Jayapalan, N. History of India. p131-32.
10. Lang, *Wanderings In India.* p183
11. Gupta, H.R. History of the Sikhs. Munshiram Manoharlal, 1998. Print.
12. Lang, *Wanderings in India.* p194
13. Ibid. p189
14. Lang, *Wanderings in India.* p189
15. Ibid. p189.
16. Forbes-Mitchell, W. *Reminiscences of the Great Mutiny 1857-1859.* Macmillan, 1893. Print.
17. Ibid. p155
18. Ibid. p156
19. Allen's Indian Mail. 17 June, 1851. p360
20. Allen's Indian Mail. 18 October, 1851. That Lang was in Simla when he appointed Wilby as his editor, is told by Lang himself in the case against him in Calcutta.
21. Forbes-Mitchell, W. Reminiscences of the Great Mutiny 1857-1859. Macmillan, 1893. Print. p158
22. Ibid.
23. Ibid. p159
24. Cook, J.D., et al. The Saturday Review of Politics, Literature, Science and Art. J.W. Parker and Son, 1894. Print. p499
25. *The Ladies' Repository.* L. Swormstedt and J.H. Power, 1869. Print. p269
26. Vizetelly, H. Glances Back through Seventy Years. 1893. Print. p8
27. Ibid. p9

28. Lang, *Wanderings in India.* p102
29. Vizetelly, H. *Glances Back through Seventy Years.* 1893. Print. p9
30. Ibid. p195-196
31. Ibid. p198-199
32. Ibid.
33. Khandelwal, Brij. 'Agra's heritage being bulldozed to dust.' News 24. 12 August 2008. Web. (http://www.news24online.com/%5C/ViewDetails.aspx?NewsId=7491) as viewed on 10 April, 2011
34. Brij Khandelwal told me these particulars in an interview. 15 June, 2011.
35. A court case relating to the property states that A. John was the owner of the property.
36. See 'Girish Chandra Gupta And Another vs Gambhir Mal Pandya (P.) Ltd. Co.' 1998. Web. (http://www.indiankanoon.org/doc/1479781/) As viewed on 10 April, 2011
37. Indian Textile Bulletin. 1892. Print. p159
38. Brij Khandelwal told me these particulars in an interview. 15 June, 2011.
39. Gould, W. *Hindu Nationalism and the Language of Politics in Late Colonial India.* Cambridge, 2004. Print. p62
40. Dodd, G. The History of the Indian Revolt and of the Expeditions to Persia, China, and Japan, 1856-7-8: With Maps, Plans, and Wood Engravings. W. and R. Chambers, 1859. Print. p435
41. *The Spectator.* Volume 24. 1851
42. 'Memorandum: Inclosure 10 in No.4' Fort, Agra, 19 August, 1857. Cited in *Accounts and Papers of the House of Commons.*1858. Print.p158
43. Lang, *Wanderings in India.* p192
44. Martin, R.M. *Our Indian Empire and the Adjacent Countries.* 1879. Print. p358
45. Frost, Thomas. *Complete Narrative of the Mutiny in India.* 1857. Print. p374
46. Ibid. p363
47. Ibid.
48. See Accounts and Papers of the House of Commons. Ordered to be printed, 1859. Print. p75-76
49. Selections from the Calcutta Review. T.S. Smith, 1882. Print. p374
50. Thornhill, M. *The Personal Adventures and Experiences of a Magistrate During the Rise, Progress and Suppression of the Indian Mutiny.* John Murray, 1884. Print. p258
51. Ibid. p259
52. Ibid. p261

53. Calcutta Review. University of Calcutta, 1873. Print. p24
54. Lewin, M. *The Way to Regain India.* London: James Ridgway, 1858. Print. p10
55. See *The Indian Law Reports: Calcutta Series.* West Bengal Govt. Press, 1925. Print. p323
56. See Kempson, M. Report of the Progress of Education in the North-Western Provinces. 1866. Print. p162
57. The Freemasons Quarterly (Magazine and) Review [Afterw.] the Freemasons' Monthly Magazine. [Continued as] the Freemasons' Magazine and Masonic Mirror. 1859. Print. p356
58. Allen, W.H. Allen's Indian Mail. 1863. p535
59. Yule, H., A.C. Burnell, and W. Crooke. A Glossary of Colloquial Anglo-Indian Words and Phrases: Hobson-Jobson. London, 1903. p570
60. Campbell, G. 'On the Races of India, as traced in existing tribes and castes.' Paper read on 9 March, 1869 for Ethnological Society of London. See The Journal of the Ethnological Society of London. Trübner, 1869. Print.
61. Ecker, A., et al. Archiv Für Anthropologie: Zeitschrift Für Naturgeschichte Und Urgeschichte Des Menschen. F.Vieweg und sohn, 1870. Print. p178-179
62. Sherring, M.A. *Hindu Tribes and Castes.* 1872. Print. p279
63. *The Englishman.* 19 February, 1870.
64. Peterson, A.T.T. *Essays from the Unseen, Delivered through the Mouth of W.L., a Sensitive, and Recorded by A.T.T.P.* London: J. Burns, 1885. Print.
65. Ibid. p119
66. Ibid. p123
67. Ibid.
68. Ibid. p132
69. Ibid. p124-125
70. Ibid. p125
71. Ibid.
72. Ibid.
73. Anon. 'Romantic Tales of Indian War: Blockade of Agra in 1857.' *The Chamber's Journal.* 1894. p715-718
74. Ibid. p716
75. Ibid.
76. Ibid.
77. Ibid. p717
78. Ibid.
79. Ibid. p718

80. A Mere Phantom'. *The Magic Lantern, How to Buy and How to Use It*, by 'a Mere Phantom'. Also, How to Raise a Ghost. London: Houlston and Wright, 1866. Print. p78-79
81. Parlour Magic. London: W.Kent, 1858. Print. p26
82. Anon. 'Romantic Tales of Indian War: Blockade of Agra in 1857.' The Chamber's Journal. 1894. p718
83. Ibid.
84. *The Mofussilite*. 25 February, 1857.
85. 'From Major W. C. Erskine, Commissioner, Saugor Division, to C. B. Thornhill, Esq., Officiating Secretary to Government, North-West Province, Agra. Jubbulpore, 5 March, 1857.'
86. In the book: Ball, C. *The History of the Indian Mutiny: Giving a Detailed Account of the Sepoy Insurrection in India* : And a Concise History of the Great Military Events Which Have Tended to Consolidate British Empire in Hindostan; Illustrated with Battle Scenes, Views of Places, Portraits, and Maps, Beautifully Engraved on Steel. London Printing and Publ. Co., 1858. Print. p39-40
87. Steinbeck, John. *The Pearl*. Viking Press, 1947. Print.
88. Sharma, S.K., and U. Sharma. Documents on Sikkim and Bhutan. Anmol Publications, 1998. Print. p185
89. Cited from *The Truth About Bootan*. Metropolitan Press, 1865. Print.
90. Ibid. p185
91. The Trial of Lalla Jotee Pershad and Others: Reported for the Delhi Gazette. Printed at the Gazette Press, by Kunniah Lall, 1851. Print.
92. *Allen's Indian Mail*. 18 April, 1851. p190
93. *The Mofussilite*. 18 April, 1851. p242
94. Lang, *Wanderings in India*. p190
95. Ibid. p191
96. *The Delhi Gazette*. 16 November, 1850.
97. Cited in *Allen's Indian Mail*. 18 February, 1851. p191
98. Ibid.
99. Ibid.
100. *The Delhi Gazette*. 22 February, 1851
101. *Allen's Indian Mail*. June 1851.
102. Ibid.
103. Campbell, G. *Modern India: A Sketch of the System of Civil Government, with Some Account of the Natives and Native Institutions*. J. Murray, 1853. Print. P256

104. Allen's Indian Mail. June 1851.

105. The Delhi Gazette. 24 April, 1851.

106. *Allen's Indian Mail.* 17 June, 1851. p360

107. Cited in *Allen's Indian Mail.* June 1851. p347

108. Ibid.

109. Lang, *Wanderings in India.* p192.

110. Lewin, M. The Way to Regain India. London: James Ridgway, 1858. Print. p10-13

111. Allen's Indian Mail. June 1851. p394

112. Lahore Chronicle. June 1851

My Friend's Wife, or Lang You're Wanted

1. Lang, John. *My Friend's Wife,* Or *York You Are Wanted.* London: Ward and Lock, 1859.
2. Allen, WH. *Allen's Indian Mail.* 1863. 535
3. *The Englishman.* 19 February, 1870.
4. *Madras Athanaeum.* Cited in *Allen's Indian Mail.* June 1851. P347
5. Cited in *Allen's Indian Mail.* 30 June, 1851. p 377
6. Ibid.
7. *Allen's Indian Mail.* 1851. 357
8. *The Mofussilite.* 18 April, 1851.
9. Reade, C., and R.R. Macmullen. *A Record of the Redes of Barton Court, Berks: With a Short Précis of Other Lines of the Name.* Jakeman and Carver, 1899. Print. 84
10. Hodson, V.C.P. *List of the Officers of the Bengal Army, 1758-1834: L-R.* Constable. Print. 1927. 203
11. Ibid p203
12. *Allen's Indian Mail.* 1851. 606
13. *The Gentleman's Magazine.* 1833. Print.p370
14. Purnell, Thomas. 'Mr Tom Taylor'. *Dramatists of the Present Day.* London: Chapman and Hall, 1871. Pp113-114
15. Elwin, Malcolm. *Charles Reade.* London: Jonathan Cape, 1930. 19
16. *Imperial Gazetteer of India: Provincial Series.* Superintendent of Government Printing, 1908. Print. 385
17. See also Michell, G., and P. Davies. *The Penguin Guide to the Monuments of India: Islamic, Rajput, European.* Penguin Books, 1990. Print.
18. *The Queen, on the Prosecution of Col. Mactier v. John Lang.* Supreme Court of Calcutta, 19 August 1851. Reported in *Allen's Indian Mail.* 18 October 1851

19. *The Mofussilite.* 15 August 1851.
20. Ibid. Also cited in Critten, Victor. *John Lang.* Canberra: Mulini Press, 2005. P 126-7
21. *Allen's Indian Mail.* 1851. 476.
22. Ibid.
23. *The Hurkaru.* 21 August 1851.
24. *Allen's Indian Mail.* 1870. 291.
25. *The Mofussilite.* 27 June 1851.
26. *Allen's Indian Mail.* 19 November 1851. 669.
27. *The Englishman.* 26 August 1851.
28. *The Optimist.* 1 October 1851.
29. *Lahore Chronicle* cited in. *Allen's Indian Mail.* 1851. 732.
30. *The Mofussilite.* 16 September 1851.p588
31. *The Mofussilite.* 6 April 1852.p221; also Crittenden, Victor. *John Lang.* Canberra: Mulini Press, 2005. p130.
32. The fact of Lang beginning the sequel after his jail stint is conjectured by Victor Crittenden in Crittenden, Victor. *John Lang.* Canberra: Mulini Press, 2005. p129.
33. Lang, John. 'An Experience of Austria'. *Household Words.* Bradbury and Evans. 18 April 1857. 381-384.
34. Lohrli, A. *Household Words: A Weekly Journal 1850-1859.* University of Toronto Press, 1973. Print.
35. Ibid. P338
36. *John William Earnshaw (1921-1971)–papers.* MLMSS 4126, Box H4369. Mitchell Library, Sydney.
37. 'Introduction'. Crittenden, Victor. In Lang, John. *An Experience of Austria.* Canberra: Mulini Press, 2006. 5
38. Household Words. 1857. p381
39. Ibid.
40. Ibid.
41. Ibid. p382
42. Ibid.
43. *The Literary Gazette: A Weekly Journal of Literature, Science, and the Fine Arts.* H. Colburn, 1851. Print. 95
44. Household Words. 1857. p383
45. Ibid. p384
46. Rajendran, V. OSM. 'FAQ on Indian Freemasonry'. *The Grand Lodge of AF and AM of India.* Web. (http://www.masonindia.org/index10.html) as viewed on 22 March, 2011

47. See Gruber, Hermann 'Masonry (Freemasonry)'. *The Catholic Encyclopedia. IX.* New York: Robert Appleton Company. 1910
48. *The Freemasons' Quarterly (Magazine and) Review* [Afterw.] *the Freemasons' Monthly Magazine.* [Continued as] *the Freemasons' Magazine and Masonic Mirror.* 1859. Print. P356
49. Torrens, H.W., and J. Hume. *A Selection from the Writings, Prose, and Poetical, of the Late Henry W. Torrens: With a Biographical Memoir.* R.C. Lepage, 1854. Print. P182
50. *The Mofussilite.* 16 March, 1854.
51. *The Mofussilite.* 11 October, 1849.
52. Lang, J. *Captain Macdonald; or, Haps and Mishaps at Capias Castle.* Ward and Lock, 1856. Print. p206-207
53. Lang, John. *The Ex-Wife.* 1859. Print. p146
54. Lang, John. *My Friend's Wife, Or York You Are Wanted.* 1859. Ward and Lock. Print. 14
55. Ibid. p28
56. Marryat, F. *Newton Forster; or, the Merchant Service.* 1838. Print. p156
57. Morton, Thomas. *The Slave, a Musical Drama in Three Acts.* 3vol, 1816
58. Journals, Oxford. *Notes and Queries.* Oxford University Press, 1866. Print. p355
59. *York, You're Wanted: To Which Are Added, the Irish Wedding. My Peggy Is a Young Thing. Lochaber No More.* Printed for the booksellers in town and country. 1823. Print.
60. Cited in *The Nation.*The Nation Company, 1868. Print. p414
61. Lang, John. *My Friend's Wife, Or York You Are Wanted.* 1859. Print. P1
62. Ibid. 10
63. Ibid. 11
64. Ibid. p60-61
65. Lang. *Wanderings In India.* p294.
66. Lang. *My Friend's Wife.* p65
67. Ibid. p66-67
68. Ibid. p69
69. Ibid.
70. Ibid. p76
71. Ibid. p83
72. Ibid. p77
73. Ibid. p4
74. Lang, John. *Too Clever by Half: Or, the Harroways, by the Mofussilite.* 1853. Print. 124

75. *The Literary Gazette: A Weekly Journal of Literature, Science, and the Fine Arts.* H. Colburn, 1858. p563
76. Lang. *Too Clever By Half.* 1853. 124
77. Lang, John. ed. Victor Crittenden. *Love's Last Sacrifice* (1863). Canberra: Mulini Press, 2007.
78. Ibid. p3
79. Lang. *Plot and Passion.* 3
80. Ibid. p15
81. Lang. *Will He Marry Her?*. 64.
82. Lang. *Plot and Passion.* (2008). pp25
83. See *Allen's Indian Mail.* 1850. P285-6
84. Lang, John. *The Wetherbys, Father and Son.* London: Chapman and Hall, 1853. 156
85. Ibid p137
86. Mackenzie, Mrs. Colin *Life in the Mission, the Camp and the Zenana; or Six Years in India.* 3 Vols. London, 1853. Cited in *Calcutta Review,* 1853. 437
87. Ibid. 434
88. *Allen's Indian Mail.* 1852. 252
89. *Allen's Indian Mail.* February 1857. 109

The Tale of Two Wives

1. Lang, John. *The Secret Police; or, Plot and Passion.* Ward and Lock, 1859. Print.
2. Lang, John. *Botany Bay, or, True Tales of Early Australia.* J. Walch, 1859. Print. (Also London: William Tegg)
3. Lang, John. *Clever Criminals: Recollections of Botany Bay.* Ward, Lock and Tyler, 1871. Print. (1859)
4. Lang, John. *Fisher's Ghost: And Other Stories of the Early Days of Australia.* E.W. Cole, 1920. Print.
5. Crittenden, Victor. *John Lang: Australia's Larrikin Writer.* Canberra: Mulini Press, 2005. 193. Crittenden has not cited his source.
6. Ibid. 192.
7. Ibid. 195
8. *The Mofussilite.* 26 January, 1860.
9. Ibid. 13 April, 1860.
10. Crittenden, Victor. *John Lang: Australia's Larrikin Writer.* Canberra: Mulini Press, 2005. 196
11. *The Mofussilite.* 17 July, 1860.
12. Crittenden, Victor. *John Lang: Australia's Larrikin Writer.* Canberra: Mulini Press, 2005.p197

13. Lang, John. *My Friend's Wife, Or York You're Wanted.* London: Ward and Lock, 1859. 3
14. *The Mofussilite.*13 February, 1862.
15. *The Mofussilite.*1 November, 1862.
16. *The Mofussilite.* May 1863. Cited in Crittenden, Victor. *John Lang: Australia's Larrikin Writer.* Canberra: Mulini Press, 2005.p206
17. *The Mofussilite.* August 1845, p113.
18. *The Mofussilite.*5 December, 1861.
19. Ibid p29
20. *The Mofussilite.* 25 August, 1862.
21. *The Mofussilite.* 26 August, 1864.
22. Crittenden, Victor. *John Lang: Australia's Larrikin Writer.* Canberra: Mulini Press, 2005.p73
23. Dickens, C. *A Christmas Carol in Prose: The Chimes; the Cricket on the Hearth.* B. Tauchnitz, 1846. Print.
24. Critten, Victor. 'Mazarine: John Lang's 1845 novel.' *Margin No 66.*July-August 2005. 30
25. 'Reminiscences'. Dowling Papers. Mitchell Library. C194.
26. Roderick, Colin and John Earnshaw. 'John Lang: First Australian-born Novelist' *Journal and Proceedings of Royal Australian Historical Society. Vol 49, Part 2.* Sydney: 1963. P112
27. Dowling Papers. Mitchell Library. C194. Also a copy in Earnshaw Papers. Mitchell Library. H4369
28. Ibid.
29. Ibid.
30. Dowling Papers. Mitchell Library. C194. Also a copy in Earnshaw Papers. Mitchell Library. H4369
31. Ibid.
32. Roderick and Earnshaw. 'John Lang: First Australian-born Novelist' *Journal and Proceedings…. Vol 49.* 112
33. Charnock, M.A.E. *Legendary Rhymes, and Other Poems*. Longman, 1843. Print.
34. See Chapter 8.
35. Wagner, K.A. *The Great Fear of 1857: Rumours, Conspiracies and the Making of the Indian Uprising.* Peter Lang, 2010. Print. 111
36. Smyth, G.C. *A History of the Reigning Family of Lahore: With Some Account of the Jummoo Rajahs, the Seik Soldiers and Their Sirdars*. W. Thacker and co., 1847. Print.

37. See Khurana, G. *British Historiography on the Sikh Power in Punjab*. Allied Publishers, 1985. Print.
38. Charles Mosley, editor, *Burke's Peerage, Baronetage & Knightage, 107th edition, 3 volumes* (Wilmington, Delaware, U.S.A.: Burke's Peerage (Genealogical Books) Ltd, 2003), volume 1, 696.
39. *The Bankers' Magazine and Journal of the Money Market*. 1870. Print.
40. *The Clergy List For 1866: Containing Complete Lists of the Clergy in England, WalesScotland, Ireland& the Colonies*. Kelly's Directories, 1866. Print. 427
41. Knowledge, Society for Promoting Christian. *Theology*. Society for Promoting Christian Knowledge., 1927. Print. 22
42. Lang, *Ex-Wife*. p154
43. Ibid. p156
44. Karskens, Grace. 'Resurrecting Chapman.'*Journal of the Australian Jewish Historical Society*, Vol XVIII, Part 1, June 2006, pp.8-21.

Ahead of His Times

1. Lang, John. Ex-Wife. London: Routledge, 1859. 236
2. Stanley, P. *White Mutiny: British Military Culture in India, 1825-1875*. Hurst, 1998. Print. 215
3. Keene, H.G. *A Servant of 'John Company': Being the Recollections of an Indian Official*. W. Thacker & co., 1897. Print. pp122-23
4. Ibid. p123
5. Ibid.
6. Ibid. p124
7. See *Reports from Committees*. 1853. Print.pp287-95
8. Buckingham, J.S., et al. *The Athenæum: A Journal of Literature, Science, the Fine Arts, Music, and the Drama*. J. Francis, 1893. Print.p597
9. Laurie, W.F.B. *Sketches of Some Distinguished Anglo-Indians: With an Account of Anglo-Indian Periodical Literature*. W.H. Allen, 1875. Print.p199
10. Anon. *Narrative of the Indian Revolt from Its Outbreak to the Capture of Lucknow*. G. Vickers, 1858. Print.
11. Wanderings in India. 235
12. Ibid. p236
13. Ibid. p236-237
14. See Keene, H.G. *Here and There: Memories, Indian and Other*. Brown, 1906. Print.
15. Napier, C.J., J. Mawson, and Great Britain. Army. *Records of the Indian Command of General Sir Charles James Napier, G. C. B.* R. C. Lepage and company, 1851. Print.pp173-6

16. Vizetelly, Henry. *Glances Back Through Seventy Years. Volume II.* London: Kegan Paul, Trench Trubner and Co Ltd, 1893. 7
17. *The Atlas* (Australian Newspaper). Vol 2. 18 April 1846. p190. 'Lang thrown into the crowd.'
18. Vizetelly, H. *Glances Back through Seventy Years.* 1893. Print.p8
19. See Levi, J.S., and G.F.J. Bergman. *Australian Genesis: Jewish Convicts and Settlers, 1788-1860.* Melbourne University Press, 2002. Print.
20. Roderick, Colin and John Earnshaw. 'John Lang: First Australian-born Novelist' *Journal and Proccedings of Royal Australian Historical Society. Vol 49, Part 2.* Sydney: 1963. P103
21. Interview with Crittenden. Canberra, May 2010.
22. *Sydney Gazette.* 21 January, 1835
23. Parkinson, Liz. *The Underwoods: Lock, Stock and Barrel.* Sydney: Lady Lizard, 1989. Pp212-226
24. Roderick, Colin and John Earnshaw. 'John Lang: First Australian-born Novelist' *Journal and Proccedings of Royal Australian Historical Society. Vol 49, Part 2.* Sydney: 1963. 107
25. Sardesai, Kalyani and Venkatraman, Deepa. 'Alice Richman's Grave'. http://cities.expressindia.com/fullstory.php?newsid=231501. 13 April, 2007.
26. http://freepages.genealogy.rootsweb.ancestry.com/~hcastle/transcripts/bev_edmonds/ transcripts/page8. htm.*Bulletin,*Sydney. 21 January, 1882

Bibliography

Primary Sources:

Prose Works:

Lang, John. *Violet the Danseuse: A Portraiture of Life and Passion.* Colburn, London: 1836. (Originally appeared as a serial in *The Mofussilite* in 1848.)

______. *Raymond.* 1840. Canberra: Mulini Press, 2004. (Originally appeared as a serial in Blackwood's *Edinburgh Magazine* in 1840 and in *The Mofussilite* in 1862.)

______. *Legends of Australia. Frederick Charles Howard.*1842. 1st edition Sydney, James Tegg, 1842 (in parts) 2nd edition Canberra, Mulini Press, 1989.

______. *Legends of Australia. James Nox.*1842.Sydney, James Tegg , 1842 (not completed)

______. *Recollections of the Late Jack Weatherly by his brother Geoffrey.* 1845 (A serial in *The Mofussilite*, of which only 8 episodes appeared)

______. *Mazarine.* 1845. Canberra, Mulini Press, 2004.

______. *Passages in the life of an undergraduate.*1846-47.Meerut (India), G.A. Gibbons, 1847.

(Originally a serial in *The Mofussilite* in 1846-47; in 1862 with the title of the undergraduate.)

______. *Lucy Cooper.*1846. Canberra Press, 1992 (Originally a serial in Sharpe's *London Magazine*,1846, *Cairo Chronicle*, 1848 and *Illustrated Sydney News*, 1853.)

______. *Jenny Dale.* 1847, London, Ward Lock, 1854 (Originally a serial in *The Mofussilite* in 1847; numerous editions including an Australian and an American edition followed.)

______. *Too Clever by Half or the Harroways* . 1847-48, London, Ingram, 1953.

______. *Livy Lake* .1849. (A serial in The Mofussilite (attributed to John Lang). No evidence has yet been discovered that this is by John Lang or that it ever appeared as a book)

______. *The Wetherbys or chapters of Indian Experience.* 1853. Meerut, Mofussilite Press, 1861.

______. *The forger's Wife.* 1853. London, Ward Lock, 1855; London W. Tegg 1959.

______. *My Furlough by Robert Wetherby.* 1854. (An incomplete serial in *The Mofussilite* in 1854; a sequel to the *The Wetherbys.*)

______. *The Ex- Wife.* 1858. London , Routledge, 1858. (Originally a serial in *The Mofussilite* titled *Passages in the Life of a Divorcee by herself*, 1856.)

______. *The Secret Police or Plot and Passion.* London, Ward Lock, 1859. (Originally a serial in *The Mofussilite* and *Welcome Guest* both versions simply called *Plot and Passions* after a play of the same title.)

______. *Captain Macdonald or Haps and Mishaps at Capias castle.* London, Ward Lock, 1858. (Originally a serial in *The Mofussilite.*)

______. *Hester Banfield* . 1857. Not published as a book. (A serial in *Fraser's Magazine* 1857 and *The Mofussilite* 1857.)

______. *Will He Marry Her? a Novel* . 1858. London, Ward Lock, 1859 (Originally a serial in *The Mofussilite*,1858.)

______. *My Friend's wife or York You're Wanted.* London, Ward Lock. 1859.

______. *Botany Bay or True Tales of the Early Days of Australia.* 1859. Canberra. Mulini Press,1989. (A series of sketches in *Household Wards* from 1853 and the *Welcome Guest*, 1859, published as a book by London, W. Tegg, 1859 Later editions by various publishers sometimes called *Clever Criminals* or *Fisher's Ghost.*)

______. *The Detective.*1861. Not published as a book. (As a serial in *The Mofussilite*)

______. *Ellen Wareham.* 1862. Not published as a book. (As serial in *The Mofussilite*)

______. *Wanderings in India and Other Sketches of life in Hindostan.* 1859. London, Routledge, Warne & Routledge, 1859 2nd edition 1861 (Series of sketches in *Household Words*, from 1853 and *The Mofussilite*, 1859)

______. *Assigned to His Wife: Or, the Adventures of George Flower, the Celebrated Detective Officer*. New South Wales Bookstall. Print.

______. *The Convict's Wife: A True Tale of Early Australia.* J. Walch. Print.

______. *Fisher's Ghost: And Other Stories of the Early Days of Australia.* E.W. Cole, 1920. Print.

Poetical Works:

Lang, John. *Geraldine . A Ballad*, London , Chapman and Hall, 1853. (in parts in *The Mofussilite*, 1845)

______. *The Death of Ibram Hossein* Lahore, *c.*1862. (in parts in *The Mofussilite*, 1862)

______. *The Rose Garden.* Trans from the poetry Sadi of Shiraz. Canberra , Mulini Press, 1992. (in various pieces in *The Mofussilite*, 1845)

______. *Songs of the Sea.* Canberra, Mulini Press, 2000. (Originally written under the pseudonym 'Epsilon' in various periodicals, 1835-36)

Secondary Sources:-

Newspapers and Periodicals:

The Mofussilite, published in India from Calcutta, Umballa, Meerut and Agra from 1845 to 1864 is a major source for John Lang's literary works.

Accounts and Papers of the House of Commons. Ordered to be printed, 1859. Print.

Accounts and Papers of the House of Commons. Ordered to be printed, 1858. Print.

Allen's Indian Mail and Register of Intelligence for British and Foreign India, China, and All Parts of the East January-December,1851. 1851. Print.

Allen's Indian Mail and Register of Intelligence for British and Foreign India. 1868. Print.

Asiatic Journal and Monthly Miscellany. Wm. H. Allen & Co., 1835. Print.

The Asiatic Journal and Monthly Miscellany. Wm. H. Allen & Co., 1833. Print.

The Athenaeum. J. Lection, 1876. Print.

The Bankers' Magazine and Journal of the Money Market. 1870. Print.

The British Friend of India Magazine, and Indian Review. Smith, Elder, and Co., 1844. Print.

British Medical Journal: Bmj. Assoc, 1861. Print.

Bulletins and Other State Intelligence. Compiled and arranged from the official documents published in the London gazette., 1860. Print.

Calcutta Review. University of Calcutta, 1873. Print.

Calcutta Review. University of Calcutta, 1859. Print.

Calcutta Review. University of Calcutta, 1852. Print.

The Calcutta Review. University of Calcutta., 1864. Print.

The Calcutta Review. University of Calcutta, 1860. Print.

The Calcutta Review. s.n University of Calcutta., 1858. Print.

The Cambridge History of English Literature. The Macmillan company, 1939. Print.

The Clergy List For ...: Containing Complete Lists of the Clergy in England, Wales Scotland, Ireland & the Colonies. Kelly's Directories, 1866. Print.

The Dark Blue. 1862. Print.

The Eclectic Magazine of Foreign Literature, Science, and Art. Leavitt, Trow, & Co., 1868. Print.

The Edinburgh Magazine and Literary Miscellany. Printed for Archibald Constable, 1823. Print.

Everybody's Journal. 1859. Print.

For the Term of His Natural Life. 1907. Print.

The Freemasons' Quarterly (Magazine and) Review [Afterw.] the Freemasons' Monthly Magazine. [Continued as] the Freemasons' Magazine and Masonic Mirror. 1859. Print.

The Gentleman's Magazine. 1833. Print.

Gleanings in Science. Baptist Mission Press, 1831. Print.

Imperial Gazetteer of India: Provincial Series. Superintendent of Government Printing, 1908. Print.

The Indian Law Reports: Calcutta Series. Superintendent, Govt. Print., West Bengal Govt. Press, 1925. Print.

The Indian Mail: A Monthly Register for British and Foreign India, China, and Australasia. 1844. Print.

Indian Textile Bulletin. 1892. Print.

The Journal of the Ethnological Society of London. Trübner, 1869. Print.

Journal of the Society for Army Historical Research. Society for Army Historical Research., 1933. Print.

The Ladies' Repository. L. Swormstedt and J.H. Power, 1869. Print.

The Literary Gazette: A Weekly Journal of Literature, Science, and the Fine Arts. H. Colburn, 1851. Print.

The London Review of Politics, Society, Literature, Art, & Science. J.K. Sharpe, 1864. Print.

The Musical World. J. Alfredo Novello, 1853. Print.

Narrative of the Indian Revolt from Its Outbreak to the Capture of Lucknow. G. Vickers, 1858. Print.

The Nation. The Nation Company, 1868. Print.

National and English Review. 1888. Print.

Notes and Queries. Oxford University Press, 1866. Print.

Parlour Magic. 1858. Print.

The Phrenological Journal and Miscellany. John Anderson, 1839. Print.

Public Dinner at Calcutta to Mr. A.T.T. Peterson. Printed at the Baptist Mission Press, 1863. Print.

The Quarterly Review of Historical Studies. Institute of Historical Studies., 1963. Print.

Reports from Committees. 1853. Print.

Selections from the Calcutta Review. T.S. Smith., 1882. Print.

The Solicitors' Journal & Reporter. Law Newspaper Co., 1864. Print.

Town Talk. H. Tuck, 1859. Print.

Transactions of the Agricultural and Horticultural Society of India. Reprinted at Baptist Mission Press, 1839. Print.

The Trial of Lalla Jotee Pershad and Others: Reported for the Delhi Gazette. Printed at the Gazette Press, by Kunniah Lall, 1851. Print.

The United Service Magazine. H. Colburn, 1859. Print.

The Welcome Guest. 1860. Print.

The Westminster Review. J. Chapman, 1859. Print.

Books:

Agnew, J.H., and W.H. Bidwell. *The Eclectic Magazine: Foreign Literature*. Leavitt, Trow & Co., 1861. Print.

Anon. *Charles Reade*. Taylor & Francis. Print.

______. *The Magic Lantern, How to Buy and How to Use It, by 'a Mere Phantom'. Also, How to Raise a Ghost*. 1866. Print.

______. *Sir John Login and Duleep Singh*. Atlantic Publishers & Distri. Print.

______. *Theology*. Society for Promoting Christian Knowledge., 1927. Print.

______. *The Truth About Bootan*. Metropolitan Press, 1865. Print.

______. *York, You're Wanted: To Which Are Added, the Irish Wedding. My Peggy Is a Young Thing. Lochaber No More*. Printed for the booksellers in town and country., 1823. Print.

Armstrong, A. *Tobacco and Snuff, L.S.D., Potatos, and Other Poems*. Longman, Orme, Brown, Green, and Longsmans, 1840. Print.

Bachman, M.K., and D.R. Cox. *Reality's Dark Light: The Sensational Wilkie Collins*. University of Tennessee Press, 2003. Print.

Ball, C. *The History of the Indian Mutiny: Giving a Detailed Account of the Sepoy Insurrection in India : And a Concise History of the Great Military Events Which Have Tended to Consolidate British Empire in Hindostan ; Illustrated with Battle Scenes, Views of Places, Portraits, and Maps, Beautifully Engraved on Steel*. London Printing and Publ. Co., 1858. Print.

Banham Martin , Ed. *The Plays of Tom Taylor* Edited with an introduction and notes. New York: Cambridge University Press, 1985.

Bhalla, Alok and Chandra Sudhir. *Indian Responses to Colonialism in the 19th Century*. Delhi: Sterling, 1993.

Barton, G.B. *Literature in New South Wales*. T. Richards, govt. printer, 1866. Print.

Bland, W., and G. Mackaness. *Account of the Duel between William Bland and Robert Case: And the Circumstances That Led Thereto, Drawn up for Posterity*. Angus & Robertson, 1892. Print.

Boccaccio, G., and C. Balguy. *The Decameron, or, Ten Days' Entertainment, of Boccaccio*. Printed for William Sharp and Son, 1822. Print.

______. and J.M. Rigg. *The Decameron*. Digireads.com, 2010. Print.

Boehmer, E., and S. Morton. *Terror and the Postcolonial*. Wiley-Blackwell, 2009. Print.

Boldrewood, R. *In Bad Company: And Other Stories*. Macmillan, 1901. Print.

Booth, W.C. *The Rhetoric of Fiction*. University of Chicago Press, 1983. Print.

Brough, R.B. *The Welcome Guest*. G. Fall, 1860. Print.

Bulwer, E.L. *Eugene Aram: A Tale*. Bernh. Tauchnitz jr., 1842. Print.

Burton, R.F. *The Book of the Thousand Nights and a Night: A Plain and Literal Translation of the Arabian Nights Entertainments*. Privately printed by The Burton Club, 1885. Print.

Burton, R.F., *A Plain and Literal Translation of the Arabian Nights Entertainments: Now Instituted the Book of the Thousand Nights and a Night*. Printed by the Kamashastra Society for private subscribers only, 1885. Print.

Byron, G.G.B. *The Poetical Works of Lord Byron*. Henry Frowde, Oxford University Press, 1807. Print.

______. *The Works of Lord Byron Complete in One Volume*. H.L. Broenner, 1837. Print.

______. *The Corsair,: A Tale*. Printed for John Murray, ... By Thomas Davison, 1814. Print.

Campbell, G. *Modern India: A Sketch of the System of Civil Government, with Some Account of the Natives and Native Institutions*. J. Murray, 1853. Print.

______. *Modern India: A Sketch of the System of Civil Government. To Which Is Prefixed Some Account of the Natives and Native Institutions*. J. Murray, 1852. Print.

Carpenter, F.I. *English Lyric Poetry, 1500-1700*. Books for Libraries Press, 1906. Print.

Chambers, W., and R. Chambers. *Chamber's Journal of Popular Literature, Science and Arts*. W & R Chambers, 1894. Print.

Chapman, J. *Diarrhœa and Cholera*. Trübner and Co., 1866. Print.

Charnock, M.A.E. *Legendary Rhymes, and Other Poems*. Longman, 1843. Print.

Chick, N.A. *Annals of the Indian Rebellion, 1857-58*. Sanders, Cones and Co., 1859. Print.

Clemm, S. *Dickens, Journalism, and Nationhood: Mapping the World in Household Words*. Routledge, 2009. Print.

Cole, John William. *Life and Times of Charles Kean*. London: Bentley, 1859, 2 vols.

Collings, R. *Classic Victorian & Edwardian Ghost Stories*. Wordsworth, 1996. Print.

Collins, W. *Poor Miss Finch: A Novel. With Illustrations*. Harper & Brothers, 1872. Print.

Cook, J.D., et al. *The Saturday Review of Politics, Literature, Science and Art*. J.W. Parker and Son, 1894. Print.

Cooter, R. *The Cultural Meaning of Popular Science: Phrenology and the Organization of Consent in Nineteenth-Century Britain*. Cambridge University Press, 1984. Print.

Creed, B., and J. Hoorn. *Body Trade: Captivity, Cannibalism and Colonialism in the Pacific*. Taylor and Francis, 2002. Print.

Crittenden, Victor. *John Lang: Australia's Larrikin Writer*. Canberra: Mulini Press, 2005.

Crosland, N., and M.B. Foster. *Memorable Women: The Story of Their Lives*. Ticknor and Fields, 1854. Print.

Dickens, C. *Household Words*. Berh. Tauchnitz, jun., 1853. Print.

______. *Household Words: A Weekly Journal*. Bradbury and Evans, 1857. Print.

______. *The Mystery of Edwin Drood*. Chapman and Hall, 1870. Print.

______. *A Tale of Two Cities: With a Critical and Biographical Profile of Charles Dickens*. Franklin Watts, 1859. Print.

Dodd, G. *The History of the Indian Revolt and of the Expeditions to Persia, China, and Japan, 1856-7-8: With Maps, Plans, and Wood Engravings*. W. and R. Chambers, 1859. Print.

Drew, J.M.L. *Dickens the Journalist*. Palgrave Macmillan, 2003. Print.

Dutt, Romesh C. *The Economic History of India in the 19th Century*. Delhi: Routledge, 2001.

E, B.C., and C.E. Buckland. *Dictionary of Indian Biography*. Cosmo Publication, 1999. Print.

Ecker, A., et al. *Archiv Für Anthropologie: Zeitschrift Für Naturgeschichte Und Urgeschichte Des Menschen*. F.Vieweg und sohn, 1870. Print.

Flanagan, R.J. *The History of New South Wales: With an Account of Van Diemen's Land (Tasmania), New Zealand, Port Phillip (Victoria), Moreton Bay, and Other Australian Settlements : Comprising a Complete View of the Progress and Prospects of Gold Mining in Australia : The Whole Compiled from Official and Other Authentic and Original Sources*. Sampson Low, Son, & Co., 1862. Print.

Forbes, D. *The Adventures of Hatim Tai: A Romance*. Oriental Translation Fund, 1830. Print.

Forbes Mitchell, William. *Reminiscences of the Great Mutiny, 1857-59*. London, Macmillan, 1853.

______. *Reminiscences of the Great Mutiny, 1857-59: Including the Relief, Siege, and Capture of Lucknow, and the Campaigns in Rohilcund and Oude*. Asian Educational Services, 2002. Print.

Ford, W. *John Laird Mair Lawrence, a Viceroy of India, by William St. Clair*. 1887. Print.

Foucault, M. *Madness and Civilization: A History of Insanity in the Age of Reason*. Taylor and Francis, 2001. Print.

Frost, T. *Complete Narrative of the Mutiny in India*. 1857. Print.

Fullom, S.W. *The King and the Countess [by S.W. Fullom]. By S.W. Fullom*. 1857. Print.

Gardener, Brian. *East India Company: A History*. Delhi: Hart-Davis, 1971.

Gilchrist, J.B., and W.C. Smyth. *The Oriental Green Bag!!! Or, a Complete Sketch of Edwards Alter in the Royal Exchequer. (Copies of Correspondence between B. Gilchrist and W.C. Smyth, Relative to the Doctor's Publications)*. 1820. Print.

Gould, W. *Hindu Nationalism and the Language of Politics in Late Colonial India*. Cambridge, 2004. Print.

Gupta, H.R. *History of the Sikhs*. Munshiram Manoharlal, 1998. Print.

Hake, T. *The Life and Letters of Theodore Watts Dunton*. Kessinger Publishing, LLC, 2005. Print.

Halkett, S., and J. Laing. *Dictionary of Anonymous and Pseudonymous Literature of Great*

Britain. William Paterson, 1882. Print.

Hall, B.H. *A Collection of College Words and Customs*. Echo Library, 2006. Print.

Harlow, G.E., and American Museum of Natural History. *The Nature of Diamonds*. Cambridge University Press in association with the American Museum of Natural History, 1998. Print.

Hasan, Masoodul. *19th Century English Literary Works: A Bibliography of Rare Books*. Delhi: DK Publishers, 1978.

Hay, D., et al. *Albion's Fatal Tree: Crime and Society in Eighteenth-Century England*. Verso, 2011. Print.

Hemenway, S.I. *The Novel of India*. Writers Workshop, 1975. Print.

Higginbotham, J. *The Bombay Miscellany*. 1862. Print.

Hoare, P. *England's Lost Eden: Adventures in a Victorian Utopia*. Fourth Estate, 2005. Print.

Hodson, V.C.P. *List of the Officers of the Bengal Army, 1758-1834: L-R*. Constable. Print.

Hood, T., and W. Harvey. *The Dream of Eugene Aram, the Murderer*. Tilt, 1831. Print.

Humbly, W.W.W. *Journal of a Cavalry Officer: Including the Memorable Sikh Campaign of 1845-46*. Longman, Brown, Green, and Longmans, 1854. Print.

Hurry-Houghton, T., and M. Hurry-Houghton. *Memorials of the Family of Hurry of Great Yarmouth, Norfolk, and of America, Australia, and South Africa*. C. Tinling, 1926. Print.

Hutchinson, H.G. *Dreams and Their Meanings 1901*. KESSINGER PUB CO, 2004. Print.

Ingram, Edward. *In Defence of British India*. London: Routledge, 1984.

Irving, J. *The Annals of Our Time [1837 to 1868]. [with] 1871 To*. 1871. Print.

Jayapalan, N. *History of Education in India*. Atlantic Publishers and Distributors, 2005. Print.

Jerosch, R. *The Rani of Jhansi, Rebel against Will: A Biography of the Legendary Indian Freedom Fighter in the Mutiny of 1857-1858*. Aakar Books, 2007. Print.

Jerrold (William) Blanchard. *The life and Remains of Douglas Jerrold*. London , W. Kent & Co. 1859.

Jerrold Douglas. *Douglas Jerrold's Weekly Newspaper*. London, William Stevens, 1846-47.

Jerrold, Walter. *Douglas Jerrold & Punch*. London , Macmillan , 1910.

Jones, B.M. *Follies & Grottoes*. Constable, 1953. Print.

Kean, Charles. *Emigrants in Motley.*London, Rockliff, 1854.

Keene, Henry George. *Here and There, Memories of India*. London , Brown Langham & Co. 1906.

______. *Servant of John Company. Being the recollections of an Indian Official,* London , W. Thacker & Co. 1897.

Keesing, Nancy. *John Lang and the Forger's Wife. A true Tale of Early Australia.* Sydney, John Ferguson , 1979

Kempson, M. *Report of the Progress of Education in the North-Western Provinces.* 1866. Print.

Khurana, G. *British Historiography on the Sikh Power in Punjab.* Allied Publishers, 1985. Print.

Knight, Stephen. *The Continent of Mystery: A Thematic History of Australian Crime Fiction.* Melbourne, Melbourne University Press, 1997.

Lalumia, M.P. *Realism and Politics in Victorian Art of the Crimean War.* UMI Research Press, 1984. Print.

Lang, A. *The Valet's Tragedy, and Other Studies, by Andrew Lang.* Longmans, Green and Co., 1903. Print.

Laurie, W.F.B. *Sketches of Some Distinguished Anglo-Indians: With an Account of Anglo-Indian Periodical Literature.* W.H. Allen, 1875. Print.

Lebra-Chapman, Joyce. *The Rani of Jhasi: A study of female heroism in India.* Honolulu, University of Hawaii Press, 1986.

Lewin, M. *The Way to Regain India.* 1858. Print.

Linebaugh, P. *The London Hanged: Crime and Civil Society in the Eighteenth Century.* Verso, 2003. Print.

Littell, E., and R.S. Littell. *Littell's Living Age.* T.H. Carter & Co., 1853. Print.

______., and Making of America Project. *The Living Age.* Littell, son & company, 1856. Print.

Living, Edward. *Adventures in Publishing. The house of Ward Lock 1854-1954.* London , Ward, Lock & Co. 1954.

Lohrli, A., and H. words. *Household Words: A Weekly Journal, 1850-1859, Conducted by Charles Dickens: Table of Contents, List of Contributors and Their Contributions, Based on the Household Words Office Book in the Morris L. Parrish Collection of Victorian Novelists, Princeton.* University of Toronto Press, 1973. Print.

Lover, S. *L.S.D., or, Accounts of Irish Heirs Furnished to the Public.* Frederick Lover, ...; and Richard Groombridge., 1843. Print.

Luther, U.M., and M. Raza. *Historical Routes of North West Indian Subcontinent, Lahore to Delhi, 1550s-1850s A.D.: Network Analysis through Dcnc-Micro Methodology.* Sagar Publications, 1990. Print.

Lyall, Sir Alfred C. *Studies in Literature.* London, John Murry , 1915.

Lytton, E.B. *What Will He Do with It?* : B. Tauchnitz, 1857. Print.

Lytton, E.B.L. *Zanoni.* Harper & Brothers, 1842. Print.

Macaulay, J. *Stirring Stories of Peace and War, by Sea and Land.* Hodder and Stoughton, 1885. Print.

Mackenna, P.J., and W.C. Taylor. *Ancient and Modern India.* James Madden, 1851. Print.

Mackenzies, C. *Life in the Mission, the Camp and the Zenáná: Or Six Years in India.* Bentley, 1853. Print.

Márquez, G.G. *Chronicle of a Death Foretold.* Ballantine Books, 1992. Print.

______. and E. Grossman. *Of Love and Other Demons.* 1994., 1995. Print.

Marryat, F. *Newton Forster; or, the Merchant Service.* 1838. Print.

Marsh, C. *Good Magic, Spells, Potions and More from History, Literature & Make-Believe.* Gallopade International, 2001. Print.

Martin, R.M. *Our Indian Empire and the Adjacent Countries.* 1879. Print.

Mehrotra, S.R. *The Emergence of the Indian National Congress.* Vikas Publications, 1971. Print.

Merriman, Harold G. *Edward Moxon, Publisher of Poets.* New York, Columbia Unversity Press, 1939.

Michell, G., and P. Davies. *The Penguin Guide to the Monuments of India: Islamic, Rajput, European.* Penguin Books, 1990. Print.

Molony, John. *The Native Born, The First White Australians.* Melbourne , Melbourne University Press 2000.

Morgan, H.J. *Sketches of Celebrated Canadians: And Persons Connected with Canada, from the Earliest Period in the History of the Province Down to the Present Time.* Hunter, Rose & co., 1862. Print.

Morrison, E. *Engines of Influence: Newspapers of Country Victoria, 1840-1890.* Melbourne University Publishing, 2005. Print.

Morton, T. *The Slave; a Musical Drama.* 1816. Print.

Napier, C.J., J. Mawson, and Great Britain. Army. *Records of the Indian Command of General Sir Charles James Napier, G. C. B.* R. C. Lepage and company, 1851. Print.

Narasimhaiah, C.D. *An Introduction to Australian Literature.* Brisbane , Jacaranda , 1965.

Nayder, L. *Unequal Partners: Charles Dickens, Wilkie Collins, and Victorian Authorship.* Cornell University Press, 2002. Print.

Nicholl, Alladyce. *A History of Late Nineteenth Century Drama 1850- 1900.* Cambridge, Cambridge University Press, 1946, 2 vols

Outram, Sir James. *Conquest of the Scinde.* Edinburgh , Blackwood, 1846, 2 vols.

Palmer, C.J. *The Perlustration of Great Yarmouth, with Gorleston and Southtown.* G. Nall, 1874. Print.

Perkins, F.B., and H. Taine. *Charles Dickens: A Sketch of His Life and Works.* G. P. Putnam & sons, 1870. Print.

Peterson, A.T.T. *Essays from the Unseen, Delivered through the Mouth of W.L., a Sensitive, and Recorded by A.T.T.P. 1885. Print.*

______. *A Treatise on the Law of Railway Companies, in Their Formation, Incorporation, and Government, with an Abstract of the Statutes, and a Table of Forms, by Thomas Chambers and A. T. T. Peterson*. W. Benning, 1848. Print.

Poe, E.A. *The Poetical Works of Edgar Allan Poe with a Notice by J. Hannay*. 1856. Print.

______. *The Raven, and Other Poems*. Wiley & Putnam, 1846. Print.

______., and J.H. Ingram. *The Raven: With Literary and Historical Commentary*. George Redway, 1885. Print.

Prakash, B. *Indian Themes in English Fiction: A Socio-Literary Study*. Mittal Publications, 1994. Print.

Press, John. *Commonwealth Literature: Unity and Diversity*. University of Leeds: Heinemann, 1965.

Reade, C., and R.R. Macmullen. *A Record of the Redes of Barton Court, Berks: With a Short Précis of Other Lines of the Name*. Jakeman and Carver, 1899. Print.

Ritchie, John. *The Wentworths Father and Sons*. Melbourne , The Migunyah Press 1997.

Rusden, G.W. *History of Australia, by G. W. Rusden*. Chapman and Hall, 1883. Print.

Sala, George Augustus Henry. *Twice Round the clock or the Hours of the Day and Night in London*. London, Houlston and Wright , 1859; reprint Leicester University Press, 1971.

Scott, E. *Australia*. Cambridge University Press, 1989. Print.

Shakespeare, W. *The Taming of the Shrew*. Cambridge Univ. Press, 1953. Print.

Sharma, S.K., and U. Sharma. *Documents on Sikkim and Bhutan*. Anmol Publications, 1998. Print.

Sherring, M.A. *Hindu Tribes and Castes*. 1872. Print.

Simmonds, P.L., and W.H.G. Kingston. *Colonial Magazine and East India Review*. Foreign and Colonial Office, 1845. Print.

Sladen, Douglas Brooke. *Australian Poets: 1788-1888*. Griffith, 1888.

Smyth, G.C. *Secret History of the Khalsa Durbar*. National Book Shop, 2002. Print.

Smyth, Sir John. *The Rebellious Rani*. London, Frederick Muller, 1996.

Smyth, W.C. *The Hindoostanee Interpreter*. n.p., 1824. Print.

Steinbeck, J. *The Pearl*. Viking Press, 1947. Print.

Stewart, D.A. *Fisher's Ghost: An Historical Comedy*. Wentworth Press, 1960. Print.

Straus, Ralph. *Sala. The Portrait of an Eminent Victorian*. London , Constable 1942.

Tahmankar, D.V. *The Ranee of Jhansi*. London, Macgibbon & Kee, 1958.

Tait, W. *Tait's Edinburgh Magazine*. 1855. Print.

Tavernier, J.B., V. Ball, and W. Crooke. *Travels in India*. Asian Educational Services, 2001. Print.

Thomas, W., and K. Pavitt. *Book of Talismans, Amulets and Zodiacal Gems*. Kessinger Pub. Co., 1914. Print.

Thornhill, M. *The Personal Adventures and Experiences of a Magistrate During the Rise, Progress and Suppression of the Indian Mutiny*. John Murray, 1884. Print.

Thurlow, T.J.H.T.C.B. *The Company and the Crown*. W. Blackwood, 1866. Print.

Tinsley, William. *Random Collections of an old Publisher*. London, Simkins, Marshalls, Hamilton & Kent , 1900, 2 vols.

Tolles, Winton. *Tom Taylor and Victorian Drama*. New York, Columbia University Studies in English and Comparative Literature No. 48, 1940.

Torrens, H.W., and J. Hume. *A Selection from the Writings, Prose and Poetical, Of... Henry W. Torrens; with a Biogr. Memoir. By J. Hume*. 1854. Print.

Vay, B.L. *Eccentric Britain, 2nd: The Bradt Guide to Britain's Follies and Foibles*. Bradt Travel Guides, 2005. Print.

Vizetelly, Henry. *A History of Champagne. Facts about Champagne and other sparkling wines etc.* London, Vizetelly & Co. 1879.

______. *Glances Back through Seventy Years*. 1893. Print.

Wagner, K.A. *The Great Fear of 1857: Rumours, Conspiracies and the Making of the Indian Uprising*. Peter Lang, 2010. Print.

Wallace, D. *Giovanni Boccaccio, Decameron*. Cambridge University Press, 1991. Print.

Walsh, William. *Commonwealth Literature*. St. James Press, 1986.

Watson, T., and D.F. Condie. *Lectures on the Principles and Practice of Physic Delivered at King's College, London*. Lea and Blanchard, 1855. Print.

Wheeler, C. B., and J. L. Bickersteth. *Memoir of John Lang Bickersteth [by C.B. Wheeler]*. 1799. Print.

Wilson, H. *Wonderful Characters: Comprising Memoirs and Anecdotes of the Most Remarkable Persons, of Every Age and Nation*. Walker and Co., 1842. Print.

Winstanley, Eliza. *Shifting Scenes in Theatrical Life*. London , Routledge , 1859.

Worth, George. *James Hanny: His Life and Work*. Lawrence, University of Kansas Press, 1964.

Wu, C., and A. Waley. *Monkey: From the Chinese by Arthur Waley*. Allen., 1944. Print.

Wylly, H.C. *The Military Memoirs of Lieut.-General Sir Joseph Thackwell, G.C.B., K.H.; Colonel 16th Lancers: Arranged from Diaries and Correspondence*. John Murray, 1908. Print.

Periodical Articles:

Anon, "Australia's First Novelist Shocked Cambridge Dons". *Daily Mirror*, November 4, 1981.

Boldrewood, Rolf. "Heralds of Australian Literature". *Australian Association for Advancement of Science*. Report 1982, pp. 799-811.

Bond, Ruskin. "Looking for John Lang's Grave". *Blackwoods Magazine* CCCXI 1972 pp 237-42

Crittenden Victor. "John Lang and Bushrangers". *Margin* No 51 July/August 2000, pp 21-31.

______. "John Lang and Sadi of Shiraz". *Margin* No 61 November 2003, p. 40.

______. "John Lang's First Novel". *Fellows of the book* ed. By Brian Taylor (*Studies in Australian Bibliophily* No. 5) Book Collections Society of Australia, pp. 159-161.

______. "Some of John Lang's Indian Stories". *Margin* No.44 April 1998, pp. 4-12

Earnshaw, J.W. "Legends of Australia and John Lang". *Biblionews* 11:4 April 1958, pp. 1-3.

______. "First Australian Novelist". *Bulletin* September 26 1959, p 44.

______. "Famed and Forgotten Australia's Novelist". *Bulletin* 80:44 September 23 1959.

Grant, William. "Obituary of John Lang". *The Mofussilite*, August 1864.

Hoskin, Rick. Magnetic Amalgams? Joh Lan's Wanderings in India, 1859, Rudyard Kipling and Henry Lawson, *Literary Criterion* 30 1&2 1995 pp.59-80

Irvin, Eric. "Was John Lang really a four word dramatist?" *Australian Drama Studies* No.11, October 11, 1987, pp. 23-26.

Narasimhaiah, C.D. Western Writers in India, *Literary Criterion* (Mysore) XV Nos. 3-4 May-June 1992 (Quarterly Abstract of English Studies)

Roderick, C.A. John Lang 1816-1864 Royal Australian Historical Society J& 49:2 1963 pp.100-135

Society Theatre Review, Bulletin No.66 (Report on British Theatre Museum *Theatre Notebook* Vol.19 1965 pp.44-45

Acknowledgements

This research has been more of a personal journey than a professional one. It's been a journey in time as much as it's been in space, as I have travelled across India and Australia; read through 19th century newspapers more than the 21st century ones in my hunt for John Lang. I use the phrase 'hunt for' because my favourite story from the John Lang corpus is 'Love's Last Sacrifice'—which is adapted from another favourite, Boccaccio's 'Federigo and the Falcon'.

Gil Vicente, a 14th century poet, says, 'The hunt for love is haughty falconry.' This journey began with a hunt for Alice Richman, a young girl who had died in Pune in 1882. Hunt leads to hunt—it's an endless metonymic shift. I have travelled and met travellers, regaled over ale, and serendipities have struck at the most unlikely times. Acknowledgements cannot be summed up in a page; this journey perhaps calls for a travelogue to be able to thank everyone; and thank them I must for their continued support and affection.

Special thanks is due towards Victor Crittenden for giving me materials and leads related to Lang, and for being a garrulous and argumentative Lang-o-philiac; Victor has left us, but will always remain a part of fond memories. I also express my heartfelt gratitude to Dr Saugata Bhaduri for having faith in my quirky anagrammatological methodologies and engaging with this research indulgently; to Professor Sareen for inviting me to various Indo-Australian fora, and to Professor Prasad for engaging with the Alice story.

I am indebted to the Australian government for awarding me the 'Endeavour Research Fellowship' that enabled me to carry out fundamental research; to the University of New South Wales (UNSW) for hosting me as a Visiting Fellow and providing me platforms to share my work; to the Inlaks Shivdasani Foundation for a research grant in 2010; to Professor Rick Hosking of Adelaide for travelling with me to Melrose to see what gardens Alice must have picnicked at (Alice Garden in Pune, where students picnic, is unfortunately her resting place); to Dr Sean Brawley for being a great supervisor at UNSW; to Dr Paul Brown for the wonderful 'pollution awareness' trips around Sydney; to the Indian Cultural Association at UNSW for awarding me for my research; to Dr Kama Maclean of UNSW for reading my articles and sharing her vast repository of knowledge about the colonial period; to Dr Grace Karskens for her valuable insights; to Dr Stephen Muecke for all the wine and creative writing gatherings; to James Paull for asking 'Why John George Lang?'; to James Aravanitakis for being such an amazing friend; to Nick Jose at UNSW for discussions about the little-known Indo-Australian connections.

Thanks to Liz Parkinson, a remote descendant of Lang, for enlightening me about the Underwood family history; to Rabbi John Levi of Melbourne for congratulating me on my research about a 'Jewish ancestor' and inviting me to a Bar Mitzvah ceremony; to Susan and Scotty in Melbourne for being indulgent hosts and listeners.

I am also thankful to Anahaita Mukherjee for calling me 'Jhansi ki Rani ke lawyer ka scholar' and publishing an article about the same; to Rohit Kulkarni, my childhood friend, who has been sending me books from the USA upon every request; to Sutapa for showing me Alice's grave; to Madhuri for scanning documents from the National Library in Calcutta; to Sue Hosking for her tales and amazing food when I was in Adelaide; to Arindam Das for being a fellow wanderer in Sydney and a guinea pig for my career as a stand-up-comedian; to Vinod for late night dhaba and chai discussions; to Narayan for being the always-willing technological help; to Arup for feigning wonder at all the incredible stories; to Arcchit, Abhishek, and Kanika for their interest in my work; to Nayantara for listening to my sob stories; to Jennie Lang for the wonderful dinners and her statement 'you get to hang out with Jennie Lang if not John Lang'; to Samar, Namrata, Nasir, Feroze, Shashi, and Anisha for travelling to Mussoorie with me in the hunt for Lang's grave; to Ruskin Bond for Mussoorie ghost stories, and for sharing how he had found Lang's grave. I am obliged to the various media houses and universities that have shown constant interest in my research. Thanks are also due to Australia India Youth Dialogue, who have given a grant to support this book; as also to Australian High Commission in India who've always been supportive.

Last but not the least, I am deeply grateful to my family: to brothers Rakesh and Nishant, and sisters-in-law Neetu and Hitti; to little Neelabh who's been my best friend in Sydney; to Amita for being an ardent admirer of a wanderer; and, above all, thanks to my parents for being supportive of all my quirks in all my memory.

I am also grateful to Petrikoer, the Bangalore-based company, for letting me snatch their editor-writer for good six months; the snatched editor was Preeja Aravind, friend of a decade. She has done a fabulous job—she's the invisible hand that made the book succeed. Several other friends, like Aarzoo, I owe a lot to—for they took time out from their busy schedules to read, suggest, and help edit.

At this juncture, I must thank Preeti Gill, who helped me find a publisher; Nirmalkanti Bhattacharjee, the Publishing Director of Niyogi Books, who took an instant liking to my Lang-o-Mania, and Vibha Chakravarty Kumar, who edited the book while also being a judicious reader, and remained patient with the overdrawn timeline.

Plate 1

Captain Macdonald, or Haps and Mishaps at Capias Castle, or The Bailiffs Outwitted *is one of the funniest novels of John Lang. The captain is under heavy debt of Jewish bailiffs. To ward them off, he mock-fortifies his castle by putting soldiers' attires on poles to act as scarecrows; while the bailiffs try every trick to get into the castle. The novel is also important because it's a part of an important question–Was John Lang Jewish—as contended by Rabbi John Levi? (Ref. p. 320)*

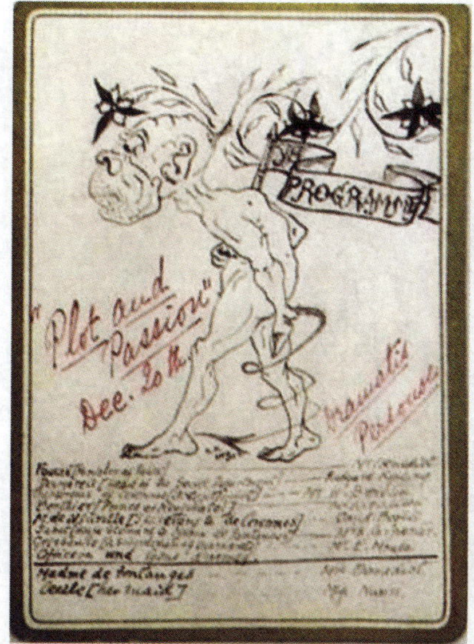

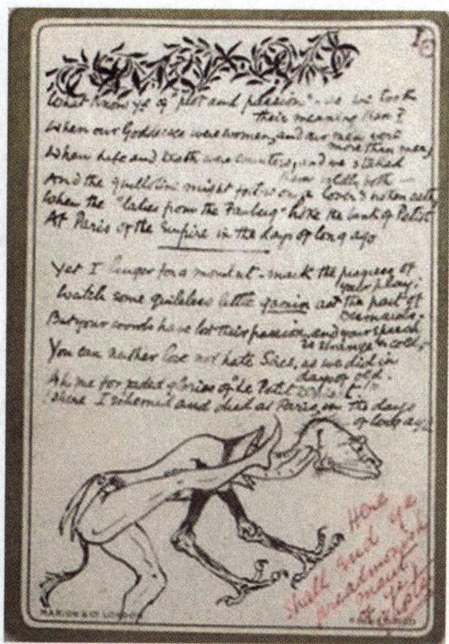

Hand-drawn invitation by Kipling for a performance of Plot and Passion, *in which he played the role of Desmartes. This performance of the play written by John Lang and Tom Taylor took place at Lahore in December 1883.* *(Ref. p. 69)*

A Chart of Phrenology. 1 Amativeness; 2 Philoprogenitiveness; 3 Concentrativeness; 3 *a* Inhabitativeness; 4 Adhesiveness; 5 Combativeness; 6 Destructiveness; 6 *a* Alimentiveness; 7 Secretiveness; 8 Acquisitiveness; 9 Constructiveness; 10 Self-esteem; 11 Love of Approbation; 12 Cautiousness; 13 Benevolence; 14 Veneration; 15 Firmness; 16 Conscientiousness; 17 Hope; 18 Wonder; 19 Ideality; 19 *a* (Not determined); 20 Wit; 21 Imitation; 22 Individuality; 23 Form; 24 Size; 25 Weight; 26 Coloring; 27 Locality; 28 Number; 29 Order; 30 Eventuality; 31 Time; 32 Tune; 33 Language; 34 Comparison; 35 Causality. [Some raise the number of organs to forty-three.]

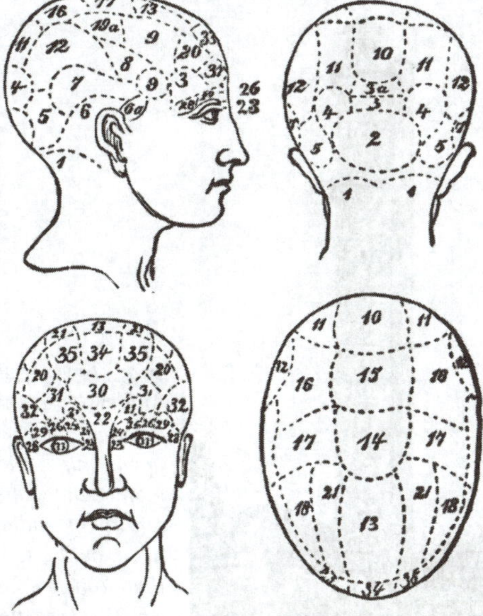

Phrenology, now ridiculous in retrospect, was considered a revolutionary science, second only to telegraph perhaps, in the mid-19th c. The human brain was mapped into zones of intelligence, criminality, etc.—and skulls of geniuses and criminals were highly valued. Lang was, however, skeptical of the euphoria around this discipline, and takes a jibe at phrenologists in the novel Will He Marry Her? *(Ref. p. 125–127)*

Plate 3

Illustration of William Lang, John Lang's son, as a thirteen-year-old boy in the first battle of Crimean War, 1854. The illustration is from Illustrated London News—*12 April 1856.*

Sway Tower built by Justice Andrew Thomas Turton Peterson at Sway, England upon his return to his motherland after years of service of India. This tower was built to demonstrate that 'concrete' is the future. At 218 feet, this is perhaps still the tallest concrete tower without any reinforcements. *(Ref. p. 117)*

Fisher's Ghost Festival. Campbelltown, Sydney, November 2010. The origins of the festival are in a John Lang story. (Ref. p. 28)

A sketch by Lang in Too Clever By Half

Plate 5

Book cover of Lang Will He Marry Her? *(1858). (Ref. p. 178)*

Lala Jotee Persaud's likeness that was passed off as Nana Sahib's in Illustrated London News *in 1857. The media was hunting for a picture of Nana Sahib, the scourge of the British in the Revolution of 1857. A reporter took away the portrait of Lala Jotee Persaud from Lang in a series of comic events. (Ref. p. 236)*

Frontispiece from a book written by 'A Mere Phantom' entitled The Magic Lantern (1866). The book describes how to use a magic lantern to raise an apparition on stage. (Ref. p. 268)

Andrew Thomas Turton Peterson, also known as ATTP, was the brother-in-law of Lang. A judge by profession, and many things by passion—phrenologist, cholera researcher, lobbyist for concrete, Spiritualist etc—ATTP is one of most colourful characters of 19th century India. (Ref. p. 108)

Original Poetry.

ELEGY

ON THE DEATH OF ———

Died Aug. —— 1845.

Et, Rose, elle a vécu ce que rivent les roses,
L'espace d'un matin.—MALHERBE.

1.

I saw them grieving o'er thy early doom,
Bearing the pall of thy untimely bier,
I saw them giving to the lonely tomb
All that remains of thee, thou daughter dear!

2.

Beauteous as the flower whose name you bore,
Chaste as the dews, which light upon it's leaves,
Wer't thou, sweet innocent, whose life is o'er,
Whose bloom departed all thy kindred grieves.

3.

Beauty is often but a dangerous dower,
And angels even, in their time, have fell,
Then let them joy thou art beyond the power
Of all the wiles in human breasts that dwell.

4.

What though life's pleasures thou must cease to know,
What though it's raptures be, by thee, unshared,
How many a scene of agony, and woe,
Mayhap, sweet flower, they early death hath spared.

5

The shafts of poverty,—and cankering care,
Malice, and envy, with their loathsome breath,
The pangs of sickness, and of dull despair,
Can ne'er break in upon thy sleep of Death.

" The Zahid, who the deepest wrong,
" With patience cannot bear,
" Disgraceth all his brethren;
" And their garments should not wear,

" The rolling river by the stone
" Doth never turbid seem,
" The holy man, who thus repines,
" Is but a shallow stream!
" Should o'er misfortune on thee fall.
" To bear it, brother, strive,
" And by forgiving other men,
" Hope God will thee forgive!
" Seeing, for certain, in the end,
" To earth return we must
" Let us embrace Humility
" Ere we become the dust."

No. 4.

GULISTAN, BOOK I—TALE 2.

ONE of the Kings of Khorasan
Had in a vision seen,
(After his death a hundred years)
Mahmoud Sebuktoreen;
His body all was scattered,
And become as e'en the mould,
Except the eyes, which glared around,
And in their sockets roll'd.
The learned all unable were
To say what meant the same,
Until at length a Derveish
In the Monarch's presence came;
And, making his obeisance,
To the Monarch made it known,
" He stareth still, when he beholds
Another hath his throne;
" Many a one of famous name,
They've buried 'neath the ground,
" Of whose existence on the earth,
No single trace is found,
" Yet this old corpse appeareth still,
Which they to dust resign'd,
" Though so decayed, that not a bone
Doth e'en remain behind;

HOR. LIB. II. CARMEN III.

Æquam memento rebus in arduis
Servare mentem.

Since, Dellius, thou wert born to die,
In times of stern adversity
Preserve an equal mind!
And, tempered in prosperity,
Let pride, and insolence in thee
No habitation find!

Whether thou lead'st a life of care,
Or happiness should be the share,
That falleth to thy lot,
With dates, and old Falernian wine,
The live-long day, at ease, recline
Within some grassy grot!

Where poplar hoar, and lofty pine
Their boughs delight to intertwine,
And form a pleasing shade,
Where gentle streams,—in mimic song,—
With ruffled surface—purl along,
Meandering though the glade!

While the black thread of " Sisters three,"
And age, and fortune suffer thee,
Bid them the wine to bring,
And perfumes, and the transcient flowers
Of grateful roses, o'er thy bowers,
Bid them profusely fling.—

For thou from purchas'd groves must roam,
From this thy Villa, and thy home,
Which yellow Tiber laves,
This heap of wealth, " now reared in air,"
Become the portion of an heir,
Who now, expectant craves!

What matters it, if thou can'st trace
E'en to the rich, and ancient race
Of Inachus, thy birth?
Or poor, and born of low degree,
Without a rag to cover thee.

Lang's newspaper The Mofussilite carried original poetry by various poets, including Lang himself (here). Lang also knew Persian very well and translated Sadi of Shiraz's Gulistaan. Here is an extract from one of the 1845 editions

Plate 9

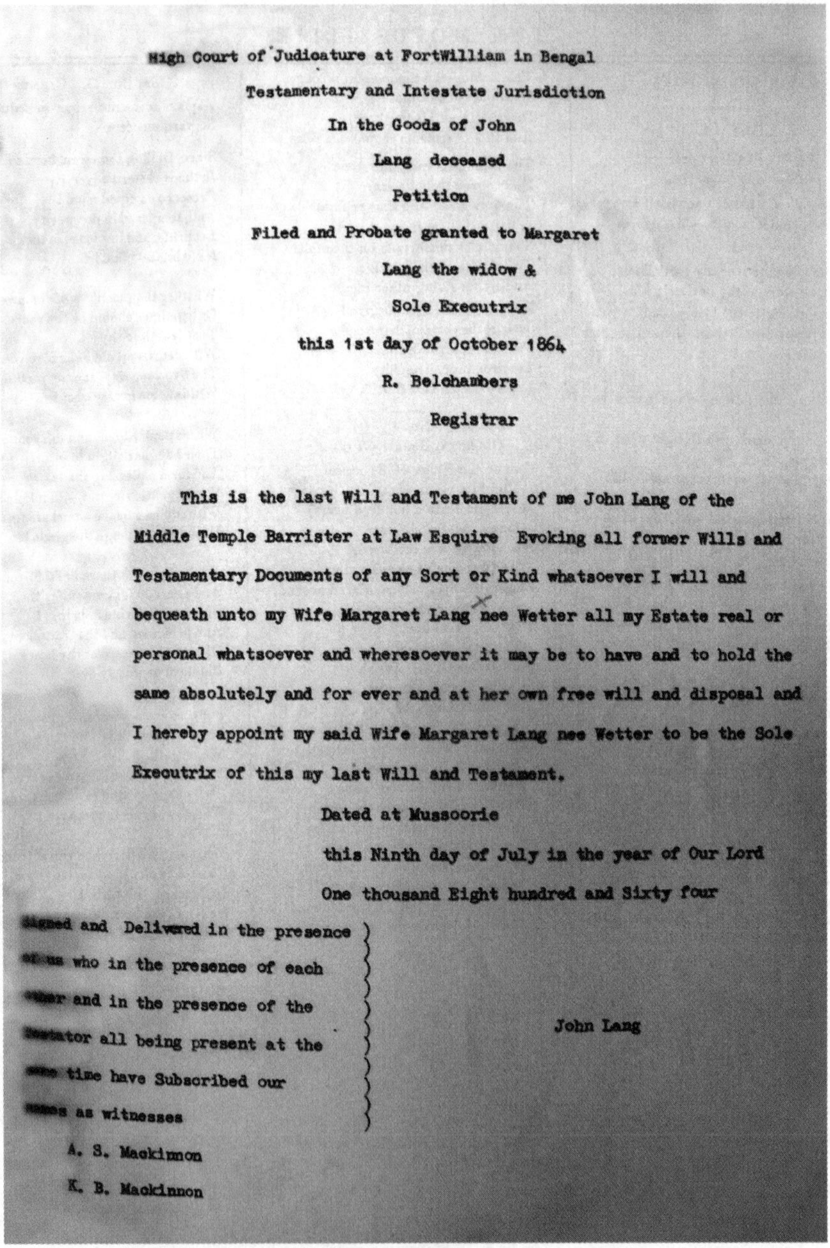

High Court of Judicature at FortWilliam in Bengal

Testamentary and Intestate Jurisdiction

In the Goods of John

Lang deceased

Petition

Filed and Probate granted to Margaret

Lang the widow &

Sole Executrix

this 1st day of October 1864

R. Belchambers

Registrar

This is the last Will and Testament of me John Lang of the Middle Temple Barrister at Law Esquire Evoking all former Wills and Testamentary Documents of any Sort or Kind whatsoever I will and bequeath unto my Wife Margaret Lang nee Wetter all my Estate real or personal whatsoever and wheresoever it may be to have and to hold the same absolutely and for ever and at her own free will and disposal and I hereby appoint my said Wife Margaret Lang nee Wetter to be the Sole Executrix of this my last Will and Testament.

Dated at Mussoorie

this Ninth day of July in the year of Our Lord

One thousand Eight hundred and Sixty four

Signed and Delivered in the presence of us who in the presence of each other and in the presence of the Testator all being present at the same time have Subscribed our names as witnesses

John Lang

A. S. Mackinnon

K. B. Mackinnon

Wetter's better: The last will of Lang, just a month before his death, bequeathing all his possessions and wealth to his second wife, Margaret Wetter.

Reuniting mother and son: The writer at Elizabeth Underwood's grave in Ashfield, Sydney. Lang never went back to Australia once he left for India; not even when his mother Elizabeth died. (Pic: Dr David Reeve)

This illustration is from The Mofussilite issue of 4 October, 1845, and signed as 'Scrooge.' Scrooge is one of the aliases Lang used. (Ref. p. 355)

Plate 11

Bengal Vol. 109 · Fol. 145 · 284

These are to Certify that the Secretary of State has in his custody a Register of **Burials** at Mussoorie A.D. 1864 ; in which Register there is an entry of which the following is a true copy :—

When Died	Year 1864	Month Augt.	Day 20th
Christian Name	John		
Surname	Lang		
Age	46		
Quality, Trade or Profession, &c., &c.	Barrister at Law		
When Buried	Year 1864	Month Augt.	Day 21st
Cause of Death ~~xxxxx~~. ...	Debility following Bronchitis		
Signature ~~or Name and Designation of Person~~ by whom Buried	R.N. Maddock Offg. Minister		
~~xxxxxxxxxx~~			
~~xxxxxxxxxxxxxxxx~~			

In witness whereof I have hereunto set my hand, at the Commonwealth Relations Office, King Charles Street, Whitehall, this eighteenth day of May in the year of Our Lord One thousand nine hundred and fifty-four.

A. M. Platt

~~Superintendent of Records~~ Commonwealth Relations Office.

(24001) Wt.23558/F.113 300 8/47 A.& E.W.Ltd. Gp.686

Death certificate of John Lang, 20 Aug 1864, Mussoorie

THE MOFUSSILITE.

PUBLISHED EVERY SATURDAY EVENING.

No. III. Vol. I.] CALCUTTA: SATURDAY, AUGUST 16TH, 1845. { *Terms of Subscription, 25 Rs. per Annum, payable in advance*

MORTALITY OF TROOPS IN INDIA.—The great mortality amongst European Soldiers in this country is a matter so frequently recorded in the newspapers, that it seemingly passes by without creating more reflection than we bestow on the most ordinary paragraphs. That many out of a large body of men should be subject to sickness—and that some should die, in a climate like this, is not to be wondered at; but when we hear of seventy, eighty, and ninety in Hospital at one time, and four, five, and six, buried in the course of two or three days, we think some special enquiry should be set on foot, and a strenuous effort made to check this thinning of the ranks.

There is no disguising the fact that European Soldiers are very badly treated in this country. They are conveyed from place to place without the slightest regard to the personal comfort, and safety of themselves, or their families; and when they arrive at their destination, they are huddled together in large numbers into tenements, far too small for their occupation—and too frequently does it happen that after a long march very many have no tenements at all provided for them, but are forced to make out in tents, the best way they can.

1st. With regard to the conveyance of troops. It would be unfair to dwell upon the serious loss H. M. 62nd sustained, when proceeding from Calcutta in September 1842. That was an accident. But what steps have been taken to prevent its recurrence? None whatever. In December last a steamer passed at Colgong a fleet of wretched country boats, which were conveying a detachment of H. M. 10th upwards, and when that same vessel returned from Allahabad, she met the same boats on

If a ship is about to take coolies to the Mauritius, great care is taken that the decks are of a certain height, and that more than a certain number do not proceed in her; in short the sympathy of the authorities is instantly,—and very properly, aroused, while any case of neglect,—be it ever so trifling—inflates the organ of the press to the very highest note; but let five Soldiers and as many women, and children, be packed into one cranky country boat, to go a distance of five hundred miles at a snails pace, and they glide away as quietly as possible.

2nd. As to the quarters of European troops. They are utterly unsuited to the climate, or the people, for this reason,—they are not sufficiently spacious, or extensive.

A case occurs, to our recollection, which will save us the trouble of entering at length into detail, or instancing Barracks, which we have seen in the interior.

About 18 or 20 months ago, a private soldier of the 10th Regt. was tried in the Supreme Court for an offence, which it is needless to mention. One of the witnesses for the Prosecution, a soldier of the same Regiment, made known that *six married men and their wives occupied one sleeping apartment.* We remember the Judge was astonished, and looked as though he discredited the statement, but several others witnesses, and one of them a Sergeant, swore to the same fact. This was in Fort William, and we have heard that children up to the age of ten years are to be found in these same apartments. Now, putting aside the disregard to morality, or the feelings of the people, is it possible that in a climate like this, where the average of the Thermometer is about 82°, health can be found in such places? or, if it be found, is

evident that his Lordship, one of her Majesty's Ministers, must have been utterly ignorant of the condition of her Majesty's troops in India. Sympathy, however, is very fickle, and seldom to be worked out by the Rule o Three. There is no saying, therefore, how this may have been.

The climate of India is assigned as the sole reason of the great Mortality in this country. This is evidently a delusion. Take the average deaths amongst a thousand Planters, or other Europeans, located in the most unhealthy districts, and compare them with the deaths in one corps,—the 20th Queen's for instance,—in the year 1843.

The climate is bad enough, we know, but the want of adaptation to it is much worse. 1,000 Rs. per month would pull punkahs for a whole Regiment during the hot weather months, but was such a luxury ever once thought of? On referring to the Army list we find rarely more than one Surgeon—and one Assistant Surgeon attached to each *Corps*. In sickly stations this can hardly be sufficient, be these officers ever so able, and active.

Nor does the Crown seem more regardful of its troops than the E. I. Company. To keep the same Regiment in this country for more than 10 or 12 years, is as unjust, as it is impolitic. Unfair both to the officers, and to the men. The former are often, after many years of Indian service, driven to effect an exchange at the sacrifice of promotion—while the latter go home so broken down in constitution, that they are utterly unfit for duty of any sort or kind.

DUELLING is a subject which most Journalists have torn to tatters, without doing any good that we are aware of; and for this rea-

One of the earliest issues of The Mofussilite, when it was still published from Calcutta instead of Meerut/Agra. Lang here highlights the abject conditions in which British soldiers lived, "six married men and their wives occupied one sleeping apartment." The climate was unsuitable to these soldiers, and plague and cholera were scourge of the times. Lang returns to this matter often in his novels, sardonically pointing out how most promotions were not because of gallantry, but because of superiors' deaths death due to illnesses. Mark how the temperature is mentioned in Fahrenheit in this article.

Lang's self-portrait with Nana Sahib (from The Mofussilite). Lang hobnobbed with the Indian royalty quite a bit, and got quite pampered with 'shampoo' etc at Nana Sahib's.

Entrance gate of Camel's Back Cemetery, Mussoorie, where Lang is buried

VIOLET;

OR,

THE DANSEUSE:

A PORTRAITURE

OF

HUMAN PASSIONS AND CHARACTER.

IN TWO VOLUMES.

VOL. I.

LONDON:

HENRY COLBURN,

13, GREAT MARLBOROUGH-STREET.

1836.

Violet, or The Danseuse (1836) is a famous anonymous novel, over the authorship of which there was a lot of debate in late 19th century. Lang ran it as a serial in his newspaper; and Victor Crittenden contended that Lang is the author of this work. If that were true, this would be Lang's earliest novel at the age of 20.

Plate 15

Sway's 218ft. tower has been sold

"Echo" Staff Reporter

BEAULIEU, Saturday.

PETERSON'S Tower, Sway, has been sold. This remarkable sentinel over Forest, heath and sea, rising 218ft. in concrete, was to have been offered for sale by auction by Messrs. Jackman and Masters, at Lymington, next Tuesday.

I was informed by the firm, today, that contracts have now been signed and exchanged for the sale of the tower privately. The new owner is Mr. G. K. Stanton, of Beaulieu.

Mr. Stanton told me that at the moment he does not know what he will do with the tower.

"I think it has great potential possibilities, but I have not got round to studying them yet," he said. "I do not know that I want to commercialise it. I think probably not."

Mr. Stanton is a large property owner, but has never before owned anything like Peterson's Tower.

"It rather appealed to me because it is such a unique property," he said.

"It is rather nice to own a thing of this sort, and that is why I bought it. The magnificence of the view from the top, too, had quite a lot to do with it. That view is well worth the climb up the winding stairs."

Mr. Stanton declined to reveal the price he paid for the tower.

News of ATTP's Sway Tower's sale. Sothern Daily Echo, 12 January 1957

CERTIFIED COPY OF AN ENTRY OF MARRIAGE

Given at the GENERAL REGISTER OFFICE, SOMERSET HOUSE, LONDON

REGISTRATION DISTRICT Wakefield Union

1839. Marriage solemnized at St. Johns Church in the Parish of Wakefield in the County of York

No.	When married	Name and surname	Age	Condition	Rank or profession	Residence at the time of marriage	Father's name and surname	Rank or profession of father
217	February 2nd	John Lang	21	Bachelor	Law Student	Middle Temple London	Walter Lang	Late Captain in the Army
		Lucy Peterson	21	Spinster	—	Wakefield	Henry Peterson	Gentleman

Married in the Church of St. John according to the Rites and Ceremonies of the Established Church by Licence by me M. J. Naylor D.D. Off. Min.

This marriage was solemnized between us, John Lang, Lucy Peterson; in the presence of us, A. T. T. Peterson, Jno. E. Charnock, Mary Eliza ...

CERTIFIED to be a true copy of an entry in the certified copy of a Register of Marriages in the District above mentioned. Given at the GENERAL REGISTER OFFICE, SOMERSET HOUSE, LONDON, under the Seal of the said Office, the 12th day of March 195..

MA 256329

Certificate of marriage of John Lang with Lucy Peterson, 1839. Lang had gone to the Peterson household to be nursed for a broken leg, and ended up falling in love and getting married with Lucy.

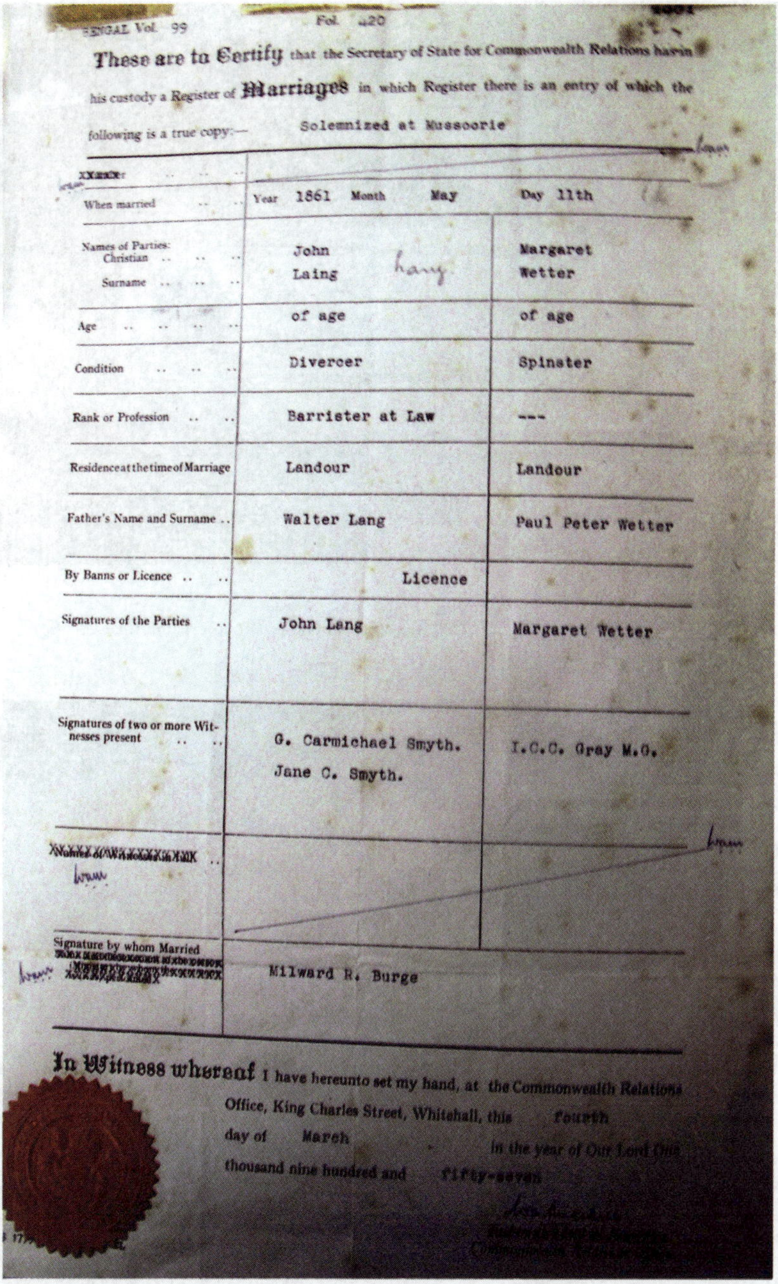

BENGAL Vol. 99 Fol. 420

These are to Certify that the Secretary of State for Commonwealth Relations has in his custody a Register of **Marriages** in which Register there is an entry of which the following is a true copy:— Solemnized at Mussoorie

XXXXXr		
When married	Year 1861 Month May	Day 11th
Names of Parties: Christian / Surname	John Laing *Lang*	Margaret Wetter
Age	of age	of age
Condition	Divercer	Spinster
Rank or Profession	Barrister at Law	---
Residence at the time of Marriage	Landour	Landour
Father's Name and Surname	Walter Lang	Paul Peter Wetter
By Banns or Licence	Licence	
Signatures of the Parties	John Lang	Margaret Wetter
Signatures of two or more Witnesses present	G. Carmichael Smyth. Jane C. Smyth.	I.C.C. Gray M.G.
XXXXXXXXXXXXXXXXX		
Signature by whom Married XXXXXXXXXXXXXXXXX	Milward R. Burge	

In Witness whereof I have hereunto set my hand, at the Commonwealth Relations Office, King Charles Street, Whitehall, this fourth day of March in the year of Our Lord One thousand nine hundred and fifty-seven

Marriage certificate of John Lang and Margaret Wetter; May 11, 1861

Alice, Alice, who the duck is Alice?
Alice Richman's grave, who fell to cholera in Pune, in 1882. The quest for Alice led the writer to John George Lang.

John Lang's grave at Camel's Back Cemetery, Mussoorie. This picture was sent by Tilak Memorial Library to George Earnshaw in the 1960s

Index

F

G

H

I